THE FUTURE OF THOMISM

American Maritain Association Publications

1988   *Jacques Maritain: The Man and His Metaphysics.*
        Edited by John F.X. Knasas. ISBN 0-268-01205-9.

1989   *Freedom in the Modern World: Jacques Maritain, Yves R. Simon, Mortimer J. Adler.*
        Edited by Michael D. Torre. ISBN 0-268-00978-3.

1990   *From Twilight to Dawn: The Cultural Vision of Jacques Maritain.*
        Edited by Peter A. Redpath. ISBN 0-268-00979-1.

1991   *The Future of Thomism.*
        Edited by Deal W. Hudson and Dennis Wm Moran.
        ISBN O-268-00986-4

1992   *Maritain and the Mystery of Israel* (tentative title).
        Edited by Robert Royal.

THE FUTURE OF THOMISM

Edited by

Deal W. Hudson and
Dennis Wm. Moran

American Maritain Association
Distributed by University of Notre Dame Press

Copyright © 1992 by

American Maritain Association

All Rights Reserved

Cover by Margaret A. Gloster

Manufactured in the
United States of America

American Maritain Association
Anthony O. Simon, Secretary
508 Travers Circle
Mishawaka, Indiana 46545

Distributed by University of Notre Dame Press
Notre Dame, Indiana 46556

To Judy and Tony Simon

The American Maritain Association and the Editors wish to thank The De Rance Foundation for its generous support of this publication.

CONTENTS

Gerald A. McCool, S.J.
   A Preface 1
Deal W. Hudson
   The Future of Thomism: An Introduction 7
Josef Pieper
   The Condition of Philosophy Today 23
Edward A. Synan
   Jacques Maritain: A Believing Philosopher 39

Part I
Thomism and Pluralism

Gerald A. McCool, S.J.
   Is Thomas's Way of Philosophizing Still Viable Today? 51
Raymond Dennehy
   The Philosophical Catbird Seat: A Defense of Maritain's
   Philosophia Perennis 65
Robert F. Harvanek, S.J.
   Discussion of McCool: From Unity to Pluralism 77
Desmond J. FitzGerald
   Gilson, *Aeterni Patris*, and the Direction of Twenty-First
   Century Catholic Philosophy 83
W. Norris Clarke, S.J.
   Thomism and Contemporary Philosophical Pluralism 91
Benedict M. Ashley, O.P.
   Thomism and the Transition from the Classical
   World-View to Historical-Mindedness 109
Vincent M. Colapietro
   History, Tradition, and Truth 123
John C. Cahalan
   On the Training of Thomists 133
Juha-Pekka Rentto
   The Postmodern Aquinas: A Fresh Start 149

Part II
Metaphysical Controversies

David B. Burrell, C.S.C.
    Jacques Maritain and Bernard Lonergan on
    Divine and Human Freedom 161

John F. X. Knasas
    Gilson vs. Maritain: The Start of Thomistic Metaphysics 169

Joseph W. Koterski, S.J.
    The Doctrine of Participation in Thomistic Metaphysics 185

Marion Montgomery
    Thomism and Romantic Confusions of the Good:
    Beauty Is Truth, Truth Beauty 197

Vittorio Possenti
    Thomism and Practical/Public Philosophy 217

Part III
Theological Contexts and Purposes

J. A. DiNoia, O.P.
    Thomism After Thomism: Aquinas and the
    Future of Theology 231

David L. Schindler
    Christology, Public Theology, and Thomism:
    Henri de Lubac, Balthasar, and Murray 247

Jude P. Dougherty
    John Courtney Murray: A Thomist on the
    Truths We Hold 265

Daniel Westberg
    The Relation of Law and Practical Reason in Aquinas 279

Romanus Cessario, O.P.
    Virtue Theory and the Present Evolution of Thomism 291

Gregory Froelich
    Ultimate End and Common Good in *Summa Theologiae*,
    Secunda Pars 301

Contributors 305

Index 307

A PREFACE
Gerald A. McCool, S.J.

The authors of these essays, as their reader will discover, are united in their admiration for the tradition of St. Thomas. Many of them, in fact, are willing to give their own philosophical allegiance to it. Yet, as their essays also show, disagreement over the correct interpretation of St. Thomas can still cause discord in the ranks of philosophers who look to him for inspiration. Thomists can still be found, it would appear, who find it hard to extend the hand of fellowship to colleagues whose understanding of the Angelic Doctor differs from their own. Disagreement among Thomists, however, can be an encouraging sign. Shared devotion to St. Thomas, combined with a readiness to disagree with their colleagues over the proper interpretation of his teaching, has always been a characteristic of thinkers in the tradition of the Angelic Doctor; and if, as these essays show, lively discussion and spirited controversy can still be found in it, the tradition of St. Thomas must still retain its life and vigor.

Indeed my own historical study of the nineteenth- and twentieth-century neo-Thomistic *movement* (as part of an older and identifiable *tradition* of St. Thomas) has given support to my own confidence in the vitality of that larger tradition. The neo-Thomistic *movement* began modestly in the nineteenth century, and, after the promulgation of Leo XIII's *Aeterni Patris*, developed into a leading force in twentieth-century Catholic thought. Reaching its high point at the middle of the century, the movement then found it difficult to retain its internal unity, and, after Vatican II, neo-Thomism was forced to surrender the position of leadership which it had enjoyed in Catholic philosophy and theology.

The beginning and end of the neo-Thomist movement, however, should not be equated with the birth and death of the broader tradition of St. Thomas in which it is included. Neo-Thomism, after all, was not the first revival movement within that tradition, nor is there any reason to claim that it will be the last. In the decades before and after the Council of Trent, an outstanding group of Dominicans restored the teaching of St. Thomas to its place of honor in their order. Because they had done so, the Dominicans, Jesuits, and Carmelites of the Second Scholasticism were able to draw on the resources of St. Thomas's thought to deal with the new set of problems confronting the post-Reformation church. In the anti-religious and anti-metaphysical atmosphere of the Enlightenment, however, the Second Scholasticism lost its vitality and influence; and, by the time that Thomism was revived again in the nineteenth century, it had been practically forgotten.

The tradition of St. Thomas then is older than the organized neo-Thomist movement, and it has survived that movement's end. Significant thinkers in the tradition of St. Thomas continued their work in the second half of the twentieth century. Some of them, like Rahner and Lonergan, were theologians influenced by Maréchal; but Maréchalian Thomism was not the only late twentieth-century claimant to the mantle of St. Thomas. William Norris Clarke and Cornelio Fabro—neither of whom were Maréchalians—developed St. Thomas's metaphysics of the person, to which Jacques Maritain had helped to call attention, and inspired the personalist Thomism of Karol Wojtyla. St. Thomas's ethics, as neo-Thomists had shown, is linked to his philosophy of the virtues and connatural knowledge, a point on which both Maritain and Rousselot were in agreement. In recent years three themes have drawn the attention of Alasdair MacIntyre and suggested the new approach to St. Thomas which we find in his later work. Despite the diversity among these thinkers, St. Thomas's influence upon their thought is unmistakable; and a new generation of ethicians has begun to look to St. Thomas for the solution to problems which post-Cartesian rationalism and empiricism cannot handle.

The tradition of St. Thomas, I am convinced, would not have survived and prospered, as it has, were it not for the contribution which the neo-Thomists made to it. Although the basic positions of Thomism are identifiable, the neo-Thomist movement did not realize its early hopes of creating a unified system of contemporary philosophy. The essays in this book will make that evident. Thomists in the tradition of Gilson and Maritain remain opposed to Thomists in the tradition of Rousselot and Maréchal on a number of fundamental issues, and, if Thomism is to be looked at as a tightly woven system, there cannot be a place for all of them within it. That does not mean, however, as MacIntyre is inclined to think, that there are "too many Thomisms" and that the movement which produced them ended in speculative failure. Much more came from the neo-Thomist movement than the historical and textual research which it stimulated. Historians, like Gilson, Chenu, van Steenberghen, and Weisheipl, have indeed enabled us to distinguish the thought of St. Thomas himself from the additions and modifications made by the Commentators of the Second Scholasticism. In addition to the work of its historians, however, the neo-Thomist movement has left us an important speculative heritage. The speculative development of St. Thomas's thought by the neo-Thomist thinkers has a lasting value in itself; and the tradition of St. Thomas would be very much the poorer if it were to be forgotten.

Contemporary Thomists, for example, can learn much from the work of Maritain. While Gilson and Chenu favored a more historical approach to Thomas, Maritain, like Gardeil and Garrigou-Lagrange, showed great respect for the tradition of St. Thomas's Second Scholasticism Commentators. Nevertheless, if Maritain was willing to work as a Thomist in that venerable Dominican tradition, he exploited his inherited resources in his own creative way. Maritain's speculative extension of Thomas's epistemology and metaphysics to the areas of speculative and practical knowledge, connaturality, aesthetics, ethics, and political philosophy remain an important part of Thomism's philosophical heritage. Years after Maritain's death, the younger ethicians and social philosophers, who have rediscovered the Aristotelian distinction between practical and speculative knowledge and, like Alasdair MacIntyre, have seen its importance for Thomistic ethics, can learn a great deal from the reading of Maritain. They will profit even more if, instead of reading isolated sections of his work, they study its whole corpus. Few thinkers of our time have been as sensitive to the richness and diversity of human knowledge and few have confronted more manfully than Maritain the problems of its integration.

In the early years of our century, when Maritain first encountered the Angelic Doctor, the possibility of a realistic metaphysics and of analogous knowledge of God had become a crucial problem for Catholic theologians. Both were required to defend the credibility of Christian revelation and the ability of the Church to make abiding dogmatic statement. Maritain, like Gardeil, Rousselot and Maréchal, endeavored to defend the possibility of both against the philosophical attacks made upon them; and, like other neo-Thomists, he did so in his own distinctive way. The neo-Thomists' remarkable defense of the philosophical foundations of the Christian faith led to disagreement among them, and the issues raised in the subsequent controversy over the epistemological grounding of metaphysics, as the essays in this book reveal, are still the fundamental issues which confront the defender of a realistic philosophy of being.

Contemporary speculative Thomism then, in many ways, is a continuation of the work begun by the great neo-Thomists. Many of its major themes, and its stress on insight, connaturality, practical knowledge and the human person, together with its use of the interplay of consciousness, concept and judgment to ground the analogy of being manifest continuity with the neo-Thomist movement. It will not be enough therefore for a younger philosopher, anxious to acquaint himself with the speculative resources of the Thomistic tradition, to confine himself to the text of St. Thomas alone. He will have to study as well, and at some depth, the works of the great neo-Thomists.

Thomism, after all, like any living tradition, has its *Wirkungsgeschichte* or effective history. It may be bad history, as Gilson remarked, to ask St. Thomas himself to solve problems which he never faced. But his greatest disciples were asked to face a number of new problems, and, in the Second and Third Scholasticism, they extended their master's thought to deal with them. When their efforts were successful, they provided the resources for further speculative work. Maritain, who knew what it was to think in the tradition of St. Thomas, was happy to draw upon the resources provided by the Dominicans of the Second Scholasticism and develop them further in his own creative work. Contemporary philosophers, like James Ross, Jorge Gracia, and Alfred Freddoso, have remarked in their works on Suarez and Molina that the Jesuits of the Second Scholasticism—who, in their minds at least, were followers of the Angelic Doctor—might have similar resources to offer philosophy today. The neo-Thomists, who continued the tradition of St. Thomas, faced many of the problems in epistemology, metaphysics, and ethics which the contemporary philosopher must still confront. And the younger Thomist benefits by reading them. The unity of this tradition will be made manifest to him by the large area of agreement which he will find expressed in their philosophy. The issues which divided the great neo-Thomists were significant ones and, alerted by those disagreements, the young Thomist can think the basic issues in Thomism through for himself and decide where he stands as a disciple of St. Thomas.

As time goes by, however, some of those disagreements may seem less central than they appeared to be at the height of the neo-Thomist movement. Contemporary philosophers have lost their faith in the Cartesian or the Kantian starting point as the guarantor of a firmly grounded philosophical method, and Thomists, as some of the essays in this volume show, are more ready than they were during the neo-Thomist movement to link St. Thomas's philosophy to his theology. The timeless thinking mind of Descartes and Kant, philosophers now admit, is at best an abstraction and, in all likelihood, an illusion. In the changed philosophical climate of our day, Thomists no longer feel themselves obliged to debate with Descartes and Kant following the rules set down by post-Cartesian philosophy. They are less concerned than the neo-Thomists were in determining whether a Thomist can work his way from the mind to reality by consistent use of transcendental method or whether an attempt like that must inevitably end in failure.

For the contemporary Thomist then some of the older distance between Gilsonian and Maréchalian Thomism may be bridged more easily. Contemporary personalist Thomists, like Norris Clarke and Karol Wojtyla, after all, neither begin their metaphysics with the grasp of *esse* in the phantasm nor work their way from consciousness to being by a transcendental method. Clarke and Wojtyla are both realists who encounter being in the activity of interpersonal community; and Clarke has seen, as Maritain saw many years ago, that reflection on the dynamic contribution of the mind to knowledge of being need not be linked to the use of a transcendental method. Now that reflection on knowledge is no longer associated with the Cartesian problematic, there may be more unity among Thomists in their approach to it and a greater readiness among them to extend the hand of fellowship to one another. As heirs of a great tradition, Thomists share a common heritage which belongs to them all and of which they can all be proud.

THE FUTURE OF THOMISM:
AN INTRODUCTION

Deal W. Hudson

Thomism usually comes in horrible wrappers.
—Flannery O'Connor

In spite of her complaint, the lady Thomist from Milledgeville, Georgia, read the *Summa* in bed every night before going to sleep. It was only *where* she read St. Thomas that was unusual. In fact, when she was reading St. Thomas and complaining about Thomism, his name was often heard and welcomed in Catholic circles. Twentieth-century disciples like Jacques Maritain, Étienne Gilson, Josef Pieper, Mortimer J. Adler, and Yves R. Simon were much in vogue, informing what we would now call the "mainstream" of Catholic thought. All of this influence, it can be noted, in spite of the bad packaging.

These days Thomism plays a minor role in philosophy at large, though a somewhat greater one among Catholic and Christian philosophers. It is hard to say whether Thomistic exteriors are as gruff now as they once appeared to the author of *Wise Blood*, or whether its image is even the problem. We now enjoy access to a "readable" abridged *Summa Theologiae* in English with the form of the articles removed.[1] Who knows whether putting St. Thomas into modern prose will do the trick of making him popular again? There must still be readers coming to the *Summa* for the first time who find themselves anachronistically attracted to the old layout, objections, *sed contra*, response, replies, the spaces in between providing the silence for reflection and anticipation.

But for those who love St. Thomas any attempt to let him speak to the present age has to be appreciated: because something has gone amiss. A number of the papers in this volume paint a fairly dismal picture of contemporary Thomism. Comparisons are made between the present level of interest in St. Thomas and that of the 1920s and 1930s. We are constantly reminded that Thomism declined through the 1950s and deteriorated rapidly in the 1960s and 1970s. At present, St. Thomas and his interpreters receive only limited attention in Catholic philosophy

---

1. St. Thomas Aquinas, *Summa Theologiae: A Concise Translation*, ed. and trans. Timothy McDermott (Westminster, Maryland: Christian Classics, Inc., 1989).

and theology, in its colleges, universities, and seminaries, in the American Catholic Philosophical Association, and in Catholic culture at large. The fact of philosophical pluralism, all agree, now confronts us. St. Thomas, for better or for worse, "has receded into the background and become something more remote," no longer *the* teacher in the theological schools but once again simply *a* Father of the Church.[2]

For those who grew up with the memory of Thomism's ascendancy the comparisons to bygone days are apropos. They remind us of the indebtedness of Catholicism to the tradition of St. Thomas; they point out the necessity of recognizing the ways Thomistic thinking has informed the fabric of the Church's magisterium. Regardless of what one thinks about St. Thomas and Thomism, both must be understood to grasp the substance of the Church's teaching about nearly everything, from the relation of nature and grace to the sacraments, from natural law to justice in the social order.[3]

Yet for those who have come to Thomism outside of official channels, as it were, the penchant for looking back feels obtrusive. One wonders whether readers coming to this volume, who are unfamiliar with the gossip of Catholic philosophy, will be dismayed by the prospect of reading about the future of a moribund movement? Fortunately for the reader, and for Thomism, first impressions, like "horrible wrappers," can be overcome. These essays go well beyond their either lamenting or celebrating the passage of neo-Thomism. The tradition of St. Thomas lives despite its lack of relative visibility within the Catholic church and its institutions. *Aeterni Patris* (1879) undoubtedly stimulated much of the twentieth-century work on St. Thomas, but there has been, as they say, hell to pay in its aftermath, the price for making Thomism official. Yet the Thomistic revival of the nineteenth century was already under way when Leo XIII issued his encyclical. The "third Scholasticism" might well have proceeded ahead without the official sanction of St. Thomas as the "common doctor" of the Catholic church.

This is not to wish that Leo XIII had done less to promulgate the *perennial philosophy*. He, after all, is not to be held responsible for the authoritarian excesses of later pontiffs,[4] or those who ignored the charge

---

2. Karl Rahner, S.J., "On Recognizing the Importance of Thomas Aquinas," *Theological Investigations*, XIII, trans. David Bourke (New York: Crossroad Books, 1983), p. 4.

3. See Avery Dulles, S.J., "Vatican II & Scholasticism," *New Oxford Review* 57:4 (May 1990): 5-11.

4. See James Weisheipl, O.P., "The Revival of Thomism as a Christian Philosophy," *New Themes in Christian Philosophy*, ed. Ralph McInerny (Notre Dame, Indiana: University of Notre Dame Press, 1968), pp. 164-85.

of his encyclical to engage modernity. At the turn of the century, Josiah Royce greeted the encyclical as a progressive moment in Catholicism, an unleashing of the potent spirit of St. Thomas against "conservative officialism" and textbook style in its schools.[5] And sixty years later, James Collins called Leo XIII the Pope of "the open tradition in philosophy."[6]

Thus, whatever happened to twentieth-century Thomism cannot be laid at the feet of Leo XIII. But Thomists should be encouraged to accept the inevitability of the encyclical's aftermath, to take a wider view, and, as a result, to stop lamenting about the glory days. Such an intellectual hegemony, often enforced with ecclesial power, was bound to crumble. If we no longer ride at the crest of Thomism, we can at least enjoy the intellectual fruits of that renascence, especially its scholarly, and sometimes saintly, example.

It can also be said that, given the long view, the news of Thomism's death has been greatly exaggerated. Many of the "old hands" around the world of Catholic philosophy and theology express surprise at the swell of interest in St. Thomas and his contemporary interpreters. Twenty years ago some assumed that interest in St. Thomas and Thomism would be completely dead by now. Not only has this not occurred, but there also are signs of a modest revival in the air. Philosophy departments are once again advertising for and hiring specialists in St. Thomas. The texts of St. Thomas are returning to the curriculum. Only ten years ago a teacher had very few texts of Aquinas from which to choose—now the choice is wide and getting wider.[7]

There is no lack of good scholarship in English about St. Thomas and Thomism. The 1970s saw the completion of the sixty-volume Blackfriars *Summa Theologiae* edited by Thomas Gilby, O.P. Previously unedited or untranslated works by Maritain, Gilson, Simon, Pieper, Lonergan, and

---

5. Josiah Royce, "Pope Leo's Philosophical Movement and Its Relations to Modern Thought" [1903], *Fugitive Essays* (Freeport, New York: Books for Libraries Press, Inc., 1968 reprint), pp. 408, 418-19.

6. James Collins, "Leo XIII and the Philosophical Approach to Modernity," *Crossroads in Philosophy* (Chicago: Henry Regnery Company, 1962), p. 301.

7. The selections by Vernon Bourke, Anton C. Pegis, Mary T. Clarke, A.M. Fairweather, Thomas Gilby and John Oesterle remain in print, to which have been added: Paul E. Sigmund, *St. Thomas Aquinas on Politics and Ethics* (New York: W. W. Norton & Company, 1988); William P. Baumgarth and Richard J. Regan, S.J., *On Law, Morality, and Politics* (Indianapolis, Indiana: Hackett Publishing Co., 1988); Christopher Martin, *The Philosophy of Thomas Aquinas: Introductory Readings* (New York: Routledge, Chapman & Hall, Inc., 1988); Simon Tugwell, O.P., *Albert and Thomas: Selected Writings* (Mahwah, New Jersey: Paulist Press, 1988); Mark D. Jordan, *On Faith: Summa Theologiae 2-2, QQ.1-16 of St. Thomas Aquinas* (Notre Dame, Indiana: University of Notre Dame Press, 1990); and Peter Kreeft, *A Summa of the Summa* (San Francisco: Ignatius Press, 1991).

Rousselot are being published.[8] Interest in reprints remains high, and a complete edition of Lonergan is underway, as is the French edition of Maritain. The highly original work of the Lublin Thomists is being translated.[9] A steady stream of books examine the thought of modern Thomists,[10] while Gerald A. McCool has begun to stimulate interest in

---

8. Jacques Maritain, *An Introduction to the Basic Problems of Moral Philosophy*, trans. Cornelia N. Borgerhoff (Albany, New York: Magi Books, Inc., 1990) [a translation of *Neuf leçons sur les notions premières de la philosophie morale*, 1951]; *The Story of Two Souls: The Correspondence of Jacques Maritain and Julien Green*, trans. Bernard Doering (New York: Fordham University Press, 1988); in addition a selection of the voluminous correspondence between Maritain and Simon is being prepared for publication, and John Dunaway has edited the correspondence between Maritain, Caroline Gordon, and Allen Tate to be published by the LSU Press; mention should also be made of Judith Suther's *Raïssa Maritain: Pilgrim, Poet, and Exile* (New York: Fordham University Press, 1990). Also, Yves R. Simon, *Practical Knowledge*, ed. by Robert J. Mulvaney (New York: Fordham University Press, 1991); *An Introduction to Metaphysics of Knowledge*, trans. Vukan Kuic and Richard J. Thompson (New York: Fordham University Press, 1990); *An Introduction to Moral Virtue*, ed. Vukan Kuic (New York: Fordham University Press, 1986); Etienne Gilson, *Methodical Realism*, trans. Philip Trower (Front Royal, Virginia: Christendom College Press, 1990); *Thomistic Realism and the Critique of Knowledge*, trans. Mark A. Wauck (San Francisco: Ignatius Press, 1986); *Linguistics and Philosophy*, trans. John Lyon (Notre Dame, Indiana: University of Notre Dame Press, 1988); *From Aristotle to Darwin and Back Again*, trans. John Lyon (Notre Dame, Indiana: University of Notre Dame Press, 1984); *Letters of Etienne Gilson to Henri de Lubac*, trans. Mary Emily Hamilton (San Francisco, California: Ignatius Press, 1988); Josef Pieper, *No One Could Have Known, An Autobiography: The Early Years*, trans. Graham Harrison (San Francisco, California: Ignatius Press, 1987); *Problems of Modern Faith: Essays and Addresses*, trans. Jan van Heurck (Chicago: Franciscan Herald Press, 1985); *On Hope*, trans. Sister Mary Francis McCarthy, S.N.D. (San Francisco, California: Ignatius Press, 1986); *Living the Truth*, trans. Lothar Krauth and Stella Lange (San Francisco, California: Ignatius Press, 1989 [contains newly translated *The Truth of All Things* and previously published *Reality and the Good*]; *Josef Pieper: An Anthology* (San Francisco, California: Ignatius Press, 1989); Bernard Lonergan, S.J. *Understanding and Being*, ed. Elizabeth A. Morelli and Mark D. Morelli (New York: The Edwin Mellen Press, 1980); and Pierre Rousselot, S.J., *The Eyes of Faith & Answer to Two Attacks*, trans. Joseph Donceel, S.J. and Avery Dulles, S.J. (New York: Fordham University Press, 1991).

9. Mieczylaw A. Krapiec, *I-Man: An Outline of Philosophical Anthropology*, trans. Marie Lescoe, Andrew Woznicki, Theresa Sandok, et al. (New Britain, Connecticut: Mariel Publications, 1983); see also Andrew Woznicki, *Being and Order: The Metaphysics of Thomas Aquinas in Historical Perspective* (New York: Peter Lang, 1989).

10. Deal W. Hudson and Matthew J. Mancini, *Understanding Maritain: Philosopher and Friend* (Macon, Georgia: Mercer University Press, 1989); and Ralph McInerny, *Art and Prudence: Studies in the Thought of Jacques Maritain* (Notre Dame, Indiana: University of Notre Dame Press, 1988) see also the series of books published by the

charting the overall history of contemporary Thomism.[11] W. Norris Clarke continues to publish, as do Joseph Owens and Frederick Wilhelmsen.[12] In addition to his historical studies, Ralph McInerny has persuasively addressed the present generation of students with texts for the classroom.[13] Studies of Thomas's metaphysics, epistemology, and philosophy of God continue to appear,[14] while the study of Thomistic ethics,

American Maritain Association and distributed by the University of Notre Dame Press; also, Laurence K. Shook, *Etienne Gilson* (Toronto: Pontifical Institute of Mediaeval Studies, 1984); John M. McDermott, S.J., *Love and Understanding: The Relation of Will and Intellect in Pierre Rousselot's Christological Vision* (Rome: Universita Gregoriana, 1983); Thomas Sheehan, *Karl Rahner: The Philosophical Foundations* (Athens, Ohio: Ohio University Press, 1987); Vernon Gregson, ed., *The Desires of the Human Heart: An Introduction to the Theology of Bernard Lonergan* (Mahwah, New Jersey: Paulist Press, 1988).

11. Gerald A. McCool, S.J., *From Unity to Pluralism: The Internal Evolution of Thomism* (New York: Fordham University Press, 1989), *Nineteeth-Century Scholasticism: The Search for a Unitary Method* (New York: Fordham University Press, 1989).

12. W. Norris Clarke, S.J., *A Philosophical Approach to God: A Neo-Thomist Perspective* (Winston-Salem, North Carolina: Wake Forest University, 1979); *The Universe as Journey: Conversations with W. Norris Clarke* (New York: Fordham University Press, 1988); Joseph Owens, C.S.s.R., *Human Destiny* (Washington, D.C.: The Catholic University of America Press, 1985), *Towards a Christian Philosophy* (Washington, D.C.: Catholic University of America Press, 1990); John R. Catan, ed., *St. Thomas Aquinas on the Existence of God: The Collected Papers of Joseph Owens* (Albany, New York: State University of New York, 1980); and Frederick D. Wilhelmsen, *Being and Knowing* (Albany, New York: Preserving Christian Publications, Inc., 1991).

13. Ralph McInerny, *Being and Predication: Thomistic Interpretations* (Washington, D. C.: The Catholic University of America Press, 1986), *Boethius and Aquinas* (Washington, D.C.: The Catholic University of America Press, 1990), *St. Thomas Aquinas* (Notre Dame, Indiana: University of Notre Dame Press, 1982), *A First Glance at St. Thomas Aquinas: A Handbook for Peeping Thomists* (Notre Dame, Indiana: University of Notre Dame Press, 1990), *Ethica Thomistica: The Moral Philosophy of St. Thomas Aquinas* (Washington, D.C.: The Catholic University of America Press, 1982).

14. Robert J. Henle, S.J., *The Theory of Knowledge* (Chicago: Loyola University Press, 1983); Mortimer J. Adler, *Intellect: Mind Over Matter* (New York: Macmillan Publishing Company, 1990); Leo Elders, *The Philosophical Theology of St. Thomas Aquinas* (Leiden: E. J. Brill, 1990); Jan Aertsen, *Nature and Creature: Thomas Aquinas's Way of Thought* (Leiden: E. J. Brill, 1988); W. J. Hankey, *God in Himself: Aquinas's Doctrine of God as Expressed in the Summa Theologiae* (New York: Oxford University Press, 1987); John F. X. Knasas, *The Preface to Thomistic Metaphysics* (New York: Peter Lang, 1990); David B. Burrell, C.S.C., *Knowing the Unknowable God: Ibn-Sina, Maimonides, Aquinas* (Notre Dame, Indiana: University of Notre Dame Press, 1986); Christopher Hughes, *On a Complex Theory of a Simple God* (Ithaca, New York: Cornell University Press, 1989).

thanks in part to Alasdair MacIntyre, appears to be a growth industry.[15] And historical, medieval, and comparative studies are published regularly.[16]

So although the giants among us may seem fewer than in previous days (and what endeavor is exempt from this), there is little reason to gnash one's teeth over the future of Thomism. Thomists will have to make extra efforts to locate one another because they may no longer be at the American Catholic Philosophical Association but at home in Crawford, Georgia. Indeed, one can say without much exaggeration that Thomism now exists in a *diaspora* and the sooner we recognize this the sooner we can take comfort in it. The dispersion of Thomism beyond Catholic universities, into secular and Protestant colleges, and beyond the Northeast corridor means that it is flourishing again without the help of official sanction and without extrinsic pressure. The tradition of Thomism, we are finding out, stands on its own two feet.

---

15. Stephen Theron, *Morals as Founded on Natural Law: The Existence of Moral Truths and What Is Required for This Existence* (New York: Peter Lang, 1988); Jean Porter, *The Recovery of Virtue: The Relevance of Aquinas for Christian Ethics* (Louisville, Kentucky: Westminster/ John Knox Press, 1990); Lee H. Yearley, *Mencius and Aquinas: Theories of Virtue and Conceptions of Courage* (Albany, New York: State University of New York Press, 1990); John Finnis, *Natural Law and Natural Rights* (Oxford: Clarendon Press, 1980); Russell Hittinger, *A Critique of the New Natural Law Theory* (Notre Dame, Indiana: University of Notre Dame Press, 1987); Michael Novak, *Free Persons and the Common Good* (Lanham, Maryland: Madison Books, 1989), and recent or forthcoming books by three of our contributors: Juha-Pekka Rentto, *Prudentia Juris: The Art of the Good and the Just* (Turku: Acta Universitatis Turkuensis, 1988); Romanus Cessario, O.P., *The Moral Virtues and Theological Ethics* (Notre Dame, Indiana: University of Notre Dame Press, 1991) and Daniel Westberg, *Right Practical Reason: Aquinas on Prudence and Human Action* (Cambridge: Cambridge University Press, forthcoming); as well as the paper edition of Yves R. Simon's *The Tradition of Natural Law* with a new introduction by Russell Hittinger to be released in 1992 by Fordham University Press.

16. John L. Farthing, *Thomas Aquinas and Gabriel Biel* (Durham, North Carolina: Duke University Press, 1988); Arvin Vos, *Aquinas, Calvin, and Contemporary Protestant Thought: A Critique of Protestant Views on the Thought of Thomas Aquinas* (Grand Rapids, Michigan: Christian University Press/ W. B. Eerdman's, 1985); Mark D. Jordan, *Ordering Wisdom: The Hierarchy of Philosophical Discourses in Aquinas* (Notre Dame, Indiana: University of Notre Dame Press, 1986); Scott MacDonald, ed., *Being and Goodness* (Ithaca, New York: Cornell University Press, 1991); John F. Wippel, *Metaphysical Themes in Thomas Aquinas* (Washington, D. C.: The Catholic University Press, 1984); John Caputo, *Heidegger and Aquinas: An Essay on Overcoming Metaphysics* (New York: Fordham University Press, 1982).

II

These papers also contain specific proposals for ensuring the future of Thomism through its revitalization. All of these writers agree that Thomism offers something unique and urgently needed in the throes of modernity and the dawning of postmodernity. The differences among their proposals come down to issues of thematic emphasis and fidelity to the historical St. Thomas. For some, who have been called, somewhat unfairly, "Thomists of the strict observance," the contemporary relevance of St. Thomas increases as you resist the temptation to update it. For example, Edward Synan, in a personal reflection, points out that while Maritain's "activity of refusal" toward modernism was sometimes excessive, this posture was more than offset by his commitment to truth without a "chronological criterion." Indeed, critics of the Maritain-Gilson brand of Thomism often complain of an unwillingness to accept postclassical (Kantian) presuppositions. Desmond J. FitzGerald responds to this charge, implied by McCool's ambivalence toward Gilson and Maritain, by reminding us that the Gilsonian emphasis on the hylomorphic unity of the human person and the *esse* of the human soul continue to provide vitality for Thomistic studies.

For a number of "existential" Thomists, the Kantian starting point is like a line in the sand, cross it and you are no longer doing Thomism. For this reason, Raymond Dennehy considers Thomas's epistemological realism the key to its future. It is not enough to celebrate the dynamism of the intellect underlying its affirmational judgment. For philosophy to be properly Thomistic the human intellect must be able to form necessary concepts. He rebuts McCool's claim that judgments can be immutable while the concepts through which these judgments are made can be contingent and mutable.[17] We mistakenly assume from the contingency of objects that their concepts lack all necessity. Such historical contextualism, for Dennehy, belies the materialization of the intellect in which concepts have been reduced to representations of objects. Without direct contact with the sensible world, the philosophical catbird seat is lost, the mind locked in a Cartesian cyclorama.

Marion Montgomery considers that the self must be "opened to being" if the intellect is to recover its ordinate relation to being. It is Thomism's concern for the "present moment" of the individual soul that makes it modern. But the health of the soul depends upon the ability to break from the entrapment of the self and memory. The modern reliance on *ratio* has destroyed the intuitive roots of our direct contact with the extramental real. In the work of Romantic poets like Keats and

---

17. McCool, *From Unity to Pluralism*, p. 211.

Wordsworth, and the later Eliot, we encounter attempts to overcome this common dilemma. These are the "prudent Romantics" who realize the pretense to absolute creativity comes at the cost of melancholy and despair. What Montgomery calls their Romantic impulse is an unrealized Thomistic intuition which each of us must discover in our journey toward the Other.

Perhaps it was partly Maritain's own intimate relations with poets that led him to posit an "intuition of being" as the foundation of metaphysics. But John F. X. Knasas, seeking to mediate a family quarrel among modern Thomists, argues that such an intuition is impossible given that the intellect is wedded to the sensible singular. We have knowledge of *esse* only insofar as we have knowledge of an individual existent. Only God's essence is identical with existence, and this divine *esse* is beyond the intuitive power of any created mind. Since there is no sensible image of *esse* itself from which to take the intuition, the starting point of metaphysics cannot be an "intuition of being." Metaphysics begins with *habens esse*, the judgmental grasp of the *esse* of things.

In the contemporary arena of practical philosophy, Vittorio Possenti welcomes the revival of the Aristotelian-Thomistic tradition, its emphasis on virtue and the relation of practical to theoretical reason. He argues that this revival was warranted due to the "deprecation of nature" in modern ethical theory. Enlightenment and post-Enlightenment ethics threw out the human *telos* making the task of moral science, as Possenti remarks, that of Sisyphus. But he warns against adopting a version of Aristotle and St. Thomas that severs the connection of ethics and metaphysics, as seen in MacIntyre. A thin theory of the good that omits the final end and natural law cannot do the job of restoring ethics to its proper task.

Other contributors to this volume, and not necessarily "transcendental Thomists," claim the work of St. Thomas carries within itself suggestions for its own authentic *ressourcement*.[18] They are quick to point out, just as Lonergan often does, that Aquinas's own thought beginning with the *Commentary on the Sentences* underwent development. It is both artificial and unrealistic, they argue, to deter further legitimate development. To this argument, someone like Dennehy would respond by inquiring about the limits of what can be called "Thomism."

In fact, an interesting feature of the essay by Benedict Ashley is that the ground for updating he finds in Aquinas is the same as that which Dennehy uses for his stricter observance. In calling for a move from the

---

18. On the comparison of *ressourcement* with *aggiornamento*, see J. A. DiNoia, O.P., "American Catholic Theology at Century's End: Postconciliar, Postmodern, Post-Thomistic," *The Thomist* 54: 4 (October 1990): 499-518.

classical paradigm of timeless knowledge and immutable concepts, Ashley appeals to the sense-oriented design of the Thomistic intellect. "Historical-mindedness" is required of us, he argues, because truth belongs to minds and human minds are immersed in history: "truth in its existentiality is perspectival." For Ashley, this personal, historical side of knowing was introduced into modern Thomism by Maréchal, Gilson, and Maritain, but they did not go far enough in overturning the dominance of a rationalist metaphysics in the various branches of philosophy, thereby returning to the example of St. Thomas. More must be done to free the empirical and social sciences from their subordination to metaphysics. Metaphysics itself will profit from carrying less of the burden: for example, by the proof of a first cause offered by natural science.

A return to the historical Aquinas, some think, will turn up a number of central themes undeveloped among contemporary interpreters. Gregory Froelich, like John F. X. Knasas, revives an important and unresolved Thomistic controversy and reveals its continued relevance. The communal aspect of the common good, he argues, has been mistakenly ignored by interpreters such as Veatch and Maritain. The result is that the goods of the city have come to be viewed as mere means to an individually conceived beatified state. If interpreted correctly, the idea of the common good both fortifies our notion of the imperfect happiness in this life and exposes as unnecessary the distinction often drawn between political community and individual good. The city is an intrinsic good worthy of our investment as well as a participation in and preparation for the eternal city to come.

The view that participation is a neglected idea in modern Thomism is expressed repeatedly in these papers. Joseph Koterski thinks that the lack of attention to Aquinas's metaphysics of participation creates a serious lacuna in Thomistic thought. Participation may be nothing less than the key to overcoming the recent rejection of Thomism. Participation metaphysics, as described by Koterski, is friendlier to the theological Aquinas; it requires a kind of efficient causality rooted in exemplary, not formal, causality, and one not strictly dependent upon the movement from potency to actuality. He shows how the vestiges of formal causality, the Platonic "somehow" so anathema to Aristotle, disappear in Aquinas to be replaced by a version of participation emphasizing creatureliness and the dependence of all things on God. His Christian universe allows Aquinas to develop a participation metaphysics where Aristotle cannot.

One of the surprising aspects of this collection is the number of contributors who address the need for Thomism once again to draw from its theological wells. A number of commentators on the neo-Thomist movement, including McCool, have regretted a philosophy "separated" from theology and spirituality, and the consequent slide toward rationalism. Josef Pieper, for example, writes, "insofar as a Christian philosophizes in existential seriousness, to that extent, he is neither able nor allowed to leave the truth of revelation out of his consideration." The data of revelation claim to be a legitimate aspect of the philosopher's object—reality. Pieper quotes Whitehead's famous remark "exactness is a fake" to support his insistence that philosophy cannot be antiseptically pure; the reality it seeks to contemplate is not all of a single order. Their preoccupation with method excludes a priori the very answers that philosophers seek.

The attempt to remove all theological tracings from Thomistic philosophy has contributed to its demise in both camps. J. A. DiNoia proposes rectifying this loss of currency with a "'post-neo-Thomistic' theological appropriation of Aquinas." The mistake of the neo-Thomist movement was in giving the impression that Aquinas's philosophical system had to be accepted totally before one could engage him theologically. Philosophy plays no such role in the *Summa*, he argues, where philosophical analysis comprises "moments intrinsic to theological thinking." The result is not a closed system but an open-ended complex of "interrelated dialectical arguments," one that makes itself vulnerable to the best of opposing arguments. Philosophical reflection takes its place in the broad sweep of a theological argument; it cannot be treated independently of its theological context without skewering it, as in the case with the treatise on God is split in half between the treatment of the divine essence and the distinction of persons. The undoubted pull between the particularity of revelation and the universality of philosophy must give way toward the theological project.

The work of John Courtney Murray, as Jude P. Dougherty shows, illustrates how the intellectual tradition of the Catholic church, and particularly its natural law ethics, offers the resources for shaping a public philosophy. Such a philosophy does not have to win the field but simply keep alive the belief that the order of nature can be understood and the good for human beings delineated. To encourage the formation of a new American consensus there must be some agreed-upon common ground for discussion: the natural law view of human nature provides that intellectual platform. Dougherty, like Josef Pieper, warns against approaches that absolutize process at the cost of solutions; an insistence on ensuring a false individual freedom multiplies social pluralism to the breaking point.

One present hope in mediating some of the pluralism is the revival of virtue ethics. However, the treatment of the virtues in Aquinas, as Daniel Westberg shows, exists in tension with the treatise on law. He looks to the theological structure of the *prima pars* itself to elucidate this relationship, explaining that law is an extrinsic rather than intrinsic guide to human action and motion, a participation in the providential purposes of God for the creation. The concept of participation brings together virtue with law, prudence with providence, the interior with the exterior: "When we know and desire the proper *fines* of human life, then we share in the light of the eternal law." Law and practical reason explain human action from different points of view—the agent's and God's.

Interest in a Thomistic ethics of virtue has also taken hold in Europe. Romanus Cessario chronicles its Augustinian mood: St. Thomas, we are told, is being read as if he were St. Bonaventure. The value of this reading for Cessario is its added dimension to virtue theory, as revealed in its interpretation as the *ordo amoris*, its relation to the gifts of the Holy Spirit and the beatitudes, and an emphasis on the crucial distinction between the infused and acquired virtues. As Thomistic ethics rediscovers both its teleological and Christocentric dimensions, the active pursuit of happiness, not the fulfillment of duty, is once again being considered a reliable guide for Christian living.

Some contributors appeal less to a lost tradition in Thomism itself than to the loss of our appreciation for tradition generally. This concern underlies John Cahalan's suggestion that teachers of Thomism have not taken contemporary Thomists seriously, as philosophers in their own right, and have tended to regard their work as commentaries on the historical St. Thomas. Until contemporary Thomists are taught for their own sake, Cahalan argues, students are unlikely to treat the tradition as a viable option for themselves.

Juha-Pekka Rentto is in favor of treating St. Thomas Aquinas as a "postmodern." Aquinas's premodern "ontological rapport of ought and is" can be turned into a postmodern critique of modernity, helping to resolve its dichotomies between reason and will, theory and practice, individual and community. Thomistic ethics are holistic yet personal. Moral rightness is grounded in a metaphysics of human nature, but rather than gathering everyone under a net of universalization, the idea of virtue focuses on two natures of human beings: on what is the same, according to the species, and on what is different, according to the acquired characteristics of individual persons.

One philosopher who has respected the distinctive voices in modern Thomism is Gerald A. McCool. His history of contemporary Thomism, however, is not encouraging: he begins with the assumption that the leading players at the beginning of the Thomistic revival misunderstood their tradition. *Aeterni Patris* codified this mistake with positing a "rigidly unitary system" of theology which was passed unchanged from generation to generation, beginning with the Patristic Age and extending into modernity. Thus, the neo-Thomist movement, McCool comments, "began with a misunderstanding and ended with disappointment." But what can be gleaned from this development, and the splintering of the Thomistic tradition itself, is a clearer understanding of the tradition and a better grasp of the themes—the dynamism of intellect, connatural knowledge, personal being, the act of existence—that are the most viable for contemporary philosophy.

McCool's longtime Fordham colleague, W. Norris Clarke, also welcomes the decline of "triumphal Thomism" and the dethroning of St. Thomas as an authority figure. Thomists can now learn new skills of "peaceful, even creative co-existence," not only with the pluralism of world philosophy but also with each other. Clarke makes concrete suggestions for Thomistic collaborations with phenomenology, hermeneutics, linguistic analysis, and neo-Kantianism. Clarke himself, however, draws the line at deconstruction.

Robert Harvanek goes farther than either McCool or Clarke in warning Thomists about their future. Thus far, Thomism has failed to respond to the advantages of philosophical pluralism. Thomism must eschew its concentration on metaphysics and move toward a greater emphasis on a social philosophy and phenomenology that will inoculate the tradition with the social and dialogical aspects of human knowledge. As it stands, neo-Thomism cannot succeed because it does not serve the needs of contemporary theology or provide the basis for an autonomous philosophy. Thomists have been obsessed with systematics, have disseminated an outmoded matter/form distinction, and have ignored the relational aspect of both substance and person.

Most of the contributors would agree that too great an emphasis on demonstrative knowledge has resulted in the rationalism of so-called textbook or manual Thomism. Vincent Colapietro contends that the Thomistic stress on the immutable character of truth and the transcendent capacity of reason can be corrected by taking tradition and self-appropriation into account. Using Maritain's idea of "fellowship" in seeking the truth, Colapietro reflects on "the ineradicably traditional character of all human knowing." Philosophizing is not like spinning out a learned catechism; it belongs to the give-and-take of a tradition in which "we must see for ourselves" before we acquire our own voice. Tradition, once secured, cannot be discarded: it exists in an ongoing dialogue that gives our propositions their philosophical force.

Many a student coming to Thomism has wondered about he lack of dialogue among certain of its major proponents. David Burrell asks just such a question: what kept Maritain and Lonergan apart? Why did they never read one another's work or draw upon them in any way? For an answer Burrell takes a look to the tangle of the Thomistic tradition, finding his clue in the isolation of the Dominican from the Jesuit world in the seventeenth century. The issue, of course, was divine sovereignty and human freedom. Maritain was schooled in the Bañezian tradition of physical premotion, while Lonergan in his early articles on operative grace sought to move beyond the dead end of the Bañez-Molina controversy. In addition, Burrell thinks this also explains why Maritain overrated his work on evil and free will. Mislead by the Bañezian premotion, Maritain's explanation consists of "postulations tailored to the event to be explained" and violates his own distinction between created and uncreated being. The lesson to be learned from Lonergan's account is that some things, such as divine activation, can only be asserted as a theorem: "the *how* escapes us." God is more the cause of creatures' actions than they are, not by divine activation but by "intelligible dependence of the act on God is greater than it is on us." We do not need an explanation in mechanistic terms to show how it works. Burrell concludes that Thomists must learn to recognize where questioning ends because we have reached the "point of unknowing." At least on the issue of freedom, Lonergan was more respectful of the mystery than Maritain.

III

Some might expect that this introduction would seek to adjudicate these different recommendations for "The Future of Thomism." But like a good host who wants to treat all of his guests equally, I will resist that temptation. Before anyone begins such a project they should consider Pieper's warning against seeking methodological purity. They should also consider some practical matters. The different strains of Thomism are going to continue in existence, regardless of which one we might choose; to be preoccupied with the failings of other Thomists can undermine the possibilities of future philosophical cooperation. Also, the choice risks contradicting the way many of us have been schooled as Thomists—we risk turning our backs on the variety of teachers who have taught us about St. Thomas.

In regard to the last of these reasons: it is not unusual for the Thomistic neophyte to receive stern warnings from Gilsonians about reading Maritain, from Maritainians about reading Lonergan, from Lonerganians about reading Aristotle, and from medievalists about reading anyone but St. Thomas. However, even the neophyte may have felt something vaguely unsettling about these warnings: like the kind of condescending connoisseurship of a Wagnerite warning the untutored against listening to, say, Gluck. The neophyte may have already noticed that preeminent modern Thomists when they did find fault seemed to have read their opponents closely and sought to understand them. Genuine scholarly engagement is one thing, curt dismissal quite another. Those drawn to Thomism as an alternative to modernism may be disappointed to find Thomists less concerned with the world-at-large than with trumping one another. Finally, these internecine quarrels seem to bespeak a closed mind, something less than the mind's openness to reality about which Thomists are always speaking. Maritain wrote about his disappointment in Thomists who

> use the formulas they have been taught in order to save themselves from regarding the thought of others, and to criticize it all the more peremptorily because they expect it to display only error. The universe of intelligible objects, to which first and foremost we owe our loyalty, is not that universe of verbal conclusions which serve all too often as material blinders which keep a man from gazing into the eyes of other men.[19]

That Maritain's advice on Thomistic manners from a half a century ago is still pertinent is cause for some regret. There remains to be a large patch of common ground shared by what Henri de Lubac calls "The Big Family of Thomists." Their resemblances are so obvious, one must ask what discourages their cooperation on issues like the human person, the rational soul, its unity with the body, the importance of sense experience, the primacy of *esse*, the virtues and character, justice and the social order, and the interdependence of philosophy and theology? Is it the result of political and ecclesial pressures stemming from *Aeterni Patris*, as noted earlier? Is Maritain's accusation of rationalism still germane? That diagnosis seems reinforced by MacIntyre's observation that concentration on epistemological differences threatens to multiply *Thomisms* along the lines of modern philosophies.[20] Certainly the underlying intellectualism of modern Thomism is the much-needed antidote for the deconstructionist critique of logocentrism.

The present generation of Thomists can look forward to the end of politicized posturing only if students refuse to reenact the prejudices of their teachers. MacIntyre's recommendation to overcome the present deadlock is intriguing. He suggests the adoption of "unthomistic means," such as the genealogical analysis (Nietzsche) of intellectual history, to engage contemporary philosophy.[21] If Thomists can trace back the

---

19. Jacques Maritain, "Philosophical Cooperation and Intellectual Justice," in *The Range of Reason* (New York: Charles Scribner's Sons, 1952), p. 47.

20. Alasdair MacIntyre, *Three Rival Versions of Moral Inquiry* (Notre Dame, Indiana: University of Notre Dame Press, 1990), p. 75.

21. Alasdair MacIntyre, *First Principles, Final Ends and Contemporary Philosophical Issues* (Milwaukee, Wisconsin: Marquette University Press, 1990), p. 57. His empha-

evolution of philosophy to its rejection of Aristotelian-Thomistic teleology and offer contemporary philosophers the means for a narrative self-understanding, then those philosophers will be caught in a dilemma. Either they accept their dependence upon narrative, thereby contradicting their rejection of teleology, or they will remain in the dark. MacIntyre's optimism, based upon his own version of the drive of the mind to know, is rooted in a recognition of the human propensity for storytelling, for discovering the coherence among the beginning, middle, and end of life's journey.

Poets, philosophers, and painters at the turn of the last century found themselves drawn to the Middle Ages precisely for its capacity to help them envision the whole beyond the sum of the parts. Although the romantic project of retrieval went astray through an increasing preoccupation with the virtuosity of selfhood, expressions of its ambitions are scattered throughout this volume. The notion of participation, the emphasis on tradition and individual experience, the rejection of rationalism, the smudging of boundaries between religion and philosophy, the impatience with anything less than ultimate finality, give witness to a continuing search in this generation for Keats's "unheard melodies." It would be surprising, would it not, if the future of Thomism lay in recovering its deep affinities with "prudent" Romanticism.

---

sis on historical, narrative appraisal may be a soft version of teleology, but the analysis he recommends has not been absent from the work of modern Thomists. Gilson's *Dante and Philosophy* is a good example of a genealogical study. One also thinks of Maritain's largely unread *Moral Philosophy*, Cornelio Fabro's *God in Exile*, James Collins's *God in Modern Philosophy*, Vernon Bourke's *History of Ethics*, and Marion Montgomery's recent Thomistic critique of American culture, *The Prophetic Poet and the Spirit of the Age*, 3 vols. (LaSalle, Illinois: Sherwood, Sugden & Company, Publishers, 1981-84).

THE CONDITION OF PHILOSOPHY TODAY

Josef Pieper

There is something peculiar and even strange in the situation of philosophy today. For, this situation is obviously characterized not so much by a specific emphasis on one or another properly philosophical problem, not by the predominance or by the recession of certain philosophical topics or questions; it is characterized much more decisively by *the position of philosophy in general* within the whole of society and especially within the whole of human search for truth, within *la recherche collective de la vérité*. This place, rank, and status of philosophy itself has become more and more problematic. Why philosophy at all? This question, most aggressively asked from outside, has become, as it seems, much more urgent than the specifically philosophical questions themselves—no matter whether formal logic is concerned or philosophical anthropology or linguistic analysis. Of course, the distinction between the "exterior" and the "interior" situation of philosophy is somewhat inexact and provisional. For, the question of what is the good and the use of philosophy itself and what it is for and what philosophy means with regard to the life of human society—this question itself is of course an eminently philosophical question. And nobody is able and competent to answer it or to try to give an answer—nobody but the philosophizing man himself. Like any other philosophical question, it forces us to take into consideration the whole of human existence; and whoever intends to discuss the question cannot avoid bringing into the play and declaring (like at the customs, at the border), his own ultimate convictions. The reason why this is unavoidable is that also *the objections against* philosophy as a whole are based on a "Weltanschauung," which means, on a conviction which explicitly concerns the whole of reality and existence.

The questions to be discussed here are in fact countless. I should like to restrict myself to the discussion of *three points* which, I feel, have indeed a special topical interest. Perhaps those three points could be formulated in the following provisional way:

(1) philosophy within the modern world of work;
(2) philosophy and the ideal of scientific exactness; and
(3) philosophy and theology.

Before I try to discuss these points one after the other I should like to say as clearly as possible, in which meaning the term *philosophy* shall be used here—whereby I explicitly resign any claim of originality. By philosophy I understand nothing else than that which the great tradition always has understood by it, namely: the consideration of (perhaps I should rather say: the attempt to take into consideration) the entirety of what we encounter and meet with. But I think it might be good to elucidate a bit more the three main elements of this description, which perhaps may be called even a definition of philosophy. These three elements are the terms *consideration, entirety* (totality) and *encounter*. All of them express something which seems to me to be a matter of rather great consequence.

First: "consideration" (or: to take into consideration) means something like this: that, with a kind of amazement and astonishment, I keep awake a question; consideration is at any rate rather the search after an answer than its discovery. This term *consideration* excludes from the beginning the opinion that philosophy could be something like a positive "doctrine" (for instance the doctrine or theory of being as such, of being as being). With this it is already clear, that this concept of philosophy is fighting in two directions: first against the idea of "scientific philosophy" which maintains or postulates that the philosophizing man ought to bring to bear the principles of the exact sciences within the field of philosophy; but it also stands against the claims of the speculative "system-philosophy," which understands itself as "the comprehension of the Absolute" (as Hegel says) or as "the science of the eternal archetypes of things" (as Schelling puts it). Further, when I said, the philosophizing man should have to deal with the *entirety and the totality* (of what we encounter), this does not mean that a truly philosophical question would be asked only in that case, in which the totality of world and existence is formally made the topic and the theme of discussion; but it does mean that the topic of a philosophical question, however concrete or particular this topic may be, has to be viewed against the horizon of the whole of reality and that the object has to be considered under every possible aspect (whereby it may be left open and undetermined just what a "possible aspect" is).

I am speaking here of exactly the same thing as Alfred North Whitehead had in view, when he said: that the specifically philosophical problem, which never will be solved definitely and once for all, consists in this: to conceive a *complete fact*; I could also say: to conceive a fact *completely*. Thirdly, I said that philosophizing means the consideration of all we *encounter and meet with*. By this I wish to emphasize the necessary relation of philosophy with experience, but at the same time I try to exclude any limitation and restriction to what usually is called the empirical fact in the plain and compact sense. I can possibly encounter something, which I do not simply experience. That which I encounter is something which offers resistance; possibly it does not show itself, and I cannot simply observe or state it, but nevertheless I am not able to discuss it away. I can possibly ignore it for a while or I can misinterpret it—let us say out of some vital or ideological interest. But, in the long run, and if I do not completely turn away the eyes of my soul, it brings itself to my recollection if only with some scruples (as with fish hooks); uncompromisingly and stubbornly it presents itself to my look. And I should say whatever our cognition encounters in this manner is the subject-matter of philosophy, *only* this and *all* this.

These previous remarks have not only, as I hope, made it somewhat more conceivable how and why it could happen that the position of philosophy and its relation to the modern world of work, to the exact empirical sciences, and to theology became problematic at all; they have, moreover (which, I hope, shall become evident later on), paved the way a bit for an answer, which may show and advocate the *independence* of philosophy as well as its *necessity*.

I

The objection against philosophy from the side of the modern working world is, considered as a theoretical argument, not especially impressive; its weight lies in its practical, life-determining power. The objection, put into an abbreviating formula, goes like this: philosophizing is senseless and, above all, disadvantageous and detrimental, because it does not serve for anything and even hinders the active realization of the aims and needs of life. This argument has, so to speak, several different degrees of radicality and, of course, it does not at all need to be formulated always explicitly. Those degrees may reach from the naive involvement in the workaday practice to the deliberate claim, that the *bonum utile*, the mere utility should be something absolute and, what is the same, to the explicit indifference to truth. The most extreme case is the practitioner of power, resisting every "useless" knowledge.

First of all, one ought to see that the emergence of the modern working world cannot be attributed to mere human wantonness; on the contrary, it is something simply unavoidable and so far something legitimate. Mankind is indeed confronted, up to a quite new degree, with the task of securing the means of existence; and it is not only the fight against hunger which forces us to make the most intense use of all energies available, it is also the preservation of political freedom, which rightly requires all our capacities. Sometimes one may be tempted, quite understandably, to ask oneself whether it is really right to insist on the claim that it nevertheless belongs to the elements of a truly human life to keep present and alive the question of the ultimate meaning of the whole of reality, which means: to philosophize.

On the other hand: the strangeness of the philosophical act within the modern working world is nothing but a sharper degree of that incommensurability that exists ever since between philosophy and the normal practice of everyday. Normally, man does not feel in the mood to ask for the ultimate meaning of reality as a whole. As long as our attention is absorbed by the active realization of purposes, we are *not* in the mood to consider philosophically the whole of existence. Whoever is conducting a case before the court, normally is not just interested in the philosophical question what justice in general *is*. There is needed, ever since, a shock, a violent push, a concussion of the normal average attitude to world and life—so that philosophizing, which means the consideration of the whole of reality may be put into motion at all. A concussion of this kind is for instance the experience of death, and also the other great power of existence, Eros, can possibly strike a man in such a way, that the pertinent occupation with the necessities and needs of daily life becomes suddenly unimportant to him or even impossible because the *whole* of existence comes into the picture. And indeed, man philosophizing has this in common with the other one, who has been shaken by the experience of death and also with that one who has been touched by the power of Eros and, by the way, also with the man in prayer and the poet, even with one who perceives and assimilates a poem in a poetical way, which means, in the only adequate way—like all these figures man philosophizing, too, does not unquestionably fit in with the functioning of the workaday practice. Man philosophizing, too, sees things "differently" in comparison with the man of practice, who is engaged in the realization of purposes.

This inadequacy and discrepancy has existed, as I said, *ever since;* and it will *never* disappear. There is, however, *something new* in the case of the contemporary working world. What is *new* is not only the sharper radicality of that quite natural incommensurability. *New* is the explicit theoretical (one might even say: philosophical!) argumentation, intended to show that philosophy, in the ancient sense, is something meaningless and even something unseemly; such argumentation is also intended to do away with that old incommensurability; but in fact it does away then with philosophy itself.

This attempt, which after all is quite conceivable, has been undertaken, as it seems, *at all times,* at the latest since the sophists. But again, the radicality of this attempt has become always sharper. Obviously the sentence out of the Great Soviet Encyclopaedia, according to which the final objective of even the most abstract sciences consists in the satisfaction of the needs of society, this sentence, I think, is only a more radical formulation of Descartes's postulate, that the old theoretical philosophy, ought to be replaced by a new "practical" philosophy, which should enable us, to become the masters and owners of nature, *maîtres et possesseurs de la nature*. And whenever in the totalitarian working state not only the sciences but also philosophy (or what passes for philosophy) has come into the trying situation of being forced to answer constantly the inquisitorial question, what its contribution is to the Five-Year-Plan, then, I should think, this is nothing but the strictest consequences of that Cartesian demand for a practical philosophy; and the dictator of the utility-plans in nothing but the contemporary modern form of the *maître et possesseur de a nature*.

This position, untheoretical on principle and based on pure will to power, clearly cannot be shaken by theoretical arguments. There is, however, one argument, an *existential* argument, so to speak, to which the human being, precisely within the totalitarian working world, seems to be extremely sensitive. The argument is: freedom.

At this point it comes to light at the same time, that we ourselves have to think anew, at least to *formulate* anew one fundamental thought to the great philosophical tradition—a thought which has, as it seems, more or less disappeared out of our range of vision. I am speaking of the Aristotelian thesis: that of all human activities the philosophical alone has the quality of freedom. This idea which at first sight indeed sounds somewhat strange, shows its enormous timeliness precisely in the confrontation with the totalitarian claim of the modern working state. This idea itself, to be sure, includes a whole philosophy of life, which cannot be explained here. But I must speak of two elements of that philosophy. The *first* element is the conviction that cognition of truth and freedom belong together in a very definite way; the *second* element is the conviction that the will to truth nowhere manifests itself more radically than in the philosophical act.

Concerning point *one*, (freedom and cognition of truth), I should like to mention an experience I had some years ago in a discussion group with students from the totalitarian world. Almost incidentally one of the participants mentioned a Russian novel, at that time everywhere spoken of, today already more or less forgotten. The friends from the other side of the Iron Curtain said that this book could not be printed and published in their own country because the truth about the Russian Revolution allegedly had been grossly distorted. To this we replied: perhaps one could find out how things really are—or not? Therefore, it is true, it would be indispensable to discuss the matter in question absolutely *independently*—independent of every official direction and instruction. Moreover, a "free room" in the midst of society would be needed—a range, in which such a discussion could take place without interference. This was the point at which several things suddenly became clear to *all* members of the group. First, it became clear what it means whether in a political community this "free room" does or does not exist—a room, *nota bene*, within which all practical purposes and interests (be they collective or private, political, ideological, economical) are explicitly suspended. Moreover, it was suddenly evident for everybody, that this asylum, this place of immunity (in the old juridical sense) had certainly to be protected and guaranteed from outside, by the political power, but that, above all, the freedom of this asylum had to be made possible and even constituted *from inside*: by nothing but the will to truth, which is, and be it perhaps only for this one moment, interested exclusively in one thing: to find out how things really stand. That and how much this (this: to be able not only to think, but also to *say*, how according to one's own best knowledge things really are and stand)— how much this means: freedom, not the whole of freedom, but a very essential indispensable piece of freedom. On this point we needed not waste a singe word, at that time, in Berlin. By the way; this freedom from any service of practical aimings and purposes, by this same freedom is meant the old concept of *liberal* arts; *artes liberales*, St. Thomas says (in his commentary on that same passage of the Aristotelian metaphysics), *artes liberales* are called only those human activities which are related to the knowledge of truth.

But now we have to discuss the *second* element of that Aristotelian conception: Why and how should "theoria," how should this will to truth and nothing but truth be a distinguishing mark of *philosophy*? Does not *every science* aim at exactly this: to see things as they really are? Do not therefore science and freedom belong together in exactly the same way as freedom and philosophy?

(As you see, at this point the topic "Philosophy and Science" comes already into the play; and it is indeed *not* a mere chance, that the demand to nullify the distinction between philosophy and science has been proclaimed just on the basis of the modern *working* world.)

We said, "theoria" in the old sense means that attitude toward reality, in which there is only one thing that matters: that man gets sight of reality and that things are seen as they really are. But since this manifestation of reality means exactly the same as *truth* (for truth is nothing but reality's coming to man's sight), therefore one can say also: the theoretical attitude to the world is directed to truth and nothing else.

This will to truth, further on, manifests itself *by silence*; for, only the silent is able to listen. And in *this* consists the *difference* between *philosophy* and *science*: to philosophize means to listen so completely and totally, that this listening silence is disturbed or interrupted by nothing, not even by a question. Science, on the other hand, is *not* silent, it *does* ask a question. And it is precisely this question, explicitly formulated under a specific particular aspect, by which science *constitutes* itself as *this* special science. The scientist explicitly wants to hear something quite definite, which lies within a formally limited range; and also his silence is only *partly* a silence; it is, in this sense, a *particular* silence. But the silence which has to be realized in the philosophical "theoria" (and the empirical individual never will succeed in realizing it *perfectly*), this silence should fill the soul entirely. This presupposes an unbiased openness, which is much more than the famous "scientific objectivity." It might rather be characterized by Goethe's formulation "complete renunciation of any pretension." Even more to the point would be the biblical phrase of the simplicity (or: singleness) of the eye: "If thy eye is single, the whole of thy body will be lit up" (Matt. 6. 22). The scientist, even if he would be hunting ever so passionately after a solution of a problem, the scientist need not be engaged to *such* a degree and not in the *existential* center of his person. That is to say, science is not to such an extreme degree "theoria" as philosophy is. A scientific physician, for instance, may conduct excellent investigations of what happens physiologically when a man dies (regarding respiration, circulation, brain function), and he may nevertheless, at the same time, close his mind to the question, what else happens whenever a man dies, what on the whole and altogether is taking place there, not only physiologically, but in *every* possible respect. Here that openness on the whole is necessary, which alone could possibly enable him, to get sight at all of the dimensions of the subject-matter of philosophy. Not only the very special kind of "critical attitude" is here coming to light, which makes all the difference between scientist and philosopher and which means not so much to refuse everything that cannot be exactly verified, but rather to be anxious that not one single aspect of reality be suppressed or forgotten. Not only this comes to light here, but also the other fact (as John Henry Newman puts it): "knowledge . . . is then especially liberal or sufficient for itself . . . when and so far it is philosophical." This is so because philosophy alone (although the sciences, of course, also have *to deal with truth*)—because philosophy alone, as Aristotle says, is *science of truth* in the strict sense, *maxime scientia veritatis*.

In fact, science, compared with philosophy has a specifically different relation to *freedom*. There exists not only a special kind of intellectual unfreedom, which, as it seems, can only befall the scientist (I am speaking of the self-restriction to what is exactly knowable). But moreover science, because of the essential *practicability* of its results, quite legitimately *serves* and can be *taken into service* of purposes which lie outside of science. And the modernity of all those old truths becomes evident as soon as one tries to defend the right of pure "theoria" and philosophical contemplation against the totalitarian claim of the contemporary working world.

II

When Karl Jaspers said in 1960 (in an academic address) that philosophy had become an embarrassment for all, he had in view the situation of philosophy not within the working world but within the *University* of today, which clearly subordinates itself more and more to the standard and measure of the exact sciences. Again, this discord cannot be put out of the world—unless philosophy itself would be put out of the world. In philosophy something happens which is, considered scientifically, indeed scandalous and even impossible, provided that you understand by philosophy the same as Plato and Aristotle and the great tradition up to Karl Jaspers have understood by it.

On the other hand, scientific research and philosophy have never been an obstacle to each other; strictly speaking, not the sciences themselves are the adversaries of philosophy, but those who maintain that exact science is the only binding and norm-giving model of all occupation with reality and truth. However, debates like this in the history of ideas (*Geistesgeschichte*) usually do not come about by a mere chance or by sheer frivolity. And it may be good from time to time to check up and to formulate anew the position of both parties. I have to limit myself here to a kind of catalogue of complaints and differences, from which the controversy usually catches fire.

The first point is: the philosophizing man and the scientist are in a radically different sense "on the way" to the answer they are searching for. Whoever undertakes to consider world and existence as a whole has set his foot on a way, on which he never will come to an end; he will *remain* "on the way"; his question will never be answered completely, nor his hope satisfied and stilled. The physicist on the other hand, who tackles a special problem, does not enter upon an unfinishable way; one moment he will have accomplished his way and his question will be answered. Of course, immediately new questions arise, but then this will be a new story again. In the manifesto of the Vienna Circle (entitled: "Wissenschaftliche Weltauffassung"—Scientific Worldview) it has been said: we do not know any insoluble mysteries; questions whose unanswerability is clear are no longer scientific questions; they will be immediately put aside. Why ask questions which cannot be answered? The reply from the side of philosophy will be: couldn't it be that as long as you are really asking the question, and perhaps only then, you keep yourself open to your infinite object; could not this be perhaps the only way to remain, so to speak, at its heels? And the philosopher will be inclined to add that the centric existence of the earthly historical man also means "being on the way"; and his existence, too, not unlike philosophy, has the structure of hope. Probably this conviction of the nonperfectibility of the historical man and of human society belongs to the existential presuppositions of a conception of philosophy which includes in its very definition the impossibility of an adequate and final answer to the philosophical question.

A *second* conflict between science and philosophy, again not easily to be settled, is the basically different idea of the greater or smaller perfection of human knowledge in general. From the viewpoint of science, it will be said: knowledge is perfect to the same degree as it is possible to grasp a reality or a fact with clear concepts and to express it in a precise formulation. The view of the philosophizing man is quite different.

It is, I think, not only a humanly moving event, but also a highly characteristic one, that Alfred North Whitehead, whose career had begun under the sign of the *Principia Mathematica*, at the end of his life as a philosopher in the great style of the occidental tradition had to confess: "The exactness is a fake." (Professor Nathaniel Lawrence, who wrote a well-founded book on Whitehead's philosophical development and who attended that famous farewell-lecture, which the eighty-year-old Whitehead finishes with that same sentence—Lawrence told me, that "he spoke it with all the vigour that he was able to put into his high, frail voice; and with a benign radiance that made you think he was about to say 'The Lord is my shepherd'; and maybe he was.") There can be not a shade of the suspicion that the former cofounder of modern mathematical logic could have proclaimed here or even conceded any kind of irrationalism. No, what comes to light here is a *changed* idea, namely, the *philosophical* and not any longer a scientific idea of the perfection of human knowledge. This idea means that not the *modus* of perceiving is decisive but the rank of *what* you perceive; wherefore, as Aristotle and Thomas Aquinas say, "the least insight one can obtain into sublime things is more desirable than the most certain knowledge of lower things."

A *third* point of quarrel: All results of science have the character of discovery, that is to say, of the disclosure of something that up-to-then was simply unknown. Under this aspect, it must appear as a kind of scandal that philosophy in fact does not only not satisfy this claim, but that it explicitly does not even make such a contention or pretense. Philosophy aims at something absolutely different—different from the extension of our knowledge of the external world. Of course, whoever views, in a philosophical way, a phenomenon like "guilt" or "freedom" or "death"—of course does intend to obtain a deeper insight into that phenomenon. Yet what in fact happens is that the philosophizing mind, in its deeper understanding, would not get sight of something absolutely *new*, of something which it simply did not know before at all. So far Wittgenstein's sentence, at least in its negative part, is quite correct: "The result of philosophy is not a number of 'philosophical propositions'"; but Wittgenstein is *not* right when he continues that this result should consist in clearing up the propositions of science. What happens in philosophy, or better, in the *philosophical act*, is rather that something that we did already know becomes more perspicuous and evident; what happens is that *re*conquest of something forgotten, which we call "remembrance." Even the great so-called discoveries in the history of philosophy have *au fond* the structure of a *re*cognition. And this, of course, is scarcely an impressive thing, if you consider it from the viewpoint of sciences, which every day triumphantly bring something new before the eyes of men—before their eyes and into their hands.

"Progress"—the glory of sciences—is indeed in the sphere of philosophy a rather problematic category; if "progress" means that the total sum of knowledge should become *eo ipso* greater and richer—*eo ipso*, that is to say: in a direct proportion to the passing of time.

Nevertheless, the philosopher ought to accept the scientific criticism at least in two points, even if this criticism should not be completely justified. The two points are: the philosophical language and the relation to experience.

Often enough, on the side of science, the criticism of philosophical language is taken all too easy. The reason is, I think, that the scientist just does not know the demand with which the philosopher always is confronted: namely, to speak of something which he undeniably encounters, but which at the same time, he is not able to voice or describe exactly; and to make perceivable in his philosophical utterance and together with his positive statement the ultimate incomprehensibility of his object. However, it is not just a little that philosophy may learn from the language of science. Even in the most complicated scientific treatise, it is, strictly speaking, not the language which makes the understanding difficult; whereas, as everybody knows the difficulty of reading a philosophical book is not too rarely caused by its language and by nothing else; language itself is the obstacle; perhaps I should rather say: the obstacle is the misuse of language. But this not only violates the spirit of science; it is likewise in contradiction to the style of the great occidental philosophy itself. Wherever the common linguistic usage is replaced by terminological arbitrariness, there has been left the realm of the *recherche collective de la vérité* (which does certainly not exclude, but rather even promotes the formation of followings).

Thus, clarity of speech is demanded not only from science but also from philosophy. But clarity is not the same as preciseness. At any rate, there is a special kind of precision, which philosophy in fact not only *has* never reached, but which philosophy cannot even *wish* to reach. This is the reason (*one* of the reasons) why philosophy can never accept the suggestion to renounce the use of natural historical language and to produce instead of it an artificial formalized terminology as the exact sciences did. "Precise" means: "cut off." The precision of the artificial term consists in this: under a certain, clearly defined aspect it cuts and snips a special partial phenomenon out of a complex fact; and the technical term offers this partial phenomenon like an isolated specimen for observation purposes. But just by this procedure, the complex fact, the "whole," with which philosophy by definition is concerned, is more or less obscured; whereas, on the other hand, the natural, historical, naturally grown language is just keeping present this complex whole. An example: the term *exitus*, used sometimes by physicians, in order to designate the physiological fact of death, the mere ceasing of the vital functions of the body—this term is "precise"; the word of natural language corresponding to this term *exitus*, is *death*. This word is much less "precise," but it is much more "clear" because "death" means and designates the whole of what really happens, when a man dies. What is important in the philosophical utterance is this: to make audible the full power of designation which is contained in the natural language and which *au fond* is known to everybody, to make it audible in such a way that, beyond all precision, the great object of human search for wisdom, concerning everybody, becomes and remains conspicuous.

Besides the allegedly lacking precision of language, the most objectionable peculiarity of philosophy seems to be its questionable relation *to experience*. And, I think, it is indeed hopeless, but also not worthwhile to try to defend as "philosophy" the countless essayistic or systematizing forms of a merely constructive-speculating thinking. The proposition of the manifesto of the Vienna Circle, "There is no way to substantial knowledge beside the way of experience" (which, after all, by no means is an empirical finding), this statement is, in the main, absolutely correct. Of course, it depends upon what you understand by experience. My suggestion would be to define experience as knowledge that comes about through an immediate contact with reality. But the organ and the infinitely sensitive and differentiated reflector of such a contact is the whole man alive. And if really our purpose is to come, on the way of experience, to a deeper and more universal knowledge of that which is, nothing of which this reflector registers must be left out of account; again I am quoting Whitehead: nothing can be omitted, experience sleeping and experience waking, experience happy and experience grieving, experience in the light and experience in the dark, etc.

Therefore, if I accept altogether the critical demand that philosophy should legitimatize itself by going back to experience, I insist at the same time on the "de-dogmatization" of the concept "experience," to whose contents everything belongs that Whitehead spoke of, and perhaps even something more.

III

The most "problematic" problem I have saved for the conclusion. There is not much controversy about the necessity, that whoever nowadays is dealing with the "essence" of man is not allowed to take no account of evolution (for instance). But there certainly will come up much controversy, if somebody would maintain (as I do): that a philosophical consideration of man is not allowed either to ignore the statement of sacred tradition which says that, in the earliest beginning of human history, something extremely fateful happened to man—something the consequences of which determine the existence of historical mankind up to this day. The general question is the following: Does it belong or not to the strictly philosophical business of man philosophizing to include into his consideration informations about world and existence which come out of a region, that could be designated by names like "revelation," "sacred tradition," "faith," "theology"? My answer to this question would clearly be: *yes*, the inclusion of such informations into the philosophical discussion is not only legitimate, but it is indispensable and necessary.

But first I should say more expressly, what to understand by those names revelation, tradition, faith, theology. *Revelation* means here the primary, absolutely incomprehensible act of communication, in which a divine speech, a *theios logos*, becomes audible; it is what Plato has called "the bringing down of a divine message by an unknown Prometheus." *Sacred Tradition*: this is the process of handing down and receiving, by which that revelation, once given, is kept historically present through the generations. *Faith* is the personal act of assent by which man accepts the divine speech as truth, for the sake of his superhuman origin. *Theology* is the attempt to interpret the documents of revelation and sacred tradition and to grasp their real meaning.

But my thesis is still exposed to so many misunderstandings that I should like to begin by saying what it does *not* mean. First, I am *not* speaking here of the general phenomenon, that whoever tries to make up his mind about the ultimate meaning of world and existence goes actually and unavoidably back to informations which have the character of a statement of belief (even if the negation of "sacred tradition" and "revelation" has been explicitly formulated as a principle). Always again it is surprising how little, for instance, J.-P. Sartre seems to notice this. Apparently he is not at all aware of how uncritically he presupposed the nonexistence of God, much more "believingly" at any rate, than the traditional occidental philosophy has ever presupposed that the world is creation. Nevertheless, Sartre's thinking, because he "declares" expressly his own preceding fundamental "convictions of faith," possesses that immediate existential relevance, which always is the distinguishing mark of a seriously performed philosophizing.

Further, I do *not* speak here of "the" philosophy, but of the philosophical *act* and of the philosophizing *person*. I do not deal here with the question, whether, in a systematic exposition of the problems of philosophy, theological statements ought to be included or not in the discussion. What I maintain is only this: *if* the philosophizing person in fact considers certain super-rational statements on world and existence to be *really informations*, that is to say, if he actually does not doubt their truth, he would cease philosophizing seriously in the very moment in which he would leave them out of account *because* he would, from that moment on, no longer consider his object under every possible aspect! What I have in view is only the case of a philosophizing person, who is expressly at the same time a believer, which in our Western civilization normally means: one who is a Christian. But I explicitly *dis*regard here the problem whether there can be or not a Christian philosophy. What I maintain is, once more, only this: insofar as a Christian philosophizes in existential seriousness, to that extent he is neither able nor allowed to leave the truth of revelation out of his consideration.

Against this, there are in modern philosophy two weighty "cons," both of high typical value: I am speaking of Martin Heidegger and Karl Jaspers.

Heidegger's counterargument goes thus: to philosophize means to ask a question: the question, in the asking of which, according to Heidegger, the philosophizing consists, is: why is there being at all instead of nothing? Now, whoever considers the biblical myth of creation to be true, Heidegger says, is *eo ipso* unable to ask seriously this question, since he is claiming to know the answer, which means, he is unable to philosophize.

Jaspers, on his part, does not say that the believer should be unable to philosophize but, quite inversely, that the philosophizing man should be unable to believe. For belief means to rely on someone else, who is acknowledged as authority; but authority is, as Jaspers says, the proper enemy of philosophizing.

If one investigates a bit closer the concept of philosophy, which is behind those two statements, it becomes clear that Heidegger as well as Jaspers both emphasize an aspect which in the traditional conception of philosophy from Plato to Kant is of almost no importance, if it is mentioned at all.

Heidegger with provoking radicality insists on the postulate that philosophizing essentially be *asking a question*. It is true that also in the great philosophical tradition it has been said always again that the philosophical question after the ultimate meaning of world and existence will never be quieted or satisfied by a final absolute answer. But: to ask a question means *here*, to *aim at an answer* and to remain open to an answer. Whereas, in the case of Heidegger, to ask a question seems to mean rather: to refuse on principle every possible answer and to close the mind against it because of the question's remaining a question.

Jaspers, on the other hand, emphasizes especially the independence of philosophy. The philosophizing man certainly is longing for an answer, but not that unconditionally, that he would be willing to accept it from someone else. This idea is, to be sure, not altogether foreign to the old concept of philosophy; but it never has had by far such an importance.

Both points of view, that of Heidegger and that of Jaspers, have one thing in common: the almost jealous vigilance to prevent any possible contamination of the formal property of the philosophical act; the methodical "purity" of philosophy seems to be more important than the solution of the philosophical question. And this marks the difference of the attitude of the great occidental philosophy which never considered itself to be a special, cleanly limited academic discipline and which, paradoxically speaking, never was interested in "philosophy" at all. Instead, it was interested, with an energy of mind which completely consumed its attention, only in this: to bring before the eyes and to keep in view what it ultimately means to be real, to be a man, to be just, to be free, and so on. The great figures of the philosophical tradition are concerned with nothing but an answer to questions like these—the answer may be ever so "unprotected" and may even come from somewhere else (be it even from a superhuman sphere).

Socrates never hesitates to confess that he does not know by his own the last truths on which human life is based, but that he got to know them only "ex akoos," by virtue of hearing; and the neighborhood of rational argumentation and mythical tradition, characteristic for almost all Platonic dialogues, means the same. In Aristotle's much more "scientific" philosophy, it is not so evident; Werner Jaeger, however, has shown, that (as he says) the *credo ut intelligam* stands also behind his (Aristotle's) *Metaphysics*. Even with Immanuel Kant the same tradition is still in force, which again is not immediately evident. But how surprising it is, eight years after the *Critique of Pure Reason*, he calls the New Testament an "imperishable guide of true wisdom," wherefrom reason gets "a new light with regard to all, that always remains in darkness but about which nevertheless it needs instruction."

How exactly this connection of what we know and of what we believe could be described—this is a new and a very difficult question which cannot be discussed here and now. Moreover, it is nowhere written that it possibly could be answered at all in a handy theoretical formula. What is in question here is not only a difficulty of thinking. But above all, this combination has to be realized under the conditions of concrete existence. Conflicts are not only likely but simply unavoidable; they are the natural companions of intellectual progress.

It could be called even the criterion of a true philosophical education, to be prepared for those discords and to be ready to sustain them and to resist hasty harmonies as well as premature resignation—which is quite in conformity with the great sentence: that the superiority of a philosophy which incorporates every attainable information does not so much consist in smoother solutions, but in showing more evidently, that reality is a mystery.

Jacques Maritain: A Believing Philosopher

Edward A. Synan

My collar justifies my beginning with a text. This evening that text is taken from the introductory words with which Professor Jacques Maritain gave his view of a youthful project on which he had come to entertain second thoughts:

> La philosophie Bergsonienne was my first book; it was published forty years ago when I was young, and did not hesitate to rush in where angels feared to tread.[1]

The unmistakable rustle you have just heard was the cautionary spreading of his wings by my guardian angel—as brakes to stop his flight. He fears understandably to join me in presuming to speak of Jacques Maritain to this distinguished reunion of the American Maritain Association.

Still, extenuating circumstances can be listed.

First, Professor Deal Hudson invited me; the Holy One, in his infinite mercy, will surely forgive him and, it is to be hoped, you will too.

Second, like many of you, but fewer as the years slip by, I knew Maritain and, what is more, he knew me—as you will hear.

Third, my supervisor when I was a student in Toronto, in dialectic a Greek of the Greeks, once skewered me in Socratic fashion on whether Maritain was a "philosopher" or a "theologian." This evening, forty years later, it will be possible to nuance my answer, for on the face of it, I was wrong in making Maritain a theologian rather than a philosopher.

Fourth and last, if Aristotle is best interpreted "through Aristotle," *Aristoteles per Aristotelem*, it will be possible and also acceptable to appeal to what Maritain has said and written in an effort to catch his intentions. Not one of us would be a member of this Association were we immune to the lure of this wise man.

---

1. "La Philosophie bergsonienne est mon premier livre. Il a paru voilà quarante ans, alors que j'étais jeune et que je n'hésiterais pas à foncer là où les anges craignent de s'aventurer," *Jacques et Raïssa Maritain. Oeuvres complètes* (Paris/Fribourg: Editions universitaires/Editions saint-Paul, 1986), 1: 7; Maritain here cited Alexander Pope, *An Essay on Criticism*, Part 3, line 66.

Since my personal contacts with Professor Maritain were during my time as a graduate student in Toronto, it ought to be mentioned that from the early 1930s Étienne Gilson and his colleagues there had made strenuous efforts to attract him to the staff of the Institute of Mediaeval Studies. Those efforts enjoyed only limited success. He did visit and he gave the occasional lecture; he often advised graduate students on their dissertations. A kind of malevolent myth grew up on the campus that he and Gilson had frequently disagreed on the advice he had given. We new students were assured by the older ones that those disagreements had been acerbic. Maritain had spoken of a "critical realism" to the distress of Gilson; he promoted the notion of an "intuition of being" quite unacceptable to our Director of Studies. Some students, we were assured, had been delayed for years as they rewrote what Maritain had recommended and Gilson had deplored. No concrete case of such a nightmare for a graduate student was ever proffered. Truth to tell, the two great Frenchmen did not agree on everything but they knew how to disagree on a civilized plane.

One remembers, for instance, the lines of Gilson on Maritain's use of the expression "critical realism." True enough, Gilson thought the term an unfortunate one: "it would be better to say it differently," but this did not prevent his saying that what "the more perspicacious among them wish to say" coincided with his own favored expression "realism" without qualification, *réalisme tout court*.[2]

A day came when Maritain and Gilson met in the presence of us students. They were cordial, each obviously interested in the other's work. In contrast to the evidently robust Gilson, Maritain was fragile, delicate, elegant. His long scarf, worn in all weathers, was imposed by Raïssa; she was exercised lest he catch a cold or worse. Her fears and his absences . . . ?

We students who were also priests were welcome in the Basilian Fathers' Common Room and there someone introduced me to Professor Maritain. He inquired graciously about my work; on whom was I working? What sort of figure was that man? A year later some well-meaning Basilian introduced me to Maritain once more. "Oh yes," he said, "you are the one who is working on a fourteenth-century English logician." How much of Maritain was in that single sentence: his genuine interest in a doctoral candidate, met in casual circumstances a year before, his precise and retentive memory, his capacity to deal without awkwardness with one inferior to himself in scholarship and

---

2. " . . . les plus clairvoyants d'entre eux veulent dire . . . it vaudrait mieux le dire autrement," Etienne Gilson, *Réalisme thomiste et critique de la connaissance* (Paris: J. Vrin, 1947), p. 37.

fame and accomplishment, yet, in his view, a superior thanks to sacramental priesthood. For me the experience was flattering and humbling and memorable. Jacques Maritain had been a fabled name from my undergraduate time at Seton Hall College; no reader of *Commonweal* and *America* in those prewar years could fail to know both Maritain's name and his always striking stance, above all on the Civil War in Spain and on the worsening plight of Europe's Jews. Those who lived through those days will know how his stance was at odds with the common wisdom of so many and of such influential Catholic circles. My friends and I then thought him a saint and a savant, a living justification of our faith and of our nascent, limited, learning. Despite all that has happened since, I think we undergraduates were right in our estimate.

"All that has happened since"?

It would be fatuous to pretend that nothing has happened to Maritain and to his reputation in the years between. From an admitted "liberal" in the most positive sense of that ambiguous term, Maritain now represents what is widely thought of as excessively "conservative," as dated, in the common parlance of the days when I was young as "old hat."

One need not entertain a Chestertonian respect for the common parlance of the Common Man to concede that there is something to this. Maritain (and we may say Chesterton as well) is in fact "old hat." Undergraduates in this decade are unlikely to read either one with the fervor that moved us; professors of philosophy are not likely to give courses based upon the books of either one. For no section of church or of society does Maritain, to say nothing of the Master of Paradox, continue to embody "liberal" ideals and aspirations. And yet, and yet . . .

Is there anything in Maritain's astonishing *oeuvre*, in that regiment of books and articles and letters, to give us pause as we concede what, it seems, must be conceded, yet might justify our persistent respect, even reverence, for Jacques Maritain?

One passage has long maintained itself in my memory:

> . . . the system of Einstein has replaced that of Newton, that of Copernicus had replaced that of Ptolemy.
>
> The temptation to generalize is enormous, to think that this sort of progress extends by right to the total domain of spiritual activity...
>
> Very frequently have we responded that this is to fall into a gross confusion: to confound the art of the philosopher with that of

the tailor or of the dressmaker. In addition, Truth does not recognize a chronological criterion.³

Words written or, at least, published in 1934, the year in which my Seton instruction began. Worse yet, it was the year in which I had graduated from high school. Would anyone today speak of the "art" of the philosopher? Who would say that "Truth" recognizes or does not recognize a criterion? Does not the reference to Einstein smack of a 1930s effort to be up-to-date, paradoxically in 1990 a confession that the author who has made it is now dated. All of this is true, but it is not the whole truth. Maritain has here put his finger on a most crucial distinction.

Some human activities, to be sure, are time-bound and it would be hard to find one more evident than is fashion in clothing. Last year's dress or last year's lapels are like last year's calendar; fluctuating hemlines and whether men wear hats date old movies with precision; chain mail gave way to plate armor, the bustle has become comic, tailors on side streets advertise that they are ready to widen (or to narrow) our old ties. More fundamental human achievements follow a comparable pattern: technology presides over an evermore rapid advance by substitution.

How absurd to transfer this perception to literature—to abandon Homer because he wrote in a dialect already old in Plato's day or to jettison Chaucer because *The New Collegiate Dictionary* does not have his terms, his spellings, his syntactical practice. Is the Parthenon out of date because it has no elevators, Notre Dame because structural steel might have allowed its towers to thrust higher?

Philosophy is like the second, not like the first. *Modus ponens* still does what *modus tollens* cannot do; "being," already an old question in the day of Aristotle, continues to pose enigmas to phenomenologists and Thomists and Hegelians and logicians.⁴ This was the chosen field of Maritain; it was no accident that this philosopher by profession was also a voice of poetry and painting, even, to a point, of theology and mysticism and prayer. Because neither he nor any other son of Adam, no

---

3. " . . . le système d'Einstein a remplacé le système de Newton; celui de Copernic avait remplacé le système de Ptolémée . . .

"La tentation est grande de généraliser, de penser que ce genre de progrès s'étend de droit " tout le domaine de l'activité spirituel . . .

3. Nous avons repondu bien souvent que c'est là tomber dans une confusion grossière, confondre l'art du philosophe avec celui du tailleur ou de la modiste. Et qu'au surplus la vérité ne reconnaît pas de critère chronologique," *Sept leçons sur l'être*, in *oeuvres*, 5: 527.

4. *Metaphysics* Z, 1; 1028b 3; see also Plato *Sophist* 244A.

daughter of Eve, escapes the human condition, Maritain's philosophical insights have been expressed in language that is redolent of his long, but finite, life. To speak in his own vocabulary, that time-bound language expressed what transcends time. Maritain was a wise man and his wisdom with its beauty comes through what he wrote in French conditioned by his education, by his philosophical masters, by his reading, by the necessity of speaking to his time in the language of that time.

There is a sense in which Maritain is, in fact, "old hat," but for those of us who wish to talk sense, this does not matter. Philosophy is a love of wisdom in a human person and wisdom is immune to aging and to death. Precisely to the point that Maritain achieved something in his lifelong love of wisdom, Maritain transcends death and aging.

But, it will be objected, his vision of wisdom is a vision of another time; he was willing to be a "Thomist" and the Thomism he cultivated has had its day. Perhaps the honored burial of Brother Thomas ought to be matched with an equally honorable, but also equally definitive, burial of his doctrine, so redolent of another age.

Should this solution not be adopted then, at least, let Thomism be renovated; have we not thinkers capable of doing for Thomism what the Common Doctor did for Aristotle—help him to say more than he could have known, develop the latent truth more relevant to our world?

Something of the sort occurred when Maritain was still alive to respond or, better, to react. In the days that followed on the ending of the Second World War no philosophical stance was more modish than the "existentialist"; its *angst* and its freedom, its impatience with the static, with "nature" and with "essence" matched the allure of its positive emphasis on "existence" in all its unpredictability and contingency. More than one Thomist excitedly rejoiced in what can hardly escape a Thomist of any complexion: the Common Doctor had more than a little to say about existence too; had he not given *esse* precedence over *essentia*, made of the act of being the perfection of perfections? Was he not Sartre before Jean-Paul and, what is more, was he not Sartre without the atheism, without the ambiguity in moral perspective?

Maritain responded and his response was a reaction:

> This brief treatise on existence and the existent may be described as an essay on the existentialism of St. Thomas Aquinas ... utterly different from that of the "existentialist" philosophies propounded nowadays. If I say that it is, in my opinion, the only authentic existentialism, the reason is not that I am concerned to "rejuvenate" Thomism, so to speak, with the aid of a verbal artifice which I should be ashamed to employ, by attempting to trick out Thomas Aquinas in a costume fashionable to our day.

Not only did Maritain wish to avoid a cosmetic existentialism, neither did he wish to embrace the currently dominant Thomism:

> I am not a neo-Thomist. All in all, I would rather be a paleo-Thomist than a neo-Thomist. I am, or at least I hope I am, a Thomist.

This old philosopher here too has appealed to the illustration we have heard him use:

> For more than thirty years I have remarked how difficult it is to persuade our contemporaries not to confuse the philosopher's faculty of invention with the ingenuity that inspires the art of the dress designer.[5]

Maritain's voice was too personal to be submerged in any other, be that other the voice of Aquinas himself. Surely he must have been conscious of this as he wrote on current political issues, on new currents in the art of poetry and of painting. The term "invention" to characterize the activity of the philosopher was hardly accidental; he was persuaded that to be faithful to a master worth his salt was to be himself, formed by his master to be sure, but taking responsibility in a world his master could not have known.

Furthermore, there is an activity of refusal in the work of Jacques Maritain that is no less essential to him than was his affirmation of the values he felt he had found in Thomism. Here, often enough, to me at least, he seems excessive. One need not be a Cartesian to think he has been harsh on Descartes. Witty perhaps, but how unfair to write that "The shop of clear ideas is the Five-and-Ten, le *Bon Marché*, of Wisdom"![6] Yet more unfair his harsh description of Descartes's appearance: "A head pridefully heavy and violent, a low forehead, a prudent eye, obstinate, chimerical, a proud and earthly mouth; a strange and secret

---

5. "Ce court traité de l'existence et de l'existant peut êre regardé comme un essai sur l'existentialisme de saint Thomas d'Aquin . . . tout différent de celui des philosophies qu'on nous propose aujourd'hui; et si je dis qu'il est à mon avis le seul existentialisme authentique, ce n'est pas que je m'applique à *rajeuner* le thomisme par un artifice verbal dont j'aurais quelque honte, et en essayant d'affubler Thomas d'Aquin d'un costume à la mode. . . . Je ne suis pas un néo-thomiste, à tout prendre j'aimerais mieux ,tre an paléo-thomiste; je suis, j'espère être un thomiste. Et voilà plus de trente ans que je constate combien il est malaisé d'obtenir de nos contemporains qu'ils ne confondent pas les facultés d'invention des philosophes avec celles des artistes des grandes maisons de couture," *Court traité de l'existence et de l'existant* (Paris: P. Hartmann, 1947), pp. 9, 10.

6. "Le magasin des idées claires est le Bon Marché de la Sagesse," *Trois réformateurs* (Paris: Plon, 1925 [re-edition 1947]), p. 94.

life as well as one marked by ruses, but still, strong and great,"[7] a description, no doubt, of the Frans Hals portrait of Descartes included in his *Trois reformateurs*. Luther was handled more roughly still with three dated portraits, 1520, 1526, and 1532, followed by a drawing of Luther dead. He had surrendered to the flesh, wrote Maritain, "following a progress it is permissible to note in a series of portraits, the last of which are of an astonishing bestiality."[8] Better to have written with Chesterton:

> We must be just to those huge human figures who are in fact the hinges of history... our own controversial conviction... must never mislead us into thinking that something trivial has transformed the world. So it is with that great Augustinian monk... whose broad and burly figure has been big enough to block out for four centuries the distant human mountain of Aquinas.[9]

In any event, Maritain saw himself as a Thomist who was not, like Brother Thomas himself, a theologian.

When the question was put to me on a stairwell in the Pontifical Institute of Mediaeval Studies, I answered off the cuff that he was. For Maritain had claimed to be Thomist and Thomas was a Regent Master in the Faculty of Theology of Paris and Naples; Maritain had promoted the value of apparitions of Mary at La Salette and, it was said, had renounced the human joys of marriage for the austere joy of ascetic renunciation; he lectured and wrote on the *Summa Theologiae* with authority—I had heard him recommend that the so-called "treatise on law" in that work be extended, not by rehashing episodes and personalities, but by exercising the queenlike prerogatives of theology and enlisting the collaboration of ethnologists on how human societies in South Pacific islands interpreted "natural" inclinations. To tell the whole truth, both he and Gilson seemed to protest too much when they would almost ceremoniously defer to graduate students who were also priests on the smallest theological issue: I knew they both knew better than I what greater theological themes meant and now mean for the Church.

---

7. "Tête superbement lourde et violente, front bas, oeil prudent, obstiné, chimérique, bouche d'orgueil et de terre; étrange vie secrète et cauteleuse, mais tout de même forte et grande," *ibid.*, p. 76.

8. "... suivant une progression qu'il est loisible de constater sur la série de ses portraits, dont les derniers sont d'une bestialité surprenante," *ibid.*, p. 15; here Maritain refers his reader to a series of nine from which he had selected four in the work of Denifle-Paquier, *Oeuvres*, 4:237; and also to H. Preuss, *Lutherbildnises* (Leipzig, 1912).

9. *St. Thomas Aquinas: The Dumb Ox* (New York: Image Books, 1933), p. 195.

Still, Maritain's consistent claim that he was a philosopher only must be accepted. It is not possible for one of his stature to be a theologian or anything else in spite of himself. What I had taken to make him a theologian was no more than his conscious working out of philosophical wisdom in the presence of a faith so intelligent that he seemed to possess and to exercise an authentic grasp of the higher wisdom . . . seeking to understand humans in the world created by the Holy One, Maritain (and Gilson too) easily gave the impression that what they were doing was the classical theological enterprise: attempting to understand what they believed. In their own view what they were doing was "Christian philosophy," a reflective, rational examination of all that is in the presence of their biblical and ecclesial faith.

In concluding, my mind goes back to Maritain's impatience with the impatience of Descartes concerning the Greek and Roman classics. For this dinner reminds me, and there is good reason to think it has reminded our Fordham hosts, of that classical dinner, the banquet of Trimalchio.

There is a positive and a negative side to this reminiscence.

In a positive way we have been provided with a meal that transcends the human need for sustenance by making an art, if not quite a fine art, of ordering, cooking, and serving us.

That our Fordham hosts might remember Trimalchio's triumph is not without a basis in history. No one else you might have invited would be likely to know that in 1934-1935 Fordham inveighed one of Seton Hall's best classics professors, John Savage, away from us just before I should normally have taken his courses. Of course we had to hire another, and Seton Hall did well on that: She managed to attract a bright new Ph.D. from The Catholic University of America—not in a larcenous way, but for his first appointment, James O'Donnell.

With the classical tradition nurtured by the likes of Savage, there ought to be Fordham people in this room who remember that Trimalchio favored his guests with the epitaph he had chosen for himself and that in it, after some boasting of financial and political triumphs, he ended with a mention of our guild:

Pompeius Trimalchio Maecenatianus hic requiescit.
Huic seviratus absenti decretus est.
Cum posset in omnibus decuriis Romae esse, tamen noluit.
Pius, fortis, fidelis, ex parvo crevit,
sestertium reliquit trecenties,
nec unquam philosophum audivit.
Vale: et tu.[10]

---

10. Petronius arbiter, *Satyricon* 71: "Gaius Pompey Trimalchio, a freedman of Maecenus rests here. To him was decreed (even though he was not present!) status

The crucial last line, literally construed tells is that "he never listened to a philosopher"; less literally, but more accurately, it may be construed as "he never took a course from a philosopher."

Tonight, perhaps, you can make the same claim in the sense that in hearing me you have hardly heard the voice of wisdom.

But in another sense, you have. It is not possible to deal with Maritain's work, yet escape the wisdom of his voice. My last word must be one of thanks for an invitation which was not only an invitation to a splendid dinner, but also an invitation to renew acquaintance with the great man to whose work our Association is dedicated.

---

as a priest, a sevir, of the Emperor. Although he could have been on every council in Rome, he did not wish to. Pious, brave, faithful, he grew great from a small start; he has left 30,000,000 sesterces! He never took a course from a philosopher. Farewell; you too . . . "

Part I
Thomism and Pluralism

IS THOMAS'S WAY OF PHILOSOPHIZING STILL VIABLE TODAY?

Gerald A. McCool, S.J.

The title of this is not an affirmation. It is a question, and those who, like myself, would be willing to give an affirmative answer to it are not as numerous as we used to be. As to the question's relevance, I cannot assume that a large number of philosophers outside the Thomist community would see much point in entertaining it. In fact, even in the larger Catholic community, I suspect, a fair number of philosophers might be counted for whom finding an answer to my question would not rank high on their intellectual agenda.

The Flowering of the Neo-Thomist Movement

That, of course, would not have been true when the American Catholic Philosophical Association was founded in 1926. By the third decade of this century neo-Thomism had become a vigorous and promising movement in North America. In the first four years of the society's existence Étienne Gilson had established himself in North America, the Institute of Mediaeval Studies at Toronto had received its pontifical charter, the Institute Saint Thomas d'Aquin had opened its doors at Ottawa, Laval University had set up a distinguished Thomistic graduate faculty in Quebec, and The Catholic University of America, the home of the independent group of American Thomists, who were the driving force behind the founding of the Association, had celebrated its fiftieth anniversary.[1]

The young and promising North American neo-Thomist movement could not have established itself as quickly as it did were it not for an earlier flowering of neo-Thomist philosophy on the other side of the Atlantic. Leo XIII's Encyclical, *Aeterni Patris*, published in 1879, is generally taken as the *magna charta* of neo-Thomism; but, despite the impetus which Leo XIII gave to the Thomistic revival, the neo-Thomist movement did not really pick up momentum until the final decade of the nineteenth century and the first two decades of the twentieth. In

---

1. Gerald A. McCool, S.J., "The Tradition of St. Thomas in North America: At 50 Years," *The Modern Schoolman* 65 (1988): 185-206.

those three decades Désiré Mercier founded his Higher Institute of Philosophy at Louvain, and set it on firm footing. Mercier, and the faculty which he had chosen and trained himself, were hard at work on Louvain's twofold agenda: historical recovery of Thomas's medieval heritage and the modernization and development of Thomas's philosophy in order to deal with the problems presented to Catholic intellectuals by the physical and social sciences.[2] From the 1930s to the 1960s many American Thomists received their graduate training at Louvain and the whole American Thomist community was indebted to its Higher Institute for the historical work of Maurice de Wulf, Fernand van Steenberghen, and Georges Van Riet, and for the speculative expansion of St. Thomas's thought by Désiré Nys, Nicolas Balthasar, Albert Dondeyene, Louis de Raeymaeker and Jacques Leclerque, for as our older philosophers may recall, a fair number of Louvain publications were translated into English and made available to readers in the United States and Canada.

In the same three decades a brilliant group of French Dominicans, all of whom had some connection with the renowned House of Studies at La Saulchoir, countered the challenge to St. Thomas's realistic philosophy of being posed by idealism, pragmatism, and Bergson's intuitionistic epistemology and process metaphysics. The founder of this Dominican school was Ambroise Gardeil and two of his better known disciples were M.-D. Roland-Gosselin and Réginald Garrigou-Lagrange.[3] As a group, they worked out a French Dominican approach to Thomism whose influence on Jacques Maritain is quite evident in the latter's *The Degrees of Knowledge*.

At the same time, Jesuit Thomists in France and Belgium took a very different approach to idealism and Bergsonian philosophy, and two of them, Pierre Rousselot and Joseph Maréchal, laid the foundations for another neo-Thomistic tradition which was later given the name of Transcendental Thomism.[4] By the 1920s Jacques Maritain had begun his

---

2. Georges Van Riet, "Kardinal Desire Mercier (1851-1926) und das philosophische Institut in Lowen," in *Christliche Philosophie im katholischen Denken des 19. und 20. Jahrhunderts*, ed. Emerich Coreth, S.J., Walter M. Neidle, George Pfliegersdorfer and Heinrich M. Schmidinger (Graz: Sytria, 1988), pp. 206-40. Attention should also be called to Armand Maurer's excellent monograph on Étienne Gilson in this volume, pp. 519-545.

3. For the philosophies of Gardeil, Roland-Gosselin and Garrigou-Lagrange see Georges Van Riet, *L'Épistemologie thomists* (Louvain: Publications de l'Institut Supérieur de Philosophie, 1946), pp. 249-62, 425-31: 432-72: 338-49. For the theologies of Gardeil and Garrigou-Lagrange see Roger Aubert, *Le probleme de l'acte de foi* (Louvain: Warny, 1950), pp. 393-435; 443-50.

4. See Gerald A. McCool, S.J., *From Unity to Pluralism: The Internal Evolution of*

independent work on the integration of knowledge through the epistemology and metaphysics of the Angelic Doctor, a project which would carry him in the course of his long career into moral and political philosophy, aesthetics, and philosophy of the person and community. And, by the year in which the ACPA was founded, Étienne Gilson had won an international reputation as a historian of medieval philosophy, and he had begun to work out his original interpretation of St. Thomas's epistemology and metaphysics, an interpretation which would lead, in the years after World War II, to the Gilsonian conception of Christian philosophy and to Gilsonian existential Thomism.[5]

During the next thirty years, between 1930 and 1960, the neo-Thomistic movement continued to flourish in Europe and North America. New Thomistic traditions arose to contest its leadership by French Dominican, Maritainian, and Transcendental Thomism. Among them were Gilson's existential Thomism and a current of personalist Thomism influenced by Gabriel Marcel. The important place which Platonic participation metaphysics had played in St. Thomas's own philosophy was rediscovered and changed the older conception of Thomism as a Christian Aristotelianism through the historical work of L.-B. Geiger and Cornelio Fabro,[6] and through the speculative metaphysics of Louis de Raeymaeker.[7] Graduate faculties in North America reflected the diversity of these European neo-Thomistic currents. Gilson's influence, for example, was strong at the Mediaeval Institute at Toronto and at Saint Louis University; Maritain's influence made itself felt at Notre Dame; Transcendental Thomism, the more recent Thomistic personalism, the new interest in the Platonic element in Thomism, and Gilson's existential Thomism were all represented in the graduate instruction at Fordham.[8] After the Second World War North America produced its

---

Thomism (New York: Fordham University Press, 1988), pp. 39-113.

5. For an excellent summary of Gilson's philosophy and a collection of texts see Anton C. Pegis, ed., *A Gilson Reader* (Garden City, New York: Doubleday-Image Books, 1957). For Gilson's Christian philosophy see Armand Maurer, "The Legacy of Étienne Gilson," in *One Hundred Years of Thomism*, ed. Victor B. Brezik, C.S.B. (Houston, Texas: Center for Thomistic Studies, 1981), pp. 28-44. For Gilson's existential Thomism see his *Being and Some Philosophers* (Toronto: Pontifical Institute of Mediaeval Studies, 1952).

6. L. B. Geiger, *La participation dans la philosophie de s. Thomas d'Aquin* (Paris: Vrin, 1953). Cornelio Fabro, *La Nozione Metafisica di Participazione secundo S. Tommaso d'Aquino* (Torino: Societa Editrice Internazionale, 1950).

7. Louis de Raeymaeker, *Philosophie de l'être* (Louvain: Publications de l'Institut Supérieur de Philosophie, 1942). English translation: *The Philosophy of Being* (St. Louis, Missouri: B. Herder, 1954).

8. McCool, "The Tradition of St. Thomas in North America: At 50 Years."

own distinguished group of neo-Thomists. Among them were the historians and speculative thinkers whose names are associated with the Mediaeval Institute at Toronto: Gerald Phelan, Anton Pegis, Vernon Bourke, Joseph Owens, Armand Maurer, and Edward Synan. There are other distinguished historians, of course, among the North American neo-Thomists. The names of James Collins and James Weisheipl, for example, come readily to mind. Other Thomists of reputation, George Klubertanz, to name but one, brought out clear and concise speculative expositions of Thomism for use in the North American classroom.

For a while I was afraid that our collective memory of neo-Thomism's contribution to Christian philosophy would be lost, but, fortunately, in the past few years its history has begun to be written. Father Laurence Shook's magnificent biography of Étienne Gilson was published in 1984. More recently, in 1988, another significant contribution to the history of neo-Thomism was made in Austria. The second volume of *Christian Philosophy in Catholic Thought in the Nineteenth and Twentieth Centuries* [*Christliche Philosophie im katholischen Denken des 19. und 20. Jahrhunderts*] was brought out in Graz by a team of editors headed by Father Emerich Coreth.[9] In a series of concise and scholarly monographs this volume recounts the whole history of neo-Thomism from its early days to the present time. And, as some of you may know, I have been at work myself, in a more modest way, on the history of European and North American neo-Thomism.[10] Some record will remain then in accessible form of this important period in Catholic intellectual life and in the history of our own Association.

Has the Tradition of St. Thomas Ceased to be Relevant?

But what does the history of the neo-Thomist movement tell us who have spent some time studying it about the viability of St. Thomas's philosophy in a new intellectual climate in which the Angelic Doctor no longer plays a major role in Catholic thought? Is it true, as we have been told, that St. Thomas's metaphysics of being has lost its relevance because it cannot deal with historical reality as a contemporary philosophy must do? In a world in which we are told that philosophers have no work left to do beyond judging the coherence of diverse language games, what work is there left for Thomas? After Heidegger's destruc-

---

9. See note 2.
10. Notably two books, *Catholic Theology in the Nineteenth Century: The Quest for a Unitary Method* (New York: Seabury, 1977, republished as *Nineteenth-Century Scholasticism: The Search for a Unitary Method* [New York: Fordham University Press, 1989]), and *From Unity to Pluralism*.

tion of metaphysics, can St. Thomas, any more than Plato or Aristotle, still claim to have grasped the authentic meaning of truth and being? In a post-Heideggerian, post-foundational deconstructionist age, why should anyone in his right mind look to St. Thomas for useful philosophical ideas? These are daunting questions for a disciple of St. Thomas. Yet, in spite of them, a case can still be made, I would argue, that, even in a vastly changed philosophical world, St. Thomas has still a few words left to say. One of the reasons for my confidence is that, thanks to the historical study of neo-Thomism, which is still going on, St. Thomas's disciples are learning to identify those words more surely and to understand why they are still worth hearing.

It may seem strange for a historian of neo-Thomism to say that, given the history which he has studied. It is disturbing for him to realize that he might never have had a neo-Thomist movement to study, if the first neo-Thomists had not misunderstood both the nature of St. Thomas's thought and its relation to the Second Scholasticism, the great Scholastic revival in Spain and Italy in the decades before and after the Council of Trent. As a result, the success of the program of medieval studies which Leo XIII linked to the neo-Thomist movement progressively undermined the conception of the tradition of St. Thomas which had moved the pope to launch it. Far from being the common philosophy shared by all the medieval doctors, Scholasticism turned out to be little more than a common name under which a plurality of systematically diverse philosophies could be grouped. And what was true of the First Scholasticism turned out to be true of the Second Scholasticism as well. Suarezianism and Second Scholasticism Thomism, which Leo's advisers took to be essentially the same philosophy, were shown to be irreducibly distinct systems. More unsettling still, significant divergences from St. Thomas's own thought were found in the systems of Thomas's great Dominican Commentators. And so, in their philosophy of knowledge and being, and in their theologies of grace and nature, the great Thomistic systems of the Second Scholasticism and St. Thomas's own philosophical theology were not, as the early neo-Thomist thought, identical. Furthermore, to complete the demolition of Leo's view of the tradition of St. Thomas, the transition between patristic and Scholastic thought in the thirteenth century had not taken place, as *Aeterni Patris* would have us think, with no notable change in method or loss in content. The change which it had worked in philosophical and theological method has been radical and, in the areas of history, spirituality, and even doctrine, losses of no small moment counterbalanced the gains which St. Thomas's scientific rigor had brought to Catholic philosophy and theology. These disturbing facts, of course, have been known for decades. Neo-Thomists did not learn them from their enemies. They learned them from the historical research of scholars like Étienne Gilson, Marie-Dominique Chenu, Henri de Lubac, and Henri Bouillard, all of whom were affectionate disciples of the Angelic Doctor. The outcome of their work was a progressive and profound change in the self-understanding of the tradition of St. Thomas.

Thomists could no longer confuse the wisdom of the Angelic Doctor with a rigidly unitary system of theology which remained unchanged in its essentials from the age of the Fathers up to the present day. And, if history had shown that there had been pluralism in what Leo XIII described as the wisdom of St. Thomas, the evolution of that wisdom in its dialogue led to another manifestation of pluralism. Neo-Thomism did not develop into a strongly unitary system of modern philosophy as Leo XIII had hoped. It evolved instead into an irreducible diversity of competing Thomistic systems. Thomists differed with one another, for example, about Thomas's relation to Plato and to Aristotle. One leading Dominican Thomist, Gallus Manser, argued that the essence of Thomism was to be found in Thomas's Aristotelian metaphysics of act and potency.[11] Earlier on, the Jesuit neo-Thomist had taken the opposite tack. For Rousselot, Thomas's significant contribution to philosophy was an epistemology of insight of *intellectus*, reminiscent of St. Augustine, which the Angelic Doctor had linked to a Platonic participation metaphysics.[12] Whether Thomas was a Platonist or not was an issue which divided his disciples on this side of the Atlantic too. Anton Pegis, as you may recall, was not receptive to the idea of a Platonic Thomism. On the other hand, my Fordham colleague, William Norris Clarke, emphasized the importance of what the Irish Thomist Arthur Little had called the Platonic heritage of Thomism.[13]

From the early years of the century Kantian idealism and the usefulness of Kant's Transcendental Method had become another apple of discord in the neo-Thomist movement. Étienne Gilson told Thomists to steer clear of Kant. Rightly understood and consistently applied, Kant's Transcendental Method, he assured them, was a straight path to idealism. Any Thomist who thought that Kantian method could lead him to realism was a victim of either historical ignorance or intellectual

---

11. Bernhard Braun, "Gallus Manser (1866-1950)" in *Christliche Philosophie*, 2: 623-29.

12. Pierre Rousselot, S.J., *L'intellectualisme de Saint Thomas* (Paris: Beauchesne, 1924). The first edition was published in 1908.

13. W. Norris Clarke, S.J., "The Limitation of Act by Potency: Aristotelianism or Neo-Platonism?" *The New Scholasticism* 26 (1952): 167-94.

confusion.[14] But Joseph Maréchal and the Transcendental Thomists who followed him took a more optimistic view. Kant landed in idealism, they explained in soothing tones, only because he had not been consistent enough in the use of his own method. Once you went all the way with it, and took Kant's method as far as consistent use of it would let you, it led with logical necessity to Thomas's realistic metaphysics of being.[15]

After World War II, Thomas's metaphysics of existence led to another Thomistic "division of the house." Once Gilson had worked out the consequences of his metaphysics of existence and defined the role which he claimed that the judgment of existence must play in our grasp of being, Gilsonian Thomism, which had already separated itself from Transcendental Thomism, could no longer be reconciled with the Dominican Thomism, in the tradition of Gardeil, whose best known representative was Garrigou-Lagrange. Maritain admired that Dominican tradition and his own Thomism had been influenced by it. Gilson and Maritain were never eager to discuss their philosophical differences but that did not mean that their versions of Thomism always fitted easily together.

By mid-century then it was clear that irreconcilable differences, in their interpretation of the tradition of St. Thomas had emerged among the neo-Thomists. Some Thomists in fact were not content simply to observe that fact. Philosophical pluralism within Thomism, they claimed, was a legitimate exigence of St. Thomas's own epistemology and metaphysics. That, at least, was the position defended by the Jesuit Transcendental Thomists, Henri Bouillard and Jean-Marie Le Blond, in their well publicized debate with Garrigou-Lagrange and with two other Dominican Thomists, Marie-Michel Labourdette and Marie-Joseph Nicolas, whose understanding of Thomism had been shaped by Maritain's *The Degrees of Knowledge*.[16] With this radical division in its ranks, at the time of the "New Theology" crisis, the neo-Thomist movement, understood as the quest for a single, rigidly unitary, philosophical system, came to its end.

---

14. Étienne Gilson, *Thomist Realism and the Critique of Knowledge* (San Francisco: Ignatius Press, 1986), pp. 129-48. Original French version, *Réalisme thomiste et critique de connaissance* (Paris: Vrin, 1939).

15. See Joseph Donceel, S.J., *A Maréchal Reader* (New York: Herder and Herder, 1970).

16. For the details of this debate see McCool, *From Unity to Pluralism*, pp. 200-33.

The Clearer Self-Understanding of the Tradition of St. Thomas

Why should that history of a movement which began with misunderstanding and ended with the disappointment of its early hopes lead me to the optimistic view that the tradition of St. Thomas still remains a live option for a contemporary philosopher and that St. Thomas still has something to say to our contemporary community? One reason is the more accurate self-understanding which the tradition has acquired precisely through the historical and speculative work done in the neo-Thomist movement. We know now that St. Thomas was a highly original philosophical theologian, original enough to be condemned in 1277 and largely neglected after that. The link between Thomas and the Thomists of the Second Scholasticism was not a link of unbroken continuity. The Second Scholasticism was the revival of a long forgotten Thomas in a changed intellectual world faced with a new set of philosophical and theological problems. The Third Scholasticism of the neo-Thomist movement was a second revival after a second long period of oblivion. At the dawn of the nineteenth century St. Thomas was virtually unknown. The world of the Third Scholasticism was completely different from the world of the Second. It was the intellectual universe which antifoundationalist and postmodern philosophers call the modern world, the world whose view of reality is shaped by the concerns of modern science and by the post-Cartesian philosophy created to deal with them.

If Gilson, Chenu, de Lubac, and Lonergan are right, no philosophical theology of the Second Scholasticism could be totally identified with Thomas's own thought, and the same, I think, can be said of the diverse philosophies of the neo-Thomist movement. Philosophical pluralism within Thomism is a fact. Yet, despite that fact, a clearly discernible unity marks all its leading philosophers and theologians as followers of the Angelic Doctor. All are in the tradition of St. Thomas. Despite their misunderstandings of St. Thomas and the disagreements caused by their effort to adapt St. Thomas's thought to problems which he had never tried to solve, the Thomists of the Second and Third Scholasticism, without exception, claimed St. Thomas as their master. And not without evidence to vindicate their claim. For in their philosophy of knowledge, man, and being, the systems of these Thomists could clearly be distinguished from the rival philosophies of Augustinians, Scotists, Ockhamites, Cartesians, Empiricists, Kantians, Husserlian phenomenologists, and Whiteheadian process metaphysics. Thomists of Second and Third Scholasticism might be criticized for deficiencies in their interpretation of St. Thomas. No follower is the equal of a great master but, if these Thomists were not in the tradition of St. Thomas, what were they? They were closer to their master than to anybody else.

A discernible unity in their philosophy of knowledge, man, and being linked them both to St. Thomas and to one another. Since they were not intellectual archaeologists but practitioners of a living, working philosophy, they extended and modified what they took to be St. Thomas's thought and, at times, failed to do it full justice. But that occurs in every great tradition, whether the tradition be that of Plato, Aristotle, Kant, or Hegel. Traditions are great traditions precisely because, although disciples constantly endeavor to make their master's thought their own, no one of them or no group of them can exhaust that thought or indeed do it full justice.[17]

Disciples of a great master should not be scorned. It can make great sense at times for a philosopher engaged in serious philosophizing of his own to turn to a great tradition for the resources which he needs to cope with the problems of his time. In the tradition of St. Thomas philosophers turned to the Angelic Doctor twice in two distinct revivals of his thought, the Second and the Third Scholasticism. For that reason there are two histories of St. Thomas: the history of his own thought, and the "effective history," or *Wirkungsgeschichte*, of St. Thomas's thought reflected through the philosophies and theologies of his disciples. To appreciate the relevance of the Angelic Doctor's thought, I would argue, we should study both. The effective history of St. Thomas, as it passed through two great revival movements, is instructive. It has shown us that the unity and the vitality of this great tradition should not be confused with the unity of any individual's interpretation of St. Thomas's thought or with the uniformity sought by a revival movement within it. The same can be said of the vitality of this great tradition. The life span of a revival movement within a tradition should not be equated with the life span of the tradition itself.

The Relevance of Thomas's Philosophy of the Person

Traditions remain alive or come back to life when philosophers find in them resources they need to address the problems of their time. One of the reasons then why I am still optimistic about the viability of the tradition of St. Thomas is the recovery and speculative development of St. Thomas's philosophy of the person we owe to a number of neo-Thomists. Thomas's human person, they have shown us, was an autonomous human nature. But, in the tradition of the Fathers, that person was

---

17. See Gerald A. McCool, S.J., "Neo-Thomism and the Tradition of St. Thomas," *Thought* 62 (1987): 131-46.

also the image of God ordered to union with his infinite Creator through a life of sensitive, intellectual, and volitional activity lived in a community of faith. Thomas inherited his Platonic participation metaphysics from Augustine and from his own master, Albert the Great; but he also took over from Albert an uncompromisingly Aristotelian philosophy of man. Thus, although Thomas's participated act of existence was limited by the essence which received it, in man that human essence was composite of primary matter and a single substantial form. There could be no place in Thomas's epistemology then for the mitigated form of divine illumination which the medieval Augustinians linked to their plurality of substantial forms. Knowledge of reality in the judgment—even of divine reality—relied on the concepts which an Aristotelian active intellect abstracted from sense experience. Nonetheless, in sharp opposition to what was perhaps the more authentic Aristotelianism of Averroes, Thomas maintained that the human knower knew himself, the world, and God. The reason was that Thomas's knower could perform the act of understanding. *Hic homo intelligit*.[18]

In other words, as Thomas explained in *De Veritate* 1.9, each individual human, moved to achieve its end as God's image by knowing and loving the Infinite *Esse* in which it participated, had immediate implicit awareness of its own activity. That immediate awareness was due to the intuitive intellectual power which Aristotle called *nous* and which Thomas called *intellectus*. Reflecting on the activity understood through *intellectus* the mind could come to know its own finality; and, when it did, it would realize that, as a faculty of knowing, it was ordered to a knowledge of being made present through its abstracted concept. And a mind which could know being could know all reality, even infinite reality.

Despite their differences about its speculative extension, neo-Thomists found themselves constantly drawn back to the epistemology of *De Veritate* and to the role assigned in it to Aristotelian *nous* and to Aristotelian finality in its account of our knowledge of being. Joseph Kleutgen turned to *De Veritate* in his nineteenth-century neo-Scholastic epistemology. Ambroise Gardeil used it in a very different theory of knowledge to justify the analogy of being. Pierre Rousselot built his intellectualism and his theology of faith on it. Maritain extended it to develop his aesthetics, ethics, and philosophy of the person. Without it

---

18. In *De unitate intellectus contra averroistas pariensienses* written about 1270. For the background of this work see James A. Weisheipl, O.P., *Friar Thomas d'Aquino: His Life, Thought and Works* (New York: Doubleday, 1974), pp. 272-82. See also Fernand van Steenberghen, *The Philosophical Movement in the Thirteenth Century* (Edinburgh: Nelson, 1955), pp. 75-93.

Bernard Lonergan would have no basis for his new method in theology.[19]

Nous, intuitive *intellectus*, and the freedom of the will, both made possible through the ordination of the mind and will to infinite truth and goodness as their goal, distinguished Thomas's ethics from the ethics of post-Cartesian rationalism and empiricism. In St. Thomas's philosophy of art and prudence, as Jacques Maritain showed us years ago in *Art and Scholasticism*, truth does not consist in the conformity of an impersonal intellect to the ready-made essences mirrored in universal concepts.[20] For, in Thomas's Aristotelian practical intellect, *nous* or *intellectus*, directed by right appetite, gains intellectual knowledge of a singular, a concrete work to be made or done. Furthermore, as Maritain reminded us in his aesthetics, and as Rousselot pointed out in his theological classic, *The Eyes of Faith*, *nous* or *intellectus*, when it operates in the realm of faith or of artistic and moral values, depends for the soundness of its knowledge on past free choices made by a personal agent.[21] And it depends as well on the influence of the community in which that personal agent lives. For soundness in artistic and prudential judgments requires sensitivity to moral and cultural values acquired by the agent's connaturality to them. If you want a sound judgment about chastity, St. Thomas tells us in a famous text, ask the chaste man.[22]

Jacques Maritain was well aware of that. In Thomas's practical science of ethics, he pointed out, moral universals are reached by generalization from the prudential judgments of good men connatural to the values at stake. Thus ethics ascends to its general principles from the *nous* and connaturality operative in good free agents; and it must descend to its concrete applications by the same route. For St. Thomas then ethics is not—and cannot be—the impersonal purely deductive science which John Locke, and many philosophers after him, imagined that it was. Practical science though it may be, St. Thomas's ethics depends on personal knowledge. Sound ethical knowledge for the

---

19. Lonergan's epistemology, metaphysics, and his method in theology have been inspired to a large extent by Lonergan's textual study of *intellectus* in St. Thomas. See Bernard J. Lonergan, S.J., *Verbum: Word and Idea in Aquinas* (Notre Dame, Indiana: University of Notre Dame Press, 1967).

20. Jacques Maritain, *Art and Scholasticism and the Frontiers of Poetry* (Notre Dame, Indiana: University of Notre Dame Press, 1974). See also Ralph McInerny, *Art and Prudence: Studies in the Thought of Jacques Maritain* (Notre Dame, Indiana: University of Notre Dame Press, 1988).

21. Pierre Rousselot, "Les yeux de la foi," *Recherches de Science Religieuse* 1 (1910): 241-59; 44-75.

22. Rousselot, *L'intellectualisme de Saint Thomas*, pp. 70-2.

Angelic Doctor is due to connaturality to the virtues on the part of free agents. And, since connaturality is affected by the interaction of agents in a community, sound ethics depends on interpersonal communal knowledge too. Maritain knew that too when he subordinated his practical science of ethics to moral theology.[23] Maritain's ethics was the ethics of a believer who lived in a community of faith.

Earlier in the century Pierre Rousselot argued that the wisdom of St. Thomas was an intellectualism linked to a philosophy of the person. Since Thomas's pure act of existence was personal, our knowledge of being in its most perfect form meant sharing in the life of another person.[24] Following the same inspiration more recently, William Norris Clarke has argued that personal being should be the model of reality on which a Thomistic analogy of being is built.[25] Furthermore, Clarke tells us, the mind's intuitive grasp of its own judging and evaluating activity through *intellectus* provides the ground on which our analogous knowledge of God is justified.[26] It follows then that, like Thomas's practical science of ethics, Thomas's speculative science of metaphysics and his philosophical theology operate inside a larger framework. They are surrounded by the personal and interpersonal knowledge of a free agent living with other free agents in a community. Inside that framework abstract impersonal knowledge is illumined, fed, and supported by personal knowledge.

Thomas and Foundationalism

That is why Thomas could never be a Cartesian or a Post-Cartesian foundationalist.[27] The Cartesian project would have no appeal to him. Nourished by the personal and interpersonal life of a religious community in the larger community of a Church, the Angelic Doctor responded to God's free call through the believer's free assent of faith. Consequently Thomas would find the Cartesian call for apodictic certainty—acquired

---

23. Jacques Maritain, *Science and Wisdom* (New York: Charles Scribner's Sons, 1940). For more of Maritain's ethics, see McCool, *From Unity to Pluralism*, pp. 141-45.

24. Rousselot, *L'intellectualisme de Saint Thomas*, pp. x-xii.

25. For Clarke's original Thomistic synthesis see Gerald A. McCool, S.J., ed., *The Universe as Journey: Conversations with William Norris Clarke*, S.J. (New York: Fordham University Press, 1988).

26. William Norris Clarke, S.J., *The Philosophical Approach to God* (Winston-Salem, North Carolina: Wake Forest University Press, 1979), pp. 49-61.

27. Alvin Plantinga and Nicholas Wolterstorff have argued that Thomas can be charged with foundationalism. For a firm denial of this accusation by Henry Veatch and others see Leonard B. Kennedy, C.S.B., ed., *Thomistic Papers IV* (Houston, Texas: University of St. Thomas, 1987).

through methodic universal doubt—incompatible with his own lived experience. In the life of a community, the other persons, encountered through the symbols of art, the signs of love, and the shared prayer of the liturgy, cannot be bracketed. The men and women who share their love in a community know through *intellectus*'s knowledge of the singular both *that* they love and *who it is* they love. Knowing this, they also know that Cartesian apodictic foundationalism cannot be the only norm of truth. The knowledge of our selves and of the free persons we love, given to us by *intellectus*, is too rich to be restricted to a lifeless world of universals. For Thomas Cartesian foundationalism would lead to a separated philosophy, separated not only from theology but separated from life.

The personal knowledge made possible by *intellectus* can do more than preserve us from foundationalism; it can unify our knowledge of the transcendent God and of human history. As William Norris Clarke used insight or *intellectus* in the mind's intuitive grasp of its own activity to vindicate analogous knowledge of God against the objections of linguistic philosophers, Bernard Lonergan extended Thomas's epistemology of *intellectus*, which Lonergan called the act of insight, to show how a nonrelativistic Thomistic philosophy of being could still control the meaning of philosophical and theological statements, even if those statements had been made in logically disconnected form within diverse historical frameworks. Hermeneutics and metaphysics need not be taken as antithetical to one another. For, as these two Thomists have shown us, resources remain in the tradition of St. Thomas to reconcile transcendence and abiding truth with history.[28]

There are resources also, I believe, in Thomas's philosophy of personal and interpersonal knowledge to answer some of the difficulties of more recent antifoundationalist philosophers. In an interpersonal world the Cartesian lonely mind is seen to be an illusion. If other persons cannot be bracketed, the problem of "constituting other persons" does not arise. Neither does the failure of post-Cartesian foundationalism imprison us in a set of ungroundable language games.[29] For Thomas's free person, who *understands* both himself and the other person whom he loves, as real interacting persons, there is always more to know than can be expressed in a language game.

---

28. Bernard J. F. Lonergan, S.J., *Method in Theology* (New York: Herder and Herder, 1972), pp. 57-99.

29. Richard Rorty, "Epistemological Behaviorism and the De-Transcendentalization of Analytical Philosophy," in *Hermeneutics and Praxis*, ed. Robert Hollinger (Notre Dame, Indiana: University of Notre Dame Press, 1985), pp. 89-121.

Some Concluding Reflections

The Third Scholasticism may have gone its way like the Second Scholasticism before it, and the neo-Thomist movement may well be over. Not everything in it was of lasting value. Before the distinction between a rigid system and a philosophical tradition was understood, too much time may have been spent deciding which philosophers could be called authentic Thomists. Too much time may have been spent as well debating whether or not St. Thomas's philosophy of being and the person, which transcends the narrow limits of Cartesian foundationalism, could be justified within the constraints imposed on it by a Cartesian or a Kantian method. Those may be quarrels of the past. No historian of the neo-Thomistic movement, however, can deny that, for the better part of a century, the work of the neo-Thomists enriched an already rich tradition. The thought of a forgotten philosophical genius was recovered, adapted, and speculatively extended. The tradition of St. Thomas, as it still exists today, has inherited from the neo-Thomists a number of valuable resources, among which, I would argue, one of the greatest is Thomas's philosophy, if younger philosophers still exist with the historical knowledge, speculative skill, and intellectual courage required to think independently in the tradition of St. Thomas.

The Philosophical Catbird Seat: A Defense of Maritain's *Philosophia Perennis*

Raymond Dennehy

Introduction

As the title of this article announces I intend to offer a defense of Maritain's claim that Thomism, as he interprets it, is the perennial philosophy. The inspiration for this project came from Father McCool's learned and stimulating book, *From Unity to Pluralism* (New York: Fordham University Press, 1989), wherein he presents the development of Thomistic philosophy and theology from the time Leo XIII issued *Aeterni Patris* up to the time of the initial decades of the twentieth century. The title of Father McCool's book gives his thesis in a nutshell: contrary to the assessment of Leo XIII and other "Thomists," such as Maritain, the development of Thomistic thought since *Aeterni Patris* reveals a plurality of theological and philosophical systems, not an exclusively single Thomistic theology and philosophy that is true for all times and places.

I mention this not only to provide a context for my presentation and not only because it gives me the opportunity to acknowledge, at the outset, how greatly I have profited from Father McCool's incisive and illuminating handling of the subject; but also to explain the apparently narrow focus of my presentation. Constraints of time make it impossible to do justice to the players in the drama, Le Blond, Rousselot, Maréchal, etc. I have therefore decided to confine myself to a critique of a single topic: the claim that "the judgments through which the first principles of metaphysics are affirmed" are "immutable," but the concepts through which these judgments are made are "contingent" and "mutable" (*From Unity to Pluralism*, p. 211).

You may have noticed that above I referred to this concentration as an *"apparently* narrow focus." I say "apparently" because it seems to me that this topic is anything but narrow in its consequences. I am convinced that the whole question of whether there is, or can be, a single Thomistic philosophy, a *philosophia perennis*, turns on the question of the human intellect's capacity to form concepts that are necessary rather than contingent, immutable rather than mutable. If any debate can be said to have galvanized Maritain's return to philosophy as a young man and his subsequent philosophical investigations, it is that one.

The Concept

What does it mean to say that "the judgments through which the first principles of metaphysics are affirmed" are "immutable," but the concepts through which these judgments are made are "contingent" and "mutable"?

All concepts originate in our perceptions of the sensible world. The objects of these perceptions are concrete, particular things. Granted, these things are contingent, for nothing in their essential being necessitates that they exist. Here two points command attention. First, although their existence is contingent, they are not devoid of necessity. For if Joe Montana exists, certain necessities follow. As a member of the human species, he is necessarily rational, autonomous, capable of laughing, learning, and teaching; hence, his existence bespeaks contingent necessity; not absolute necessity, to be sure, but necessity nonetheless. Thus to know that Joe Montana is a man is to possess certain and necessary knowledge about him: the man, Joe Montana, who exists on 25 October 1990, is necessarily rational, autonomous, and risible.

Second, it is not absolutely necessary that Joe Montana be the quarterback for the San Francisco "Forty-niners" in 1990, since he might never have been born, might have chosen never to play football, and having chosen to play football, might not have recovered from the back injury he suffered in 1987. But he was born, did choose to play football, did become the quarterback for the San Francisco "Forty-niners," did recover from the injury of 1987, and has been playing at that position for the "Forty-niners" ever since. Consequently, it will *always* be true that Joe Montana was quarterback for the San Francisco "Forty-niners" on 25 October 1990. If Joe Montana is quarterback for the San Francisco "Forty-niners," on 25 October 1990, it is *necessarily* true that he is the quarterback for the San Francisco "Forty-niners" on 25 October 1990. Because finite, material beings enjoy only a contingent existence, they come into existence and pass out of existence: they exist but do not have to exist. But to exist at a given time is to be *actually* existent at that time; to pass from one state of being to another is to have been *actually* in those states at the successive moments. For all time, it is *necessarily* true that they were *actually* what they were when they were actually what they were.

These observations lead me to conclude that the only plausible meaning that can be assigned to the assertion that our concepts are contingent is this, that they are the human intellect's expression to itself of contingent things. You can, of course, say that any knowledge of contingent things has an object that is subject to change and that therefore, if the object of knowledge is subject to change, so must the knowledge of these objects be subject to change. But since change is the passage of a thing from one actual state at t1 to a different actual state at t2, and because everything is what it is and not another thing, if follows that at t2 the thing was *necessarily* what it actually was at t1.

The impossibility, or at least dubiety, of there being a perennial philosophy, such as Maritain's Thomism, cannot accordingly be supported by the appeal to "contingent" and "mutable" concepts. From the contingency and mutability of the *object of the concept*, you cannot legitimately infer that the *concept of the object* is contingent and mutable.

Historical Conditioning

Might not the claim that our concepts are contingent and mutable find support in the fact that we are creatures of time and place and thus that our concepts are historically conditioned? Advocates of this position might argue that our concepts are contingent and mutable in the sense that they are shaped by the worldview of our particular historical epoch so that we impose on our perception and interpretation of things the presuppositions of our culture. We would thus know things in a particular historical context and our concepts could only express things in the manner we have been conditioned to express them. Because historical contexts change, it would follow that our concepts are contingent and mutable in relation to changing historical contexts.

If the claim that our concepts are historically conditioned is to support the claim that all our concepts are contingent and mutable, it must be joined with the premise that it is impossible for us to transcend our particular historical context to arrive at concepts that express the essential being of things. Thus our concepts would be contingent and mutable because:

(i) one cannot know outside of an historical context;
(ii) the concepts that we derive from our perceptions of the world vary as the historical contexts in which these perceptions occur vary.

From these two premises, however, it does not follow that we cannot derive veridical concepts; that would require the addition of one or another of the following:

(iii) the historical context distorts our concepts so that what we take to be veridical is not;
(iv) the historical context does not in itself distort our concepts of things but rather restricts us to a limited perspective, when in fact there are other possible perceptions, thereby permitting us to form veridical concepts

which are only perspectival, so that seemingly competing conceptions of the same thing might be equally veridical since they represent different historical perspectives;

(v) the historical contexts of the various epochs offer us various concepts of things, but since we can never extricate ourselves from historical context, there is no way to tell which, if any, conception is veridical.

Premise (iii) cannot be reconciled with premise (i) since, if we cannot obtain concepts except from within historical contexts, there would be no way to tell which concepts are veridical and which not. Premise (ii) is also incompatible with premise (i) for the same reason: if the historical context conditions our concepts, as its proponents insist, where do we find the criterion for judging which concepts are veridical and which not, even in the qualified sense of premise (iv), namely, that it is veridical from the standpoint of the historical context in which it is obtained? Insofar as both premises (iii) and (iv) presuppose a criterion that is historically unconditioned, they contradict premise (i), namely, that all our concepts are historically conditioned. But we have seen that premise (i) is absolutely necessary to the claim that all our concepts are contingent and mutable.

This leaves us with the final candidate, premise (v). But it presupposes an assertion that is not evident, namely, that *any* historical context is incompatible with the formation of veridical concepts.

But from the proposition that our concepts vary as our historical contexts vary it does not follow that none of these conceptions is veridical. The history of Western philosophy testifies to the dependence of the human mind on historical context. The fifth century B.C. was indeed a privileged era. Its auspicious social, economic, political, and general cultural conditions no doubt allowed the flowering of the Greek genius for observation and clear thinking. In a different historical context, the Greeks might never have discovered the *logos*, the pure idea, and Plato might never have beheld so clearly the difference between knowledge and sensation. In a context different from that produced by the interaction of Christianity and Greco-Roman civilization, the West might never have seen the dignity of the human being as a person or understand God as the First Efficient Cause, the creator and conserver of being. Nevertheless, the statements "Knowledge depends on historical context" and "We can attain veridical concepts of things" are not mutually incompatible. If all my concepts are derived in one or another historical context, the most that can be inferred from this is that context is a *necessary* condition for the acquisition of veridical concepts. But a necessary condition is *that without which the result or end cannot be realized*. It does not ensure the result, for it is not the *sufficient* condition. On the face of it, it is equally plausible that auspicious cultural conditions permit us to acquire concepts that express the essential being of things veridically. Of all the possible cultural conditions, it is neither conceptually evident nor experientially established that there are no cultural conditions which, when combined, enable us to derive veridical concepts. In other words, if it is necessary that we derive all our concepts in some historical context, it is not therefore necessary that that context prejudice the veridical nature of those concepts.

For my own elucidation, I thought it necessary to enter upon the above analysis before adverting to a more fundamental difficulty with historical contextualism. The challenge to the possibility of our obtaining veridical concepts based upon historical contextualism is nothing more than a variant of good old-fashioned philosophical relativism. Just as the latter self-destructs in trying to appropriate to itself mutually contradictory propositions, so does contextualism. I have argued above that the only defensible sense of historical contextualism rests upon three premises: (i) it is impossible for us to derive concepts outside an historical context and thus our concepts are historically conditioned; (ii) the concepts that we derive from our perceptions of the world vary as the historical contexts in which these perceptions occur vary; (iii) the historical contexts of the various epochs offer us various concepts of things, but since we can never extricate ourselves from historical context, there is no way to tell which, if any, conception is veridical. These premises bring us face to face with historicism's fatal flaw. It is simply a variant of relativism and thus suffers from the latter's fatality; it contradicts itself. You cannot assert that all our concepts are historically conditioned without either one or the other of two decidedly infelicitous consequences. Either you are committed to an assertion whose concepts are conditioned by the inevitable context in which you advanced it, in which case you are scarcely in a position to make transhistorical assertions; or you make a transhistorical assertion, in which case you contradict the assertion that all our concepts are historically conditioned. Clearly, the historicist wishes to make an assertion about all human knowledge: he claims to occupy the catbird seat after he has already denied its existence. It won't do for him to try to dodge this fatality by appealing to the meta-language/object-language distinction since that distinction—as when one speaks about the formal rules governing the validity of a given proposition in mathematical logic from within a universe of discourse not governed by those rules—can only apply to a specific area of knowledge, not to the very nature of the concept. Statements about knowledge itself are transcendental, which is to say, *transhistorical*, statements.

But if we are capable of forming veridical concepts, and if we cannot form them outside a historical context, and if historical contexts vary, what is the criterion of the veridical? The heart and soul of realism is that *things are the measure of mind; mind is not the measure of things*. There is no way of demonstrating that we form veridical concepts since demonstration operates entirely in the realm of pure concepts, and you cannot use concepts to justify the veridical nature of other concepts. For what could the putative confirmatory concepts display that the dubious concept lacked? On the contrary, the only way that concepts can be identified as veridical is by the primitive and direct apprehension of their veridical nature. I am persuaded that what makes this criterion seem an unwarranted assumption to the historicist is a failure to appreciate what it means to say that, for the epistemological realist, epistemology *follows from* our knowledge of things and is the rationally systematic *reflection* on that experience. If you do not start philosophizing with that primitive, direct experiential knowledge, you are left with the intellect and its concepts as your starting point. In the introduction to his book on Kant's theory of causality, Ewing draws the telling analogy that Kant's philosophical method was like that of an astronomer who, rather than starting with the study of the stars by scanning the heavens, starts with an examination of his telescopic apparatus to determine just what kind of data the latter is capable of attaining. I have never taken the time to find out how far this analogy can be pressed, but it seems to me an apt characterization, at least, of Kant's procedure. But while it obviously makes sense to check out the design and operation of your equipment before using it to make sure that it does not produce distortions or illusions, that procedure does not work so well in epistemology. By starting within the intellect, you have walled yourself in with concepts. You are then left with the task of trying to determine whether your concepts match any extramental reality. And this, as I have noted above, is impossible. Perhaps you have seen the commercial currently being shown on television wherein two groups of cats are shown standing eagerly in front of what seems to be two tanks containing fish. A spokeswoman for the advertisement, who happens to be one of the current film celebrities, informs us that only one of the fish tanks is real; the other apparent tank is, in fact, merely a picture of a tank containing fish on a television screen. Her sponsor's television sets produce such clear and vivid pictures, we are told, that even the cats are fooled into supposing that they are gazing at real fish. We, the television viewers, are, of course, in no position to know why the one group of cats is clustered in front of the television screen. But given the peculiar organization of the cat's eye, it is highly improbable that the cats in question would be attracted to, let alone deceived by, a two-dimensional representation. At all events, the reason that we are deceived, the reason that we see no difference between the real fish tank and the television depiction of a fish tank is that, on *our* television screen, there is no difference between them, for the simple reason that they are both pictures. Neither one bespeaks any more affinity with the real than the other. We must therefore accept the spokeswoman's word that one is real and the other a mere picture on a television screen.

This example exactly parallels what happens when you start your epistemological inquiry with concepts rather than with things. You are inevitably forced into a representationalist epistemology, since being walled in by concepts, you can never get into the catbird seat which would allow you to compare your concept with the object it allegedly expresses to see if the former is a veridical expression of the latter. The concept of the object and the object of the concept have become one!

This explains how one could be led to suppose that our concepts are contingent and mutable. If the object of my knowledge is the concept, if what I know is the concept, then either one of two conclusions follows: (i) all I can be said to know is myself and my ideas; I have no way of knowing if there are other intellects or, if there are, whether they know the same things that I know; or the weaker conclusion, (ii) other people may have different subjective experiences from mine, but, because all members of the human species have the same intellectual structure and consequent a priori concepts and principles, we can be said to have objective concepts that are universal to us all. The first conclusion is subjective and solipsistic; the second is Kantian and intersubjective.

Either conclusion is consistent with the claim that our concepts are contingent and mutable in the sense that they would or might vary from individual knower to individual knower or vary from one species of knowers to another. Recall Kant's observation in his *Critique of Pure Reason* that while we can know things only as they appear to us and not as they are in themselves, there may be rational beings elsewhere in the universe who know things as they are in themselves.

These considerations lead me to say that the claim that our concepts are contingent and mutable is incompatible with the essential tenet of epistemological realism, namely, that *things are the measure of mind; mind is not the measure of things*. For, as I have argued above, the only defensible sense in which concepts can be said to be contingent and mutable is as the intellect's *representations* of things. As representations, they inevitably interpose themselves between the knowing subject and the putatively known thing. The object of knowledge thus becomes *intramental* rather than *extramental* and this destroys the claim that the intellect knows *things*, for it cannot be reconciled with the claim that the intellect knows things directly.

Representationalism also accounts for the challenge to the claim that there is, or can be, a single Thomistic philosophy that is true for all times and places, a *philosophia perennis*. Whether the representationalist embraces either subjectivism or Kantian intersubjectivism, he can only know what is an object of knowledge for him or for intellects like his. Consider the following premises:

> (i) What I know are not things but my *representation of things*; thus, my *representation of things*, not the things themselves, is the only object of my knowledge;
> (ii) the criterion of the veridical is the conformity between the intellect and the thing known; but the thing known is *by representation* of the thing;
> (iii) it follows that all my concepts are *relative* to the unique knowing subject that I am (subjectivism) or to the intellectual structure peculiar to the human species to which I belong (Kantian intersubjectivism);
> (iv) consequently, I have no rational basis for declaring that there is, or can be, for the human intellect, an exclusively single philosophy that is true for all times and places.
> (v) therefore, representationalism is inimical to the very notion of a *philosophia perennis*; the latter requires an epistemological realism, that is to say, one which affirms the principle, *things are the measure of mind; mind is not the measure of things*; and this, in turn, requires the affirmation that our concepts are veridical; for, as I have argued above, if they are veridical, they must be necessary and not contingent.

The Concept in Epistemological Realism

As I noted already, realism takes our experiential knowledge as a given: we know and what we know are things, and *we know* that we know things. Philosophy, in this instance epistemology, is an act of reflection on that experiential knowledge. Therefore, contrary to the Kantian methodology, realism does not start philosophizing with an examination of the intellect and its mechanism and then proceed to discover what and how this mechanism can know. Rather it starts out with knowledge of things and then proceeds to ask how this knowledge takes place.

From the premise that our knowledge of the sensible world is certain and evident, you cannot avoid the conclusion that our concepts are immaterial, for there is no other way to account for our knowledge of extramental things since this latter requires the formation of veridical concepts by our intellects. And here is the nub of the whole controversy surrounding the concept: if our concepts are not immaterial expressions of extramental things, they are material expressions of them; and if they are material expressions of them, then they cannot be veridical. The materialization of the intellect underlies every representationalist epistemology because it is matter that predisposes a faculty to operate according to individuating conditions, as our external senses are specified so as to apprehend only one or two properties of things. To hold the position that our concepts are shaped, not by the essential being of the thing known, but by the biases of the knowing subject, whether they be the inherent operations of the intellect or a culturally determined psyche, is to affirm, at least implicitly, that the intellect is a material organ.

But, on the realist's premise that we know extramental things and that we know that we know them, the intellect must be immaterial. Such knowledge would be impossible otherwise. How else could it perform a substantially immaterial operation, the formation of veridical concepts? To know that the being emerging from the locker room of the San Francisco "Forty-niners" is the man Joe Montana is to apprehend in his material being the essence man or manness. I can form this concept only because my intellect can free the intelligible structure, that is the specific essence of Joe Montana, from the constrictions of matter. By doing so, the intellect raises that intelligible structure to its own level of immaterial being.

Now to say that these concepts are veridical is to say that they are objective. And if knowledge is objective, that must mean that the intellect *becomes*, on the *intentional* level, the thing known. The alternative—that the intellect does not know the thing directly but instead knows the concept of the thing—is absolutely incompatible with epistemological realism insofar as it interposes a third thing between the knowing subject and the known. In short, the veridical nature of our concepts and the objectivity of our knowledge go hand in hand; you cannot have one without the other.

Ontological and Sensational Knowledge

None of the above denies the influence of historical conditioning of our knowledge. That we are creatures of time and place, let there be no doubt. Our perceptions, concepts, and way of experiencing the world are powerfully shaped by our time and place in history. So decisive is this shaping power that it is often, if not always, impossible for me to perceive, conceive, or experience objects of another time and place as they were then and there confronted. As a child, I believed in Santa Claus, but do so no longer. If I dedicated myself to the task, I could by intense reflection arrive at an increasingly more accurate understanding of what it was like for me to entertain that childhood belief. But I could never recapture that exact experience because too much water has gone over the dam between then and now. Although I am the same person, too much has changed, both within me and in my environment, to enable me to retrieve my childhood objects of experience and to perceive, conceive, and experience them as I did then. If I cannot accurately recapture my own past experiences, how could I hope to recapture those of other people, living in other times and places?

For example, as a sailor in the United States Navy, I would walk patrol in Keelung with Frank Chi, a master sergeant in the Taiwanese Army. We would frequently pass the long evenings on patrol by exchanging accounts of our respective cultures. How much did we each really understand about the other's culture? No doubt, the concepts I formed of Chinese culture, as Frank Chi related them to me, were sifted through the cultural presuppositions of my Western and American heritage, leading me to impose meanings on his descriptions that were, I am sure, frequently different from those that he wished to impart. Born and raised in San Francisco, the first-generation son of Irish, Catholic parents, I could not possibly have experienced and thus conceived the world into which he was born and raised, pre-Communist Shanghai.

Not to put too fine a point on the topic, we surely do not conceive the body politic the way the Athenians of Socrates' day conceived the *polis* or conceive the relation of God to his universe as a fifteenth-century Florentine did.

These limitations occur within the polarity of intellect and imagination, concept and image. My images originate in what I have directly experienced and in the personal and cultural environments that have conditioned me to associate particular experiences with particular images. Although anachronistic, Rembrandt's painting of Aristotle in Renaissance attire does not overwhelm the artist's conception of a great genius engaged in inquiry.

Our difficulty in overcoming spatio-temporal conditioning originates in the fact that we are not pure intellects but materially embodied intellects that must gain their concepts by abstraction from repeated contact with individual, material things. That is a significant limitation. We cannot know the subjective experiences of others, and even our own previous subjective experiences become increasingly opaque to us because we cannot enter into our former states of mind. Such experiences must be lived to be known.

If all our knowledge consisted of the perception of mere sensible properties, we would, indeed, be slaves of our historical context. But our perceptions of the sensible world convey to us more than mere sensations; they convey the *being* of things: essence, existence, and the principles of being as well. Such knowledge—what I mean by "ontological" knowledge—escapes enslavement to historical context. No matter how things differ and vary, no matter how often they change from one state to another, they remain *ways of being*, and what belongs to *being as being* cannot be reduced to the prejudices of historical context and its material conditions.

This is not to say that we can know being perfectly; even the being of the humblest individual thing has so far defied our efforts to know it exhaustively. But, on the ontological plane, our knowledge of things progresses, not so much by the acquisition of new sensible data, as occurs in the sciences, but by the ever-deepening penetration of our intellects into the metaphysical core of being. That, I take to be Aristotle's meaning when he says that "In the beginning children call all men 'father' until they learn the difference."

Although there is very much more to say about the nature of ontological knowledge, I believe that I have said enough since the task of this presentation was to show the indefensibility of the claim that our concepts are "contingent" and "mutable," and I am persuaded that I have accomplished it.

Conclusion

I said in the introduction that the question of whether there is, or can be, a *philosophia perennis* turns on the question of the human intellect's capacity to form concepts that are necessary rather than contingent, immutable rather than mutable, which is to say, concepts that are veridical rather than not. It seems to me that this assertion can now be inferred, as a conclusion, from my ensuing argument. I have tried to show that if we cannot derive from our perceptual experiences of the world concepts that are veridical, then it follows that not only are our concepts contingent and mutable, but they are representational as well. And if they are representational, then it follows that there will be as many philosophical interpretations of the world as there are representations. Not being able to peek around these representations to see if they match the things of which they are the putative representations, there is no catbird seat upon which we can perch to observe what is veridical and what is not. The representationalist cannot simultaneously be a realist; whoever holds that our concepts are contingent and mutable is a representationalist; therefore whoever holds that our concepts are contingent and mutable cannot simultaneously be a realist.

Finally, whoever is not a realist is not a Thomist; for, by any reasonable interpretation, whatever else Thomistic philosophy may be, it is a realism. Therefore, any attempt to argue, by appealing to the position that our concepts are contingent and mutable, that there is, or can be, a pluralism of Thomistic philosophies fails because it is an appeal to what is the antithesis of realism.

I have chosen to argue in my own terms on behalf of Maritain's claim that there is a single, Thomistic philosophy, a *philosophia perennis*. But, if you wish to see how much importance Maritain attached to the role of the concept in this matter, you can do no better than to consult his book, *From Bergsonian Philosophy to Thomism*. In that youthful work, he takes off the gloves and slugs it out with Bergson and others who deny that our concepts are veridical. I say that Maritain won by a knockout.

Discussion of McCool, From Unity to Pluralism

Robert F. Harvanek, S.J.

At an earlier meeting of the Maritain Association in Toronto celebrating the 100th anniversary of *Aeterni Patris*, I remarked that it was a good occasion because we could study the beginning, the progress, and the end of the neo-Thomist revival. This was in a hall in the Mediaeval Institute. My paper was received in silence. Fr. McCool has demonstrated the truth of that perception in an amazingly thorough and insightful history of neo-Thomism.

My argument in Toronto was from history and culture. History has shown that philosophical movements are not sustained forever. They catch on, develop, hang around for a while, seem to be the answer to all the questions, and then, sometimes suddenly, they are no longer there anymore. Some, many philosophies continue to have influence and some have revivals, but the revivals also have a limited lifetime. The sign of the disappearance of neo-Thomism as a movement was the absence of new books on the shelves on Thomism, and what books there were had moved from metaphysics and epistemology to ethics and social philosophy.

Fr. McCool's thesis is an internal one, namely, that neo-Thomism self-destructed rather than that it was overcome by external enemies. The extraction of a philosophy distinct from theology from the work of Thomas and his synthesis of that philosophy attempted by the classical Thomist commentators and reduced to 24 Theses after the 1918 Code of Canon Law proved to be developments of some of Thomas's insights and principles but not true repetitions. They were rather different Thomisms and *Thomism* was a collective term for a pluralism of philosophies with common historical roots.

There were other dynamisms at work, and one of the strongest was the desire or need to be contemporary and to deal with the questions that were being raised in Western modern philosophy as they were being raised and in the context of the issues and philosophies that were alive in the philosophical community. This desire for contemporaneity was evident from the beginning of the neo-Scholastic movement at Louvain in the attempt made by Désiré Mercier to relate Thomas to contemporary psychology and epistemology. It was also evident in Henri Bouillard's assertion that a philosophy was not true if it were not relevant. And toward the end of his career Karl Rahner affirmed the need to respond to questions of the moment and dropped the designation of his own thought as Thomist or Scholastic. Many a Catholic philosopher or theologian escaped to patristic studies in order to be free of the restraints of a Church-sponsored Thomism. In the end I think it was this need to be in the mainstream that accounts for the demise of the Thomistic revival.

I would like to indicate several areas where neo-Thomism does not seem to respond to contemporary issues.

The first is that it was not able to respond to the needs of contemporary theology. The great value of Scholastic and Thomistic philosophy in the seminary was its integration with Scholastic theology. For the clergy the truth of Scholastic philosophy was that it clarified the mysteries of faith. Two examples were the distinction between essence and existence and the substance-accident metaphysics of physical and creaturely being. The real distinction offered an explanation of the two natures-one person in Christ. In the theory accepted by Cardinal Billot and taught at the Gregorian University in Rome, the human nature of Christ does not have its own existence, but is actuated by the existence of the Second Person of the Trinity and consequently Christ is both God and man. The substance-accident distinction also was a handy explanation of the Eucharist, since the human imagination could understand the endurance of the appearance of bread and wine along with the transfer of substance to the body and blood of Christ.

But what happened was that theology was undergoing a development of its own and turning to historical, linguistic, and social studies to explain the Scriptures and the Faith. Systematic studies based on metaphysics dwindled. They were replaced by Scripture, Liturgical, and Sacramental theology. The integration between what the Scholastic philosophy seminarians were taught and the theology they later experienced was no longer there. Moreover theologians were using contemporary nonscholastic philosophies for their theology and making neo-Scholasticism even more irrelevant. Neo-Thomism was largely a philosophical, not theological, movement and it is not now receiving the support of theology.

This leads to another failure of neo-Thomism, that is, to be true autonomous philosophy in the sense of the age of reason or Enlightenment philosophy while at the same time claiming the title of Christian Philosophy. It certainly depended on faith, not only by being supported by the teaching authority of the papacy and the Vatican, but also in the theories of Gilson, Maritain, and others. Faith supplied what reason could not give and theology completed the limitations of philosophy.

This has resulted in two moves. One, the most common, is to enter into the non-Catholic world of philosophy in secular universities and learn its methods and its questions and take up its arguments. Catholic doctoral students in philosophy have moved *en masse* to non-Catholic universities. When they have returned to teach in Catholic universities they have brought secular philosophy with them. At the same time philosophy departments in Catholic universities have brought in professors who are secularists with little or no knowledge of Thomism. In the context St. Thomas becomes another philosopher along with Hume and Kant, Hegel and Heidegger, Ayer and Wittgenstain, and sometimes is forgotten altogether.

The other move is to return Christian philosophy to its context within Christian theology. Michael Buckley, in his learned book on the origins of modern atheism, argues that the root of modern atheism lies in the separation of reason from faith and abstract rational argument apart from the history of religion and specifically the history of Christ. I might add with the Fathers of the Church that philosophy without Christ can only end in skepticism or in Nietzschean nihilism. Deconstructionism, it has been argued, is the inevitable result of the Enlightenment. This means that philosophy within Christianity is a different kind of knowledge than secular philosophy. (Note Lonergan's view that the arguments for the existence of God should be taught within the theology department.)

I would like to note briefly several other areas where neo-Scholasticism has problems. One is the understanding of philosophy as a system. The debate in neo-Scholasticism, as McCool has made clear, is whether or not one version or other of Thomism is the true system, and if there is a pluralism. It is a pluralism of systems. But there are philosophies, and Christian philosophies, which are not systems. I have in mind Kierkegaard and Marcel. Kierkegaard was a vigorous opponent to Hegel's systematizing and failure to recognize the individual and the unique. Marcel expressed amazement at the amount of order Troisfontaines was able to give to his phenomenology of the concrete.

Second is several problems in the area of substance in Aristotelian philosophy. One is the scheme of hylomorphism as applied to physical substance from minerals to the human person. It is difficult to maintain the philosophy of matter and form in the face of modern science with its atomism and wave theory which seem to be so successful. The success of transplants in modern medicine seems easier to explain with Whitehead's social theory of organisms than with matter and form. The same is true of evolutionism.

Next is the isolationism of individual substance. This may be more of a problem with the concept of individual and person in Aristotelian

Thomism. Scholasticism defined individual in terms of the ordinary language of division: "undivided in itself and divided from everything else." It is true that a primary category among Aristotelian accidents is relation, but it still allows the imagination to think of an isolated substance, "able to be created by God so it stands alone," rather than recognizing the interrelatedness of all created things to each other and to the Creator. The concepts of flow and wave, together with Peirce's agapism, a sort of dynamic net with knots of cohesion, seem more pertinent. Whatever difficulties Hegel's systematization may have, his notion of relation seems to be necessary.

This is also pertinent to the notion of person in the Aristotelian tradition from Boethius to Aquinas. Something like Aquinas's theory of person and relation in the Trinity seems necessary on the human level also. The interpersonalism of Macmurray and Buber and Marcel seems to call for a relational notion of person. Karol Wojtyla has been calling for a reading of anthropology along the lines of the phenomenology of Max Scheler. These moves seem to require at least an adjustment of the concepts of substance, individual, and person.

In my view this isolationist view of individual and person seriously hampers Thomistic epistemology. Aristotelian Thomism does not need other persons in communication to explain human knowledge. Physics seems to have dominated the imagination of Aristotle in his treatise on the soul. All one needs is the physical universe including the biological and sensitive world with an agent and passive intellect to explain human knowledge. Robinson Crusoe could be what he was without having been developed in human society. It is only after concepts are produced that language comes into the picture. The philosophy and science of language today seems to reverse that view. Without communication and language there is no conceptualization, or at least only the pragmatic conceptualization of the tiers of animals.

It is true that Fr. McCool describes true knowledge as had only in the judgment, but the judgment is understood only as affirmation or negation and not as the act of saying something to another. The reference to speech is there, as for instance in Aristotle, who describes truth as "saying what is," but it is not made use of in the theory. C. S. Peirce describes the judgment as the act of witnessing to others (he uses the composition of place of the court room) that if they were to consider the evidence they would come to the same conclusion. This clearly makes the judgment a triadic act, that is, knowing is explaining (interpreting) something to someone, instead of the classic dyadic relation of knowing subject and object.

Once one sees human knowledge as social and dialogic, it is an easy step to understand philosophy in the same way. Plato understood this.

Aristotle understood the historical character of philosophy, but the history stopped with himself, as it did with Hegel. But philosophy is a dialogue and not one single system or perspective. It is therefore intrinsically pluralistic, though the language of pluralism still continues the imagination of individualism that I have criticized. It is better to say that philosophy is communitarian.

There are different circles of community. Thomism operates within the circle of medieval Catholicism with its surrounding and infiltrating context of Islam and Judaism. There are different communities within Catholicism, in philosophy and theology, frequently within the traditions of a religious order. Transcendental Thomism is almost entirely Jesuit. Maritain gathers lay Catholic philosophers around him. Today's Western philosophy is divided between Anglo-American linguistic analysis and Continental post-bellum philosophy. In our global universe the circle broadens to enclose the East and the Far East. The influence of Hinduism and Buddhism is very evident among us, especially in Catholic spiritual movements.

I would like to mention briefly one other area, the philosophy of religion. Religion belongs to the philosophy of man, and has received attention much beyond what it had in the Middle Ages and Aquinas. In our age anthropology has replaced metaphysics in the philosophy of God. The Five Ways of Thomas are still in the anthologies, but more attention is given to the Ontological Argument or to forms of the Kantian pragmatic argument.

Within Catholic circles theism is seen by some to be inadequate. Whitehead has a dual notion of God, which seems to reflect the Incarnation and the Mystical Body. An English Jesuit author has argued philosophically for a trinitarian conception of God. Raimundo Panikkar's book, *The Trinity and the Religious Experience of Man*, did the same thing. And beyond the Trinity there is Mystery, Rahner's late name for God. It seems that it is necessary to understand God on ascending levels from theism to trinitarianism to mystery. This of course involves going beyond the Greek or Hebrew or Islamic worldview, which pretty much circumscribes neo-Scholastic as well as deistic natural theology.

I have been talking about Thomism as a movement. There is of course Thomas and every philosopher would do well to include him in the sources of his own philosophy. And there continue to be Thomistic revivals. We are seeing a mini one now (MacIntyre), but in ethics and social anthropology rather than metaphysics and epistemology. What Thomas's place will be not so much in the future but in our own time will, I'm sure, be the subject of the rest of this conference.

Gilson, *Aeterni Patris* and the Direction of Twenty-First Century Catholic Philosophy

Desmond J. FitzGerald

There have been moments since Vatican II when some of us teachers with a Thomistic background have wondered if the Thomism of our youth could carry beyond our century.

Those of my generation recall the enthusiasm we devoted to the study of St. Thomas Aquinas in those years of World War II and in the decades afterwards; we remember how eagerly we sought each new book by the interpreters of Thomas: Maritain, Gilson, Pegis, Bourke, Owens, Maurer, Klubertanz, Henle, and hastened to pass on their insights to our students. But today we are concerned that we have failed to ignite the generation of our students with the fire we caught from our teachers. Yes, there are exceptions and the graduate schools of the Catholic University of America, Marquette, St. Louis, Toronto and Notre Dame will point proudly to those exceptions in their letters of recommendation.[1]

As Joseph Owens noted in 1979 at the University of St. Thomas's celebration of the centenary of Leo XIII's *Aeterni Patris*: "The centenary occurs unfortunately at a low ebb in general Thomistic interest. For the most part, teachers and writers in philosophy at the moment do not seem to like Aquinas, and students are not being attracted to him."[2]

And yet as Owens goes on to imply, this may be the best time to focus on our need to reflect on the place of St. Thomas as our metaphysical teacher.

There are a number of events that give hope that we are passing out of a phase where enthusiasm was declining and entering a new phase where more students are being turned toward Aquinas and meeting him as if they were his discoverers. The translation and publication of

---

1. Cf. James Collins, "Thomism in the College," in *Three Paths in Philosophy* (Chicago: Henry Regnery, 1962) for a discussion of the transition Catholic universities and colleges were going through at the beginning of Vatican II in 1962.

2. Owens, "The Future of Thomistic Metaphysics," in *One Hundred Years of Thomism, Aeterni Patris and Afterwards: A Symposium*, ed. Victor B. Brezik (Houston, Texas: Center for Thomistic Studies, University of St. Thomas, 1981), p. 146.

the Catholic University of Lublin textbooks led by my colleague, Fr. Andrew Woznicki, and Fr. Francis Lescoe;[3] the founding just over a dozen years ago of this Maritain Association and its significant conferences and publications, and the meeting here this week on the "Future of Thomism."

Now our meeting in a special way has Fr. Gerald McCool's *From Unity to Pluralism: The Internal Evolution of Thomism* as its focal point. As has been noted, Fr. McCool's study is the continuation of his 1977 *Nineteenth Century Scholasticism: The Search for a Unitary Method* (originally *Catholic Theology in the Nineteenth Century*).

Fr. McCool first studied the revival of so-called Scholastic theology in the 1800s in which the persons of Liberatore and Kleutgen were among the leaders culminating in the encyclical *Aeterni Patris* of Leo III in 1879.[5] Now his present volume has analyzed how in our twentieth century the unity anticipated by the directives of Leo XIII has evolved into the plurality of Thomisms of today.

Fr. McCool's thesis is that the expectations of *Aeterni Patris* that Thomistic philosophy would serve the progress of theology in the twentieth century have not been realized. The unity that was anticipated has not been achieved and now at the end of this century we are disappointed.

As Fr. McCool says: "Or, to put it in more forceful terms, the hope that had animated *Aeterni Patris* at the very beginning of the neo-Scholastic movement had no real support in the philosophy of St. Thomas himself."[6]

If one were to pick landmarks to identify changes in the roadway, Vatican II through the early 1960s stands there as a recognizable marker. This pastoral council in its return to Scripture for its inspiration seemed

---

3. See Mieczylaw A. Krapiec, *I-Man: An Outline of Philosophical Anthropology*, trans. Marie Lescoe, Andrew Woznicki, Theresa Sandok et al. (New Britain, Connecticut: Mariel Publications, 1983). An abridged version by Francis Lescoe and Roger Duncan was published in 1985.

4. *From Unity to Pluralism: The Internal Evolution of Thomism* (New York: Fordham University Press, 1989); *Nineteenth-Century Scholasticism: The Search for a Unitary Method* (New York: Fordham University Press, 1989). During the discussion Fr. McCool mentioned he was putting together a text on "The Neo-Thomist Movement" for the Outstanding Christian Thinkers series, Chapman Press.

5. The text of *Aeterni Patris* is available in *One Hundred Years of Thomism*; the Etienne Gilson-edited *The Church Speaks to the Modern World: The Social Teachings of Leo XII* (Garden City, New York: Doubleday Image Book, 1954); as an appendix in Jacques Maritain, *St. Thomas Aquinas* (New York: Meridian Books, 1958); and of course collections of the encyclicals of Leo XIII.

6. *From Unity to Pluralism*, pp. 228-29.

to have less use for St. Thomas Aquinas, whose work, while profoundly based on Scripture, reflected the more straightforward reading of the Bible that characterized Catholic teaching before the watershed encyclical on Scripture, the *Divino Afflante Spiritu* of Pius XII in 1943.[7] The scriptural sophistication of the experts who prepared the documents of Vatican II seemed independent of the so-called Scholastic training these experts would have had to have had, given that they were the products of seminaries of the post-modernist crisis early in our century.

As McCool writes:

> As the history of theology after Vatican II was to show, the future lay with the "new theologians," and the form of Thomism which LeBlond used to vindicate the place of history and pluralism in theology is the form of Thomism which survived the demise of the Neo-Thomist movement in the theologies of Rahner and Lonergan.[8]

As I am not a theologian nor have I had the basic training in theology that prepares even the ordinary assistant pastor for the priesthood, I defer to others on these theological issues. I note that Fr. McCool puts more emphasis on the crisis of the "new theologies" of the late 1940s occasioned by the publication of Fr. Henri de Lubac's *Surnaturel* than on Vatican II as such, but, of course, there is a continuity in these events.[9] So with respect to the development of Catholic theology into the next century, I have a sense of speaking as an outsider, like someone attentive to a conversation relating to a topic in which he has no expertise but who ventures a remark or so based on common experience and some years of teaching in areas which are the core of college studies and are fundamental to the preparation of theologians. As the document from Vatican II on Priestly Formation says:

> Then, by way of making the mysteries of salvation known as thoroughly as they can be, students should learn to penetrate them more deeply with the help of speculative reason exercised under the tutelage of St. Thomas.[10]

The footnote to this remark reviews the repeated recommendations of recent popes to study St. Thomas as a principal guide, and, of course,

---

7. *Divino Afflante Spiritu* can be found in vol. 4, *The Papal Encyclicals*, ed. Claudia Carlen (Wilmington, North Carolina: McGrath Publishing Company, 1981).

8. *From Unity to Pluralism*, p. 225.

9. Cf. the discussion of *Surnaturel* by Gerard Smith and Anton C. Pegis in *Proceedings of the American Catholic Philosophical Association* 23 (Washington, D.C., 1949).

10. "Decree on Priestly Formation" (*Optatam Totius*) in *The Documents of Vatican II*, ed. Walter M. Abbott (New York: Guild Press, 1966), p. 452.

these recommendations continued in the later days of Paul VI and John Paul II.

So given that in some sense St. Thomas's theology continues to be our guide, we have the question of which St. Thomas to follow. For as Fr. McCool's study shows, there are a plurality of St. Thomases as far as his interpreters go. These are basically reducible to two schools: the so-called Transcendental Thomists who directly or indirectly were inspired by the work of Fr. Joseph Maréchal, and for Fr. McCool this comes down to today to Karl Rahner and Bernard Lonergan, or the direct realists such as Jacques Maritain and Étienne Gilson. As to the differences between the latter, McCool has ably underlined their differences on the use of commentators, the attention given to the philosophy of nature, and one might add the differences in the analysis and appreciation of works of art.[11] Yet despite these differences they stand together in their affirmation of the reality of Christian philosophy, their emphasis on the importance of *esse*, the actuality of essence in the metaphysics of Aquinas, their direct realism in epistemology, and their understanding of St. Thomas's theory of the human person as a hylomorphic composite of body and soul.

Since my colleague Professor Dennehy has replied to Fr. McCool out of his own background as a student of Maritain, I have chosen to give my emphasis to the value of using Gilson's interpretation of St. Thomas as a way of fulfilling the intentions of Leo XIII with respect to the development of Catholic theology.

Here, perhaps, is the place to remark that many philosophies have served the theologian; obviously St. Augustine made use of Plotinus, and St. Bonaventure remained in the Augustinian tradition while using the language of Aristotle and so on. Different tools can be used for the work of theology, but we can reflect on whether or not some philosophies may work better than others. My contention is that the philosophy contained in the theological writings of St. Thomas can continue to be a fruitful source for theological analysis into the twenty-first century. And

---

11. Jacques Maritain, *Creative Intuition in Art and Poetry* (New York: Pantheon, 1953); Etienne Gilson, *Painting and Reality* (New York: Pantheon, 1957). The American Maritain Association devoted a session of its 1980 meeting in St. Louis to the different approaches of Maritain and Gilson to painting with papers by Robert McLaughlin, Desmond FitzGerald, and Laurence K. Shook. My paper suggested Maritain approached contemporary abstract expressionism as an epistemologist and questioned the intelligibility of the painter's product; Gilson approached the paintings as a metaphysician and accepted the being of the painting as something made; on the whole in their own book illustrations, Maritain seemed more sympathetic to the work of his contemporaries.

further, the emphasis that Gilson gave to these Thomistic principles can continue to serve theology.

Any one of us could compose a list of features of Gilson's writings which would characterize his philosophy. For my purpose I have chosen only a few: the affirmation of Christian philosophy, the underlining of *esse*, the act of being in Thomistic metaphysics, the realism of his epistemology, and as a special feature, his representation of St. Thomas's philosophy of the human person. These are solid achievements which the theologian can use in the work of faith seeking understanding.

With so much written on Christian philosophy it hardly needs to be reexplained here.[12] As has been noted, one establishes its possibility from the fact that it does exist. Without returning to the often quoted text of Exodus (3: 14) calling attention to the fact that when asked his name God replied in terms of existence: I AM WHO I AM, the very fact that in the light of revelation St. Augustine and St. Thomas looked at this world of experience as a "created world" rather than one which had always existed, meant that they were looking at something that happened to be rather than had to be. Thus they could be legitimate philosophers who experienced the world differently than did Plato and Aristotle in virtue of their faith. They were experiencing the world as philosophers do but they were alerted to experience a contingent world, one in which the things in it had been given existence. Thus there was this sensitivity to *esse* in Christian thinkers which distinguished them from their Greek predecessors.

Another area in which it seems clear that Gilson as a twentieth-century Thomist is closest to his master is epistemology.[13] Where other students of St. Thomas sought to modernize Aquinas after the fashions of Descartes and Kant, Gilson rejected this and returned to the direct realism of his master.

---

12. One can begin with *Christianity and Philosophy*, trans. Ralph MacDonald (New York: Sheed and Ward, 1939) [*Christianisme et Philosophie* (Paris: J. Vrin, 1936)]; and then go on to the "Introduction" in *The Christian Philosophy of St. Thomas Aquinas*, L. K. Shook's translation of *Le thomisme: Introduction à la philosophie de Saint Thomas d'Aquin*, 5th ed. (Paris, 1949); and "Revelation and the Christian Teacher," Part 1 of *Elements of Christian Philosophy* (Garden City, New York: Doubleday, 1960). Shook is completing his translation of *Le thomisme*, 6th ed. (1955), and its publication will be through the Pontifical Institute of Mediaeval Studies, Toronto.

13. The classic source is *Réalisme thomist et critique de la connaissance* (Paris: J. Vrin, 1936) and *Le réalisme methodique* (Paris: Pierre Téqui, 1936). There is a translation of the first by Mark A. Wauck, *Thomist Realism and Critique of Knowledge* (San Francisco: Ignatius Press, 1586), and the second, *Methodical Realism*, has been translated by Philip Trower and is available from Christendom Press, Front Royal, Virginia, 1990.

For Gilson human knowing begins with the recognition that something is. As he affirmed in his autobiographical *The Philosopher and Theology*, he was preoccupied with *things*.[14] This affirmation of a direct realism is not a naive realism. One who has an intimate knowledge of the range of philosophy, modern as well as medieval thought, cannot be regarded as naive with respect to the problems of knowledge. But a direct realism is one wherein the knower grasps the intelligibility of the thing known through one's human knowledge which is a simultaneous sensio-intellectual experience. What Gilson challenged so much in his epistemological writings of the 1930s were the various attempts by so-called neo-Thomists to dress Aquinas in the fashions of Descartes and Kant. These controversies of over sixty years ago are largely forgotten; the articles and books exist, of course, but they are intriguing only to the historian of the revival of Thomism in our century. Our students are surely not concerned about them. To read about the controversies serves as a reminder of the vitality and concern of the Scholastics before World War II, and I find a nostalgia for the time when our intramural disputes were taken so seriously. Fr. McCool is excellent in his review of Gilson's accomplishments in this and other areas such as the controversy over "Christian philosophy." But in the final paragraph of his assessment of Gilson, there is an ambivalence. For all the credit he gives Gilson for clarifying the meaning of an authentic Thomism, he does not follow through and nominate Gilson as the model or guide for the next century's philosophic support for theology.

> As Gilson himself observed, if his criteria for determining Thomism are the right ones, there can still be Thomists but there can be no Neo-Thomists. For the authentic disciple of the Angelic Doctor progress can consist only in his ever-deepening understanding of what St. Thomas himself has written. Progress for the Thomist cannot consist in devising new and different philosophies and claiming St. Thomas' support for positions which were never his own.[15]

In a very special way Gilson's philosophy of man or philosophical anthropology serves to present to our times and to the next century an understanding of the human person which is one part of the foundation of theology. Another way of saying this is to affirm that a sound understanding of the human person is fundamental to the investigation of man's relation to God.

---

14. Gilson, *The Philosopher and Theology*, trans. Cécile Gilson (New York: Random House, 1962), p. 18.

15. *From Unity to Pluralism*, p. 197.

Dr. Anton Pegis, one of Gilson's early students in North America, never tired in his writings of returning again and again to the theme of the unity of man in Aquinas.[16] Of course this unity was a composite unity of matter and form, but as Pegis pointed out again and again, in St. Thomas's theory of man, you had that unique level of the hierarchy of being wherein a subsistent form, man's soul, is also the form of a body. In one stroke St. Thomas had resolved what was Descartes's greatest stumbling block: how to defend personal immortality and at the same time to affirm the unity of man.

In Gilson's *Christian Philosophy of St. Thomas Aquinas*, and in the later textbook written for undergraduates *Elements of Christian Philosophy*,[17] this special feature of Aquinas is made central: the human soul endowed with *esse*, a subsistent form, comes to be as the life of a particular body, an individual quantity of matter, conferring on the body the act of living and making with it a living human person.

Paraphrase cannot begin to do justice to the magisterial way Gilson presents the philosophy of Aquinas in *Elements of Christian Philosophy*. It begs for quotation. Yet such is the presentation that one would be tempted to quote not paragraphs buy whole chapters. Suffice it to say that this work written late in his career is both a metaphysical textbook and a historical treatise blended in an extraordinary way. Gilson had always been a historian of philosophy but there emerged out of his epistemological controversies of the thirties, a confident teacher totally immersed in his subject—the doctrine of St. Thomas—and able to present it in a dynamic, exciting way.[18]

The discussion of the problem of the demonstration of personal immortality may be taken as an example. Here Gilson shows how Aquinas could start with Aristotle's theory of man as a composite of body and soul, but in virtue of recognizing that the human soul has an *esse*, an act of being, go far beyond Aristotle's theory. This makes the soul a subsistent entity as well as the form of the body. Gilson goes on to show how neither Scotus nor Cajetan realized this point in their failure to appreciate the originality of Aquinas in his transformation of Aristotelian principles. Thus Gilson's chapter on "The Human Soul" is not just

---

16. Cf. "The Notion of Man in the Context of Renewal" in vol. 1, *Theology of Renewal, Renewal of Religious Thought*, ed. Laurence K. Shook (Montreal: Palm Publishers, 1968); and "Some Reflections on *Summa Contra Gentiles* II, 56" in *An Etienne Gilson Tribute*, ed. Charles J. O'Neil (Milwaukee, Wisconsin: Marquette University Press, 1959).

17. *Elements of Christian Philosophy*.

18. Cf. Desmond J. FitzGerald, "Etienne Gilson: From Historian to Philosopher," in *Thomistic Papers, II*, ed. Leonard A. Kennedy and Jack C. Marler (Houston, Texas: Center for Thomistic Studies, University of St. Thomas, 1986).

an exposition of what Aquinas taught but it is, further, a lively analysis of the sixteenth-century debates in which Pietro Pomponazzi and Thomas de Vio, Cardinal Cajetan, were such central characters.[19]

Without going into the details of these chapters, the treatment of "Man and Knowledge" and "Man and Will" are written in the style of the master teacher and so make for Aquinas's philosophy of knowledge and choice an exposition comparable to the discussion of the immortality of the human soul.

In "Neo-Thomism and the Tradition of St. Thomas,"[20] Gerald McCool reviews the revival Thomism in our century, and notes the falling off of attention to "the tradition of St. Thomas" in our present time. McCool treats of Gilson's role in this revival especially clarifying the differences between Aquinas and various later Scholastics such as Suarez, Cajetan, and John of St. Thomas. McCool always treats Gilson with great respect and does an excellent job of presenting the features of Gilson's contributions to contemporary Thomism. But when all is said and done, in his conclusion he ends up favoring Karl Rahner and Bernard Lonergan as the best hope of neo-Thomistic philosophy serving theology into the twenty-first century.

Since I cannot make a claim to any special knowledge of Rahner or Lonergan, I cannot dispute his preference. But I am puzzled at his failure to include Gilson's Thomism. Having granted that Gilson probably comes closest to an "authentic Thomism" in his grasp of St. Thomas's actual teaching, I fail to appreciate why he is not on the final list.

As Leo XIII says toward the close of *Aeterni Patris*:

> Let carefully selected teachers endeavor to implant the doctrine of Thomas Aquinas in the minds of students, and set forth clearly his solidity and excellence over others.[21]

According to my understanding of the expectations of *Aeterni Patris*, Gilson, as well as Maritain, should be among those "carefully selected teachers" we can use as theology moves into the twenty-first century.

---

19. The graduate students of Paul Osker Kristeller, Professor Emeritus, Columbia University, have explored this controversy in a number of doctoral studies. Cf. Martin Pine, *Pietro Pomponazzi: Radical Philosopher of the Renaissance* (Padua: Editrice Antenore, 1986).
20. *Thought* 62 (June 1987).
21. *Church Speaks to the Modern World*, p. 50.

Thomism and Contemporary Philosophical Pluralism

W. Norris Clarke, S.J.

I have been asked to speak on some aspect of Thomism today, in view both of Fr. Wade's* and my own long connection with it. And I am indeed pleased to do so. This happens to be precisely my fortieth year as a teaching and writing Thomist, 1949-1989. During those forty years the place of Thomism on the Wheel of Fortune has changed quite a bit, and finds itself in quite a new philosophical environment and with new tasks today, compared with those early years of my own teaching. Since it is not often that venerable Thomistic campaigners like myself can be found around to tell the tale of old campaigns and still be deeply involved in some of the new ones, as I still am, I thought it might be of interest to you to recall briefly the rather painful transition period we have now come through since 1950 and then—as the main focus of my address—examine some of the new tasks and new attitudes a vital Thomism is called upon to assume today.

Thomistic Triumphalism

When I grew up as a young teacher of Thomistic metaphysics, after my M.A. at Fordham (where, by the way, I did a thesis under the rigorous mentorship of that most convinced of Thomists, Anton Pegis, for whose training, demanding as it was, I have always been grateful), and then after my Ph.D. at Louvain under Fernand van Steenberghen, Thomism was the confidently reigning orthodoxy of the day in American Catholic philosophical circles. It was the era of what, looking back, we now call "Thomistic Triumphalism." In the annual conventions— almost every one of which I have attended over those forty years—this could not have been clearer. The topics were preponderantly Thomistic, as well as the speakers, the questions, and the answers. It was an exciting and fruitful time of intelligent American assimilation and development of the latent riches of Thomism, especially the existential Thomism newly recovered by Gilson, De Finance, and others (Gilson's famous

---

*This is a revised version of the William Wade Philosophy Lecture, delivered at St. Louis University, February 12, 1989. This article originally appeared in *The Modern Schoolman* and is reprinted with the kind permission of its editors.

fifth edition of *Le Thomisme*, with its new chapter on existence, and De Finance's *Etre et agir* came out in the same year, 1939) and the Neoplatonically inspired participation dimension of St. Thomas's metaphysics, which I helped to make known in this country. What came to be called "existential Thomism" had only recently made a not always unbloody entrance into the American Catholic philosophical world, in seminaries and universities, as some of you well remember here, in the case of the at first embattled Fr. Renard.[1]

But if you were not within this Thomistic circle, it was evident enough that you would feel a bit out of place, somewhat like Ruth amid the alien corn. I even remember clearly one striking occasion, when some youngish Franciscan philosopher had put forth a rather challenging question during the question period after a paper, a question coming from a Scotistic perspective quite different from that of St. Thomas. I remember very clearly the Chairman looking down at the questioner as though he were a visitor from somewhere in outer space, and replying that this question obviously did not come from a Thomistic perspective and as such was not really of interest to this convention. Thus authoritatively squelched, the questioner and his question sank back into reluctant oblivion. This was a bit much, and protests were later made, in the name of the tolerance that was a hallmark of St. Thomas himself. Things did begin to change then, but slowly. The peak of Thomistic triumphalism was passing.

The attitude toward other modern philosophers outside the Thomistic tradition was certainly not as harsh or outspoken as that expressed by Mortimer Adler in his famous acceptance speech on receiving the Aquinas medal from the ACPA, when, I am sure many of you recall, he said he had learned nothing from modern philosophers except how to avoid error. There was indeed the willingness to appropriate from them and integrate into the Thomistic system any bits of truth they had discovered or rediscovered since his time, but also the hope that if our expositions of Thomism were cogent enough, those who were still under the blight of Descartes, Hume, Kant, Hegel, and the like, not to mention Pragmatists, would soon come into the orbit of the Thomistic sun and flee those foggy swamps for the invigorating air and sunny peaks of essence and existence, matter and form, act and potency, and, of course, the agent intellect.

---

1. For a more scholarly history of contemporary American Thomism, see Gerald. A. McCool, S.J, "A Tradition of St. Thomas in North America: At 50 Years," *The Modern Schoolman* 65 (1988): 185-206; and his larger work, *From Unity to Pluralism* (New York: Fordham Univ. Press, 1989).

Decline of Thomism

But in the sixties and early seventies, with the Second Vatican Council, and the general revolt against authority and the weight of the past in all fields, quite different winds began to blow, and major sea changes began to appear within Catholic intellectual circles, too. Over some ten or fifteen years a sudden and rather precipitous decline took place in the prestige and predominance of Thomism among Catholic circles in both philosophy and theology. St. Thomas as authoritative touchstone of orthodoxy, especially in philosophy, was sometimes quietly, sometimes stridently, dethroned, at least outside of the seminaries. Young Catholic philosophers going into graduate work did not so much argue with St. Thomas or refute him as simply move away from his whole systematic metaphysical approach into other more contemporary ways of doing philosophy, principally into phenomenology, often in existentialist and personalist directions. The teaching of St. Thomas still continued to maintain a certain primacy in the now shrinking world of seminary education for priests, but was no longer the great dominant, almost exclusive force it had been in the wider Catholic university and college world. A steady but thinning stream of dedicated Thomistic scholars still kept the thought of St. Thomas sturdily alive and growing, but Thomism was now just one among a number of other philosophical approaches. Pluralism was now the established order of the day, even in Catholic circles. That is the way things still stand today, with the Thomistic share slowly shrinking as it is harder to find competent young Thomists—although there does seem to be a mysterious turnaround in the demand for them during the last few years, as the desire for a return to roots gains more strength in our American culture today.

The reasons for this decline are many and complex, some of them so interwoven with the whole movement of twentieth-century culture that it would have been difficult for any one group to stem their tide. Certainly one reason was an overemphasis on the almost exclusive authority of St. Thomas in philosophical matters as though the answers to all significant philosophical problems could and must be found somewhere within his system, with the resulting lack of integration of what was genuinely new and fruitful in other traditions, and especially methods, of doing philosophy. This was bound to provoke a negative reaction eventually.

The historian Philip Gleason, of Notre Dame, has made a particularly insightful analysis of the historical process at work, which, while I do not agree with it in every respect, seems to me well worth calling to your attention. He entitles it: "Neoscholasticism as Pre-conciliar Ideology."² Following the lead of Clifford Geertz, he understands "ideology" in a somewhat special non-pejorative or value-neutral way: it is "that part of a culture which is actively concerned with the establishment and defence of patterns of belief and value."³ Ideology is distinguished from the intellectual enterprises of science and philosophy in that, whereas the latter aim at disinterested understanding and explanation, the former implies commitment and is intended to motivate action. It is not that ideology implies some sort of false philosophy or some purely political motive in its promotion, but rather that its doctrinal content, sound or unsound, has taken on a new cultural role, that of supporting a cultural way of life.

Professor Gleason then goes on to show how neo-Scholasticism, which in practice meant primarily some form of neo-Thomism, took on such a role in twentieth-century pre-conciliar American Catholic culture. As he puts it:

> Neoscholasticism functioned as an ideology ... by providing the rational grounding for the Catholic worldview or collective "philosophy of life." By that I mean that Neoscholasticism constituted the technical philosophical system that could be called upon to explain, justify, and elaborate the interlinked, but technically informal, set of beliefs Catholics held concerning the nature of reality, the meaning of human existence, and the implications of these beliefs for personal morality, social ethics, political policy, and so on.⁴

As evidence Gleason cites the Presidential Address of Fr. John McCormick, S.J., of Marquette University, to the American Catholic Philosophical Association Convention in 1929:

> We have a system of philosophy to teach, and this system is for the most part fairly definite and has very definite relations to the whole of Catholic thought and a very definite value in building up a Catholic world-view.⁵

Another revealing statement is that of Fr. Charles Hart, for many years Editor of the *New Scholasticism*, the official organ of the ACPA, when he called neo-Thomism "the great fountainhead of Catholic energy ... Catholic Action in the sphere of thought." Even more revealing is the

---

2. It is printed in the *Catholic Commission on Intellectual and Cultural Affairs Annual* (Notre Dame, Indiana: CCICA): 15-25.
3. *Ibid.*, p. 17.
4. *Ibid.*, p. 18.
5. *Proceedings of American Catholic Philosophical Association*, III (1929), 18-19.

judgment of Fr. James Macelwane, S.J., geophysicist at St. Louis University, in a critical self-study of current Jesuit education in 1932.

> It is recommended that the professors, especially of externs [lay students], bring out clearly how Scholastic Philosophy is a stable, universal, and certain system of thought, a real philosophy of life, something to which they can anchor all their views and thoughts and knowledge. No other system of thought in the world has this universality, cohesion, logic, and strength.[6]

A 1935 editorial in *The Modern Schoolman* gives voice to this same aspiration to renew and unify contemporary culture with the help of neo-Scholasticism:

> There is need of a return to first principles in order to bring together the heterogeneous elements of our civilization. There is need of a "refreshing" of Scholasticism itself in order the better to apply it to modern problems. The Neo-Scholastics, therefore, *must* rethink and *re*generate and *re*live their philosophy. They must study it in all its ramifications and see how it serves as a unifying bond whereby the specialized sciences are given their true places in the whole scheme of things.... Only after the particular sciences have been rooted in the common ground of Scholasticism's primary truths can we set about this great work of restoring, at least in part, the intellectual and cultural unity of the Middle Ages.[7]

This overtight linking of the unity of Catholic belief and life with the unity of neo-Scholastic philosophy does indeed seem to contain within it the seeds of its own backlash—too much of a good thing, even an ardent Thomist might have warned. Gleason traces the decline of the privileged place of neo-Scholastic philosophy to several factors. (1) The upward mobility of Catholics and their movement out of Catholic ghettos into the wider stream of American society, with the new, more independent critical thinking that resulted, began to break down the older, more monolithic unity of Catholic thought and action, so that it was no longer plausible that there was "*the* Catholic viewpoint" on everything. (2) The opposed "unity" of neo-Thomism was itself splitting off intellectually into several major streams. Tension was developing as well within Catholic theology, not only between different schools of Thomists, but between the claims of systematic theology versus those of

---

6. *Report of Commission on Higher Studies of the American Assistancy of the Society of Jesus, 1931-32*, (Mimeo, St. Louis University), p. 145.

7. "Toward Unity—Editorial," *The Modern Schoolman*, 12 (may, 1935), 95. Robert J. Henle, S.J., was Editor at the time.

the newly arising biblical and kerugmatic theologies. (3) "As the philosophical and theological scene became increasingly diversified, the goal of synthesis, or the ordering of all knowledge in an intelligible unity, grew correspondingly remote, and was by 1960 effectively abandoned." Gleason points finally to the Second Vatican Council as the catalytic agent that propelled the whole process into high gear:

> In retrospect it seems clear that pressures had been building up below the surface for a long time. The calling of the Council provided the opening they needed. The Council itself quickly took on the character of a volcanic eruption. That eruption, combined with the more general cultural earthquake of the 1960s, reshaped the older Catholic worldview and shattered its intellectual underpinning, Neoscholastic philosophy.[8]

There is much of value to be pondered in the above analysis, though I would prefer to rephrase the last sentence to read: " . . . shattered *the privileged authoritarian position* of Neothomism." The latter has far more intrinsic strength of its own than merely its role as an ideology. At any rate, for good or ill we now have to live for the foreseeable future in the new atmosphere of pluralism in all fields, cultural, philosophical, theological, etc.

There was much that was inevitable in this rapid evolution, and much that is good in the resulting pluralism. No one philosophical approach or methodology can any longer handle all philosophical problems in all areas of interest. There must be complementarity and collaboration. The complementarity of Thomistic metaphysical analysis and phenomenology is a leading example, to which we shall return later. Another good result is that the oppressive burden of official authority figure in philosophy and theology as "Common Doctor" of the Church, laid on St. Thomas by Pope Leo XIII in his famous Encyclical letter *Aeterni Patris* (1879) on the restoration of the study of St. Thomas, has now in large part been lifted from the shoulders of poor Thomas, who in his own time, as you know, was almost always cast in the role of embattled innovator. Most students when they come to the study of Aquinas now are not even aware that he is supposed to be an authority figure. All too many have never even heard of him before. One of our Fordham students, for example, when asked if he knew who Thomas Aquinas was said he was an early Jesuit thinker who got in trouble with the Pope! As a result, younger people are now able to approach him as worth studying for his own sake, and not a few, I can testify personally,

---

8. Gleason, "Neoscholasticism ...," p. 22.

are rediscovering him with surprise and considerable intellectual satisfaction.

Thomism in a Pluralistic Context

But granted the new pluralistic setting, what is the role that an alert Thomism can play therein, where it must now carry on its work not only with many other traditions in the wider philosophical community but also cheek by jowl within the same department? For this is now the case in most large departments, even in higher institutions of Catholic inspiration and tradition, such as Notre Dame, Marquette, St. Louis, Fordham, Loyola of Chicago, Boston College, etc.—and also now, it seems, in most middle and smaller size departments? Thomists must now learn the skills, not just of polemics, as of old—which they have always been good at—but rather of peaceful, even creative co-existence.

What are the basic possible types of relationship between Thomistic philosophy and the other main philosophical currents today? Since Thomistic natural law ethics already holds a clear-cut place among other ethical systems, I will focus principally on metaphysics (including the philosophy of God as its crown) and philosophical anthropology. If one puts the question in political terms, I suggest that the main kinds of relationship can be reduced to four.

1) There can be *competition* within the same field with those who share roughly the same objectives. Thus St. Thomas and Whitehead are head-on competitors in the same general field of *metaphysics*, both admitting the legitimacy of the great metaphysical questions and of metaphysical-type answers to them, e.g., What is the nature of the real? etc. This is an old and well-known relationship that has been with us since the beginning of Western philosophy, with Plato, Aristotle, Aquinas, Leibniz, Spinoza, Hegel, etc., all proposing their own metaphysical systems competing in a common forum and with recognizably similar general objectives. There is no need to elaborate further on this type of relationship, except to note that about the only serious competitors with St. Thomas in this field today are thinkers like Hegel, Whitehead, Ivor Leclerc, Paul Weiss, Justus Buchler (with his Ordinal Metaphysics), Errol Harris, David Weismann, Robert Neville, and perhaps a few others. Several of these might well be called fellow-travellers of St. Thomas on a number of points. To relate fruitfully, however, to such competitors, Thomists today cannot be content to stay in their own corner, lecturing to their own, but must make the effort to understand reasonably well what these others are up to, and learn to present their own positions in language accessible to their contemporaries. We might call this type of relationship one of *peaceful but competitive co-existence*.

2) The second type goes beyond this peaceful but still competitive coexistence to a relationship of positive *complementarity and collaboration*. This *should* be the relationship, I think, between Thomism and phenomenology, though unfortunately it is not always or even often the case, for reasons we shall see later. Thomists should in principle have no quarrel with phenomenology and should welcome its contributions as complementary to its own work. For St. Thomas does not ordinarily lay out in great detail a phenomenological description of the data from which his metaphysical analysis begins. He usually sketches this very briefly, taking for granted that we are acquainted with the relevant data from our ordinary human experience, e.g., the various kinds of change, the exercise of efficient causality, human emotions, etc. The main exception is in ethics, where he does lay out a detailed phenomenology of the various virtues and their interrelationships, which contemporary ethicians are now drawing upon more and more as a rich quarry. The rich and insightful analyses of contemporary phenomenology can be a wonderful complement to enlarge and refine Thomas's own base of analysis, especially with regard to relations between human persons (personalist existentialism, etc.). Many forms of linguistic as well as hermeneutic analysis should be able, it seems to me, to co-exist peacefully in such a complementary relation with Thomistic metaphysics and philosophy of man, though this is by no means always the case.

3) Then there is the relationship of what we might call *border disputes* between Thomism and certain other philosophical approaches, where one tries to take over part of the territory of the other, maintaining that it has a more legitimate claim to it than the other. We often see this occurring between phenomenology and Thomism—more often from the side of phenomenology, it seems to me. It also occurs between Thomism and linguistic analysis, often from both sides, and sometimes, at least, based on a misunderstanding.

4) The fourth relationship is one that we might call *total warfare*, where one party wishes to wipe out the other's sovereignty entirely and either take over its territory completely or perhaps even obliterate it. This is the kind of relationship that tends to prevail between Thomism (or any properly metaphysical position) and the various forms of *empiricism* still flourishing among us today, sometimes in disguise, which in principle will not tolerate any kind of metaphysical analysis that professes to transcend experience. The two parties may cooperate in other areas, but on this point there can be no compromise. Some forms of phenomenology may take on this empiricist tinge, as well as some modes of linguistic analysis, for whom, to use a well-known example, "descriptive metaphysics" (describing the basic categories of our experience expressed in

language) is "in," whereas "explanatory metaphysics" (the postulation of something beyond experience to explain what is within experience) is "out." This would also be true, in my opinion, of various forms of *Kantianism* or *neo-Kantianism*, often called *anti-realism*, according to which we cannot really know in any objective way the real world in itself. I would also group under the same general heading various forms of strong (or extreme) *relativism* now current among us, whether of the historical, conceptual-linguistic, or hermeneutical type (radical hermeneutics), including such aggressive newcomers on the street as Deconstruction and Postmodernism. Again, there is much to be learned from these movements in the form of caution against overconfidence in the use of reason (in particular against autonomous, self-sufficient reason of the Enlightenment type). But in their extreme forms they undercut all serious, especially metaphysical, use of reason, and cannot live in peaceful, even competitive, co-existence with a metaphysically oriented Thomism.

The Complementarity of Thomism to Phenomenology

Let me return to what seems to me the most significant challenge and opportunity for Thomism today, its relationship with phenomenology. We have already noted above how phenomenology can complement Thomism by providing it with a richer basis for its metaphysical analyses. Let us consider now the more controversial side of how Thomism can complement phenomenology. What is it that phenomenology itself cannot handle and Thomism can provide? Let me single out just two basic questions, which are in fact closely interconnected.

I. *Questions of Existence and Action.* By this I mean foundational questions of the very existence itself of the framework of interaction between the knower or subject and his world, the world that offers itself to him for description. This must be in principle presupposed by phenomenological analysis as the always-already-given before it starts its work. There is no way it can raise questions about the very existence of its own framework that it must presuppose in order to carry on its work. Questions like, "How come there is a framework at all of this actually existing world (or *Lebenswelt*, if you wish) plus a self-conscious knowing subject, so intrinsically attuned to one another that one can be known by the other?" There is no way phenomenology can even raise, let alone answer, such a question, since by its method it must restrict itself to the description of what actually presents itself in consciousness. It cannot raise questions about the basic *conditions of possibility* of experience itself. Yet, unless we artificially inhibit the natural unrestricted drive of the mind to know, when we reflect in depth we are naturally led at some point to such radical questions.

Nor can phenomenology identify *action* as the ultimate condition for the self-revelation of one real being to another, without which knowledge of the real would be impossible. For, to recognize the presentation of the object in consciousness as the sign of a real being presenting itself, the mind must interpret the action and point back through it, in an act of *interpretive judgment*, to the real source existing in itself *beyond* our consciousness. If one wishes to raise such basic questions, recourse to the metaphysics of being and knowledge is indispensable. Certain forms of existential phenomenology do, I admit, seem to be willing to extend their analysis into this realistic grounding of knowledge (perhaps Heidegger?). This is fine, and I welcome it. But it is important that the practitioners of it be aware of what they are doing and that they have extended their methodology beyond the original strict bracketing of real existence insisted on by Husserl.

Thus we find Heidegger criticizing Western philosophy generally and metaphysics in particular for their "forgetfulness of Being," that is, of the radical "shining forth" of beings to man which grounds our propositional knowledge of them as true or false. There is much truth in his critique, though I do not think it applies as much to St. Thomas as to other Western thinkers. But we still do not find Heidegger himself ever getting around to answering the more basic question, "Why are there any beings around to shine forth at all, and why do they thus shine forth to us as though mind and being were made for each other?" For Being itself is not an independent cause producing them; it depends on them as they on it. Heidegger raises, but never really answers, the radical question, "Why is there anything at all rather than nothing?"[9]

II. *Causal Explanation*. One of the striking omissions in the kind of intellectual operation allowed by the methodology of phenomenology is that of causal explanation, i.e., explanation by recourse to an *efficient cause* or causes. By this I do not mean the emasculated empiricist version of causality propagated by Hume, where efficient causality means only the regularly repeated sequence in time of two events such that given the first, the second regularly follows. This type of relation does indeed allow predictability, which is ordinarily enough for the purposes of science. But it does not imply any relation of *dependence* of the effect on the cause either in its being or its coming to be, nor does the cause actively produce or bring into being in any way what is called its effect.

---

9. Cf. B. Riouz, *L'Être et la vérité chez Heidegger et Thomas* (Paris: Presses Universitaires de France, 1962).

Hence the cause is not properly explanatory of the effect; it does not provide the sufficient reason *why* the effect is actually present.

This more robust understanding of the efficient cause as that which is *responsible by its action* for the being or coming into being of an effect, either in whole or in part, has been used as a primary mode of explanatory thinking down the ages not only by classical metaphysicians since Aristotle (and even Plato, with his Demiurge), but also by ordinary people in the carrying on of daily life, and is in fact indispensable there. Any questions such as, "Who or what broke the window?", "Who killed Martin Luther King?" etc. are all seeking for the efficient cause in the strong classical, not the Humean, sense. All police investigations rely on it: Someone has been killed. It becomes clear on investigation that he could not have killed himself. Therefore someone did it; and the police proceed to eliminate possible candidates one by one till they find the appropriate one, the only one that provides the *sufficient reason* required to render the even intelligible, i.e., to "make sense" out of it. To accept that the event has no sufficient explanatory reason at all, just does not make sense at all, is absurd, is not an intellectually or practically acceptable way to live in the real world.

But notice how this mode of explanation works. It begins with an empirically observable datum of some kind, which turns out to be incapable of explaining (rendering sufficient reason for) itself. We then seek for something adequate to explain it—its efficient cause—*outside* of present experience, not now in the consciousness of the investigators (the police do not observe the murder being committed). But such a procedure is in principle impossible for phenomenology as such to involve itself in, for the simple reason that it limits itself to the description of what is already actually present in consciousness. An efficient cause that is beyond the reach of present consciousness is in principle outside its reach entirely. It might perhaps describe the psychological process of searching for a cause as this process manifests itself in consciousness, but it cannot carry out the actual search itself.

There is no difficulty in phenomenology's admitting that it cannot carry on such a search by its own methods, that this is not its domain. But there is trouble when phenomenologists go on to claim, as some do, that such a search has no intellectual validity in itself, cannot be done validly or with certainty by anyone. Such a phenomenology has made an empiricist turn that needs to be called clearly in question by Thomistic metaphysicians.

Although there is no need in principle for phenomenology to make such an empiricist turn, it does seem to me the case that in fact there is in much contemporary phenomenology an implicit, not always conscious perhaps, empiricist attitude or underlying commitment at work: namely, that it is not possible for the human mind to transcend the horizon of experience. Whatever can be known by more than mere conjecture must be either within the circle of actual human experience or in principle be capable of being grasped within it. This implicit empiricist commitment to experience as the limit of human knowledge extends in fact far beyond phenomenology to be one of the most widespread methodological commitments permeating a great deal of contemporary philosophical thinking today. I am thinking not just of professed empiricists but also of many linguistic analysts, pragmatists, etc., many of whom do not at all look on themselves as empiricists.[10] Here is a prime example of where Thomists must smoke out and bring into the open the fact and the implications of this implicit commitment and question its legitimacy, as an ungrounded and arbitrary constriction of our natural drive to know.

Heidegger is an interesting example. He insists that we are all locked as humans within the finite horizon of human experience and cannot transcend it by any philosophical effort to reach something that in principle lies beyond this finite circle, such as God. God, if he exists, he tells us (which he does not deny in his later works), can indeed come to us, reveal himself to us. But we cannot, by our own powers of reason, break through our finite horizon to reach him. This always puzzled me. Why not use a causal argument, sufficient reason and efficient causality to reach beyond our finite horizon and affirm the exigency for an Infinite Being as required to ground our finite world? It is true that as a phenomenologist Heidegger could not in principle make such a move. But why not make it as a metaphysician, or at least why block others from doing so, on the grounds of our human condition? Heidegger really gives no answer.

Curious about this, I tried to track down, if I could, just why he refused to use, or apparently allow, any causal arguments to God. He is curiously reticent about the question in his writings. But I finally tracked down one former student of his who had been in one of his seminars (unfortunately I did not hold onto his name), who told me that he himself had had the same difficulty and had pressed Heidegger on it. For a long time the Master refused to answer the question, but at last, under persevering pressure, he broke down and made this admission,

---

10. Thus even an analytical metaphysician like Anthony Quinton does not hesitate to say, "For a causal inference is only legitimate if it is at least possible to obtain evidence for the existence of the cause which is independent of the events it is said to explain." "The Problem of Perception," in *The Philosophy of Perception*, ed. G. Warnock (Oxford, 1967), p. 62.

as reported to me: "All right, I'll tell you. I'm still too much of a Kantian to accept efficient causality as revelatory of the real. The revelation (or 'mittence') of Being that includes efficient causality belongs to a medieval epoch of Being that is no longer accessible to us."

This seems to me most illuminating, "revelatory" in its own way. But my response would be: Who has the right to declare what revelation Being is making to us today? Could it not be that Heidegger himself has gotten locked in the past and is not hearing the new message of Being, "Look, the Humean-Kantian epoch of denigration of efficient causality is now past and gone. Now is the time to restore efficient causality to honor again"? Since Being itself does not talk in our language, it can only be we who are its interpreters, which means that is we who must take the personal responsibility for thinking out the exigencies of Being at any time. It is a cop-out, it seems to me, to lay the blame on some inscrutable force like Heidegger's Being, hidden behind the passage of history, for holding or rejecting any philosophical position. At any rate, it seems clear to me that one of the most significant contributions Thomism can make in the contemporary pluralist scene is the restoration of the validity of explanation by efficient causality, in particular when the cause required must by its nature transcend the horizon of our ordinary experience. It is perfectly legitimate philosophically to explain something in our experience by recourse to a cause outside of it. I do not have the time here to show in detail how this can be done. But I believe it certainly can be done, and I have tried to do it myself elsewhere.[11] *Pace* Hume and Kant, there are no good reasons for abandoning realistic efficient causality and many compelling ones for restoring it to a place of honor.

Thomism and Kantianism

In some form or other the influence of the great Immanuel Kant is still very much with us. The old unchanging a priori forms of understanding, the same for all human beings, may be gone. But they have been replaced by other, more nuanced types of a priori forms, e.g., linguistic, cultural, historical, hermeneutical, etc., which, while no longer unchanging or the same for all people, are still a priori for those within their framework and still, at least in their strong forms, prevent the human mind from coming to know the real world as it is. Notwithstanding his contributions to many fields, especially ethics, it seems to me that

---

11. See my *The Philosophical Approach to God: A Neothomist Perspective* (Wake Forest, North Carolina: Wake Forest Univ. Press, 1979), Chap. 2; see also Galen Strawson, "Realism and Causation," *Philosophical Quarterly*, 37 (1987), 253-77.

contemporary thinkers in general are still too intimidated by the great Immanuel in the fields of epistemology, metaphysics, and natural theology. On basic questions like the realism of knowledge, efficient causality, and arguments for the existence of God, his thought, especially his arguments, are severely flawed and not at all coercive. It is timely for Thomists to speak out vigorously and throw off the heavy hand that has for so long crippled our self-understanding as human knowers.

Kant's understanding of *efficient causality* and the principle of causal explanation is one important case in point. Although certainly an improvement on Hume, it is still a confused compromise between Humean temporal sequence and the older classical notion of the efficient cause as the active producer of its effect and therefore the explanatory ground or sufficient reason for it. The mere introduction by the mind of a necessary link between cause and effect does not yet restore the actively productive role of the cause and the ontological dependence resulting therefrom, which is the core of the classical—and ordinary life—understanding of efficient causality and grounds its explanatory character. To do so he would have to reject the Humean two-event, temporal process model of causality and replace it with the original Aristotelian single-event model, where the causing and the being caused are the one identical event, but with different relations, one as in the effect, the other as from the cause: for example, the cutting of the orange and its being cut are identical ontologically, located *in* the orange as *from* or by the knife (*actio est in passo*), as Aristotle brilliantly analyzed the categories of action and passion. But Kant could never quite bring himself to give up the Humean two-event model, which indeed fitted so well with Newtonian scientific explanation.

Another key example is his attempted refutation of the supposedly classical *cosmological argument* for the existence of God. Even among religious thinkers, when speaking philosophically, all too many today are still intimidated by the famous "Kantian Critique," and are willing to concede much too readily that "of course Kant has shown that arguments to the existence from the world cannot be valid; so we will take another approach." The fact of the matter is that Kant on this point has simply gotten the classical forms of the cosmological argument all wrong; he has refuted only some rationalist form of it perhaps found in his own time but one that is proposed by no classical thinker and would have been vigorously repudiated in principle by a realistic metaphysician like St. Thomas. The first part of the cosmological argument, as Kant proposes it, is accurate enough, proceeding from the fact of contingent being to the necessity of a Necessary Being. But then comes the second part, the passage from Necessary Being to Infinitely Perfect Being, or *Ens Realissimum*, as he puts it. Here is the crucial flaw, Kant insists, involving an implicit recourse to the invalid ontological argument. To make the passage, Kant argues, we must be able to *deduce* the concept of Necessary Being from that of *Ens Realissimum*, which involves deducing existence from a concept. But he has exactly reversed the procedure of the classical argument. St. Thomas, as a typical example, argues that Necessary Being, which he has already shown must actually exist, necessarily implies Infinitely Perfect Being, because nothing finite can be self-sufficient (necessary). Hence the *Ens Realissimum* is in fact "deduced" (Thomas would prefer to call it a *reductio*, or drawing back of something to be explained to its ground) from Necessary or Self-sufficient Being, not the contrary, as Kant supposes. The procedure which Kant criticizes is indeed invalid, but I know of no well-known classical theist who proposes such an argument. The classical arguments remain in the order of existence all the time. Kant has refuted a straw man. There may be other difficulties with the cosmological argument; but this should not be one of them.[12]

The third and most important point on which Thomists must vigorously stand up against Kant concerns his refusal to allow the human mind knowledge of the real world as it is, on the grounds that all we can know is the world as it appears to us phenomenally, which is made intelligible by the imposition of our own a priori forms of sense and understanding. The single greatest lacuna in his epistemology, to my mind, is his failure to draw the consequences of action as the *self-manifestation* of being, *the* mediator between the real and our minds. Kant himself is caught in a kind of self-performatory contradiction or incoherence here. He admits on the one hand that we do not create the objects we know; they must present themselves to our cognitive apparatus by action. But on the other hand he will not admit that action can be revelatory of anything about the thing in itself, even its real existence, otherwise we would know something about the thing in itself. "Being" or "existence" is only the result of our positing of the conjunction between the manifold of sense and our a priori forms; it can never reach outside our consciousness to attain the real. So at the same time we must recognize the existence of the object we know, on the basis of its action (to know we are not merely making it up), and yet we cannot affirm the object's existence in itself, because this would be knowing something objective about the thing in itself.

---

12. Immanuel Kant, *Critique of Pure Reason*, trans. N. K. Smith (New York: St. Martin's Press, 1929), Chap. III, Sect. 5: "The Impossibility of a Cosmological Proof of the Existence of God," pp. 505-18.

Furthermore, action that is absolutely non-revelatory of its source, that tells us nothing whatever about it, not even that it *is this kind of actor*, is unintelligible, cannot be made sense out of. I suspect that what made Kant so blind to the implications of action for a realistic epistemology is his rationalist ideal of knowledge of the real as requiring that we know what a thing is like in its own essence as it is in itself *apart from any action* on others. Of course such an ideal is unrealizable for us who are not creative of what we know. But a more modest, yet real and objective knowledge of the real is open to us, a *relational realism* that reveals to us the objective relations of the world to us, i.e. what kind of habitual *actors* things are towards us and other beings, which is equivalently to reveal what kind of *natures* they have in themselves. This, to my mind, is the core of the "moderate realism" of St. Thomas, and it reveals what after all is what we really want to know about the world: what kind of *difference* do things make to us.[13]

Thomism and Hermeneutics

Here is one of the most significant adaptations that Thomism must make, it seems to me, if it is to live realistically in our contemporary pluralistic context. It is no longer possible to return to a pre-hermeneutic state of innocence. The ideal of a timeless system of thought, free of historical conditioning or presuppositions, that carries conviction by the sheer impersonal, objective rigor of its reasoning, without initiation into a living tradition of interpretation, should now be recognized as unrealistic, unrealizable in our concrete human condition. As Polanyi as well as Gadamer have shown, all *focal* human perception or intellectual knowledge of any kind always comes surrounded and supported by an aura of *peripheral* knowledge that is lived existentially but can never be fully and explicitly articulated. To enter into any system of thought, especially at a later time, we must be initiated into a tradition of interpretation, operate a fusion of horizons between our own contemporary perspectives and interests and those of the original creators of the system, and retrieve the truths therein, which may indeed be timeless in their intelligible core, in terms of our own points of view and familiar language. This must always be done by a personal judicious use of intelligence, for which we take personal responsibility. Everyone brings his or her own aura of implicit suppositions, lived experience, needs,

---

13. Cf. my essay, "Action as the Self-Revelation of Being: A Central Theme in the Thought of St. Thomas," in Linus Thro, ed., *History of Philosophy in the Making*: Essays in Honor of James Collins (Lanham, Maryland: University Press of America, 1982), 63-80, esp. pp. 75-76.

interests, tradition of interpretation, etc. to any text or system of thought, and it is theoretically impossible to spell out explicitly all that is contained therein. Husserl's Cartesian ideal of finally analyzing clearly and distinctly all human knowledge is indeed a dream, and an inhuman one at that.

Contemporary Thomists, therefore, must accept and learn to be comfortable in the realization that their system of thought, like all others, is subject to the conditions and limitations of hermeneutical interpretation, involving a fusion of horizons that recognizes the limitations of background, historically conditioned perspectives and interests, as well as language, of the original system's own historically situated moment, plus a positive initiation into a living tradition of interpretation beyond the bare impersonal words of the text by itself. But such a hermeneutical approach does not, as some seem to fear, block objective understanding or fatally relativize it. As Polanyi has well shown, I think, especially in the case of perception, the aura of peripheral knowledge does not block or cripple focal knowledge; it positively supports and *enables* it. This point seems to be persistently overlooked by Deconstructionists, who keep appealing to the indefinitely expandable background of any text to cast doubts on our ability to know anything with certainty. They forget the self-conscious intentionality and living skill that we bring to any act of explicit judgment. But it still remains that the dream of completeness and immutable methodology or language must be given up. In a word, Thomism today must have a new humility, a self-consciousness of its own built-in limitations. I see no difficulty in an alert Thomism's assimilating the attitude of a realistic, moderate hermeneutics.

Thomism and Relativism, Deconstruction, Postmodernism

I must perforce be brief here. There is much to be learned from all these movements as regards *caution* against the overconfidence of reason in its own unaided powers. Their special focus of attack is against the pretensions of Enlightenment Reason, as capable of solving all problems worth solving by the autonomous self-sufficient use of a rigorous, impersonal scientific method. There is no loss in the dethronement of such an idol, of what they call the excessive "logocentrism" of the West.

But once they move to an extreme position that pretends to block all access to universal truth for the human mind, they self-destruct in self-referential fallacies.[14] For it is the fatal flaw of all relativisms, conceptual-

---

14. Cf. James L. Marsh, "Strategies of Evasion: The Paradox of Self-Referentiality and Post-Modern Critique of Rationality," *International Philosophical Quarterly*, 29 (1989): 335-50.

linguistic, historical, cultural, or otherwise, that to make any significant statement about the limitations of human knowledge they *must* affirm their statement to be of *universal* validity, applying to *all* periods and cultures in human history. Otherwise their strictures might apply just to some radical circles in Paris, New York, or Berkeley in the late twentieth century, and the rest of us would not have to take them seriously. One could always then retreat to Philadelphia, or St. Louis, or Buffalo and there set up philosophical institutes and universities which could tranquilly proceed to proclaim universally valid philosophical *dicta* of all kinds. Unless the limitations on knowledge proposed by the relativists applied to *all* philosophers, irrespective of time, place, or culture, as part of the universal human condition itself, the position would be irrelevant, self-trivializing. But any universalizing of its own position must necessarily at once undermine and contradict—by a *performative*, not logical contradiction—the explicit content of what they are affirming. There is no self-consistent way of blocking all access to the truth of a careful, self-critical, responsibly exercised human intelligence. As Maritain has put it somewhere, mind and reality are in "a nuptial relation," or, as the Sufis express it even more poetically, mind and reality "sing a marriage song together."

In conclusion, I think it is not only quite possible but even good for its health that an alert, self-critical Thomism accept its role of one voice in the contemporary philosophical community, making its own distinctive contribution in this broadly pluralistic context. It must work positively with phenomenology, linguistic analysis, hermeneutics, and many aspects of Pragmatism, but vigorously resist and critique all strong forms of empiricism, Kantianism, and contemporary relativisms of all stripes. And, of course, it must listen attentively to, learn from where appropriate, and dialogue with other contemporary metaphysicians.

Thomism and the Transition from the Classical World-View to Historical-Mindedness

Benedict M. Ashley, O.P.

Bernard Lonergan's analysis of our century just closing as a transition from what he called "the classical world-view to historical mindedness"[1] is often thought to be the explanation of the decline of Thomism in America. Is not the Thomistic tradition of philosophy and theology redolent of the "classicist" mentality? And is not such a mentality utterly unable to deal with the dynamic, subject-centered, existentialist, personalist, and pluralist mind-set of our times, which Vatican II called Catholics to address positively?

If Thomism is to have a future, therefore, it must shed its classicist mentality and assume historical-mindedness without losing its integrity and uniqueness. Since what is described as classicist in the thought of the past is best typified by Platonism and its *essentialism*, and since Maritain, Gilson, and others in the first half of this century seem to have firmly established the *existential* character of Thomism, such a renewal seems possible.[2]

Historical-mindedness in philosophy is the recognition that truth exists only in the minds of persons.[3] Hence, when these persons are human, it exists only in historical events of knowing, each of which is conditioned by the experiences of the past, the pragmatic situation of the present, and anticipations of the future. Consequently, truth in its existentiality is perspectival, that is, it is an envisioning of reality from

---

1. Bernard J.F. Lonergan, S.J., "The Transition from a Classicist World-View to Historical Mindedness," in *A Second Collection*, ed. W. F. J. Ryan, S.J., and B. J. Tyrell, S.J. (Philadelphia: The Westminster Press, 1974), pp. 1-9.

2. For a history and analysis of this achievement see Gerald A. McCool, S.J., *Catholic Theology in the Nineteenth Century* (New York: Crossroad/Seabury, 1977), pp. 241-67, and *From Unity to Pluralism: The Internal Evolution of Thomism* (New York: Fordham University Press, 1989), pp. 114-99. See also Helen James John, *The Thomist Spectrum* (New York: Fordham University Press, 1966); and Georges Van Riet, *Thomistic Epistemology*, 2 vols. (St. Louis, Missouri: B. Herder, 1963).

3. "Such is the objectivity of truth. But do not be fascinated by it. Intentionally it is independent of the subject, but ontologically it resides only in the subject: *veritas formaliter est in solo judicio*" (Lonergan, "The Subject," in *Second Collection*, p. 3).

a particular point-of-view determined by the knower's historical situation. Thus inevitably human truth is one-sided. The achievement of truth is a social activity in which a plurality of points-of-view must be brought into a reasonable conversation. For such a conversation to proceed, no one point-of-view can claim *a priori* a superior validity, unless a super-human participant intervenes.

Why, then, do we Thomists have so much difficulty entering into the intellectual dialogue in this concrete time in history, a time when historical-mindedness and acquiescence to the pluralism of truth are so in style? My suggestion is that it has been our "metaphysicism," our tendency to reduce philosophy to metaphysics, a tendency foreign to Aquinas himself, and of fairly recent origin, which has stultified us and caused the post-Vatican II decline of Thomistic influence in Catholic life.

In Greek and medieval thought,[4] and in Aquinas's own texts,[5] the term "philosophy" was taken broadly to include the entire range of human disciplines (other than the *sacra doctrina* of Christian theology) from logic to metaphysics. The last was, indeed, philosophy *par excellence*, but it did not absorb, indeed it presupposed, the other kinds of philosophy. So true was this, that in the medieval schools, metaphysics was ordinarily not an item in the curriculum, since it seemed to overlap with sacred theology, which for Christians had replaced metaphysics or natural philosophy as queen of the sciences.[6]

We need to recall that it was not until Christian Wolff, a follower of Leibnitz, working in a Cartesian perspective, that the division within *physica* between a philosophy of nature and an empirical science of nature was introduced.[7] Only then did the field of philosophy begin to

---

4. See John Passmore, "Philosophy" in *Encyclopedia of Philosophy*, ed. Paul Edwards (New York: Macmillan/ Free Press), 6: 216-30.

5. *Index Thomisticus*, ed. Robert Busa, S.J. (Stuttgart-Bad Cannstaat: Frommann-Holzboog, 1974), 17, n. 62201. See also James A. Weisheipl, "Classification of the Science in Mediæval Thought," *Mediæval Studies* 28 (1965): 54-80.

6. James A. Weisheipl, "Curriculum of the Faculty of Arts at Oxford in the Early Fourteenth Century," *Mediæval Studies* 26 (1964): 143-85, finds no statutory mention of a requirement to study metaphysics before 1407. Nancy G. Siraisi, *Arts and Sciences at Padua: The Studium of Padua before 1350* (Toronto: Pontifical Institute of Mediæval Studies, 1973), pp. 109-142, shows that the study of Aristotle's *Metaphysics* at that university was linked with the study of his *Physics* and given only secondary importance.

7. This metaphysicism has a long history. Suarez, whose Scotistic tendencies are well known, in *Disputationes Metaphysicae, Opera Omnia* (Paris: Vivès, 1877), vol. 25, Dist. I, Sect. iv, 13, p. 29, attributes the reduction of the other sciences to material parts of metaphysics to Giles of Rome (I *Metaphysics*, q. 22 and beginning of *Posterior Analytics*) but himself advocates the traditional order of learning. In fact, however, his

THOMISM AND TRANSITION • 111

be set over against the field of the sciences, natural and humane. Furthermore, Wolff, while recognizing a philosophy of nature, and of man, etc., reduced them all to branches or applications of metaphysics. When Thomism was revived by Leo XIII in its neo-Scholastic form, many Thomists, notably Cardinal Mercier and the Thomistic Institute of the University of Louvain which dominated the first period of this revival, accepted and refined this notion.[8]

In the second phase of the Thomistic revival, under the leadership on the one hand of Joseph Maréchal, and on the other of Jacques Maritain and Etienne Gilson, closer attention to the text of Aquinas and its historical setting, gradually eliminated this Wolffian notion. Maréchal and his followers, however, accepting the Cartesian "turn to the subject" and the Kantian transcendentalism, also accepted a dichotomy between philosophy as transcendental, and the sciences as categorical or empirical, and thus continued to identify philosophy with metaphysics (or the critique of metaphysics). While they admitted the possibility and desirability of a "correlation" between the two realms of knowledge, they viewed them as completely autonomous.[9]

Gilson, while quite unsympathetic to Transcendental Thomism, shared with it the identification of philosophy with metaphysics, and has even been accused of identifying metaphysics with Christian theology. Certainly he justified his position on this issue by insisting that Aquinas was a theologian. Hence for Gilson, although St. Thomas

---

Metaphysics absorbs much of philosophy, and this Wolff carried out in full, *Discursus Praeliminaris de Philosophia in Genere*, 3 (Verona: Haeredes Marci Moroni, 1779), nn. 56, 8687. See also Richard Blackwell, "The Structure of Wolffian Philosophy," *The Modern Schoolman* 38 (1961): 203-318; and Jose Ferrata Mora, "Suarez and Modern Philosophy," *Journal of the History of Ideas* 14 (1953): 528-47.

8. The evolution of views at the Institute Supérieur de Philosophie of the University of Louvain on the philosophy of nature can be traced in widely used textbooks: Desire-Joseph, Cardinal Mercier, *Cours de Philosophie* (1905), 1: 26-30, attacked Wolff's views as "un divorce desastreux" (p. 26, n.l) but followed him in distinguishing the "sciences of observation" from the philosophical disciplines of cosmology, psychology, and natural theology which were their "complement." Fernand Renoirte, *Cosmology: Elements of a Critique of the Sciences and Cosmology*, 2nd ed. (New York: Joseph F. Wagner, 1950), p. 175-81, returned to the Wolffian conception of cosmology as "metaphysical."

9. See Gerald A. McCool, S.J., *From Unity to Pluralism*, pp. 87-113. Robert J. Henle, S.J., "Transcendental Thomism: A Critical Assessment" in *One Hundred Years of Thomism*, ed. Victor B. Brezik, C.S.B. (Houston, Texas: Center for Thomistic Studies, 1981), pp. 90-116, argues that Transcendental Thomism is really not Thomism, but he notes (pp. 92-93) that Marechal did not intend this transcendental approach to replace but only to complement that of Aquinas.

recognized a formal distinction between philosophy and theology, existentially his philosophy subsists only within the structure of his theology, and is definitively formulated only in the *Summa Theologiae*.¹⁰ Consequently, for Gilson, the other human disciplines simply are not philosophy at all, although philosophy, that is, metaphysics, has the right to criticize them when they illicitly make metaphysical claims.¹¹

Maritain never accepted this reduction of philosophy to metaphysics, as his *The Degrees of Knowledge* and his *The Philosophy of Nature* clearly show.¹² He recognized the existence of a variety of disciplines, including a philosophy of nature, an ethics, a politics, and an esthetics, which can properly be called "philosophy" by analogy to metaphysics as *prima inter pares*. These are not, as Wolff thought, mere applications of metaphysics, since each of these disciplines has its own self-evident first principles not reducible to those of metaphysics. Maritain not only defended this position of Aquinas but he exemplified it in essays that

---

10. Gerald A. McCool, S.J., *From Unity to Pluralism*, pp. 161-200; and John F. Wippel, *Metaphysical Themes in Thomas Aquinas* (Washington, D. C.: The Catholic University of American Press, 1984), chap. 1, "Thomas Aquinas and the Problem of Christian Philosophy," p. 133, see notes 71 and 76 of that work for other authors on this issue. Wippel (*Metaphysical Themes*, pp. 26-29), while disagreeing with Gilson, seems to me too cautious when he requires corroboration in Aquinas's other philosophical works to accept safely any position in the Aristotelian commentaries as Aquinas's own. I prefer the view of James A. Weisheipl, *Friar Thomas d'Aquino: His Life, Thought, and Works* (Garden City, New York: Doubleday, 1974), pp. 281-85. Medieval authors so respected the *auctoritates* that in their commentaries they either interpret them benignly to fit their own conviction as to the truth; or, if, they doubt the truth of the text, carefully distance themselves from it (as St. Albert the Great frequently does in his Aristotelian commentaries), but seldom simply report the meaning of the text, as modern commentators often do. It seems to me anachronistic to attribute this modern "objectivity" to Aquinas. See also John M. Quinn, O.S.A., *The Thomism of Etienne Gilson: A Critical Study* (Villanova, Pennsylvania: Villanova University Press, 1971), pp. 94-124; and S. Elders, "S. Thomas D'Aquin et Aristote," *Revue Thomiste* 88 (1988): 357-376.

11. In *The Philosophy of St. Thomas Aquinas*, translation of 3rd edition of *Le Thomisme* (New York: Dorset Press, 1986), chap. 9, pp. 186-203, Gilson simply follows the *Summa Theologiae* in order, method, and content in presenting Aquinas's views of subangelic reality. It should be noted, however, that Gilson used his interpretation of Thomism in writing brilliantly on literary, esthetic, and even scientific topics. For example his *Painting and Reality* (New York: Meridian Press, 1959) and *From Aristotle to Darwin and Back* (Notre Dame, Indiana: University of Notre Dame Press, 1984).

12. "The Philosophy of Nature" in his *Science and Wisdom* (New York: Charles Scribner's Sons, 1940); *Distinguish to Unite or the Degrees of Knowledge*, 4th ed., trans. G. B. Phelan (New York: Charles Scribner's Sons, 1959), pp. 21-70; 136-201; and *The Philosophy of Nature* (New York: Philosophical Library, 1951) with the review of Maritain by William H. Kane, O.P., *The Thomist* 16 (1953): 127-31.

contributed positively and originally to many of these diverse philosophies in their own proper terms.[13]

Nevertheless, Maritain was not able to free himself completely from the prevailing notion that the modern sciences, whether natural or humane, are postmedieval "new" sciences quite unlike their medieval counterparts in principles and methods. Instead he accepted the autonomy of these new sciences and tried to explicitate exactly what their proper objects and proper principles were in contradistinction to those of the correlative types of philosophy. Thus for him, just as for Wolff, there is a formal distinction between the philosophy of nature and the empirical sciences of nature. The former was *dianoetic* having first principles of a philosophical type, while the latter was *perinoetic*, and was subdivided into *empiriometric* or *empirioschematic* depending on whether it used or did not use mathematical models.[14] Unfortunately, this interesting but dubious proposal of Maritain, based largely on an inadequate knowledge of the history of science, has overshadowed his defense of the plurality of philosophies.[15] As a result, Gilson's radically reductionist view has been much more influential.[16]

Thomist philosophy in the period immediately before Vatican II was thus presented chiefly as a metaphysics. This alone guaranteed its decline in the United States where analytical philosophy looking back to the empiricism of Hume and native pragmatism have produced a culture in which metaphysics is dismissed as "nonsense" or at least "irrelevant."[17] But even where the Cartesian-Kantian tradition of continental Europe has been dominant, transcendentalized Thomism, has been caught up in the steady march toward the "forgetfulness of being,"

---

13. The range of Maritain's thought is manifest in the essays on his work in *Jacques Maritain: The Man and His Metaphysics*, ed. John F. X. Knasas, American Maritain Association (Notre Dame, Indiana: University of Notre Dame Press,1988).

14. See references in note 12 above and James A. Weisheipl, "Commentary on 'Maritain's Epistemology of Modern Science' by Jean-Louis Allard" in *Conference Seminar on Jacques Maritain's "The Degrees of Knowledge,"* ed. R. J. Henle, S.J., et al. (St. Louis, Missouri: The American Maritain Association, 1981), pp. 174-84.

15. For such a discussion see *Theologies of the Body: Humanist and Christian* (St. Louis: Pope John Center, 1958), pp. 253-344; and William A. Wallace, O.P., *From a Realist Point of View* (Washington, D. C.: University Press of America, 1979).

16. See J. F. X. Knasas, "Immateriality and Metaphysics," *Angelicum* 65 (1988): 44-76, for recent literature.

17. For what the noted historian of philosophy Frederick Copleston, S.J., calls the "recurrent waves of metaphysics and anti-metaphysics" (p. 130), see "The Nature of Metaphysics" in his *On the History of Philosophy and Other Essays* (New York: Barnes and Noble/Harper and Row, 1979), pp. 116-30.

as Heidegger named it, ending in the present lamentations over "the death of philosophy."[18]

In both empiricist and Kantian traditions, philosophy has been identified with metaphysics, and metaphysics with an analysis of the conditions of knowledge, while the *content* of knowledge has been surrendered to the nonphilosophical sciences. Certainly Thomism has important things to say about the subjective aspect of knowledge, but for Aquinas this is so sharply subordinated to the objective content of knowledge, that a Thomism which has been restricted in this way to metaphysics, or to "cognitive theory,"[19] can have little to say in any contemporary conversation about the topics which dominate our historical perspective.

The way out of this dead-end, I would suggest, is a ressourcement, a return to Aquinas's own point-of-view. Historical-mindedness not only calls our attention to our own historical situation and concerns but also frees us from our clinging to our own restricted point-of-view, so that there can be a "fusion of horizons."[20] Today we are imprisoned in a set of fixed convictions that philosophy and science are two utterly diverse enterprises, that philosophy is metaphysics, that if certitude in knowledge is possible at all it is only by a transcendental critique, and that modern science is so successful it could only be hindered in its progress by a radical philosophical critique of its basic principles. Aquinas shared none of these restrictive presuppositions. For him the proper object of the human intelligence are material things as they are known through the senses.[21] In studying such things, we must first establish their existence by sensible observation, primarily by the sense of touch.[22] Our intellectual concepts have scientific relevance only through

---

18. On the current "death of philosophy" see the essays in Hugh J. Silverman, ed., *Philosophy and Non-Philosophy Since Merleau-Ponty*, Continental Philosophy I, (New York/London: Routledge, 1988).

19. Developed by Bernard Lonergan in his *Insight: A Study of Human Understanding* (New York: Philosophical Library, 1957). For his account of his own relation to Marechal see his essay, "Insight Revisited," in *A Second Collection*, pp. 263-78.

20. Hans-Georg Gadamer, *Truth and Method* (New York: Seabury/ Continuum, 1975), pp. 269-74, 337-38, 358.

21. Aquinas compares the human intellect to that of God and angels and then says, *Est autem alius intellectus, scilicet humanus, qui nec est suum intelligere* [as is God's], *nec sui intelligere est objectum primum ipsa eius essentia* [as is an angel's, or the separated human soul], *sed aliquid extrinsecum. scilicet natura materiali rei*. (S.Th. I, q.87, a.3 c.; cf. III *Sent.*, dist. 23, q.l, a.2, ad 3; C.G., II, 75; *De Ver.* q. 10, a.9; *In de Anima*, II, 6.

22. See Charles De Koninck, "Sedeo, ergo sum," *Laval Theologique et Philosophique* 6 (1950): 343-48.

reduction to such existential facts, and the principles of our scientific knowledge are judgments verified in such existential facts, never simply in nominal concepts.[23]

Although our sense knowledge shows us a world of great variety in a constant process of change, our intelligence can analyze this world only by a step-by-step process of insight by which we separate the randomly variable aspects of reality from the more stable and uniform aspects, the natural from the chance or artificial, going always from general, vague insights toward more and more specific, precise ones, yet never losing sight of the fact that the beings we are considering are changing beings, *ens mobile*, knowable by us only through their changes.[24] So much for the classicist mind obsessed with fixed essences! For Aquinas the goal of science is not the intuition of essences but the establishing of causal relations which explain the coming into existence and perishing of sensible realities.[25]

Yet the more detailed our exploration of the world the more difficult it becomes to separate the essential from the nonessential and to discover these causal relations. Only by the use of careful observation and experimental isolation of phenomena, and by dialectical reasoning based on hypothetical models, especially mathematical models, can we

---

23. The "order of questions" discussed in the *Posterior Analytics* (cf. Aquinas, *In Post. Analyt.*, II, lect. 1) requires that the question *quid sit* be answered affirmatively before the question *quid sit* can be raised. Only then will a definition be a "real" rather than a "nominal" one, and only real definitions can be used in scientific demonstrations. Hence (contrary to common misconceptions) Thomistic philosophy is never an essentialist deduction from mere concepts, but is always existential, and presupposes critical acts of judgment concerning the existence of the things defined.

24. For Aristotle and Aquinas sense knowledge always requires a change in the sense organ by the action of the sensible object, hence the object is immediately known precisely as it enters into the process of change through its active qualities (*sensiblia propria*). Other spatio-temporal aspects (*sensiblia communia*) of the object are known only mediately through these qualities. Hence, the human intellect because its own proper object is changeable being knows the physical world not as something static but precisely in its dynamism (cf. *In De Anima*, II, lect. 13, 386-394).

25. The goal of science is to answer the question *propter quid*, i.e., the causes of the fact studied (*In Post. Analyt.* I, lect. 4, 30-43 bis). This answer is to be found in the essential definition of some subject, but this definition must be a real, i.e., existential, definition. Thus scientific method always moves from establishing the existence of a subject and of its properties and finishes by finding an essential, causal relationship among them. All existential definitions must be reduced to sense knowledge, and ultimately to the sense of touch.

26. Dialectical reasoning is employed by Aristotle and Aquinas to arrive at a discrimination of the essential features of a state of affairs from the accidental

make progress.²⁶ Fortunately, there are no limits to this progress.

As we build up a scientific understanding of the natural world around us, the need for other sciences and their possibility becomes evident. First of all, the difficulties we meet, and the divergences of opinion which arise among our fellow explorers of nature, lead us to see the need for rigorous modes of thinking and the exact use of language. Thus we discover the logical disciplines as necessary to progress in learning.²⁷ These disciplines, although instrumental to natural science, have principles distinct from those of natural science, because they are concerned not with existing, sensible realities and their relations, but with mental and linguistic constructs and their relations. The condition of such logical sciences, however, is that we have no mental relations except between concepts derived from the physical world, and no language whose ultimate reference is not to that same world.²⁸

The need and possibility of mathematics also emerges from natural science, when it demonstrates that all sensible things are quantitative (that is, they can be measured and counted) and we discover in the

---

features. The "controlled experimentation," characteristic of modern science and of which Aristotle and Aquinas knew only a few rudimentary examples, would have been accepted by them as a technology (art) in the service of dialectical thinking. If dialectic succeeds, it makes possible an act of *intellectus* (insight) expressed in a real definition. Such a definition is then a principle of scientific (as distinguished from dialectical) argument. An example of this process is provided by Aristotle's search for a definition of "soul" at the beginning of the *De Anima* (cf. Charles De Koninck, "Introduction a l'etude de l'âme," *Laval Théologique et Philosophique* 3 [1947]: 9-65; and Emile Simard, "Le hypothese," *ibid.*, pp. 89-120).

27. *In De Trin.* (Decker), q. 5, a.1, ad 2. That logic originated in the difficulties met in studying nature is clear from Aristotle's dialectical procedure in *Physics* I, and *De Anima*, I.

28. The object of logic is the purely mental relations formed between "objective concepts" by intellectual acts. Such concepts are ultimately derived from the material changeable things which are the proper object of natural science. The logician does not know these relations as psychological objects (that pertains to natural science of which psychology is only a subdivision), but precisely as mental relations (e.g., the relation of predication) which cannot exist in the real world but only in the process of our thinking about it. Such relations, however, imitate real relations found in nature, as exemplified in Venn diagrams—circles standing for relations of logical classes. Thus the validity of logical rules presupposes our knowledge of the material world; it is not *a priori*. For example, the principle of contradiction as a logical rule is grounded in the principle of contradiction as an existential ("ontological") assertion about the consistency of our experience of the sensible world. Only subsequently can metaphysical reflection on this sensibly grounded principle show it to have absolute (metaphysical) necessity as applying not merely to *ens mobile* but to *ens commune*.

process of doing this that the human intelligence, because it is served also by the interior sense we call imagination, has the ability to idealize quantities by a mentally constructive process which results in abstract figures and numbers which differ from physical figures and numbers in that they are absolutely uniform and unchanging, hence not subject to efficient or final causality, and having only mental existence.[29]

Because of its fixity, simplicity, and precision of relations, mathematics makes possible an application of logic much more elaborate than that in natural science and permits the perfecting of logic as a discipline. Moreover, mathematical models, although they apply only approximately to the existing physical world, are very helpful in forming hypotheses about that world and testing them dialectically. They can even produce certitude that some hypothetical physical situations are impossible.[30] Thus for Aquinas the theory of the "liberal arts" provides instruments for the successful development of natural science.[31]

Natural science in its own proper development arrives at two important conclusions, which make clear that the realm of material things which it studies and which supplies the conditions of the other sciences I have mentioned, is not identical with all that is. These are the famous demonstration that although all existing material things require a cause of their existence other than themselves, the First Cause of them all—though of course it too must exist in order to cause them to exist—is not material. Hence the sense of the term "being" must be analogically extended to signify not just *ens mobile* but *ens commune*, that is, being

---

29. *In De Trin.*, q. 5, a.3. The most thorough treatment of Aquinas's views on mathematics is by Bernard Mullahy, C.S.C., "Thomism and Mathematical Physics, 2 vol. (Dissertation, Laval University, 1946), typescript, partially published as "Subalternation and Mathematical Physics," *Laval Théologique et Philosophique* 2 (1946): 89-107; cf. also Charles De Koninck, *The Hollow Universe* (London: Oxford University Press, 1960).

30. On the "subalternation" of natural science to mathematics see *In De Trin.*, q. 5, a.3, ad 6 and 7 and the article of Mullahy above.

31. The chief texts of Aquinas on this subject are listed in Pierre H. Conway, O.P., and B. M. Ashley, O.P., *The Liberal Arts in St. Thomas Aquinas* (Washington, D. C.: The Thomist Press, 1959), pp. 62-64. See also Pierre H. Conway, O.P., *Principles of Education* (Washington, D. C.: The Thomist Press, 1960). Armand Maurer's introduction to his translation, *The Division and Method of the Sciences: Q. V and VI of Aquinas's Commentary on the De Trinitate of Boethius*, 4th rev. ed. (Toronto: Pontifical Institute of Mediæval Studies, 1986), has many useful bibliographical notes on this topic.

32. The summary presentation by Aquinas of the fundamental proof from motion in S.Th., I, q. 2, a.3 must be read with the much fuller development in C.G., I, 13-16. For an accurate exposition of the argument and discussion of why it has not been rendered obsolete by modern physics, see Vincent E. Smith, *The General Science of*

common to material and immaterial existents.[32]

The second demonstration is that there exists substantially united with the material human body an immaterial subsistent form, namely, the human soul. This second proof presupposes the first, since the former establishes (a) the existence of a First Cause and therefore, (b) that not all being is material; while the latter establishes another instance of such immaterial being, namely the human soul, which depends on the First Cause for its own existence.[33]

The existence of immaterial being raises the question of whether a science of being in this new inclusive sense is possible, but it also indicates the great difficulties the formation of such a science would entail, since the immaterial realm is not within the proper object of our intelligence, that is, is meta-physical. If it were, then "being as such" (usually said to be the proper object of metaphysics) would be *ens mobile* and natural science would be "first philosophy" not only *quoad nos* but *in se*.[34]

Because of these difficulties about developing metaphysics as a science, there has to be a sufficient reason for its pursuit. This reason is provided when we consider that the fact of the immateriality of our intelligence means that we differ from all the other things of the material world in that our activities are not wholly determined by nature, but at least in part are a matter of *free choice*.[35] Hence, the need for the ethical disciplines by which our intelligence guides free human actions, and the technologies by which it invents and produces artifacts.[36]

The ethical disciplines develop the theme of the *summum bonum* both for the individual and for the society in which alone the human individual can achieve actual freedom, and Aquinas comes to the conclusion that this *summum bonum* proper to human beings is the achievement of wisdom and above all such knowledge of the First Cause as is possible for us by human efforts.[37] Since such knowledge, however difficult, is the goal of human existence, the need and possibility of a meta-physics as the first philosophy is established. The proof of the existence of the First Cause by the science of nature is the necessary condition of such a

---

Nature (Milwaukee, Wisconsin: Bruce Publishing Co., 1958). For discussion of common misunderstandings of Aquinas's argument see Thomas C. O'Brien, *Metaphysics and the Existence of God* (Washington, D. C.: The Thomist Press, 1960).

33. S.Th. I, q. 75, a. 1-2, a. 5-6; q. 89. See Anton C. Pegis, *The Problem of the Soul in the Thirteenth Century* (Toronto: St. Michael's College, 1934).

34. *In Meta.* (Marietti), III, 6, 398; VI, 1, 1170; 11, 7, 2267.

35. S.Th., I, q. 83; *De Ver.*, q. 24, a. 1-2; *De Malo* , q.6.

36. *In Ethic.*, I, lect 1, 1-6 (Marietti).

37. *In Ethic.*, VI, lect. 5, 1180-1183; X, lect. 11, 2098-2210.

science, but nevertheless metaphysics is autonomous, based, as is every science, on an intuition of its own formal subject, an intuition, however, which presupposes certain conditions.[38]

The thesis that the necessary condition of metaphysics is the proof provided by natural science that immaterial being exists provoked a heated controversy in the 1950s which still continues. In 1979 the various opinions were collected and carefully analyzed in a Catholic University of America thesis by John V. Wagner.[39] After showing the fallacies of the attempts to deny that Aquinas held the position in question, Wagner concluded, nevertheless, that the texts which expound this position do not absolutely exclude other ways of access to the subject of metaphysics. The strongest alternative is to be found in Aquinas's arguments that it is not impossible for forms that are not the forms of matter to exist. Lawrence Dewan, O.P., has recently supported this proposal, but,

---

38. This is analogous to the Thomistic doctrine that the senses are the material condition of intellection, and that rational credibility is the material condition of faith. In each case the more perfect kind of knowledge is *formally* independent, because it has its own proper principles which are known by some intuitive type of knowledge (*intellectus*), but this intuition presupposes a material condition without which it is impossible. On the nature of intuition (*intellectus*) in Aquinas see Julien L. Péghaire, C.S.Sp., *Intellectus et ratio selon 5. Thomas d'Aquin* (Paris: J. Vrin; Ottawa: Institute d'Etudes Medievales, 1936).

39. John V. Wagner, *A Study of What Can and Cannot be Determined about Separatio as it is Discussed in the Works of St. Thomas Aquinas* (Ann Arbor, Michigan: University Microfilms, 1979). Wagner's main reason for doubting that Aquinas accepts Aristotle's position without qualification is "An approach [such as Aquinas's] that describes metaphysics as beginning with the discovery of primary beings and then includes the rest of being in its field of study because it is caused by them is not the same as an approach [such as Aristotle's] that discovers an immaterial being and on the basis of that discovery widens the notion of being." (p. 353 n.56) This opposition disappears if we note that for Aristotle *and* Aquinas the proof of the First Mover in the *Physics* goes all the way to God as the primary being, whose existence is easier to prove than that of lesser immaterial beings. *Et sic terminat philosophus considerationem communem de rebus naturalibus in Primo Principio totius naturae, qui est super omnia Deus benedictus in saeculo saeculorum. Amen* (8, lect. 23, 2550 Marietti). Although for Aquinas, God (as Wagner shows correctly) is not the subject of metaphysics, but its principle, his existence known by natural science, establishes the reality of *ens commune* (common to material and immaterial beings) as its subject. There is no circularity in using this physical proof as the condition of metaphysics, and then in metaphysics showing that this same proof has not only physical but metaphysical certitude and necessity. The essentially reflective, critical character of metaphysics requires it to inquire into the facts established by the special sciences in order to determine their type of necessity or contingency.

admits that it only establishes the *possibility* that being can be immaterial.⁴⁰ If this is the case, is it not paradoxical to suppose that so "existential" a philosopher as Aquinas would anticipate Leibnitz by constructing his metaphysics on mere possibility? In my judgment, these texts which are evidently the last resort of those who want to cut Thomistic metaphysics loose from any necessary relation to natural science, do not even establish the positive possibility of immaterial being, but are intended by Aquinas simply to refute arguments that claim to prove its impossibility.

It was the great accomplishment of Gilson, to which L.-B. Geiger and Cornelio Fabro also greatly contributed,⁴¹ to bring out in a way that had become obscure even in the major commentators on Aquinas, how the Common Doctor was able to explicitate in his metaphysics the philosophical truth which Christian faith confirms, that God is the *Ipsum Esse Subsistens*, who by the utterly free act of creation calls all other existents into a participation in *esse*.⁴² Thus that by which realities are real is being in the (analogical) sense of the act of existing, known by us in an intellectual judgment.⁴³

To say that the act of existing is the ultimate reality of all things, however, is meaningful only if we also add that this act of existing in creatures is limited and specified by essence, while in God it is identical

---

40. "St. Thomas Aquinas against Metaphysical Materialism" in *Studi Tomistici*, Atti del VIII Congresso Tomistica Internazionale, vol. 14, *Problema Metafisici* (Vatican City: Libreria Editrice Vaticana, 1982), pp. 412-34.

41. Etienne Gilson, *Being and Some Philosophers*; L. B. Geiger, O.P., *La Participation dans la philosophie de S. Thomas d'Aquin* (Paris: J. Vrin, 1942); Cornelio Fabro, *La nozione metafisica di partecipazione*, 2nd ed. (Turin: Societa Editrice Internazionale, 1952). On the last see Mario Pangallo, *L'essere come atto nel Tomismo essenziale di Cornelio Fabro*, Studi Tomistici, vol. 32 (Pontificia Accademia di S. Tommaso, Vatican, Libreria Editrice, 1987).

42. It must be noted, however, that Aquinas himself believed that this Christian insight was already achieved by Aristotle, since he says quite plainly, after expounding the Stagirite's views that "From this is manifest the error of the opinions of those who teach that Aristotle thought that God is not the cause of the substance of the heavens, but only its motion" (*Ex hoc autem manifest falsitas opiniones illorum, qui posuerunt Aristotelem sensisse quod Deus non sit causa substantiae caeli, sed solum motus est, In Meta.*, VI, 1, 1164 on Aristotle, *Meta.* VI, 1026a 11-18). "Substance" here certainly includes *esse*, since substance as such can be caused only by giving it existence.

43. Etienne Gilson, *Being and Some Philosophers*, 2nd ed. (Toronto: Pontifical Institute of Mediæval Studies, 1952); Cornelio Fabro, *La nozione metafisica di partecipazione*, 2nd ed. (Turin, 1950).

44. See discussion in J. Wippel, *Metaphysical Themes*, pp. 107-161, 191-214 and literature there referred to.

with essence.[44] "Being" taken as the metaphysician takes it to cover all that exists as material and nonmaterial is an empty term until it is filled with an array of analogical and univocal concepts developed in the special sciences. To say that God is Pure Act means just as much or just as little as we have learned of him through the actualities of this world.[45]

Thus for Aquinas metaphysics is a reflective science, or better still, a contemplative wisdom [46] and if it has no content supplied by the special sciences to reflect on and contemplate, it remains merely verbal and thus otiose. Hence, if studied in isolation from the special sciences, it either suffers reduction to the natural sciences or is forced to claim transcendental intuitions which are unavailable to public discourse.

Nor is it necessary to accept the view, Platonic in its origin but reinforced today by the rapid progress of the special disciplines and the prevalence of the hypothetico-deductive method, that these disciplines can never achieve anything more than probability. In fact these disciplines have proper principles that have a genuine certitude, although of different types. Hence, they continue to accumulate a set of solid, demonstrated conclusions, although these are few in relation to the large body of shifting hypothetical conclusions which constitute the bulk of current opinion in the field.[47] Therefore, the material dependence of metaphysics on these disciplines does not imperil the certitude of metaphysics itself.

Thus the future of Thomism depends on our allowing our sense of history to let us look once more with sympathy and without apologies on the way Aquinas viewed the variety of sciences, and the manner in which he saw their unification by a trans-physical wisdom. I believe we will then find that he can, through us, enter into the modern philosophical dialogue as a living and magisterial voice.

---

45. No doubt this is why Aquinas makes so much use of the now obsolete Aristotelian sciences in his writings which today prove a source of embarrassment to modern commentators and teachers.

46. *In Meta.* I, 1, n.34.

47. See William A. Wallace, "Demonstration in the Science of Nature, " in *From a Realist Point of View*, pp. 329-70.

History, Tradition, and Truth

Vincent M. Colapietro

My purpose in this paper is to raise a question about the adequacy of a position, apparently held by a significant number of prominent contemporary Thomists (*e.g.*, Josef Pieper, Jacques Maritain, Bernard Lonergan, and Ralph McInerny), concerning how natural truths are discovered.[1] This position has a strong claim to being considered *the* traditional Thomistic approach to truth. By "approach," I mean something wider and vaguer than "definition," "concept" or "notion." The abstract definition of truth as *adequatio* may be essentially correct and a clear distinction between discovery (*inventio*) and learning (*disciplina*) may be truly indispensable for providing an account of our coming to know the truth.[2] Even so, the historical appropriations of this definition and this distinction may, nonetheless, be seriously limited and (what is worse) philosophically limiting. By the "traditional Thomistic approach to truth," then, I mean the way Thomas's own understanding of what truth is and how truth is discovered has been articulated and defended over six centuries by thinkers committed to the tradition bearing his name. In this articulation and defense, certain dominant emphases have emerged. More often than not, these have arisen in a polemical context in which one or more of Thomas's assertions about some aspect of truth were being (at least, by implication) challenged or criticized. The emphasis to which I shall attend concerns not what truth is but how it is discovered.

Here it is instructive to recall the words of Jacques Maritain: The more closely we examine philosophical controversies, the more fully we realize that

> they thrive on a certain number (increasing with the progress of time) of basic themes to which each newly arriving philosopher endeavors to give some kind of place . . . in his own system [or outlook], while at the same

---

1. By "natural truth," I simply mean a truth that is, in principle, discoverable by the natural light of human reason.

2. Thomas Aquinas, *Quaestio disputata de veritate*, q. 11, a. I. Cf. Jacques Maritain, *A Preface to Metaphysics* (New York: Mentor Omega Books, 1962), p. 10; Ralph McInerny, *Thomism in an Age of Renewal* (Notre Dame, Indiana: University of Notre Dame Press, 1968), p. 41.

time, more often than not, his overemphasis on one of the themes in question causes his system to be at odds with those of his fellow competitors—and with the truth of the matter.[3]

This insight into philosophical controversies helps us to frame the ideal of philosophical inquiry. As Maritain puts it, "The greater and truer a philosophy, the more perfect the balance between all the ever-recurrent basic themes with whose discordant claims philosophical reflection has to do."[4] In the end, philosophical adequacy is judged in terms of properly placed emphases and, we might add, properly drawn distinctions. The relevance of this to our topic is that the traditional Thomistic approach to truth needs to be assessed in terms not merely of its abstract definitions but also in terms of its historical emphases.[5]

For our purposes, the two most important emphases concern reason and truth itself. Traditional Thomists have stressed the capacity of human reason to grasp immutable truths and, thereby, to transcend historical contingencies.[6] There are weighty and, in my judgment, compelling reasons for this emphasis. Even so, the stress on the immutable character of truth and the transcendent capacity of reason has encouraged a misleading view of tradition, a view quite at odds with the way those who emphasize these points characteristically carry on their intellectual lives.[7]

It is *not* my objective here to show that St. Thomas's own understanding of truth is unable to illuminate the continuing authority which he himself is accorded in a self-conscious intellectual tradition. Do not

---

3. Jacques Maritain, *On the Use of Philosophy: Three Essays* (New York: Atheneum, 1965), pp. 29-30.

4. *Ibid.*, p. 30.

5. The work of Gerald McCool, S.J., is indispensable for assessing Thomism in this manner.

6. There are, of course, important voices in the Thomistic tradition who have challenged this emphasis. For example, W. Norris Clarke, S.J., in his Presidential Address to the ACPA in 1969, contended that "we have not yet worked out an explicit philosophical understanding and expression of the nature and limits of human truth, as actually attainable in the concrete, which is adequate to—or sometimes even [merely] compatible with—our lived experience in so many areas of 20th century life and thought" (*Proceedings of the ACPA*, Volume XLIII, edited by George F. McLean, p. 1).

7. I am reminded in this connection of a remark made by Albert Einstein in a piece included in *Ideas and Opinions* (New York: Dell, 1976): "If you want to find out anything from the theoretical physicists about the methods they use, I advise you to stick closely to one principle: don't listen to their words, fix your attention to their deeds" (p. 264).

suppose that in raising a question I am dismissing a position or a tradition, much less a thinker of Thomas's stature. Quite the contrary. One of my principal hopes is to render plausible the notion that a historical figure attains and continues to exert intellectual authority insofar as that figure is perceived as an inexhaustible resource, a source to which others can go, again and again. It *is* my contention that the role of traditional authority in the drama of philosophical life is often misunderstood, even by some of the most perceptive and eloquent defenders of tradition. In other words, an important truth about tradition has been obscured by certain traditional emphases regarding truth. This truth is that the authority of tradition is, even in fields like mathematics, physics, and philosophy, more than merely "provisional and preliminary."[8] This authority is, at least for the traditionalist, enduring or continuing.

Allow me to proceed by offering several personal recollections. These bear directly on the intimate but complex relationship between tradition and truth. Neither seekers of truth nor lovers of wisdom grow on trees; they grow out of traditions. The natural desire for knowledge needs the nurturing community of inquirers. There is, at the heart of any tradition, a personal encounter between, on the one side, individuals who embody that tradition and, on the other, those who do not or at least not yet. These encounters characteristically are face-to-face exchanges in which both moral and intellectual habits (though not necessarily virtues) are exemplified by the older generation and, in some measure, acquired by the younger. Insofar as I have any claim to the title of "philosopher" in its etymological and most authentic sense, it is largely because of my transformative encounter with several undergraduate teachers who were deeply committed to the thought of Saint Thomas.

As an undergraduate, I was encouraged by these teachers to read anything and everything by Ralph McInerny (including his novels!). His *Thomism in an Age of Renewal* was one of the works through which I was introduced to Thomism as a self-conscious philosophical tradition. Some of you might recall that, in this book, Professor Ralph McInerny devotes a chapter to "Philosophy and Tradition." Following the lead of a footnote at the end of this chapter, I discovered Josef Pieper's finely nuanced yet doggedly commonsensical examination of "The Concept of Tradition." This discovery prompted me to move in several directions—back to the writings of that thinker from whom Pieper and McInerny primarily drew their insights and also back to both the dictates of my own reason and the disclosures of my own experience. In other words,

---

8. McInerny, *Thomism*, p. 42. Here the author is quoting, possibly misquoting, Josef Pieper, "The Concept of Tradition" in *Review of Politics* 20 (1958): 474.

a dialogue was generated by my encounter with Professor McInerny's reflections on tradition and philosophy. In this dialogue, the claims of a tradition were checked against my own experiences and reflections and, in turn, these experiences and reflections were tested against these claims. In short, there was a *mutual* interrogation or cross-examination. At times, this took the form of an inner dialogue; at other times, it took the form of an actual conversation with flesh-and-blood companions.[9]

In preparing to write this paper, one of the first things I did was to reread what both Pieper and McInerny had to say about tradition. I also consulted the writings of other thinkers, paying especially close attention to what other Thomists have said about the topic. Throughout his discussion, McInerny stresses that the reader or listener possesses the resources and criteria by which to judge what is being transmitted in the name of tradition. In fields such as mathematics, physics, and even philosophy, we are not simply at the mercy of our teachers or any other transmitters of tradition; for we have independent access to what they are talking about.[10] They can supply the occasion for us becoming aware of some aspect or domain of reality but never confer upon us our awareness of this reality. This awareness is something we ourselves bring to our attempts to learn or discover the truth. While this awareness or consciousness *is* in one important sense a gift, that is, something we receive from Another, this Other is not one of our kind. Because of this gift, we have within ourselves the resources to see *for ourselves* what others are claiming to be the case. "[I]n principle at least, we could, by attending to those objects independently of the help of others, come to see what, thanks to instruction, we are being led to see."[11] A prominent feature of McInerny's eloquent defense of philosophical tradition and the Thomistic tradition in particular is an ennobling appeal to personal experience. If "the main lesson of Empiricism is," as Hegel claims, "that a man must see for himself and feel that he is present in every fact of knowledge which he has to accept,"[12] then a main lesson of traditionalism is that we learn the main lesson of empiricism—that we must see for ourselves.

---

9. This part of our initiation into tradition might be related to what Maritain calls "fellowship," a word connoting "something positive—positive and elementary—in human relationships. It conjures up the image of traveling companions, who meet here below by chance and journey through life . . . good humoredly, in cordial solidarity and human agreement, or better to say, friendly and cooperative disagreement" (*On the Use of Philosophy*, p. 33). While our intellectual traditions make *cooperative* disagreement possible, intellectual fellowship makes such disagreement endurable and, at least on occasion, delightful.

10. McInerny, *Thomism*, p. 52.

11. *Ibid.*

12. Hegel, *Logic* (Oxford: Clarendon Press, 1975), p. 61.

In one of his later writings, Jacques Maritain strikes a similar chord when he asserts that:

> Given a chance to reveal its own nature, Thomistic philosophy exhibits the gait and demeanor characteristic of all philosophy; a demeanor and gait fully at liberty to confront the real. The philosopher swears fidelity to no person, nor any school—not even, if he is a Thomist, to the letter of St. Thomas and every article of his teaching. He is sorely in need of teachers and of a tradition, but in order for them to teach him to think when he looks at things (which is not as simple as all that), and not, as is the case with the theologian, so that he can assume the whole of this tradition into his thought. Once this tradition has instructed him, he is free of it and makes use of it for his own work. In this sense, he is alone in the face of being; for his job is to think over that which is.[13]

The function of a tradition is to empower us to *think* when we *look* at things, to reflect about whatever we have encountered or might encounter and, as a result of this reflection, to grasp the widest and deepest significance of these encounters. In other words, a tradition enables us to come into full and independent possession of our own intellectual resources, in particular, our ability to attend to the disclosures of our lived experience and our capacity to reflect upon the implications of these experiential revelations.

If we turn to Bernard Lonergan's *Insight* (1957), we are confronted by a variation on this theme, albeit a variation in which the autonomy of the knower is perhaps even more decisively stressed than in either McInerny or Maritain. According to Lonergan,

> the issues in philosophy cannot be settled by looking up a handbook, by appealing to a set of experiments performed so painstakingly by so-and-so, by referring to the masterful presentation of overwhelming evidence in some famous work. Philosophic evidence is within the philosopher himself. It is his own inability to avoid experience, to renounce intelligence in inquiry, to desert reasonableness in reflection. It is his own detached, disinterested desire to know. . . . It is his own grasp of the dialectical unfolding of his own desire to know in its conflict with other desires that provides the key to his own philosophic development. . . . Philosophy is the flowering of the individual's rational consciousness in its coming to know and take possession of itself. To that event, its traditional schools, its treatises, and its history are but contributions; and without that event they are stripped of real significance.[14]

---

13. Jacques Maritain, *The Peasant of Garonne*, trans. Michael Cuddihy and Elizabeth Hughes (New York: Macmillan Company, 1968), p. 161.

14. Bernard Lonergan S.J., *Insight: A Study of Human Understanding* (New York: Harper & Row, 1978), p. 429.

What each of these Thomists is underscoring in his own way is an important implication of a truth articulated by Thomas himself and discoverable in our own experience as learners. As Maritain reminds us, human beings are, in the Thomistic view of human teaching, social animals primarily because they are in need of teaching; "and the teacher's art, like the doctor's, co-operates with nature, so that the *principal agent* in the art of instruction is not the teacher imparting knowledge to his pupil and producing it in his mind, but the understanding, the intellectual vitality of the pupil who receives[,] that is to say, assimilates, the knowledge actively into his mind and so brings knowledge to birth there."[15] Just as the organism is the principal source of its own recovery, so the understanding is the principal source of its own discoveries.

But the irony here is that, when I turned to my own experience and reason (when I turned to the sources to which Pieper, McInerny, Maritain, and Lonergan invited me to turn in order to assess the validity of what is being handed down), what these personal sources of intellectual illumination revealed about themselves is their inadequacy to perform the role demanded of them by these defenders of tradition who were also champions of reason. Did I not feel compelled to go back, once again, to authors and, indeed, texts I had read numerous times before? And was not this feeling rooted in my own experience of fallibility and nurtured by my reflections on the practical implications of my own finite, fallible nature? This suggested to me that a philosophical tradition is not a ladder we kick away after using it to ascend to the truth, enjoying the perspective provided by the catbird seat.

If I reflect upon my own practice as a philosopher, and if I observe how others (especially those who possess the humility or self-effacement to identify themselves by the name of another thinker—for example, Thomists, Heideggerians, or Deweyans) undertake the task of philosophy, what I conclude is that a living philosophical tradition is an *ongoing* dialogue between, on the one side, the claims of this tradition and, on the other, the disclosures of my own experience and the dictates of my own reason. In this dialogue, neither side is absolutely or unqualifiedly privileged: what I am able to see only with the help of others is never totally eclipsed by what I am able to see for myself.

Recall what we noted earlier, namely, that the adequacy of a philosophical outlook is to be judged in terms of whether its emphases are properly placed and its distinctions are properly drawn. My argument has been simply that the emphasis on the transcendent capacity of human reason (*i.e.*, the ability of reason to rise above the contingencies

---

15. Jacques Maritain, *Preface to Metaphysics*, p. 10.

of history) and the immutable character of some truths needs to be balanced by an emphasis on the historical rootedness of this reason and on the corrigible nature of our judgments. It is one thing to acknowledge a truth; it is quite another to accord a truth the place it deserves within our lookout. If we reflect, in the light of our own practice of philosophizing, upon the traditional roots of virtually all philosophical reflection and also upon the fallible nature of our own intellectual resources, we need to highlight our *continuing* dependency upon some intellectual tradition, even if it is not the one in which we were brought up. "Tradition as authority fulfills its role," according to McInerny, "by a flourish and exit."[16] Insofar as philosophy is a matter of demonstration in the strict sense, it is true that tradition as authority fulfills its role in this way; however, insofar as philosophy is an affair of interpretation, a struggle to make sense out of our experience, the authority of tradition is never merely provisional or preliminary. The emphasis upon demonstrative knowledge rather than hermeneutical understanding is partly responsible for our underrating of tradition and our exaggeration of the degree of autonomy from tradition which reason is able to attain.

Speaking of Socrates, McInerny notes that: "At one time he subjected himself to a philosophical tradition; later he modified what he had accepted to the point where he could say that he had repudiated his philosophical origins. There is a pattern here which shows up again and again in the great philosophers and, in however a modest way, in the philosophical growth of each of us."[17] But this is only part of the story. For when we as individuals have reached the point where we can repudiate these origins, we are confronted with a choice: we can adopt either an ahistorical approach to philosophical questions or a deliberately and self-consciously historical approach. As Michael McCarthy notes in *The Crisis of Philosophy*, tradition "is the *willed* inheritance of the past that illumines the present and future."[18] Antitraditionalism, itself a tradition going back to Bacon and Descartes, is the willed *rejection* of the past as authoritative. Pierre Duhem contended that: "It is easy to break a tradition, but not so easy to renew it."[19] It is perhaps less easy than we suppose either to break a tradition or to break *with* tradition.

"The opposite of a correct statement is," as Neils Bohr has pointed out, "a false statement. But the opposite of a profound truth may well be

---

16. McInerny, *Thomism*, p. 44.
17. *Ibid.*, p. 39.
18. Michael McCarthy, *The Crisis of Philosophy* (Albany, New York: SUNY press, 1990), p. 170 (emphasis added).
19. Pierre Duhem, *The Aim and Structure of Physical Theory* (New York: Atheneum, 1962), p. 313.

another profound truth." The opposite of the truth concerning the capacity of our minds to see for themselves, to transcend the contingencies of history and their dependency on the instruction of others, is the truth concerning tradition as an ongoing dialogue in which there occurs a mutual interrogation of what we claim to be able to see for ourselves and what others claim to be real whether we see it or not. In the final analysis, *I* judge what is so on the basis of what is revealed by my reason and through my experience. This emphasis is linked to the radical responsibility I must take for my own intellectual life. It also brings into view one of the most important bases of my dignity as a person.

But my judgments are responsible only to the extent that, in framing them, I have sought the counsel of others. As Thomas reminds us with his characteristic simplicity, it is part of wisdom to seek counsel. This does not, of course, mean soliciting anybody and everybody for their "opinion." It does mean having the courage and humility to expose our judgments to the criticism of those whom we deem to be wise.[20]

What Thomas himself did not need to emphasize in his time—because it went without saying—might need to be especially stressed in our own day—because it is rejected without thinking. This is nothing other than the *enduring* authority of our intellectual tradition, an authority from which we can never completely extricate ourselves. In the earlier stages of our adult development, we are preoccupied with taking full possession of our unique talents; in the later stages, our concern is with what has been called generativity. In the former, the focus is on taking responsibility for oneself; in the latter, it is on taking responsibility for one's tradition. We are disposed to assume responsibility for own traditions out of a sense of gratitude for the graciousness by which we were empowered to think for ourselves. A living tradition—and how could a tradition be living if the claims of the past did not have the power continuously to re-assert themselves?—depends upon the omnipresent willingness to go back, time and again, to what was uttered generations ago. In this willingess, we see exemplified the compatibility of thinking *for oneself* and thinking with *others*. To think for ourselves does not require that we think by ourselves (*i.e.*, in isolation from others). Quite the contrary. To think for myself is, if conscientiously undertaken, to think

---

20. If there is a "hermeneutical circle," there also appears to be a *critical circle*. We turn to those whom we deem wise and, in doing so, appear to be caught in a circle. But, if we take history seriously, then it is possible to see how the passage of time provides the opportunities to shuttle back and forth from the advice of others to he disclosures of our own experience. This ongoing, mutual dialogue, involving moments of cross-examination, is precisely the aspect of our involvement in tradition that, in this paper, I have tried to bring into focus.

with others, both others now living and long dead. In the abiding disposition to return continuously to my intellectual elders and, then, to weigh carefully what they have to say, I reveal myself to be a traditionalist. To see the authority of tradition as merely provisional and preliminary is, in effect, to endorse a *rationalist* conception of tradition. In opposition to such a conception, I have been arguing for a *traditionalist* conception of reason, one in which the link between reason and tradition is seen as essential not only at the outset but throughout the entirety of our fallible lives as rational animals. In terms of this conception, coming-to-know is far more of a communal and historical process than is fully recognized.

The thinkers with whom I have been in a sense arguing would, no doubt, readily grant this point. *Our* task is to be careful that, in our philosophical outlooks, each of "the ever-recurrent themes" (to use Maritain's expression once again) receives its due. My question is: Has the traditional emphasis on the transcendent capacity of human reason (the ability of us to see for ourselves and, thereby, to transcend our dependency on others) deflected our attention away from the ineradicably traditional character of all human knowing and coming-to-know? If this is so, then does this not point to the need for consulting those other philosophical perspectives (*e.g.*, pragmatism and hermeneutics) in which the communal, interpretive, historical, and even political dimensions of coming-to-know have been stressed? To acknowledge this need might help us to see more clearly that we are always in the position of learners and, thus, never free from the authority of tradition. For a Thomist, such an insight should be welcome.

The future of Thomism will be, as it has been, an ongoing dialogue in which fallible inquirers try to discover ever more nuanced and effective ways to apply the measure of the real to their judgments about reality.

On the Training of Thomists

John C. Cahalan

The period since Vatican II has seen a dramatic decline of interest in studying Aquinas among graduate students. Thirty years ago, there may not have been as much interest in Aquinas as we would have liked, but there was much more than there is now. Those who were in Catholic graduate schools then, whether as students or teachers, can testify to this change from their own experience. Those who were not there then could verify this change for themselves by, for example, comparing the number of courses in Aquinas offered at Catholic graduate schools then and now.

The reasons for the decline of interest in Aquinas are varied and complex, and not all the reasons are in the control of educators. But I will argue that there are things teachers of Thomism should have been doing a generation ago which would have resulted in greater interest in Aquinas today, and doing these things now will result in greater interest in the future. Much of what Thomistic educators have been doing is excellent, and my main purpose is not to criticize. I am making a positive proposal for improving the teaching of Thomism at the graduate level, a proposal designed to increase interest in studying Aquinas not only among present students, but even more importantly, among future students, that is, among the students of our present students. The proposal is designed to produce students who can interest their students in studying Aquinas.

I

The way graduate students were taught in the sixties was in part a reaction against the tradition of manual Scholasticism still in existence prior to Vatican II. Quentin Quesnell has recently given us a description of that milieu:

> This Scholastic thought world was one that put an extraordinary premium on logic, clarity, the mechanics of exposition, on precise divisions and subdivisions of the material. It presupposed the possibility of perfect and exact definitions of everything.... The chain of reasoning can always be followed, if one has the patience and stamina to pursue it. This was its

strength but also its weakness. For so much emphasis on form could easily allow form to replace substance. Ideas and names are always sharper and clearer than reality, and a world of definitions, divisions and logic could soon become a world of words alone. It was obvious that the system was not devised to promote innovation.[1]

Quesnell had seminary education specifically in mind, and it would be a mistake to think that this picture represents *all* Thomistic education prior to Vatican II—far from it. At my undergraduate institution, for example, many students were exposed to original works of Aristotle and Aquinas, not to mention the works of non-Thomist philosophers. Still, the manual tradition did contribute to the decline of interest in Aquinas. But even though Thomists have forsaken the manual tradition, they have not found a way to generate the kind of interest Aquinas deserves to enjoy.

Quesnell points to another failing of the manual tradition that the graduate education of thirty years ago was designed to correct: "You did not do independent historical research, reading through the originals in the context of their own times" (p. 148). In part as a remedy for the manual tradition's *a*historicism, the graduate education of Thomists preceding Vatican II usually focused on studying Aquinas's own texts. The professors were concerned to establish the correct interpretation of Aquinas's texts in their historical context, often in opposition to an incorrect interpretation of one of the classical commentators or of some modern Thomist.

This historical-textual approach to Thomism, however, was not the only alternative to the manual tradition. As we all know, the twentieth-century produced many Thomists who were neither manualists nor textual commentators but thinkers who philosophized Thomistically. They were men and women with philosophical questions who found answers to those questions in Aquinas. Their work showed how truths they found in Aquinas answered questions posed by modern philosophy. Their method was not to defend one reading of his texts against other readings but to show how philosophical conclusions could be established from the data of experience.

This philosophical approach to Thomism, however, was seriously neglected in the graduate education of thirty years ago. To see how thoroughly it was neglected, consider the following: in three years of graduate education at two highly regarded schools, the universities of

---

1. Quentin Quesnell, "A Note on Scholasticism," in *The Desires of the Human Heart: An Introduction to the Theology of Bernard Lonergan*, ed. Vernon Gregson (New York: Paulist Press, 1988), p. 149.

Toronto and the University of Notre Dame, I was not once required to read a modern Thomist. Studying Thomism meant studying the texts of Aquinas to the exclusion of studying any of his disciples. Occasionally, modern Thomists would be recommended in class, but the professors did not require the students to read any of them. And when the professors did mention modern Thomists, it was to criticize their interpretations of Aquinas at least as often as to recommend reading them. The professors were pursuing a historical approach; they were interested in establishing the correct interpretation of the texts of Aquinas, and they were interested in modern Thomists as interpreters of Aquinas, not as philosophers who had truths about reality to teach us. Modern Thomists were only secondary sources; and as good historical scholars, our job was to go to the primary sources.

If a random sampling of courses at two of the best Thomistic graduate schools is insufficient to establish that the philosophical approach to Thomism was being neglected in favor of the historical-textual approach, there is other evidence. For example, one could examine the Thomistic publications from the generation preceding Vatican II, whose authors were the teachers of that period, and the generation following Vatican II, whose authors were the students of that period. The examination would show that textual analyses predominate among those publications.[2] The fact is that in the second half of this century Thomists have produced far less literature of a creative philosophical character than in the first half. As Ralph McInerny said to me sometime in the mid-sixties, "What I want to know is where are the big Thomists of this generation." But should we have expected anything else, if young Thomists were not required to study models of Thomism done philosophically? How could we have expected them to learn and integrate Thomism philosophically, if they were not required to experience creative and philosophical Thomism?

Maritain apparently agreed with this assessment of Thomistic publications. In *The Peasant of the Garonne*, he criticized Thomists for not producing enough literature of "genuine philosophic value" and for instead producing literature that "possessed neither the gait and method, nor the light characteristic of philosophical research."[3] These remarks occur in a discussion of the manual tradition; his example is Gredt. But Maritain was aware of all the excellent historical research on Aquinas published since the time of Gredt. If he thought that those historical

---

2. And even when the intent of a work is to make a philosophical argument, the philosophy is often obscured by the historical and textual content.

3. Jacques Maritain, *The Peasant of the Garonne*, trans. Michael Cuddihy and Elizabeth Hughes (New York: Holt, Rinehart, Winston, 1968), p. 136.

studies made up for the lack of genuine philosophical value in the manuals, he should have said so. (And since Gilson's *The Spirit of Mediaeval Philosophy* is one of the few books, along with Garrigou-Lagrange's *La Philosophie de l'être et le sens commun*, Maritain put in the category of excellent *philosophy*,[4] he did not have a narrow conception of what constitutes philosophy and what constitutes history.)

In other words, Maritain was implying that neither the manual tradition nor the historical-textual approach are sufficient to make Thomism a living philosophy. The philosophical approach is also necessary. This is not to say that the philosophical approach should replace the historical. The historical-textual approach is not only valid but necessary.[5] For example, we owe our awareness of the importance of *esse* to the historical insights of Thomists like Gilson and Fabro. But the experience of the second half of this century has shown that the historical approach is not sufficient for training Thomists who can make Thomism live as a philosophy with the position of influence it should have in our culture and in the Church.

II

In particular, neither the manual tradition nor the historical approach is sufficient to maintain the kind of interest among students that Aquinas deserves. At the two schools mentioned above, for example, many students expressed a loss of interest in Aquinas because they were encountering contemporary questions that interested them, and Aquinas—at least the Aquinas they were learning about—did not appear to answer those questions.

But if the professors had required them to study modern Thomists in addition to studying Aquinas, those students could have learned that Aquinas can provide answers to modern questions. For in order to get those answers from Aquinas, one has to do more than understand his texts. One has to put two and two together; one has to transpose truths into contexts different from those where one finds them in Aquinas; one has to see the significance of Thomistic truths from a fresh perspective.

For example, Maritain recognized that Aquinas's distinction between things as things and things as objects is the crux of the problem of realism, in general, and the problem of the correspondence theory of truth, in particular.[6] But the texts of Aquinas do not apply the thing-

---

4. *Ibid.*, 136 n. 7.

5. See, for example, Maritain's remarks on history in philosophical education; *ibid.*, p. 137.

6. See Jacques Maritain, *The Degrees of Knowledge*, trans. Gerald B. Phelan (New

object distinction to those problems. For another example, Deely showed that intentional existence, not entitative existence, is the locus for dialogue between Thomism and Heidegger.[7] But Aquinas rarely refers to intentional existence by name. Yves R. Simon found his solution to the problem of civil government in a subtle distinction of Aquinas's concerning the relation of an individual's will to God's.[8] But not having Simon's precisely formulated questions in mind, few readers would have found what Simon found in that text. For another example, the *De Ente et Essentia*'s distinction between natures absolutely considered and their two *esses* can help solve Quine's problem of ontological relativity.[9] But the connection between the formulas of the *De Ente et Essentia* and Quine's position is far from immediately obvious.

That Thomistic truths are so fecund is a testimony to their profundity and universality. Training in textual analysis alone, however, does not equip us to actualize the potential of Thomistic truths. Nor can any training guarantee it. But exposure to thinkers who philosophize Thomistically is a *de facto* necessary condition for students to develop that ability. The alternative is to focus on the texts of Aquinas in one class and on contemporary philosophy in another, making appropriate cross-references. That strategy is used, but it is not adequate for students to be able to deal Thomistically with contemporary questions. I have just mentioned one reason why: to understand how Aquinas can help us solve contemporary problems, we often have to see Thomistic truths from new perspectives. Another reason is that attempting to deal with modern questions Thomistically without knowledge of prior attempts to do so creates the problem of reinventing the wheel, with the inevitable false starts.

For example, Sandra Edwards recently defended Aquinas's position on universals against some of its modern critics.[10] She displayed a

---

York: Scribners, 1959), pp. 71-108; on the correspondence theory of truth, see p. 97 n. 2.

7. See John N. Deely, *The Tradition via Heidegger* (The Hague: Nijhoff, 1971).

8. See Yves R. Simon, *Philosophy of Democratic Government* (Chicago: University of Chicago Press, 1951), pp. 40-41.

9. See John C. Cahalan, *Causal Realism: An Essay on Philosophical Method and the Foundations of Knowledge* (Lanham, Maryland: University Press of America, 1985), pp. 247-52. *Causal Realism* also shows the not immediately obvious connections between other Thomistic doctrines and a number of modern problems: the doctrine that the genus is only logically distinct from the species and the problem of deriving metaphysical concepts from sense experience (pp. 414-17); the doctrine of *per se nota* propositions and Quine's critique of analytic truth (pp. 69-76); the doctrine of material causality and Hume's critique of the knowability of efficient causality (pp. 277-92).

10. "The Realism of Aquinas," *The New Scholasticism* 69:1 (Winter 1985): 79-101.

grasp of contemporary issues and the ability to defend her position philosophically. But she reached the conclusion that Duns Scotus's theory of universals, especially the formal distinction between the nature as such and the *haecceitas* of the individual, not only is consistent with Aquinas's theory but also is able to resolve ambiguities in Aquinas's position.[11] The later Scholastics, however, had discussed the positions of Scotus and Aquinas on universals at length, and Edwards does not even refer to them. Poinsot, in particular, is well known for having shown, against Scotus, that universality requires only a negative unity of non-division, a unity a nature has in the mind, not a formal unity outside the mind.[12] If Edwards was aware of the number of modern Thomists influenced by Poinsot, she should have defended her position against his. But instead of going to a "secondary source" like him, this competent scholar had to try, unsuccessfully, to reinvent the wheel.

I do not cite this example to show that we should return to the traditional commentators as interpreters of Aquinas. Correct interpretation is not the only thing at stake; the ability of Thomists to interest future students in studying Aquinas is also at stake. To develop that ability, present students need models of Thomism done philosophically. The commentators often provide such models. Quesnell points out a crucial difference between the Scholasticism he criticizes and the kind of Scholasticism found in the commentators: modern Scholasticism was a method of exposition; classical Scholasticism was a technique of investigation and research.[13] Many of the later Scholastics were

---

11. *Ibid.*, pp. 100-101.

12. *The Material Logic of John of St. Thomas*, trans. Yves R. Simon, John J. Glanville, and G. Donald Hollenhorst (Chicago: University of Chicago Press, 1955), pp. 102-114, 130-40. Concerning the ambiguities Edwards mentions, Poinsot could have taught her that Socrates's and Plato's *individual* natures are only similar, not identical, outside the mind. But Poinsot would also say that their natures are *specifically* identical, the content of an abstracted concept being identical, as far as it goes, with what each individual is, and that Socrates's and Fido's individual natures are *generically* identical. Specific and generic identity may seem paradoxical to modern logicians for whom the identity of an individual with itself is the paradigm of identity. But Aquinas's doctrine implies that specific and generic identity are epistemologically prior to individual identity. Identity is a logical relation characterizing an individual because it has become an object of knowledge. And the specific or generic universal, not the individual, is what first falls under the apprehension of the intellect. Before intellection, the senses know individuals, but they do not know the relations of individuality or identity. Knowledge of those relations requires the intellectual grasp of specific or generic natures, and the corresponding grasp of identity between what the content of an abstracted concept is and what a sensed thing is.

13. See Quesnell, "A Note on Scholasticism," p. 145.

doing textual interpretation. But they were also concerned about philosophical issues, and they developed their interpretations while dealing with those issues. They sometimes misinterpreted significantly—as has every modern interpreter that I am aware of. But doctrinal purity, as important as it is, does not fulfill the need to show how Thomism can deal with philosophical problems, good or bad, that people actually have, or the need to produce students who can continue to show that. If graduate programs required students to read modern Thomists, the students would probably encounter Thomists who made use of philosophical insights from the commentators. And such students would be much less likely to try to reinvent the wheel.

III

Quesnell's description of the manual tradition in seminary education provides further evidence that modern Thomists who pursued the philosophical approach to Thomism were often ignored, and not only in graduate schools. What many students saw of Thomism was either the manual tradition, on the one hand, or historical-textual analysis, on the other. Since the purpose of Quesnell's article was to provide background for discussing Lonergan, reading Quesnell could give the impression that Lonergan's Thomism was a needed remedy for the manual tradition, as if no other alternative was available. In fact, the quality of Thomism prior to Vatican II was far higher than one might think just from reading Quesnell. And for many of us, the best Thomism was superior in intellectual quality to much of the philosophical and dogmatic theology done since Vatican II. I am not talking about whether one agrees with a particular theologian's positions; I am talking about the intellectual caliber of the way he or she arrives at and defends those positions. One does not have to be a Thomist, or even a theist, to share this view of the current state of the Church's intellectual life. Describing the contemporary Catholic thinkers he was familiar with, Sidney Hook said: "They don't think as rigorously as one expects Thomists to do even when they are wrong. I long for the days of Maritain and Gilson."[14]

There is no way to prove how much of this perceived decline in intellectual quality is due to the earlier neglect of the best Thomists in graduate schools. But the graduate teaching of Thomism affects more than the state of Thomism; it affects the intellectual life of the Church. And as long as philosophy plays a major role in priestly formation, the graduate teaching of Thomism will affect the quality of the Church's

---

14. Quoted in William McGurn, "Our Favorite Secular Humanist," Interview with Sidney Hook, *Crisis* 7:1 (January 1989): 38.

pastoral life as well. If Quesnell's experience is representative of seminary education prior to Vatican II, many priests were not exposed to the best that modern Thomists had accomplished. There is reason to believe that Quesnell's experience was common, at least in that respect. The aftermath of Vatican II showed, for example, that many priests did not understand Maritain's careful distinctions-without-separation between what belongs to the spiritual and temporal orders. No one was more responsible than Maritain for making the Church aware of the social dimension of her calling, as even his critics conceded. But when he reminded them that he had always subordinated social action to a personal relationship with God ("contemplation" in his terminology), the critics accused him of being unfaithful to his own insights.[15] How could we have promoted better understanding of such crucial matters as the primacy of the spiritual? Only by better preparing graduate students to make them understood. The consequences of neglecting modern Thomists in graduate schools were not trivial.

The chief concern of this essay, however, is the consequences of neglecting modern Thomists for Thomism itself. Again, the historical-textual approach to Aquinas is both valid and necessary. I am merely pointing out that it is not sufficient, sufficient, that is, for training Thomists who can interest future students in Aquinas by making Thomism a living philosophy. To achieve that end, the historical-textual approach needs to be supplemented by the philosophical. The problem at the two schools mentioned above was that textual analyses were *de facto* considered sufficient for that end. I say "*de facto*" because, if asked, most of the professors who failed to require the study of modern Thomists would probably have agreed that training in textual analysis alone was not sufficient. But those professors were leaving it up to someone else to require the students to study modern thinkers who made Thomism live in their time.

IV

I have been saying that the situation we are in today is due in part to the way Thomism was taught in graduate school thirty years ago. But why was the graduate education of thirty years ago what it was? How could the textual approach, both valid and important in itself, come to so dominate Thomistic graduate education that the philosophical ap-

---

15. For references, see Brooke Williams Smith, *Jacques Maritain, Antimodern or Ultramodern? An Historical Analysis of His Critics, His Thought, and His Life* (New York: Elsevier, 1976), pp. 21-28.

proach was not given its due? Reflecting on the historical process through which that happened can help us understand the state of Thomism today and what we must do to improve it.

Aeterni Patris was the main source for the Thomistic revival of this century. So one might hypothesize that the predominance of the historical-textual approach over the philosophical was a result of *Aeterni Patris*'s call for a renewal of historical research into Aquinas. That is possible, but not very likely. For one thing, *Aeterni Patris*

> was a purely disciplinary document... Its scope was limited to the method of philosophical instruction approved for the education of future priests in seminary and Catholic faculties.[16]

Outside of those contexts, *Aeterni Patris* imposed no religious obligation on Catholic philosophers to study or follow Aquinas, and prominent Catholic philosophers did not follow him.[17] So it is doubtful that the authority of *Aeterni Patris* alone can explain the degree of interest that once existed in studying the texts of Aquinas.

More importantly, *Aeterni Patris* did more than call for a renewal of historical research into Aquinas; it also called for "ongoing dialogue between Thomists and other contemporary philosophers," and taught that "Thomism should develop its capacity to integrate human knowledge through its dialogue with contemporary science, philosophy, and culture."[18] In a word, *Aeterni Patris* called for the philosophical as well as the historical approach to Thomism. In answer to this call, there emerged thinkers, like Cardinal Mercier and the early Garrigou-Lagrange, who were essentially trying to do philosophy in a Thomistic mode. Such Thomists supplied another motivation for studying Aquinas's texts, a motivation that Church authority alone did not provide. Substantial thinkers were using Thomism philosophically to deal with modern philosophical questions. The works of those thinkers told students that they should be studying Aquinas and backed up that claim, not with appeals to Church authority, but with persuasive philosophical arguments concerning modern questions, arguments purportedly based on Aquinas. Students need a reason for devoting much of their careers to Aquinas. Those thinkers, along with the authority of *Aeterni Patris*, supplied a sufficient reason.

---

16. Gerald A. McCool, *Nineteenth-Century Scholasticism: The Search for a Unitary Method* (New York: Fordham University Press, 1989), p. 1.

17. See Gerald A. McCool, *From Unity to Pluralism: The Internal Evolution of Thomism* (New York: Fordham University Press, 1989), pp. 39 and 60.

18. *Ibid.*, pp. 161 and 1, respectively.

Ironically, perhaps, those thinkers provided an additional, unintended motivation for studying Aquinas's texts. As McCool says:

> Neo-Thomism's dialogue with contemporary philosophy, far from promoting its own internal unity, led to the emergence of systematic pluralism among Thomists themselves.[19]

With the passage of time, interpretations of Aquinas multiplied. The more conflicting interpretations there were, the greater was the need to determine the genuine thought of Aquinas by the historical analysis his texts. If you were already interested in Aquinas, you would have wanted to know what the correct interpretation of his thought was. If you already had an interpretation, you had to do textual analysis to justify your interpretation against conflicting ones.

By the second half of the century, however, the balance had tipped so far toward the historical approach to Thomism that its publications far out numbered those of the philosophical approach, scholars could write articles attempting to do Thomism philosophically while apparently unaware of what had already been done, and a random selection of courses at two of the leading schools could find the students not being required to read any modern Thomist. Something was lost due to the predominance of the historical-textual approach, but more than that, what was lost was something necessary for the success of that approach. Once, many fine students were interested in studying the texts of Aquinas. Now comparatively few are. Is it merely accidental that interest in studying Aquinas peaked *following* the work of so many thinkers who did not do Thomism textually but used Thomism philosophically to deal with modern philosophical questions? Is it naive to believe that, because Thomistic philosophers were showing that Aquinas had much to say about contemporary problems, and doing it by producing works of philosophy, many students who otherwise would not have been interested in studying the texts of Aquinas were interested?

On the contrary, if you are already interested in Aquinas, you have a reason for wanting to know the correct interpretation of his texts. But finding the correct interpretation does not by itself generate *new* interest. For that, Thomists have to show that Aquinas correctly understood can answer the philosophical questions contemporary students actually have. But we so emphasized the historical-textual approach that we did not produce enough of the kind of thinkers needed to sustain the interest in Aquinas. We produced textual scholars, but much less often did we produce thinkers who showed how Thomistic truths could stand on

---

19. *Ibid.*, p. 161.

their own two feet in the arena of philosophical problems. Because we did not have enough thinkers who could show that Aquinas was worth studying, textual studies could not continue to flourish as they once did. By overemphasizing the historical-textual approach, we were sawing off the limb we were sitting on.

Modern Thomistic philosophers were sometimes guilty of significant misinterpretations and omissions, and the historical-textual approach was a salutary balance. But today we are off balance in the other direction, and we have to find a way to restore the balance. If we do not, the numbers of students who want to invest their efforts in studying the texts of Aquinas will continue to be too small to keep Thomism alive as an important philosophical force in the culture or even in the Church.

For those still unconvinced that the philosophical approach was necessary for historical studies to flourish as they did, those who may still think that authority of *Aeterni Patris* alone was sufficient, I can only suggest that they answer two further questions for themselves. First, *Aeterni Patris* did not just call for historical analysis of Aquinas; it also called for Thomists to do Thomism philosophically. But have we responded to *Aeterni Patris*'s call by training our students for that second task, and can we adequately train them for that task without requiring them to study models of significant previous attempts at it? Second, assuming Church authority was sufficient encouragement for studying Aquinas prior to Vatican II, can we rely on Church authority to produce a similar degree of interest after Vatican II? If the answer is no, Thomists will have to *earn* that interest by making Thomism work as a living philosophy, and that will require training students who can do Thomism philosophically.[20]

V

Of course, a reaction against the *a*historical manual tradition described by Quesnell also contributed to the emphasis on the historical approach. The result was that it became hard to find, at the graduate level, any remedy for the manual tradition other than historical analysis. Ironically, the vacuum created by that false dichotomy may have helped transcendental Thomism get established. The manual tradition substituted form for substance and technical vocabulary for depth of thought. The emphasis on history was an effort to return to the genuine substance of Aquinas's thought. And some may have believed that the best way to deal with a Maréchal, for example, was to let Aquinas speak for himself,

---

20. We can also ask how much of any current renewal of interest in Aquinas is due to the primarily philosophical work of thinkers like Grisez and MacIntyre.

by using proper historical methods. Instead, the excessive historicism that replaced ahistoricism may have made transcendental Thomism look good by appearing to be the place where Thomism was confronting modern thought philosophically and creatively. For students insufficiently exposed to other modern Thomists, transcendental Thomism could look like an attractive alternative, or, indeed, the only alternative. By not producing students who did Thomism philosophically, the historical approach left the field open to another revision of Aquinas's philosophy.

Since increasing interest in Aquinas is my topic, transcendental Thomism's failure to do so deserves comment. I submit that transcendental Thomism is insufficiently *relevant* to solving the modern problems concerning which it claims superiority to other forms of Thomism. For example, some transcendental Thomists see an opposition between Aristotelian science and the methods of empirical knowledge, especially history.[21] But the main contemporary problems about empirical knowledge concern the possibility of intersubjective and intercultural truth and, if such truth is possible, of verifying which empirical hypotheses are true. And the work of Maritain and Simon, based on Aristotelian science, is much more pertinent to these problems than is transcendental Thomism.

For example, hermeneutics raises the problem of how we can know the true interpretation of a text, and deconstruction questions the very idea of a text's having a true interpretation. Concerning the possibility of truth, Maritain may be alone among Thomists in requiring that the nature of truth be the first problem epistemology addresses, and his use of the distinction between things as things and things as objects is needed to solve that problem. For example, that distinction shows, against Quine, that how to translate a text is a genuine empirical question, in all respects. Since it is an empirical question, verifying the correct answer requires the kind of non-Kantian regulative principles Maritain spoke about, for example, that change must be caused and that similar causes have similar effects. Translation and interpretation are causal analyses. The effect to be explained is the existence of physical marks and sounds. The causal explanation is that these entities are used as signs by an agent who possesses certain thoughts and intends to communicate those thoughts by means of the marks and sounds. The verification of such causal hypotheses is founded, ultimately, on the same metaphysical causal principles that any empirical verification is founded on. The defense of those principles and the explanation of their application to experience requires Aristotelian philosophy, together

---

21. See McCool, *Nineteenth-Century Scholasticism*, pp. 260-62.

with the distinction of things from objects, Maritain's distinction of ontological from empiriological analysis, and Simon's analysis of order in analogical sets. And the same Aristotelian analyses that justify empirical knowledge answer the objections of Hume and Kant against metaphysics.[22] Transcendental Thomism's subjective starting point is tangential to solving these problems about empirical and metaphysical knowledge. Kant sought to solve them from a subjective starting point only because he could not see any other way to solve them.

To their undying credit, transcendental Thomists were and are trying to do Thomism philosophically. To respond to that attempt, we must do more than show that they were not faithful to Aquinas. We must also imitate them in producing literature that is philosophical and contemporary.

VI

To restore the necessary balance to Thomistic graduate education, wherever that still goes on, we must require students to read and be examined on a number of authors who do Thomism, *even if not under that name*,[23] philosophically. The authors chosen do not have to be from previous generations. Some people, including graduates of non-Catholic universities, have continued to do Thomism philosophically, even though there are too few of them. For example, I know of four Thomists who have written studies of Quine from a Thomistic perspective. So, if you have tried an author who did not work with your students, there are other authors whom you can try. The important thing is that, in the course of their studies, graduate students be required to become familiar with a variety of such authors, three or four at a minimum, since not every author will appeal to every student.

By an author's appeal to a student, I do not mean the student's agreement with the author's interpretation of Aquinas. I mean the

---

22. For the argument of this paragraph, see Cahalan, *Causal Realism*, especially pp. 245-66. *Causal Realism* does not explicitly address hermeneutics and deconstruction. But its reply to Quine on translation and defense of empirical verification, based on Maritain and Simon, can be extended to the problem of intersubjective and intercultural interpretation, since translation and interpretation are causal analyses.

23. I would rather call Aquinas's philosophy "Realism" than "Thomism." With Mortimer Adler, I think that using an individual's name to identify that philosophy does it a disservice by failing to express its universality as the only philosophy whose principles make it open, at least in potency, to the full range of reality and experience. See Mortimer J. Adler, *St. Thomas and the Gentiles* (Milwaukee, Wisconsin: Marquette University Press, 1938), pp. 63-65 and n. 65. I am calling it Thomism here, since interest in Aquinas himself is my topic.

appeal of the author's method of doing and writing philosophy. In fact, I assume that professors will often require students to read authors whose interpretations of Aquinas the professors disagree with on important points. This has to be assumed, because few Thomists would agree on all important points, despite their best efforts at historical analysis. In reality, historical analysis has not solved the problem of conflicting interpretations, unless we decide to use the opinion of the majority of scholars at any moment as the criterion of truth.

Of course, there are limits on the kind of authors one would consider models for doing Thomism philosophically. For the reasons mentioned above, as well as other reasons, my own bias is against the transcendental Thomists. But something is wrong if a faculty cannot find a number of authors who would do students much more good than harm, despite the authors' imperfect interpretations. If you cannot find a number of such authors and your interpretation of Aquinas is correct, something is wrong with Aquinas's philosophy, because Aquinas has not been able to inspire thinkers who both follow him and do original philosophy.

Obviously, you are free to criticize in class the modern Thomists you disagree with, as long as you criticize them with arguments that are philosophical, not merely textual. But you should be very careful in your selection of topics to dispute. One reason so many of my fellow graduate students lost interest in Aquinas was that the Thomistic professors spent so much time disputing the interpretations of other Thomists on points that appeared important to the professors, but appeared much less important to the students—and for good reason. In other classes, the students were encountering contemporary issues that challenged philosophy of the Thomistic type in incomparably more fundamental ways than interpretations of Aquinas challenged each other.[24] Thomistic professors were not discussing those more fundamental issues, or if they were, they often seemed more intent on establishing one reading of Aquinas's position against other readings than on responding to contemporary challenges. The students were intelligent enough to see that the intra-Thomistic debates were not answering their more pressing questions. They knew that there was a big philosophical world out there to confront, and they perceived Thomistic professors as ignoring that

---

24. Often, differences between Thomists existed, if not in the eye of the beholder, at least in the magnifying glass of the beholder. The De Koninck/Eschmann/Maritain debate about the common good became one of the most bitter intra-Thomistic disputes. Joseph W. Evans told me that, long after the dispute, De Koninck remarked to him that the disagreement between De Koninck and Maritain amounted only to De Koninck's wanting Maritain to state that the beatific vision was a common good.

world for the sake of confronting one another. Those students were experiencing a Thomism turned in on itself. We cannot afford to repeat that mistake.

In closing, I am not suggesting that we restore Thomism to balance by overreacting in the other direction. An historical understanding of Aquinas is necessary, without doubt, and we must continue to train students to do historical analyses. But to interest future students in the texts of Aquinas, we must also produce graduates who can write Thomism philosophically. Although I consider the proposal of this paper to be moderate and modest, our attitude toward the proposal should not be moderate. The future of Thomism is at stake.

The Postmodern Aquinas: A Fresh Start

Juha-Pekka Rentto

The recent resurgence of interest in the practical philosophy of Aquinas is highly motivated. The basic reason for this is that Aquinas's philosophy has not been at issue in most of the modern philosophical discussion: his thoughts, even if ancient, appear fresh and new when brought to bear on the philosophy of today that does not know not how it relates to its classical ancestors.

Modern practical philosophy, with its roots in the Renaissance, its birth in the Enlightenment, and its heyday in the scientific positivism of yesterday, was in the beginning an answer to problems of classical philosophy raised by the new scientific knowledge. But soon enough, as modernity became the paradigm, the continuity with classical thought was lost.[1] The result is that classical philosophy at large, and *Thomasian* philosophy in specific, has for a span of centuries been marginalized and reduced to stereotypes that have little to do with what the perennial philosophy really stood and stands for.[2]

St. Thomas has been a legitimate project of research merely for historians; for others, his philosophy has only been visible as a muddled and distorted second-hand stereotype whose only role in their theorizing is to provide an example of how the Middle Ages were less enlightened than the modern times, and an easy justification for the infinite superiority of the project of modernity to the superstitions of the past.[3]

---

1. See, for example, Alasdair MacIntyre, *Whose Justice? Which Rationality?* (Notre Dame, Indiana: University of Notre Dame Press, 1989), p. 209ff., where the process of alienation from Aristotelian background is outlined in the development of the Scottish Enlightenment. For a specific example, see p. 269ff. where the author describes how Hutcheson's work was affected by his blindness for Shaftesbury's differences with Aristotle.

2. Not only Maritain is an example of a modern philosopher who found inspiration in a discovery of Aquinas; also MacIntyre's writings show a sharp shift in tone between *After Virtue* (Notre Dame, Indiana: University of Notre Dame Press, 1984), p. 178ff., where Aquinas is treated rather stereotypically, and *Whose Justice? Which Rationality?*, where MacIntyre sees an "emerging Thomistic conclusion" (p. 403).

3. Let me only mention my compatriot Aulis Aarnio as an example. He, in his latest book *Laintulkinnan teoria* (A Theory of Legal Interpretation), lumps Aquinas together

It follows that Aquinas has for a long time been the exclusive property of the official Catholic church and those of its servants who call themselves Thomists. At the same time the mainstream of modern philosophy has journeyed on farther and farther away till it reached a point where, for all practical purposes, Aquinas was reduced to just a name in history, and his philosophy to a mere curiosity about which everybody knew that it was nonsense but nobody knew what it was all about.

But today it is the day after for modernity: the legitimacy of the modern project is questioned from various directions. The most visible critique has come from the so-called postmodern angle of deconstructivism: it is held that the modern project of constructing systematic structures of understanding and knowledge is mistaken, wherefore all structures ought to be torn down to their parts. If we take Aquinas seriously, he can offer us an alternative to the total demolition of structures by helping us understand why the structures edified by modernity are misconstrued. Then, instead of pulling down everything, we may be able to keep the viable structures while discarding the rotten ones. In this way we can turn his premodern though into a postmodern critique of modernity, and make a fresh start with better insight.

Theory and Practice

Aquinas offers us several important viewpoints that open "postmodern" possibilities for understanding problems left unsolved and unexplained by the modern political philosophy. Here I shall concentrate on a few points I consider most central: his notion of practical reason, his ontological and moral holism, and his account of virtue.

Aquinas's distinction between theoretical and practical reason is a distinction largely blurred and lost in modern thought: practical philosophy has become a theoretical discipline. With the rise of the natural sciences, their positive method and scientific ideal have been transferred to most other disciplines. On one level, this means that the scientistic standards of verifiability and truth have been received in much of the modern ethics, with the well-known results that question

---

with the deductive school of philosophy, and with the degenerated *modern jusnaturalists* of the seventeenth and eighteenth centuries, and thereby opposes Aquinas to what he calls the practical school of philosophy which he takes to consist in the modern *nouvelle rhetorique* and its successor the discourse theory of practical reason. One need not be an accomplished Thomist to see that to claim that Aquinas's thought is nothing but deduction, and that it is alien to practical reasoning, is about as misleading a characterization as can be.

the knowability of morals and make ethics appear as something less than a full-fledged science, or somewhat irrational or even senseless, because it cannot meet the scientistic criteria of truth. This has made practical philosophers nervous, and they have begun to conceive of their major task as to construct theories of the good or of the right that would come as close to the scientistic standards as possible. As a consequence, modern ethics, aside from a disproportionate preoccupation with epistemology, has a predilection for general theories, more often than not based on some notion of universalizability as the ultimate criterion of rightness.[4] In short, the universal tenability and validity of theory has become more important in practical philosophy than the evaluation of individual actions.

Now I propose that the unhappy consequence of all that is that it leads modern practical philosophy into a situation where it undermines its own position by its own progress. The more sophisticated theories it is able to produce, the clearer it becomes that there is no handy criterion by which we could judge by which theory we ought to act. This is, I propose, because on the level of theory, ethical knowledge is merely knowledge of what is the right kind of thing to do in a right kind of situation, in abstraction from all and any actual situations of individual moral choice.[5] As this is the case, we can make up all sorts of theories

---

4. This tendency is shared by utilitarians as well as Kantian philosophies of today. Where utilitarians hope to reduce ethics to a more-or-less rational calculus with universally valid units, Kantians wish to make everything turn on a notion of rational universalizability. We have naturalistic theories like Richard B. Brandt's "Theory of the Good and the Right" that try to transform ethics into psychoanalysis, or biology, or whatnot. We have theories like Lawrence Kohlberg's that try to formulate an ethic on the basis of universal structures of human cognitive development. And we have discursive theories like Jürgen Habermas's which discard the scientistic criteria of truth and try to substitute for them a method of rational discourse which would guarantee as universal a validity as possible for practical arguments and conclusions. Rather characteristic for the modern preoccupation with general theory is, I think, the scientistically inspired desire to make moral choices easy and matter-of-course with a theory that gives an appropriate answer to all moral problems. An explicit example of this is Alan Gewirth's programme on his *Reason and Morality* (Chicago: University of Chicago Press, 1978), p. 21.

5. At stake here is not only the idea that the moral tradition has been fragmented into different lines of argument that have no common code of discussion, as MacIntyre has suggested, but also—and more importantly—the modern tendency to moral legalism, to reducing ethics into a set of general rules; cf., *e.g.*, Germain Grisez, "Against Consequentialism," *American Journal of Jurisprudence* 23 (1978): 58. But knowledge of what rules require is theoretical knowledge of abstractions rather than practical knowledge of what is to be done, as Ralph McInerny, "The Basis and Purpose of Positive Law," *Studi Tomistici* 30 (1987): 137-46, points out.

according to how we define the kinds of situations in which they are intended to apply, without ever confronting an actual moral problem. But in a real situation of moral choice, it does not matter much if one acts according to a universally valid theory; what is important is that one do the thing that is right there and then. And the criteria for that particular rightness are curiously un-universalizable, as they are largely drawn from the particular context of the individual choice. Strictly speaking, a general theory of practical reason does not address a genuine practical problem at all.

Aquinas, in the Aristotelian tradition, defines practical reason as that activity of intellect whose object is that particular thing which is to be done, as opposed to theoretical, or speculative reason, whose object is the universal intelligibility of what is being known. Where theoretical reasoning concludes in a statement, practical reasoning concludes in an action. Hence the two kinds of reasoning, even if not entirely different facilities, are different enough to make it clear that the standards of success in practical reasoning must be different from those in theoretical reasoning. If we, moreover, appreciate Aquinas's point according to which it is precisely because practical reason deals with particular *operabilia*, that is, things pertaining to human action, that practical reason by its very definition is less certain than theoretical reason,[6] we can see how unreasonable it is to demand from practical reason that it meet the scientistic criteria of certainty and verifiability if it is to be considered a respectable discipline at all: to demand that which is by definition impossible is not a demand to be taken seriously. If we appreciate the *different* character of practical reason, modern ethics can perhaps be cured from the self-imposed inferiority complex from which it suffers in its relationship to the "real" science.

Ontology and Truth

If practical reasoning is different from theoretical reasoning, practical truth is also different from theoretical truth. Both are adequations,[7] but different kinds of adequations. To understand the way they are different, we must place them in context with the Thomasian ontology.

The ontology of Aquinas gives being a threefold structure: there is the actuality of things, that is, the particular things that are in actual

---

6. See, *e.g.*, *ST* I-II 94, 4. The reason for the greater indeterminacy in practical reasoning is of course to be found in the freedom of human will, which makes it impossible to make certain predictions in matters pertaining to human action.

7. For the general definition of truth as "a certain adequation of intellect to thing," see *ST* Ia 6, 1.

existence; there is the potentiality of things, that is, the formal possibility of the plenitude of being characteristic for each kind of thing; and there is the movement that connects actuality with potentiality by turning possibilities into act, that is, the way of movement characteristic for each kind of thing in existence and on its way to whatever possibilities it has ahead. The characteristic possibilities of a thing are its natural good, and when a thing moves it seeks its natural good as the end of its activity.

The human mode of movement is action; a human being seeks its end by doing things by its own choice. Hence the object of human actions is to bring into actuality whatever unfulfilled possibilities one has. Thus the point of practical reasoning is to make a possibility become an actuality by a given action. It follows that the central criterion of success for practical reason is whatever the action which is its conclusion actually changes the intended possibility into actuality; it is the *action* that must be adequate to its end, whereas in theoretical reason it is the *statement* that must be adequate to corresponding reality. Practical truth is a property of actions rather than statements. If we appreciate this insight, we can confidently give up the vain search for universally valid statements and theories of what is right and wrong, and concentrate again on the real task of practical reason, namely, doing the right thing here and now.

A further difference between theoretical and practical truth is that where truth in matters theoretical is an adequation of a statement to a reality that is in actuality prior to the statement, truth in matters practical is an adequation of an action to a possibility that can only become an actuality as a result of the action. This highlights the difference in certainty between practical and theoretical reason: practical reason cannot simply look behind and check whether it was right, it must look ahead and make an attempt at making its intention come true. But it also highlights a more fundamental characteristic of practical truth: if we phrase it in Aquinas's own terms according to which practical truth consists in conformity with right appetite,[8] we can see that it is not enough that an action is effective to whatever its end is, but it is also required that the end it seeks is a real human good, a good to which one's will rightly inclines. This insight brings to the fore a consideration modernly marginalized, namely, the equal importance of right will to right reason. Where modern ethics is most often an ethic of reason over irrational passions, Thomasian ethics is an ethic of will and reason brought into harmony. The most important consequence of this is the central role that must be reserved for virtue in a successful ethic. This question we shall return to below.

---

8. *ST* I-II 57, 5; ad 3.

Wholes Not Parts

That reason and will are not a dichotomy at potential opposition but an integrated whole is an expression for the holistic nature of Thomasian ethics. As opposed to the modern predilection for analysis and fragmentation of reality, Aquinas seeks to synthesize and integrate the seeming divisions into one reality. This is perhaps his most significant challenge to modernity. If ethics can begin to see the whole again for its parts, perhaps it can find its way back to the essential questions instead of losing itself in a dispute over various misleading dichotomies.

The roots of Thomasian holism are to be found in its ontology. That being is conceived of as a movement in which potentiality becomes actuality entails the view that the characteristic end of any being is growth in one's capacities, fulfillment of one's potential, plenitude of one's being. In short, each being seeks its wholeness. It follows that seeking one's integral plenitude, the fullness of one's whole being, has an intrinsic moral quality: that is one's ultimate good, and the ultimate end to which one's seeking of any particular ends ought to be integrated. So there is, for one thing, no significant hurdle between is and ought, or between being and value, as the two are parts of one integral reality where that which is is in movement toward that which is in its nature to seek.[9]

That there is such a hurdle is one of the fundamental tenets of modern ethics. Now it is quite correct that merely from what is in act cannot *logically* be derived what ought to be in act. But it is an overstatement to make this insight a central tenet of practical philosophy, for what is important is not the logical relationship between is and ought but their ontological rapport. The modern stress on Hume's hurdle has led ethics to overlook the point that maybe is and ought are part of one reality after all, even if they do not logically entail each other. If we can accept this insight, we can free a lot of our energy from the recurrent attempts at showing how an ought can, after all, be derived from is, and from their equally recurrent refutations, and tackle more important questions.

---

9. I do not wish to say that there is no hurdle between is and ought at all, but that if there is a hurdle, it is not a problem of ethics. Undeniably there is no logical entailment between *theoretical* is and *practical* is-to-be, and between *merely practical* directiveness and *moral* ought, as Germain Grisez, Joseph M. Boyle and John Finnis, "Practical Principles, Moral Truth, and Ultimate Ends," *American Journal of Jurispurdence* 32 (1987): 127, suggest. But entailment or not is not a central consideration at all. For, as the aforementioned authors also point out, the "is-to-be of the first principles of practical knowledge is itself an aspect of human nature," and the "moral ought is nothing but the integral directiveness of the is-to-be of practical

Another misleading dichotomy of modern practical philosophy, as well as of social theory at large, is the one between individual will and reason, which allows us to think that human beings are like machines driven to action by the reactions of a fundamentally amoral will to external stimuli, while the universal reason acts as if it were an external and apparently *objective* restraint on it. When we combine this with the modern notion of freedom as being at liberty to do whatever an individual wants to do, rather than as freedom to the right thing,[10] we land with a further modern dichotomy, namely, that supposed to obtain between individual and community.

When modernity made the individual the central theme of social thought,[11] it made the society appear as a battle-ground of different individuals against each other, and even of individuals against the community. The result is that modern societies are commonly considered not quite unlike zero-sum games where the individual preferences of individuals are at stake. I find very illuminating MacIntyre's account where he shows how the desire for finding a scientifically objective ground for political considerations, combined with modern individualism and the dualistic self-conception of modern personality, has led to the modern amoral image of the political community as an impersonal mechanism for making trade-offs between conflicting individual interests;[12] what seems important for modern citizens is that the society satisfy as many of their wants as can be, rather than help them in integrating their personal pursuits and interests into a more comprehensive scheme of common good. Therefore citizens are no longer conceived of as autonomous members of the political community, they rather appear individual subjects of egotistic pursuits, reduced into political objects that can be manipulated by a political management of the market of individual preferences, and lured to act in the desired manner by providing incentives. The unhappy result of all this is that citizens tend to lose sight of their shared responsibilities, and learn to consider it their vested right to defend their individual interests *against* those of others, and take pride in doing so. The foreseeable outcome is a moral deterioration of the political community and a dissolution of every significant notion of the common good.

From the Thomasian view, there is no incompatibility between the individual and the community, for the good of a part is the good of the

---

knowledge" (*ibid.*).

10. A good example of an argument for a liberty-freedom, and explicitly against the traditional kind of freedom-freedom, is Carol C. Gould, *Rethinking Democracy, Freedom and Social Cooperation in Politics, Economy, and Society* (Cambridge: Cambridge University Press, 1988), p. 31ff.

11. As MacIntyre, *Whose Justice? Which Rationality?*, p. 209ff., points out.

whole, and *vice versa*. The political community is a whole, and citizens are its parts.[13] It follows that it is not right for a citizen to seek his individual good, a merely partial good, at the cost of the common good, the good that in this context represents the notion of *whole* good. But it is not so that the citizen ought to seek the common good over and above his individual good. For the common good is no different from his real personal good: the common good is not other people's good, it is one's own true good, wherefore it is also the proper end of one's actions.[14] Appreciating this insight will open for us the possibility of looking at the human polity anew as a shared enterprise for the common good rather than a mere conglomerate of conflicting interests seeking short-term bargaining equilibria. With a view to the new kinds of common problems not only single societies but the whole human community is facing and will face in an ever-accelerating pace, the need for such a new direction is evident.

Virtue and Responsibility

A central component of the Thomasian holism is its view of the human being; man is an integral being, a whole where all the parts are integrated to the same end, namely, human good, and its transcendence in divinity. Most importantly, on this view is no opposition between reason and will, or between soul and body, but all are parts of one man equally directed to good. A man's life is a whole, rather than a series of disconnected accidents. A man's life has a single end in view, happiness, or beatitude as Aquinas has it, and all one's actions are to be integrated to that end. It follows that, from the Thomasian point of view, the focus of morality is on the quality of a man's life as a whole, rather than on his single actions. Therefore, morality cannot merely be about maximizing one's interests, or about abiding by a set of deontological rules: it must give adequate attention to the moral growth of a man's personality. This attention can only be provided by a theory of virtue.

Virtue, from the Thomasian view, is not just a matter for private individual morality; it is the thematic centerpiece of the moral responsibility of free man—with regard to the responsibility of the individual for his personal moral growth, as well as to that of the citizen for the moral growth of the political community. The moral freedom of man consists in his being determined to good at large, but undetermined to

---

12. *Ibid.*, p. 326.
13. *ST* II-II 58, 7; ad 2.
14. *ST* II-II 58, 9; ad 3.

any particular good:[15] in order to act, one not only can but must choose between alternatives. No one else can make one's choices for one, one is always responsible for making one's own. Whether an individual person will actually move toward his natural end in fullness of being, depends on his own choices. Whether he will actually become a good person, that is, actualize his full potential of moral goodness, depends on his own autonomous action. In this way man is unlike all other corporeal creatures: where these are moved, he moves himself. Where they have only one common nature, *natura speciei*, he has two: the common nature of the human species, and his personal *natura individui*, or second nature. This second nature, unlike the first, he acquires by his own actions.

In this context, the notion of virtue has three roles. For one thing, the second nature, one's *hexis* as opposed to one's *physis*, is one's personal habit, or habitual disposition. This habitual disposition is what we have made out of ourselves, our acquired personality, as it were. Due to the freedom of choice we enjoy, it can be either virtuous or vicious, depending on whether our choices have been good or evil, right or wrong. In this sense, virtue is the result of morally right choices: it is the virtuous disposition in which an individual person actualizes his natural potential of moral goodness. From this viewpoint, virtue appears as the end of human growth. Hence Thomasian morality, unlike most of modern ethics, is primarily about the growth of personal virtue, rather than about conflicts between one's own nonmoral good and that of others.

For another thing, no one but oneself can make one morally good: moral goodness cannot be distributed by an authority, or given to a student by a teacher, it must be acquired by one's own choices. For this purpose, our first and foremost help is our conscience. But conscience can be misled and mistaken in particular matters. Consequently it is the responsibility of every individual to practice good choices with his conscience, so that it might habituate to them and become more reliable. From this viewpoint, virtue is the appropriate method of moral growth: a virtuous second nature can only be acquired by a conscious exercise of virtue.

But the way in which one can exercise virtue depends on one's circumstances, as well as on one's personal aptitudes and inclinations: different people are apt to be good at different aspects of human excellence. Hence not only the method but also its result, the individual second nature, is different for each person. Hence each person quite legitimately conceives of human excellence in his own unique manner. It follows that, on this view, even the criteria of moral rightness are in a

---

15. See, *e.g.*, *ST* I-II 1, 7.

way fundamentally personal; the inevitable ultimate standard of choice, in this life of imperfect knowledge, is for each human being a standard he has himself participated in making up by his own previous choices, and with a view to his further personal prospects.

If we take all this seriously, modern practical philosophy is in deep trouble. If morality is about personal growth, then all other-directed utilitarian, deontological, and distributive theories of ethics miss the very point of morality. If the standards of right moral choice are inevitably personal, then all and any attempts at creating an ethic on the basis of universalization are misdirected.

And what is more, from the viewpoint of virtue, the key concepts of modern political philosophy acquire an unconventional shade that offers prospects for unconventional insight in the *raison d'être* and functioning of the political community. The political community is about fostering shared civic virtue, rather than about distributing nonmoral goods. Freedom consists in being free to act virtuously, rather than in being at liberty to act as one's passions may prompt one to act. Equality cannot be a fundamental value of society, unless it is defined as the equality of virtue shared by the citizens in a true perfect community. Democracy is not an end in itself but only one of various ways in which civic virtue can be fostered. Rights lose their status as grounds for political or moral action, as it is not one's rights against others but rather one's responsibility for oneself that is the constituent consideration of ethics. Dethroning such deified concepts is the first price modernity is to pay, if it is to yield a new self-understanding of man as a reasonable creature. But a renewed Thomasian outlook to practical philosophy promises an ample reward that will no doubt more than compensate for that superficial loss.

Part II
Metaphysical Controversies

Part II
Metaphysical issues

Jacques Maritain and Bernard Lonergan on Divine and Human Freedom

David B. Burrell, C.S.C.

This consideration of two contemporary Catholic thinkers, each writing explicitly *ad mentem Sanctae Thomae*, can be seen as an object lesson for us today, and a kind of *experimentum crucis* for the thesis of Gerald McCool's recent interpretative reading of the history of modern Thomists: *From Unity to Pluralism* (New York: Fordham University Press, 1989). The issue itself is the vexed one of our human attempts to understand the interaction of divine and human freedom: of two actors, creator and creature, each of whom is free and whose commerce must be free. The specter of Dominicans and Jesuits in a fruitless tug-of-war throughout the seventeenth century, only to have the reigning pope grab the middle of the rope to call them off, continues to cloud humane discussion of this thorny issue. For something of those polarities remain present in the very lack of exchange between two persons who might otherwise have themselves discussed the issue: Jacques Maritain and Bernard Lonergan. For while Maritain was older by some years, their productive lives overlapped, but not their spheres of intellectual intercourse. The works of Maritain which we will be considering were published in 1947 and 1963, while Lonergan's study of operative grace in Aquinas was originally published in *Theological Studies* as a series of articles in 1942-43.[1] What kept them apart? Or, I should say, what kept Maritain from even noticing Lonergan's groundbreaking work? Historians may indeed know and should tell us, but one may certainly speculate that Maritain's immersion in the Dominican school of Thomist studies might have predisposed him against thinking one might find any groundbreaking work in *Theological Studies*, then a largely Jesuit organ; or if we would credit our friend Jacques with a larger soul than

---

1. Jacques Maritain, *Court traité de l'existence et de l'existant* (Paris: Hartmann, 1947)=ET: *Existence and the Existent* (New York: Pantheon, 1948)=EE; *God and the Permission of Evil*, trans. Joseph W. Evans (Milwaukee: Bruce, 1966)=GPE—talks given at Toulouse in 1962 and originally published in French in 1963; Bernard J. F. Lonergan, *Grace and Freedom*, ed. Patout Burns (New York: Herder and Herder, 1971)=GF—from original *Theological Studies* articles.

that, the distinction of philosophical from theological approaches to this matter, which he tries assiduously to respect, would have left him dependent on his Dominican theologian friends to call his attention to the articles, and there my speculation would certainly be more plausible—in the forties! So we have set ourselves the formidable task of mediating the relative isolation of Dominican from Jesuit worlds of theological reflection, especially on this issue, where knees jerked before heads or hearts could become engaged; together with the stringent separation of theological from philosophical inquiry—itself reflecting the gap which had widened in baroque Thomism between the natural and the supernatural, whose resonances were to pit Reginald Garrigou-Lagrange against Henri de Lubac in this very decade—a battle broadcast to the entire Catholic world in *Humani Generis*. A formidable task, indeed, but one which our perspective may help us to carry through—not without challenge, I am sure!

For the issues themselves are straightforward: that God, as free creator of all that is, is at the source of all that creatures are as well as all that existing creatures do, yet without thereby being the author of our sinful actions. Yet what can be put so straightforwardly may even show in its original formulation the intrinsic difficulty of going much further, and this one certainly does. For a full characterization of this relationship would presuppose our possessing adequate terms for structuring the creator-creature relation, and that of course is precisely what we lack. Since we can count on Thomas Aquinas as a common reference point for both authors, his two assertions that the "proper effect of God's creating is the very to-be (*esse*) of things" (ST 1. 45. 5), and so it is "in their *existing* that creatures may be said to resemble the creator" (ST 1. 4. 3), forcibly remind us that we will be unable to model the creator-creature relation precisely because we cannot adequately conceptualize what it is to-exist (*esse*). Again, Maritain insists on this point again and again in *Existence and the Existent*, the first of the works which probes the issue in contention, and Lonergan accepts it implicitly in his explicit introduction of the "theorem of divine transcendence" (GF 107). The differences between their two approaches, then, do not put them at variance on the fundamental points relevant to our defining this issue; they rather spell diverse strategies for dealing with so elusive a subject—strategies imbedded in their respective intellectual formations and in part institutionalized in the way in which Maritain, at least, felt constrained to respect the division of labor between a philosopher and a theologian. We shall call attention to these especially in noticing their choice of language in speaking of what lies *ex professo* beyond our ken.

Maritain is preoccupied with the question of human freedom, and especially concerned that it neither impinge divine freedom nor be impinged upon by God's activity, as the inelegant expression "divine intervention" invariably does. Questions of *sufficient* or *efficacious* grace form but the penumbra of his account, since these are properly theological issues, but the Bañezian construct of "physical premotion" will frame his treatment throughout. It is this adherence to the Dominican school of commentators, through whom Maritain invariably approached the "teaching of St. Thomas," which will determine his choice of language and his casting of the questions. Lonergan, on the other hand, is preoccupied with the diverse distinctions drawn within the salvific activity of God called "grace," and anxious to render an account of that activity consonant with Thomas Aquinas and coherent in itself. If the first of these requirements is met, he has no worries about derogating from human freedom, but his entire inquiry is animated by the conviction that a coherent treatment of grace and freedom will be consonant with Aquinas only if the Bañez-Molina controversy is overcome and the discussion moved to a level which bypasses their *contretemps*. In short, Maritain is content to modify Bañez's treatment of the matter, however fiercely critical he may be of the "antecedent permissive decrees" of those whom he calls "hard Thomists" as "anything but an insult to the absolute innocence of God" (GPE 21-31). Lonergan, for his part, feels constrained to move beyond both of the seventeenth-century protagonists, since "the Molinist lacks the speculative acumen to make his grace leave the will instrumentally subordinate to divine activity, [while] the Bañezian has exactly the same speculative blind spot: because he cannot grasp that the will is truly an instrument by the mere fact that God causes the will of the end, he goes on to assert that God also brings in a *praemotio* to predetermine the choice of means" (GF 144). In order to do this, Lonergan must reconstruct for us the position of Aquinas himself, and in doing so has recourse to a language of "theorems" which can sound strange to students of medieval philosophy and theology. But his tactic here is strategic: to remind us forcibly that in this inquiry we must venture beyond the domain of imagination into a properly metaphysical region where we can only be guided by the *logic*, or as I would prefer, the *grammar* of the matter.[2]

Both Maritain and Lonergan insist that a sinful action, insofar as it is sinful, cannot be an action at all. Maritain is working within a framework developed by John of St. Thomas and by his own contemporaries, Jean-Hervé Nicolas and Charles Journet, in which one postulates "divine motions" and distinguishes between logical moments in

---

2. That the *mode* of metaphysics is, broadly speaking, logical, can be found in Aquinas's Commentary on Aristotle's Metaphysics: *In 4 Metaphysica* 4 [574] (Rome: Marietti, 1950).

them and in the response of a free person to them. Employing Aquinas's later distinction in the movement of the will between *specification* and *exercise*, Maritain needs a term for the nonexercise of the will, so he introduces the verb "to nihilate" (*néanter*), and distinguishes the divine activations as "shatterable" (*brisable*) and "unshatterable" (*imbrisable*), or as we would put it today, *defeasible* or *indefeasible* (EE 92). One takes these to be philosophical analogues of *sufficient* and *efficacious* grace: so the mechanics of the matter is that "if the shatterable motion is *not shattered*, it gives way of itself, as the flower to the fruit, to an unshatterable motion under which the good act will be infallibly and freely produced" (GPE 57). "Infallibly" we understand; but why "freely"? Because the creature has gone along with the original divine motion and has not "nihilated" it. A fascinating scenario, clearly constructed to "account for" a freedom which allows room for the independent nonaction of the creature, but is not committed *a priori* to an understanding of freedom as autonomy. In other words, a creaturely freedom. This allows Maritain to transform the "prior permissive decrees" of the Bañezians into a "consequent permissive decree (consequent to the instant of nihilation or of nonconsideration of the rule, where the shatterable divine motion is shattered)" (GPE 59).

Ingenious, no? What's wrong with it? Nothing, really, except that it can hardly be proposed as explaining anything, since it consists of postulations tailored to the event to be explained. There is more to it, of course, for tucks can always be taken where needed or it can be let out here and there—but to what end? Maritain recognizes, as we know he would, just how serious a matter this is, for it regards more the reality and "innocence," as he puts it, of God even more than it does human freedom. It also touches on a subject which more than any other could be a motivation for one abandoning faith in God, a kind of touchstone of modern atheism. But if that be the case, how can he find himself fiddling with metaphysical nuts and bolts, as it were, and end the Foreword to his last treatment of the issue by saying: "if in my philosophical work there has perchance been some actual contribution (however imperfectly it may have been able to be presented) to the progress of thought, and to the researches which announce a new age of culture, it is indeed, so I am persuaded, the one with which this little book has to deal" (GPE viii). When one thinks of all that he did, of the doors he opened in political thought and in aesthetics, to say nothing of metaphysics, one must ask how he might have been so misguided about his own work? That is not uncommon, of course, but it seems to me that there is a specific explanation here, and that Lonergan has hit squarely upon it. One simply must rise to a level of appropriate "theoretical" power to order the realities involved. And so long as Maritain remained wedded to the Bañezian *praemotio*, as his entire treatment of "divine activations" implies, then the *manner* of God's action has to be reflected into a created entity, and this intellectual maneuver clearly violates "the distinction" of the source of being from all that owes its existence to it, and that "distinction" is one of Maritain's controlling convictions. He was, in short, misled by the intellectual pattern taken over from Bañez and the subsequent Dominican school, which he simply accepted in order to improve upon it.

We will recall that what "physical premotion" intended to capture was Aquinas's contention "that God applies all agents to their activity" (GF 73). That is, God's granting each thing its very existence, when that existence is interpreted as esse, implies "that God moves and applies every agent" as well. But when we see this divine activity as implicit in the granting of *esse*, as the inevitable consequence of this account of the relation of the creature to its creator, then we will not need a particular "divine activation," and especially a *created* one, to account for a creature's acting. There is no image of "intervention" here, but rather a general "theorem of divine transcendence" whose intent is "to place God above and beyond the created orders of necessity and contingence: because God is universal cause, His providence must be certain; but because He is a transcendent cause, there can be no incompatibility between terrestrial contingence and the causal certitude of providence" (GF 79). It was the cosmic emanation scheme, inherited from Aristotle yet elaborated by al-Farabi and transmitted to the west by Ibn Sinâ, which formed the conceptual background for Aquinas's understanding of "premotion"—hardly a distinct created "activation" but rather the corollary to a deliberate free creation: that all things come under the purview of the creator. This cosmic vision has as *its* "corollary [that] of universal instrumentality, for an instrument is a lower cause moved by a higher so as to produce an effect within the category proportionate to the higher; but in the cosmic hierarchy all causes are moved except the highest and every effect is at least in the category of being; therefore all causes except the highest are instruments" (FG 81). We must speak here of *theorems* and of their *corollaries*, however, because we cannot determine anything in the creature which indicates that it is an instrument. (And if we can't find it, we ought not postulate it either, since we shall see that we do not need *something* created if we understand creation properly.) That is, we know that the hammer did not build the house, yet that the carpenters who did are themselves instruments as well—that we cannot see. Yet we must assert it, although we can only assert it as a theorem: because God is the source of all that is, "the idea of causing causation has its premise in creation-conservation" (GF 86).

The creating-conserving cause who freely originates the universe also cares for it, and so moves creatures to act in such a way that the divine providential purposes are fulfilled. Not, however, after the pattern of premises following from conclusions, as in the Neoplatonic emanation scheme, but after the image of "the plan or design or art in the mind of an artisan" (GF 82). So what freely comes forth from God in its very being can be brought to act freely by that same One who keeps it in existence. The how escapes us in both cases, of course, but using the language of "theorems" links us expressly to the originating activity, and so reminds us that just as the how of creation escapes us (it is not a motion), so does the manner in which God causes agents to cause by "applying causes to effects." Yet to affirm creation-conservation as we do is to affirm the latter "universal instrumentality" as well. Similarly, as Lonergan goes on to note, whoever affirms the "new creation" of sanctifying grace will be brought to affirm the concurrence of actual grace as well, for just as the One who creates us by holding us in existence cannot but—by that very fact—act in and through us as well, so the One who grants us a share in the very life of God—Father, Son, and Spirit—will so live in and through us as to allow our actions to be—like Jesus' own—God's returning thanks to God.[3] If existing is a participation in the very *nature* of God, whose essence is to-be, then the new existence of habitual grace is a participation in the very *life* of the triune God.

What secures at once "the distinction" as well as the creature's freedom is summarized in what Lonergan calls the "doctrine [or theorem] of divine transcendence: "God produces not only reality but also the modes of its emergence; among these are necessity and contingence" (GF 107-108). What is required to understand (yet never to comprehend) this doctrine or theorem is the "formal feature" of *eternity* and the master-metaphor of divine practical knowing.[4] Here Lonergan converges with Maritain's insistence on the mode of divine knowing—eternal and practical, leaving the rest of us to wrestle with this conceptually elusive relation of eternity to temporal process.[5] Yet while that remains a conundrum, the issue of God's knowing as active—"the

---

3. Cf. John of the Cross, *Spiritual Canticle*, Stanza 39, par. 3 (*Collected Works of St. John of the Cross*, trans. Kieran Kavanaugh and Otilio Rodriguez [New York: Doubleday, 1964], p. 558).

4. See my *Knowing the Unknowable God* (Notre Dame, Indiana: University of Notre Dame Press, 1986), chap. 6.

5. The recent essay by Normal Kretzmann and Eleonore Stump, "Eternity," *Journal of Philosophy* 78 (1981): 429-58, has helped to rehabilitate God's eternity, though not without criticism. See my "God's Eternity," *Faith and Philosophy* 1 (1984): 389-405, for a development of their view.

knowledge of God is the cause of things," and not vice-versa, as with us—can be elaborated in the face of our endemic tendency to presume God's knowing as speculative.[6] What both Bañez and Molina presume is a "causal influx" (familiar to us from Hume), which follows upon God's knowing, whereas causality for Aristotle and Aquinas consists in a real relation of dependence of the effect on the cause, such that the real difference between *acting* and *causing* lies not in the agent but in the effect (GF 64-79).[7] The result is that God is more the cause of creatures' actions than we are, yet not by virtue of a "divine activation" (*praemotio physica*) but because the intelligible dependence of the act on God is greater than it is on us. But all this incorporates what we can know about creation, namely that the creature depends on God for its very existing and all that flows from that act of existing. As David Braine puts it: "God is not the grammatical subject of existential statements about creatures but nonetheless remains the first and only unconditional agent of their existing."[8] Such a view, which follows as a corollary from a consistent grasp of the fact that God's knowledge is the cause of things' very being, rules out *concursus* as Molina saw it, since his conception would have us adding God's action to that of the creature as a vector-sum. And, as we have noted, Bañez' *praemotio physica* would put the difference between acting and causing in the primary agent, God, rather than in the effect. So we can see that what is needed is a theoretical grasp of these matters which does not purport to be an *explanation*, in the sense of attempting to show "how it works." For there is no mechanism at work—the act of creation is not itself a motion, so we must move beyond recourse to imaging the forces at work. The name I like to give such a strategy is "grammatical," without thereby conceding that "it is all a matter of language," but rather insisting that one needs to be guided by the

---

6. Maritain has a telling passage in which he warns us against transferring to God a theory of knowledge similar to that of Descartes, albeit inversely: "we must be careful not to imagine that in the divine 'science of vision'—where the creative will is linked with intelligence—God would attain or would properly speaking know only His own essence and His own ideas, which would be as it were *models* of the things produced in being by the creative will . . . in such a way that things would supposedly be known only because they would resemble the models in question, at which alone the divine knowledge would stop" (GPE 70). This is what James Ross castigates as "exemplarism" in "God, Creator of Kinds and Possibilities: *Requiescant universalia ante res*," in *Rationality, Religious Belief, and Moral Commitment*, ed. Robert Audi and William Wainwright (Ithaca, New York: Cornell University Press, 1986), pp. 271-88.

7. For a fruitful contemporary use of this axiom, see David Braine, *Reality of Time and the Existence of God* (Oxford: Clarendon Press, 1988), pp. 134-36.

8. *Ibid.*, p. 136.

entailments (positive and negative) of the assertions one can make, and that is all. In short, one needs to know where questioning here comes to an end, and the proper sort of knowing in such matters will involve an "unknowing" which acknowledges that one simply cannot go on. While both Maritain and Lonergan display a keen awareness of this feature of theological inquiry, one cannot help but recognize that Lonergan has translated that constraint into the grammar of his own treatment better than Maritain was able to do. I have already offered my hypothesis to locate the source of this difference: in Maritain's continued dependence on a commentary tradition which failed to understand such matters, while his mentor and Lonergan's understood them exquisitely.

Gilson vs. Maritain: The Start of Thomistic Metaphysics

John F. X. Knasas

My focus is two articles written by Jacques Maritain and Étienne Gilson late in their lives. Maritain's article, entitled "Réflexions sur la nature blessée et sur l'intuition de l'être," was the first to appear. It was published in the 1963 volume of *Revue Thomiste*.[1] In the section devoted to the intuition of being, Maritain depicts Gilson to be a proponent of the intuition of being.[2] Taking umbrage at Maritain's portrayal, Gilson presented his reflections on the intuition of being in his 1974 article, "Propos sur l'être et sa notion," published by *Studi Tomistici* in the volume *San Tommaso e il pensiero moderno*.

Though these articles raise many topics, I probe them from one angle only, namely, for their insights on how to start Thomistic metaphysics. I contend that Maritain and Gilson disagree on this topic and that Gilson's position possesses the advantage both Thomistically and philosophically.

Since both Frenchmen strive to be faithful to Aquinas and since for Aquinas metaphysics is a science distinct from others by its subject matter, I would like to set the stage with a brief sketch of Aquinas's description of the subject of metaphysics. Aquinas variously expresses the subject of metaphysics. Formulae include: *ens commune, ens qua ens,* and *ens inquantum ens*. Aquinas is on record as describing the subject of metaphysics in terms of its separateness from matter.

> However, even though the subject of this science [metaphysics] is being-in-general [*ens commune*], the whole science is said to concern what is separate from matter both in existence and in thought. For not only are those things called separate in existence and thought that can never exist in matter, like God and the intellectual substances, but also those that can be without matter, such as being-in-general.[3]

---

1. The article also reappeared in Maritain's *Approaches sans entraves* (Paris: Fayard, 1973).

2. Maritain, "Réflexions sur la nature blessée et sur l'intuition de l'être," *Revue Thomiste* 68 (1968): 18.

3. *In Meta.*, Proem; translated by Armand Maurer, *The Division and Methods of the Sciences* (Toronto: Pontifical Institute of Mediaeval Studies, 1963), p. 89.

Also:

> for something can exist separate from matter and motion ... because by its nature it does not exist in matter and motion; but it can exist without them, though we sometimes find it with them. In this way being [*ens*], substance, potency, and act are separate from matter and motion, because they do not depend on them for their existence, unlike the objects of mathematics, which can only exist in matter. Thus philosophical theology [also called metaphysics] investigates beings separate in [this] second sense as its subjects.[4]

Most generally speaking, metaphysics deals with what is separate from matter both in existence and in thought. The meaning of this formula is clear from its subdivision. On the one hand, the separate refers to what is never a body. The examples are God and the angels. In short, this first sense refers to spiritual realities. On the other hand, the separate refers to what can be apart from matter as well as in matter. Examples include *ens commune* and substance. An indication of this second kind of separateness is offered by this text:

> We say that being and substance are separate from matter and motion not because it is of their nature to be without them, as it is of the nature of ass to be without reason, but because it is not of their nature to be in matter and motion, although sometimes they are in matter and motion as animal abstracts from reason, although some animals are rational.[5]

While the first sense of separate refers to spiritual realities, the second sense refers to intelligibilities. As intelligibilities they can be compared to animal. Animal is an intelligibility common to Tom, Dick, and Harry, Fido, Flicker, and Flossy. What distinguishes the intelligible objects of being, substance, etc., from others is their range. These notions are realized in sensible things, though they need not be.

Items separate in this second sense constitute the subject of metaphysics. In fact, one among them, *ens commune* or *ens inquantum ens*, is most used to refer to the subject of metaphysics. Hence, the separateness of *ens* is the reason for calling the science "metaphysics":

> It is called *metaphysics* because it considers being [*ens*] and its attendant properties; for these objects that go beyond physics are discovered by a process of analysis as the more universal is discovered after the less universal.[6]

---

4. *In de Trin.* V, 4c; Maurer, *Division and Methods*, p. 45.
5. In de Trin. V, 4, ad 5m; Maurer, *Division and Methods*, pp. 48-49.
6. *In Meta.*, Proem; Maurer, *Division and Methods*, p. 89.

Throughout this article and with a proviso, I utilize the word "immateriality" to designate the separateness from matter found in *ens*. The proviso is that "immateriality" should not be taken to mean that the concept of *ens* is realized only in spiritual things. As open to realization both in bodies and spirits, *ens* is neither material nor immaterial. Used in its regard, "immaterial" merely focuses attention upon the ability of the concept to be realized apart from matter.

Finally, if metaphysics treats of items separate in the first sense, it is only as causes of its subject matter:

> There is one [kind of theology] that treats of divine things not as the subject of the science but as the principles of the subject. This is the kind of theology pursued by the philosophers and that is also called metaphysics.[7]

Besides immateriality, the subject of metaphysics is marked by composition. It is a composite commonality. At *Summa Contra Gentiles* II, 54, Aquinas remarks:

> It is therefore clear that composition of act and potentiality has greater extension than that of form and matter. Thus, matter and form divide natural substance, while potentiality and act divide common being [*ens commune*]. Accordingly, whatever follows upon potentiality and act, as such, is common to both material and immaterial created substances, as *to receive* and *to be received, to perfect* and *to be perfected*. Yet all that is proper to matter and form, as such, as *to be generated* and *to be corrupted*, and the like, are proper to material substances, and in no way belong to immaterial created substances.[8]

The potency-act composition has a greater extension than the matter-form composition. The matter-form composition ranges only through material substances. The potency-act composition extends to immaterial created substances as well. Furthermore, the potency-act composition divides common being. Hence, the *ens commune* mentioned here is the same *ens commune* elsewhere characterized as the subject of metaphysics. Only now a further wrinkle is mentioned. The notion is composite. It harbors a potential and an actual element.

Earlier in the chapter, Aquinas identifies these elements.

> there is in [intellectual and immaterial] substances but one composition of act and potentiality, namely, the composition of substance and being

---

7. *In de Trin.* V, 4c; Maurer, *Division and Methods*, p. 44.
8. *Summa Contra Gentiles* II, trans. James F. Anderson (Notre Dame, Indiana: University of Notre Dame Press, 1975), p. 158.

[*substantia et esse*], which by some is said to be of that which is [*quod est*] and being [*esse*], or of that which is and that by which a thing is.

On other hand, in substances composed of matter and form there is a twofold composition of act and potentiality: the first, of the substance itself which is composed of matter and form; the second, of the substance thus composed, and being; and this composition also can be said to be of *that which is* and being, or of *that which is* and that by which a thing is.[9]

The potency-act composition common to both material and immaterial things is the substance-being (*esse*) composition. Substance and being are intelligibilities that in turn comprise another intelligibility—that of *ens commune* itself. In this text, the immateriality of *ens* lies especially in its *substantia* component. *Ens* is immaterial because *substantia* can be realized as a matter-form composition or as a form itself subsisting. In either case, however, *substantia* is still composed with *esse*.

From these texts, then, Aquinas portrays *ens commune* not only as an immaterial commonality but also as a composite commonality. *Ens commune* is (1) a commonality able to be realized apart from matter as well as within matter and (2) a commonality composed of two principles, substance and *esse*. In what follows I will refer to *ens commune* in the first respect as the immaterial sense of *ens* and to *ens commune* in the second respect as the *habens esse* sense of *ens*.

II

With this background I turn first to Maritain. In the portion of his article devoted to the intuition of being, Maritain affirms as the *sine qua non* for conducting metaphysics the attainment of the third degree of abstraction. In my own terminology, for metaphysics we must at least have grasped the immaterial sense of *ens*. For Maritain, all metaphysicians, even non-Thomistic ones, are metaphysicians because they at least do this much.[10] Hence, Aristotle, in whom the intuition of being is only virtual, does succeed in bringing his notion of being beyond the meaning of presence in the physical world. What distinguishes the Thomistic metaphysician is that he reaches the third degree of abstraction in and through the power of the intuition of being (*esse*). Maritain explains it this way:

> With [the intuition of *esse*] we leave the realm of simple apprehension in order to enter that of judgment. For there is a typical character absolutely

---

9. *Ibid.*, p. 157.
10. Maritain, "Réflexions," p. 31.

and uniquely proper to this intuition. It is produced in and by an affirmative judgment of existing: "I exist," "Things exist"; but this judgment is not like others, in which a subject with a certain essence is linked by the copula "is" to some attribute or predicate known in the way of an idea issuing from the abstractive operation. On the contrary, in the unique case of which I speak, that of the intellectual intuition of being, the idea or concept of existence does not precede the **judgment** of existence. It comes after it and comes forth from it. In this case we have a judicative act (the second operation of the mind) which is of another type than all other judgments.

In effect, it does not apply an attribute to a subject. It is the subject itself which it affirms or poses in the mind in the manner in which the subject is outside the mind, in extra-mental reality. And to conduct this judicative act correctly is for the intelligence to know intuitively, or to see, in the bosom of the spiritual intimacy of its proper operation, the extra-mental being, the existing, the *esse*, of this subject. Here is the intuition of being. By it I plunge into the realm of the existing, while escaping from the realm of essences and their relations.

It is after this that a return of the first operation of the mind upon that which had been seen (but not by it) will produce for it an idea, a concept or mental word which will designate it and which will be handy for discourse. What we will then possess will be the idea (of a judicative origin and consecutive to the intuition of being) of the *esse* known as such or of the existing exercised in act outside of the mind (as when I say, for example, "the soul communicates to the body its proper existence or its proper *esse*").

In other words, in the (unique) case of the intuition of being, the concept, this concept of the *esse*, formed after I have *seen* it, is *second* in respect to the judgment of existence where and in which, while pronouncing existence in itself, my intelligence has seen the *esse*. This concept is owing to a reflective return of simple apprehension upon the judicative act in question.[11]

The nature of this second concept of *esse* is described this way.

On the contrary, when it is a question of the second concept of existence, that which proceeds from the intuition of being, we are in the register of *Sein*, which goes with the third degree of intelligibility. The assertion of the existence is not then a copulative assertion, but a properly existential one, the assertion of the existing. The being is then known as such, in its proper light, which is the revelation of the extramental existing made to the mind in the mind. It is no longer taken in its relation to the sensible world; it is taken absolutely, in its limitless and intrinsically differentiated universality which embraces all that which *is* (and *is* in a manner irreducibly varied).[12]

---

11. *Ibid.*, pp. 17-18.
12. *Ibid.*, p. 25.

Thanks to this second concept of existence, as it captures what is known in judgment, our conceptualization of *ens* itself attains the third degree of abstraction. For the concept of existence is the keynote in the concept of *ens*. Maritain says:

> It appears to me important to remark, moreover, that what I have said of the existence, it is also necessary to say of the existent (*l'existant*) or the being (*l'étant*). Today it is fashionable to oppose the being (*l'étant*) to the existence (*l'être*); this is a mistake. A being or an existent is quite evidently a subject that exists or possesses existence.
>
> There are, then, two different senses of the word *ens* or being (*étant*). In the first sense, the word refers to *Dasein* and to the plane of the first degree of abstraction.... In the second sense, the word *ens* or being refers to *Sein* and to the plane of the third degree or intelligibility.[13]

In sum, Maritain squarely rests the attainment of the subject of Thomistic metaphysics upon a heightened judgmental appreciation of the *esses* of sensible things. Such an appreciation enables the mind to frame an analogous concept of *esse* that outstrips the material and sensible order. Since the meaning of *ens* is that which has *esse*, then it too attains its immateriality thanks to the mentioned analogous concept of *esse*. In this fashion Maritain accounts for both the immateriality and essence-existence components in the subject matter of Thomistic metaphysics, namely, *ens commune*. Noteworthy is that Maritain employs the phrase "intuition of being" to designate only the judgmental grasp of the *esse* of a sensible thing. The subsequent conceptualizations of both *esse* and *ens* are not instances of what is meant by the intuition of being.

III

For the most part this final position on how to attain the subject of Thomistic metaphysics echoes what Maritain said earlier. In his *Degrees of Knowledge* (1932), he wrote:

> The metaphysical transsensible [e.g., *ens*], since it is transcendental and polyvalent (analogous), is not only free from matter in its notion and definition but can also exist without it. That is why the order to existence is embowelled in the objects of metaphysics. If ... metaphysics descends to the actual existence of things in time, and rises to the actual existence of things outside time, it is not only because actual existence is the sign *par excellence* of the intrinsic possibility of existence.[14]

---

13. *Ibid.*, p. 26.
14. *The Degrees of Knowledge*, trans. Gerald B. Phelan (New York: Charles Scribner's Sons, 1959), p. 218.

Something about the actual existence of sensible things indicates that existence need not be confined to those things. The intrinsic possibility of existence is manifested in the actual existence of sensible things. Built upon existence, the notion of *ens* manifests a freedom from matter.

The approach to metaphysical *ens* through the *esse* of sensible things is used again in *Existence and the Existent* (1947). After insisting that the concept of existence (*esse*) cannot be cut off from the concept of being (*ens*, that-which-is, that-which-exists, that whose act is to exist), Maritain says:

> When, moving on to the queen-science, metaphysics, . . . the intellect disengages being from the knowledge of the sensible in which it is emersed, in order to make it the object or rather the subject of metaphysics, when, in a word, it conceptualizes the metaphysical intuition of being . . . what the intellect releases into that same light is, here again, first and foremost, the act of existing.[15]

Something about the existence of a sensible thing informs the intellect that to have existence is not necessarily to be a body. To have the intuition of *ens* is to have the intuition of *esse*. The insight into the immateriality of *ens* is rooted in an insight into the intelligibility of *esse*.

In one respect, however, the earlier positions differ from the last. In the earlier accounts the "intuition of being" sometimes refers, not to the judgmental grasp of *esse* but to the grasp of *ens*. Examples of passages in this vein are as follows. In his *Preface to Metaphysics*, Maritain specifies the true subject of metaphysics as *ens secundum quod est ens* (*l'être en tant qu'être*). He then remarks:

> The being which is the subject matter of metaphysics, being as such [*l'être objet du métaphysicien, l'être en tant qu'être*] . . . is real being in all the purity and fullness of its distinctive intelligibility—or mystery. Objects, all objects, murmur this being; they utter it to the intellect, but not to all intellects, only to those capable of hearing. . . . Being is then seen in its distinctive properties, as transobjectively subsistent, autonomous, and essentially diversified. For the intuition of being is also the intuition of its

---

15. *Existence and the Existent*, trans. Lewis Galantiere and Gerald B. Phelan (New York: Vintage Books, 1966), p. 26. Also, "It is being, attained or perceived at the summit of an abstractive intellection, of an eidetic or intensive visualisation which owes its purity and power of illumination only to the fact that the intellect, one day, was stirred to its depths and trans-illuminated by the impact of the act of existing apprehended in things, and because it was quickened to the point of receiving this act, or hearkening to it, within itself, in the intelligible and super-intelligible integrity of tone peculiar to it" (*ibid.*, p. 20).

transcendental character and analogical value. It is not enough to employ the word being, to say "being." We must have the intuition, the intellectual perception of the inexhaustible and incomprehensible reality thus manifested as the object of this perception. It is this intuition that makes the metaphysician.[16]

Maritain repeats the point in a discussion of the "metaphysical intelligible" from *The Degrees of Knowledge*. Maritain is discussing the intelligible object predicated in saying, "Peter is a being." The general lines of the discussion follow Aquinas's analysis of *ens* at *De Veritate* I, 1c. At one point Maritain remarks:

> There is, therefore, an intellectual perception of being [*une perception intellectuelle de l'être*] which, being involved in every act of our intelligence, in fact rules all our thought from the beginning. And when this is disengaged from itself by the abstraction of the transsensible, it constitutes our primordial philosophical intuition [*notre intuition philosophique primordiale*] without which we can no more acquire the science of metaphysical realities than a man born blind acquires the science of colors.[17]

Here the intellectual perception of being is the philosophical intuition of *ens*.

Finally, Maritain continues to emphasize this meaning of the intuition of being in his *Existence and the Existent*. He writes:

> A philosopher is not a philosopher if he is not a metaphysician. And it is the intuition of being [*l'intuition de l'être*] ... that makes the metaphysician. I mean the intuition of being in its pure and all-pervasive properties, in its typical and primordial intelligible density; the intuition of being *secundum quod est ens* [*l'intuition de l'être secundum quod est ens*].[18]

As the last line makes evident, Maritain again is using "*être*" in the sense of *ens*.

In sum, in his earlier accounts of the approach to metaphysics, Maritain employs the intuition of being terminology with a twofold ambiguity. The terminology refers both to the judgmental grasp of the *esse* of sensible things and to the conceptualization of the immaterial sense of *ens*. In his last *Revue Thomiste* account, Maritain forsakes this ambiguity and precisely limits the phraseology to judgment's grasp of *esse*. Though Maritain's second sense of the intuition of being involves

---

16. *A Preface to Metaphysics* (New York: Mentor Omega Books, 1962), p. 49.
17. *Degrees of Knowledge*, p. 215.
18. *Existence and the Existent*, p. 19.

a conceptualization of judgmentally grasped *esse*, as far as I know, Maritain never calls this conceptualizing a third sense of the intuition of being. Yet, since it is the crucial element for the grasp of *ens qua ens*—the second sense of the intuition of being—it may not be too inappropriate for someone to refer to it also as an intuition of being.

The above precisions are important to make before turning to Gilson. For although Gilson is responding to an article in which Maritain is speaking of the intuition of being's first sense, Gilson criticizes no such thing. What Gilson targets as the intuition of being has more to do with Maritain's second sense as that involves the conceptualization of *esse*. To a reader Gilson's equivocating is undoubtedly disturbing. Yet it perhaps has some excuse in Maritain's own loose use of terminology. More importantly, however, Gilson's terminological incongruence with Maritain's last article indicates no philosophical failure to understand Maritain and to deliver a fatal criticism.

IV

As mentioned, Gilson in his article took umbrage at Maritain's portrayal of Gilson as a proponent of the intuition of being.[19] Gilson's various criticisms of the intuition of being are as follows.

> What is the existence (*l'être* meaning *esse*) of the existent (*l'étant*). It is not itself a being (*un être*). As such the existence of the existent does not exist. It does not have some proper existence apart from that of the substance which it makes an existent. The substance exists only by the existence, but the existence exists only in the substance and as the existence of this existent. This is even why one could not have the intuitive intellection of the existence of an existent (*d'intellection intuitive de l'être d'un étant*), because the existence is perceptible to us only in the sensible perception of the substance which it actualizes. From the act of perceiving such or such an existent, we are able to abstract the abstract notion of existence, this common and universal existence attributable to all that which exists; but the existence proper to each existent is known to us only as a cause imminent to that which it makes exist. The only *esse* perceptible in itself and as such is God, because "God is *esse* itself" (C.G. I, 22; I, 33); "the *esse* of God is his substance" (C.G. II, 52, 7); "the quiddity of God is his being itself" (C.G. I, 25, 5). No existent is such that its quiddity is its existence; it is not then necessary to take the sensible intuition of the existent for an intellectual intuition of its existence.[20]

---

19. Gilson, "Propos sur l'être et sa notion," *San Tommaso e il pensiero moderno*, ed. Antonio Piolanti (Città Nuova: Pontificia Accademia Romana de S. Tommaso d'Aquino, 1974), p. 8.
20. *Ibid.*, p. 10.

Also,

> Consequently, we apprehend existence only as the existence-of-such-an-existent, which is for us an object of sensible intuition; we never apprehend existence in itself and apart in its proper quality of existence. It is necessary to return to this text: "it is not properly said that *esse* exists but that through *esse* something exists" (De div. nom. Pera, 751). One has the intuition of things that exist in virtue of their *esse*, one could not have an intuition of an act of existence which itself does not exist.
>
> One is able to distinguish as many degrees of abstraction as one wishes; nothing will make our apprehension of existence not be an abstraction of the intellect taken from the sensible.... We see the actual existence only in the effect in which it manifests itself, which is the existent sensibly perceived and intellectually known. If the existence were perceptible in itself, as it is in the case of God and only thus, it would indeed be an object of intellectual intuition. This is not a question of degrees of abstraction if it is not that. The very nature of the human intellect is the cause: the human intellect "does not think without an image," and since there is not some image of existence insofar as existence, which is a pure intelligible, the intellectual intuition is refused here below to minds that are most skilled in metaphysical meditation.[21]

Then,

> Would we betray this thought ["and just as God's substance is unknown, so too his *esse*" (*De Pot*. 7, 2, ad 1m)] by simply saying: the *esse* of God is unknown? This is, however, the immediate and inevitable consequence of the fact that we do not have the intuition of *esse*; for since God is *esse* itself in its purity, he necessarily escapes our view.[22]

In explaining this unknowableness of God, Gilson remarks:

> it is based on the primitive fact that existence (*l'être*), the immanent formal cause of the existent (*l'étant*), is conceivable to us only in its effect.[23]

> ... the intellect is not able to represent to itself the quiddity of the act of *esse* except under the form of the existent that it causes to exist.[24]

A final critical text is:

> The intellectual intuition of *esse* as such would be an intuition of a pure intelligible; in the philosophy of Thomas Aquinas, this intuition is refused

---

21. *Ibid.*, p. 11.
22. *Ibid.*, p. 12.
23. *Ibid.*, p. 13.
24. *Ibid.*, p. 16.

to us as inconceivable with the present human condition: "the soul understands nothing without a phantasm," said Aristotle; Aquinas comments: "It is impossible that our intellect, according to the state of the present life in which we are joined to a passible body, understand something in act, except by turning itself to the phantasm." (*S.T.* I, 84, 7) The rule is founded on nature, it then allows no exception.[25]

What is Gilson saying? The key to answering that question is a grasp of what Gilson criticizes as the intuition of being. Gilson's target is not what Maritain's *Revue Thomiste* article calls the intuition of being. Undoubtedly, since Gilson is explicitly responding to Maritain's article, the reader would at first think otherwise. Nevertheless, a careful reading fails to support that impression. In the sense of the grasp of the thing's *esse*, Gilson attributes the intuition of being to a number of thinkers.

> All men who philosophize and turn their mind toward this problem push the metaphysical analysis of being (*l'être*) more or less far; Thomas has many times described their pilgrimage towards being. There comes a point where certain thinkers refuse to push beyond the existent as existent (*l'étant comme étant*); they refuse precisely because they do not recognize the intuition of being (*intuition de l'être*) as the ultimate and root of the existent (*l'étant*); such is for example the case of Duns Scotus. Others, quite rare indeed, but Avicenna, Thomas Aquinas, Bañez and their successors, attest their existence, dare to affirm as the supreme act, the *esse* in virtue of which the existent exists.[26]

Neither is Gilson quibbling with Maritain about judgment as our resource for grasping *esse*. True, in his article Gilson never mentions judgment but does affirm that the discernment of the act in virtue of which the existent exists, namely, *esse*, is "the effect of a more extended abstractive reflection."[27] With this characterization, however, Gilson repeats his words from his *Elements of Christian Philosophy*:

> [The awareness of *esse*] certainly results from a supreme effort of abstraction, since, in order to form it, the intellect must conceive, apart from the condition of being an existent, the act owing to which the existent finds itself in this condition: *ipsum esse significatur ut quiddam abstractum*.[28]

Gilson appends to this text footnote 29. It reads: "Judgment posits *esse* as separated from essence although, in finite beings, it cannot subsist

---

25. *Ibid.*
26. *Ibid.*
27. *Ibid.*, p. 14.
28. Etienne Gilson, *The Elements of Christian Philosophy* (Garden City, New York: Doubleday and Company, Inc., 1960), p. 131.

apart." Hence, Gilson's talk of apprehending *esse* by an abstraction, though at first alarming, should not be taken as opposing judgment as the original distinct grasp of *esse*. It is his repeated teaching elsewhere.[29] In sum, Gilson admits that there is an intuition of being if that means the judgmental grasp of the *esse* of things.

Neither is Gilson targeting Maritain's second sense of the intuition of being. That second sense concerned the grasp of immaterial *ens*. But in criticizing Maritain's intuition doctrine, Gilson clearly speaks about *esse*, not about *ens*. As far as I can tell, Gilson's article never discusses Maritain's second sense.

What Gilson is intent upon discussing as the "l'intuition de l'être" is in truth Maritain's second concept of *esse*. As noted for Maritain, this second concept is subsequent to the judgmental grasp of the *esses* of sensible things. It is an analogous concept and occupies the third degree of abstraction. So located, we appreciate its meaning as not limited to realization in matter. This position seems just the target of Gilson's previous remark:

> One is able to distinguish as many degrees of abstraction as one wishes; nothing will make our apprehension of existence not to be an abstraction of the intellect taken from the sensible.... This is not a question of degrees of abstraction if it is not that.

Here Gilson criticizes the intuition of being in the sense of a conceptualization of the *esse* of sensible things that reaches the third degree of abstraction. But that is Maritain's second concept of existence. My conclusion, then, is that in his article Gilson understands as the intuition of being Maritain's formation of the second concept of existence. Though Gilson uses the language differently than Maritain, Gilson

---

29. "These two distinct operations both see the real, but they do not penetrate it to the same depth: intellection attains the essence, which the definition formulates, judgment attains the very act of existing [*le jugement atteint l'acte même d'exister*]" (Gilson, *Le Thomisme: Introduction a la Philosophie de Saint Thomas d'Aquin* [Paris: Librairie Philosophique J. Vrin, 1972], p. 184). Gilson insists that only judgment can attain *esse*: "... le jugement seul peut atteindre l'existence.... l'acte de juger peut seul atteindre le reel dans sa racine" (*ibid.*, p. 185). These texts reiterate what Gilson said in *The Christian Philosophy of St. Thomas Aquinas* (New York: Random House, 1956), p. 42. Also, "... for judgment itself is the most perfect form of intellectual knowledge, and existence is its proper object" (Gilson, *Being and Some Philosophers* [Toronto: Pontifical Institute of Mediaeval Studies, 1952], p. 202). For a defense of Gilson against the charge that he rests Aquinas's metaphysics upon Revelation, see my "Does Gilson Theologize Thomistic Metaphysics?" in *Thomistic Papers V* (Houston, Texas: Center for Thomistic Studies, 1990), pp. 3-19.

still employs it to designate something Maritain espouses. In sum, though Maritain's *Revue Thomiste* article understands the intuition of being as the judgmental grasp of the *esse* of a perceptible thing, Gilson's *Studi Tomistici* article locks the phraseology on Maritain's subsequent conceptualization of judgmentally grasped *esse*.

But if we now know about what Gilson is talking, what is he saying? As I understand him, Gilson's point is that given the way we originally know *esse*, we can never claim to know it as it is in itself. In other words, we only know the analogon of analogous *esse* through its analogates, and these are sensible. This locus for the apprehension of the analogon fails to provide sufficient insight into the analogon to grasp possible immaterial instances of analogous *esse*. If Maritain is claiming an understanding of immaterial analogates, then his intuition of being must be occurring thanks to a grasp of the analogon itself. This is a grasp independent of the creaturely analogates with which we are familiar. But there is in Thomism no such type of knowledge. Gilson gives two reasons. First, for Aquinas all this life's knowledge begins from phantasms. These present existence as the act of sensible things. This acquaintance with analogous *esse* rules out a direct acquaintance with it. Second, since for Aquinas God is existence itself, Maritain's position would also mean a knowledge of what God is. But for Aquinas the divine nature remains to the natural capacities of the human intellect as something *penitus ignotum*.

As a Thomist Maritain should realize that no way exists for simply the judgmental grasp of the *esses* of sensible things to release to the intellect a concept of existence that attains the third degree of abstraction. Understood as Maritain's second concept of existence, there is no intuition of being in Thomism. It can be quickly noted that Gilson's critique also undercuts Maritain's second sense of the intuition of being—the grasp of the immaterial sense of *ens*. Since Maritain ties the attainment of this notion to the second concept of existence, then failure to attain the second concept is tantamount to failure to attain the second sense of the intuition of being. Gilson, though, does not carry his critique that far.

V

I am interested in another implication of Gilson's critique. This implication concerns the requirements for initiating Thomistic metaphysics. In his *Studi Tomistici* article, Gilson speaks of metaphysicians who lack the intellectual intuition of being that he has criticized but nevertheless possess the intuition of being in the sense of a grasp of the *esse* of sensible things. I have quoted Gilson's remark and among these metaphysicians Gilson includes Avicenna, Aquinas, Bañez, and himself. What does this mean if not that the immateriality of *ens* and all talk of attaining the third degree of abstraction are nonessentials for starting Thomistic metaphysics. I repeat, Gilson claims that Aquinas and others are metaphysicians and yet they lack what Gilson calls Maritain's intellectual intuition of being. In other words, they were metaphysicians before they attained any third degree of abstraction. What made them metaphysicians? Simply their grasp of *esse* as the most profound principle in the sensible existents before us. It appears to me that Gilson is saying that a grasp of Aquinas's *habens esse* sense of *ens commune* sufficiently distinguishes the beginning of the metaphysical enterprise. The inception of the enterprise has no need of the other immaterial sense of Aquinas's notion of *ens commune*.[30]

On the neo-Thomist scene, such an opinion is undoubtedly a singular one. Almost unanimously, other neo-Thomists regard as the *sine qua non* of metaphysics, the attainment of concepts whose meaning spans the material and immaterial orders.[31] As I have argued elsewhere,[32] this assumption presents serious philosophical and Thomistic problems. By questioning the immaterial requirement, Gilson's approach should be welcomed as a new opportunity to make the doing of Thomistic metaphysics intelligible.

I would like to respond to two obvious problems facing anyone wishing to develop Gilson's position. First, it is no objection against Gilson to note that in his commentary to Boethius's *De Trinitate*, question V, article 1, Aquinas philosophically argues for the immateriality of metaphysics. As Aquinas himself notes, any number of possibilities exist for a third speculative science whose object includes independence from matter. First, the science could deal with something that never exists in matter, for example, God and the angels. Second, it could deal with objects able to be in matter and apart from it, for example, substance, quality, being, potency, act, etc. Third, the science could deal with both the previous. These manifold possibilities should cause one to

---

30. At this point the reader can profitably turn to Gilson's earlier critique of Maritain's interpretation of how to do Thomistic metaphysics. Gilson sets aside Maritain's intellectual intuition of "real being in all the purity and amplitude of its own intelligibility or its own mystery" for a universal concept of being whose "wealth consists, first, of all the judgments of existence it virtually comprises and connotes" (*Christian Philosophy of Aquinas*, pp. 43-44).

31. For Joseph Owens as the exception, see my "Metaphysics and Immateriality," *Angelicum* 65 (1988): 54-57.

32. *Ibid.*, pp. 44-54.

hesitate to say just how metaphysics deals with what is separate from matter. Apparently for Gilson the proper thing to do is to begin with *habens esse* and to see in the unfolding of the science where immateriality emerges. It is noteworthy that at *In VI Meta.*, lect. 1, n. 1163, Aquinas presents the immateriality of metaphysics in virtue of its treating God and angels.

What then of Aquinas's already cited frequent remarks on the immateriality of the subject of metaphysics? How should they be handled? If I understand Joseph Owens correctly, the texts can be taken as expressing a circumstantial requirement rather than a philosophical statement on the entry into metaphysics. The texts express a medieval theologian's need to take Aristotelian metaphysical terminology and give it a nondivine reference. In this fashion the intellectual world is made safe for revealed theology. Owens remarks:

> All this is involved in the use of the formula "separate in being and notion" to characterize the subject of metaphysics in the new understanding brought to it by Thomas Aquinas. Presumably the interest of the theologian in assuring for sacred theology its proper place among the sciences was his dominant concern. As subject of a science, separate substance had to be reserved to sacred theology. In contrast, the philosophical theology of Aristotle had to be dealing with a different subject. Yet in conformity with Aristotelian terminology, the latter subject had also to be separate, not only in notion like the mathematicals, but in a stronger way. The formulation of this further type of separation was found in Avicenna and Albert "separate in being and in notion."[33]

This medieval theological concern to launder the Greek terminology should not lead us astray on the entry point of Thomistic metaphysics. *Quoad se, ens* is immaterial. It is realizable apart from matter. Accordingly, Aquinas emphasizes this point to give the Aristotelian terminology a nondivine reference. But *quoad nos, ens* is first appreciated as *habens esse*. This sense of *ens* is doctrinally sufficient to initiate metaphysics.

In conclusion, these two late articles by Maritain and Gilson present a provocative exchange of opposed views on the undertaking of Thomistic metaphysics. The thunder claps in the exchange should not be allowed to grow silent but should be made to echo through contemporary discussion of Thomistic metaphysics.

---

33. Joseph Owens, "Metaphysical Separation in Aquinas," *Mediaeval Studies* 34 (1972): 306. Also see Owens, "Aquinas as Aristotelian Commentator," in *St. Thomas Aquinas on the Existence of God: Collected Papers of Joseph Owens*, ed. John R. Catan (Albany, New York: State University of New York Press, 1980), pp. 4-12.

The Doctrine of Participation in Thomistic Metaphysics

Joseph W. Koterski, S.J.

The most lively front within current Thomistic debate seems to be on the battlefield of natural law. One party is vigorously contending that the first principles of practical reason are known *per se*, without any special dependence on speculative reason, metaphysics, or the philosophy of nature. The other is equally vigorous in asserting the importance of speculative reason, metaphysics, and the philosophy of nature for discussions about natural law.[1] The result has been an increasingly better understanding of the spectrum of natural law theories, depending on how much advertence is made to speculative reason by a particular theorist, or how much about the natural world can simply be assumed from cultural context, and how much needs to be explained. It is a fine debate, but too windy for my feathers.

I mention this debate here so as to call your attention to a remark by Thomas often mentioned in discussions of natural law, namely, that the natural law is nothing other than the rational creature's participation in the eternal law.[2] It seems to me that the terms *natural law* and *eternal law* tend to get most of the play when we work on this passage, trying to figure out what the relation of two blocks of content are,[3] and then we push along to a yet larger schema in which positive law and divine law are incorporated into the picture. But there are other terms here which get relatively little play: *participation* and *creature*.

It may be that their significance is simply overlooked. "Nature" and "creature" are often taken as interchangeable synonyms. "Rational

---

1. I refer to the debate between the school of Germain Grisez, John Finnis, Joseph Boyle et al. and the recent criticisms brought by such people as Russell Hittinger, Ralph McInerny, and Henry Veatch.

2. *ST* I-II, 91, 2: "Unde patet quod lex naturalis nihil aliud est quam participatio legis aeternae in rationali creatura."

3. For example, Appendix 2, "The Theological Classification of Law," pp. 162-64 of the Blackfriars edition of the *Summa Theologiae*, volume 28, by Thomas Gilby, O.P. (Cambridge, 1966). The frequent uses of *participatio* and its cognates in Thomas's treatise on law almost entirely vanish in the variety of paraphrases employed in this translation.

creature" sounds as though it is simply medievalese for saying "human being" or "person," and "participation" seems a harmless way of saying that we human beings have a powered-down version of a law that would electrocute us were there not an appropriate transformer.[4] On the other hand, there may actually be some reluctance to take the notion "participation" seriously. Even though the *Index Thomisticus* reports more than 385 instances of its use by Thomas,[5] it still sounds vaguely Platonic, and so we are hesitant to assign it any technical significance. Only a few Thomists have concentrated on participation, while others keep it at arm's length in their metaphysics.[6] In my judgment, it is one of the genuinely fruitful ways of entry into Thomistic metaphysics, ranking with approaches that have proven to be helpful by taking as their key the notions of act and potency, the real distinction between essence and existence in creatures, the analogy of being, and the primacy of the act of existing.

I will not attempt here to make a full-scale explication of the famous text on the natural law as the rational creature's participation in the eternal law, but I would like to make three observations for our discussion and to provide some background material on the subject.

---

4. *Ibid.*, p. 162: "The concept of law is analogical.... It is found at various strengths, according to the Platonic principle of the diverse participation of values, a more-and-less of being and truth and goodness which comes when a pure perfection can be communicated in various degrees by causality, not because it can be mixed with something else and, as it were, watered down. So law scales down from the pure and eternal exemplar in the mind of God to the unsteady beat of lust in human nature."

5. *Particeps* 59x, *participatio* 87x, forms of *participare* 239x, plus a tremendous number of other forms in the lemma.

6. There are two famous books on the subject, largely unread by English speaking Thomists. They came out at nearly the same time, *La nozione metafisica di partecipazione secondo S. Tomaso d'Aquino* by Cornelio Fabro (2nd ed. Turin, 1950; French edition 1961) and L.-B. Geiger's *La participation dans la philosophie de S. Thomas d'Aquin* (Paris, 1942). Both have a good reputation, but do not seem to have made terribly much impact on the general run of Thomistic thinking.

There are also a number of fine, recent books that have taken up the question of participation in Aquinas, including Leo Elder's *Die Metaphysik des Thomas von Aquin in historischer Perspektive* (Salzburg: Verlag Anton Pustet, 1985) and Jan Aertsen's *Nature and Creature: Thomas Aquinas's Way of Thought* (Leiden: E. J. Brill, 1988). See also the brief discussions in Etienne Gilson's *The Elements of Christian Philosophy* (New York: Mentor-Omega, 1963), pp. 103-112, and Joseph Owens, *An Elementary Christian Metaphysics* (Houston, Texas: Center for Thomistic Studies, 1985), pp. 99-110, and the very helpful essay by John F. Wippel, "Thomas Aquinas and Participation" in vol. 17 of the CUA series, *Studies in Medieval Philosophy*, ed. J. Wippel (Washington, D. C.: The Catholic University of America Press, 1987), pp. 117-58.

Observations

Thomas's use of the term *participation* here is not out of the blue, but has as its background the doctrine of participation in Thomistic metaphysics. In fact, this particular statement is an assertion about the metaphysical grounding of ethics, for it explains that the moral law governing human conduct, natural law, is one of the ways in which "the rational creature" shares in the divine order, that is, God's eternal law. Although "law" seems to us to be primarily a category of social thought, Thomas is taking it metaphysically as the "rule and measure" constitutive of all natures; it is the eternal law which impresses upon all things their tendencies toward their own proper acts and ends (*ST* I-II, 91, 2 c).

As creaturely, human nature is ordered to a divine plan by Providence, and as rational, its very understanding of this order is crucial to the degree of perfection to be achieved in the process of participation. This text thus speaks immediately to one of the questions current in the natural law discussions taking place today as to whether any propositions in ethics depend on propositions in metaphysics, let alone whether there is any systematic dependence. It will be an important project to spell out this relationship in terms of participation, and to remain mindful of it in articulating natural law, a project that I think will involve staying constantly mindful of (1) the human being *as creature*, (2) the ongoing *dependence* of the creature on the Creator, and (3) the *humility* involved in "being measured," in contrast to the *hubris* of some Protagorean conception of "man as the measure" of all things.

A second point to note is Thomas's choice of the term "rational creature's participation." The importance of the creation for Thomistic metaphysics as a difference from Aristotelian metaphysics would never be denied, but I think we still need to bring out the thoroughgoing significance of "creature" in the way that we already sense the significance of "rational." That is, the distinctiveness of rationality to differentiate the human being from the animal world has received much emphasis, but we would do well to emphasize also the fact of creatureliness. This is possible because of a certain antinomy in Thomistic metaphysics; at the level of material beings Thomistic thought insists on the autonomy of finite substances and the genuine efficacy of secondary causes, but it also insists that there is a larger picture in which creatures have only a relative independence and autonomy.

I think that bringing out the creaturely dimension would involve seeing the constant importance of being related to God as our source and our goal. While "being related to God" is true of all creation, the human way of "being related to God" is as "rational creature"—that is, as participating in some of the higher perfections of divine being, such as being-a-person, which Thomas and all Christian theology take to be the inner relation constitutive of God's own being.[7] The eternal relation of one divine person to another, that is, their communion with one another, suggests a relational definition of "person" that would give a more lively picture of "human person" than the Boethian definition of person so often quoted. Further, the communitarian aspects of such a definition would resist the individualism typical of our age with a decisive, polemical bite, even while protecting the truths of distinct substance and relative autonomy that at present need no defending.

Third, and more broadly for the future of Thomism, one of the prevalent reasons for the wholesale rejection of Thomism by many is its apparent extrinsicism, the sharp separation of the orders of nature and grace. In fact, the histories of Thomism recently published[8] have made clear and understandable some of the reasons for the qualified, or even the utter repudiation of Thomism today, particularly in theology. But renewed attention to Thomas's doctrine of participation may lay aside some of those objections and actually show the attractiveness of Thomas's way of thinking when we start to consider grace as the participation of our nature in the divine life, faith as the participation in God's knowledge, and charity as participation in divine love.

The Doctrine of Participation: History

Thomas clearly subscribes to Aristotle's criticism of the Platonic idea of participation (*methexis, metoche*) by denying that there are any separate, self-subsisting Forms of natural things. I take it that for Plato every pure Form (Idea) is a unity able to be "divided over many." Somehow these Forms are *present in* or *present to* the world of becoming, from which they are separate. The "somehow" remains ever unclear, and one of Aristotle's criticisms is that the friends of the clear, crisp Forms always fudge on the "somehow" in their explanations. In some of the earlier dialogues Plato uses verbs like "to be in" or "to be present in." But with the later dialogues the ideas seem to be external to things, exercising formal causality without actually entering sensible objects.

---

7. See especially John D. Zizioulas, *Being as Communion* (Crestwood, New York: St. Vladimir's Seminary Press, 1985).

8. E. g., Gerald G. McCool, S.J., *From Unity to Pluralism: The Internal Evolution of Thomism* (New York: Fordham University Press, 1989); Bronislaw Dembowski, *O filozofii chrzescijanskiej w Ameryce Polnocnej* [Christian Philosophy in North America] (Warsaw: Academy of Catholic Theology, 1989).

Aristotle's rejection of the theory of ideas as the intrusion of logical categories into the principles of being includes the rejection of "participation" as the explanation of (1) a thing's coming into being by the entry of a Form from outside and (2) its destruction by the withdrawal of the Form. This explanation would entail that notorious beast, the *regressio ad infinitum*, because an idea and a sensible object that share in the same essence would need yet another form in common, that is, a third reality beyond their own, and so on to infinity. Aristotle also criticizes Plato's confusion of substances with accidents, for Plato gives all of them subsistent reality as Forms, and he finds the participation of mutable objects in eternal forms insufficient to explain the central problem of pre-Socratic philosophy, change and movement.

Participation as a Form of Predication for Thomas

While Thomas does reject the Platonic notion of participation he found in the *Timaeus* and read about in Aristotle, he accepts the notion of participation in his own sense. Its Latin roots mean literally "to take a part of," and this points him to an ontological view: "to receive partially what belongs to another in a universal way," that is, to receive only part of what belongs to another fully, and so merely to share in it without exhausting it.[9] Beyond the merely etymological point, he wants to use this notion to address the problem of the one and the many.

He reports in his commentary on the *De Hebdomadibus* that there are three acceptable senses for the term. The weakest sense is to use it as a logical term: a less extended concept participates in a more universal one. For instance, "dog" participates in "animal." The term here describes the predication of genus and species.[10] But at the basis of this logical application is a foundation in reality, and thus a second acceptable sense of the term: a subject or a substance participates in an accident, and matter participates in substantial form. A substance can be said to share in accidents, and matter to share in form because substantial and accidental forms, which are common of their very nature, are limited when they are received in this or that subject, and do not exhaust the perfection in question. Here at this level Thomas believes there is *real composition* which can be expressed by participation, whereas at the level of logical explanation, genus and species are not ontological realities but classes of predicates. To have said that there were real participation at that level would be to take the Platonic approach that Thomas joins Aristotle in repudiating. Instead, Thomas regards this sense of par-

---

9. *In De Hebdomadibus*, lect. 2; *In I Metaph.* 1, 10, 154.
10. See *In VII Metaph.* 1, 3, 1328.

ticipation as perfectly consistent with Aristotle's "predication *per se*," the predication in which one thing is said univocally of something else.[11]

At the third level, an effect participates in its cause. This is the sense operative when we say that the creature participates in the creator, the finite being in being itself. Fr. Wippel's 1987 article catalogs many texts in which an *esse commune* is shared by substances and accidents analogically, but he also lists many texts in which there is a being that is common in another sense: not predictably common, as existence is to substance and accident, but common in the sense of a unity whose causality extends to all other beings, material and spiritual, and whose perfection (namely, that they exist) they only partially share.

In Thomas's mature doctrine of participation this third sense of participation as an effect's share in the perfection of its cause entails (1) the *genuine composition* of a receiving and limiting principle (the essence) and that which is received (existence),[12] and the role of *imitation* in participation, that is, the way in which the effect resembles or has some likeness to its cause and spends its existence operating according to its created nature, so as to return as far as possible to its Origin, so as to grow in its perfection and likeness to its cause.

Participation as a Form of Causality

In this third area it is crucial to be assured that Thomas does not fall into the Platonic trap while trying to preserve a role for participation in metaphysics. It is important to note that Thomas does not use the term to describe the causality involved in the *generation* of natural things. The causes of generation are nature, art, and chance, and causality here is always univocal. A given horse is the cause that equine nature begins to exist in a newly generated horse, and likewise throughout all of nature, according to the fourfold analysis in terms of matter, form, agent and

---

11. SCG I, 32: "Omne quod de pluribus praedicatur *univoce, secundum participationem* cuilibet eorum convenit de quo praedicatur: nam species participare dicitur genus, et individuum speciem . . . omne quod participatur determinatur ad modum participantis, et sic partialiter habetur, et non secundum omnem perfectionis modum."

12. See W. Norris Clarke, S.J., "The Limitation of Act by Potency: Aristotelianism or Neoplatonism?" *New Scholasticism* 26 (1952): 167-94. Note also the use to which Wippel puts some of Thomas's texts on participation to make an argument for the real distinction between essence and existence in a manner different than the standard proofs: *Metaphysical Themes in Thomas Aquinas*, vol. 10 of the CUA "Studies in Philosophy and the History of Philosophy" (Washington, D. C.: The Catholic University of America Press, 1984), pp. 150-56.

end. An agent in this sense has a particular effect; it causes the form to be in this matter, which is the principle of individuation.

But the cause *per se* of a nature cannot be reduced to that which participates in a nature. If it were, then the individual horse would be the cause of equine nature absolutely, and thus be its own cause. Not possible. For generation, Thomas abides by the Aristotelian set of four causes and does not use participation to name the causality generative of a nature in a new subject. And he explicitly rejects the Platonic notion that ideas external to the subject could generate these newly arising natures.

But it is also significant that Thomas preserves the notion of causality by participation when Aristotle dismisses it, and I think that Thomas's joint philosophical confidence in his proofs for the existence of God and his Christian faith in God as the Creator of a fundamentally good universe are responsible. In fact, I wonder if we do not sometimes deemphasize this cofoundation in faith to avoid the charge of fideism and to make Thomism competitive in the secular marketplace, when in fact a more prominent display of the fact would be received as a more honest and more intelligible picture of Thomism.

Thomas points out, for instance, that Aristotle's criticism of the model-function of the ideas does not prevent God's wisdom from being the exemplary cause of all things.[13] He wants to have it signify the derivation of temporal diversity from eternal unity and thus the structural dependence of the many on the one, for he sees the need to refer to a unity to explain a multiplicity.[14] But what Thomas criticizes is the Platonic notion that natural things are generated from separately existing Forms, or that material things are compounded of different forms that separately exist outside the thing.

This latter view comes up with reflection on the *ratio* of "good" since "good," like any of the trans-categoricals, is predicated of diverse categories of being. It is not that Thomas rejects a separated good, namely God, on which all good things are dependent, nor did he think that Aristotle did.[15] But as he specifies in the *De Veritate*: "Plato asserted that those things which can be separated by the intellect are also separate in reality." It is not that natural things participate in God's goodness by some extra form of goodness added to their being, but rather that created things are good because of their own forms, and their existence is a participation in the divine existence, their goodness a transcendental

---

13. *In I Metaph.* 1. 15. 233.

14. See Anton C. Pegis, "The Dilemma of Being and Unity" in *Essays in Thomism*, ed. Robert E. Brennan (New York: Sheed & Ward, 1942), pp. 149-84.

15. See *In XII Metaph.*, on the Unmoved Mover.

aspect of being. Goodness is analogically realized in each of the different classes of beings, and in each case God is the exemplary and efficient cause of the goodness which is found in each thing by its formal perfection.[16] This I take to be the heart of Thomas's doctrine of the transcendentals, namely, that a being is true, because there is a being which is true in the maximum degree, and a being is good because there is a being which is good in the maximum degree, and so on. It is a position at the basis of the Fourth Way.

How can Thomas use participation in a causal sense that is not the rejected Platonic sense? The answer resides in an explicit doctrine of *creation* which entirely surpasses the Aristotelian framework and involves another type of efficient causality than movement from potency to actuality: creation, not movement from potency to act; exemplary, not formal causality. What I think he is doing is purging the doctrine of participation of all aspects of formal causality, so as to see it as a communication of being, with no trace left of a "form divided among different subjects" as for Plato.

The proper sense of participation in Thomistic metaphysics is the dependence of all things on God. This does not mean that "creatures have a part of God's existence" but rather that "some other nature (not God's nature) is brought out of nonexistence, is made to exist." That is, the one nature of being makes all other things be, through efficient causality. This is a dependence that explains even why natures are natures (namely, that things can only have a nature is they are designed, that is, formed according to an exemplar in a creative, knowing intellect[17]) and that accounts for the doctrine of natural inclinations so crucial to the natural law debate (namely, their being-related-to-God includes their directedness back to their origin and goal[18]). Thomas can make the Aristotelian doctrine of substantial forms and prime matter a starting point for metaphysics, and agree with any Greek that "from nothing, nothing comes" in the natural order. But he also has a doctrine of creation as an equally important source of his metaphysics, and even if he entertains the possibility of an eternal world on Aristotelian grounds, he is convinced of the complete dependence of every creature on God.

---

16. *ST* I, 91, 6: "On account of this first that is being and good by its essence, all other things can be called good and being insofar as they share in it by way of a certain assimilation." That God is not the formal cause, see *ST* I, 75, 5 ad 1.

17. While we often understand "art" as an imitation of the action of nature, Thomas pushes this image further back, asking us to see nature in terms of Divine Artistry.

18. In fact, the natural law text with which we began explicitly says "all things in some way participate in the eternal law as they have an inclination to their own acts and ends impressed on them by it."

The discussion of creation in the *Summa*,[19] for instance, as the "emanation" or "procession" of creatures from God, makes two important points, that God is the first cause and final end of all beings and that Thomas prefers to explain this causality in terms of participation.[20] His reason: that whose being is what it is solely by virtue of its own essence is the cause of everything else, for anything whose being is other than its own essence is caused to exist by another. This is the compositeness we spoke of before, not just the composition of matter and form in beings of nature, which allows for a tremendous autonomy in the explanation of generation and the science of secondary causes, but a composition of essence and existence in things material and immaterial. This is also the importance of chapter 9 of *De substantiis separatis*, that even immaterial substances are creatures characterized by composition. There is for them no generation such as can be described for material beings,[21] but there is still a composition of potency and act, of essence and existence.

In the basic sense of participation, all beings *participate* in existence, that is, they share in being and its transcendental properties, more perfectly or less so, since they are caused by the one first being, which is being perfectly. Participation—taking a part, having a limited share of something else which is wholly that—expresses for Thomas the nonidentity of that which is with its being, and the inner ordering of the nature, the thing's principle of movement and rest, toward that which is the fulfillment, the completion of the movement.

In terms of existence, the generative causes are causes of being only *per accidens*, because the new being that comes about does not come to be out of absolute nonbeing. In the order of nature, "from nothing, nothing comes," for across the whole realm of categorical being there is always presupposed a preexistent subject. But when we turn to the transcendental plane and consider the coming forth which Thomas calls creation (or using that Neoplatonic term *emanation* so strange to Aristotelian ears[22]), the process is not to be conceived of as a mutation or a motion from potency to act, but as another kind of causality, an influx of being from the first principle.[23] In God (this first principle) Thomas finds an identity of essence and existence that makes the compositeness

---

19. *ST* I, 44-45.

20. See also SCG II, 15.

21. That immaterial beings bear no possibility of becoming in themselves, cf. *De Anima* q.1 a.6 ad 8; *ST* I, 61, 1.

22. K. Kremer's study, *Die neuplatonische Seinsphilosophie und ihre Wirkung auf Thomas von Aquin* (Leiden, 1971), is useful here, with caution.

23. Thus the difference between the first and the second among Thomas's Five Ways.

of existence and essence elsewhere intelligible. This, by the way, I take to be one of the most strongly defended assertions of Maritain's *Existence and the Existent*.[24]

Exactly contrary to the common supposition of Greek philosophy, that "from nothing, nothing comes," creation differs in principle from the this-worldly process. It presupposes nothing in the thing created, by contrast to the process of this worldly change, whose very explanation comes by an explicitation of the presuppositions of the process. The duality inherent to a *formatio* is replaced by the absolute sovereignty of God who produces creatures with a "received" or "participated being," a being that is composite in contrast to God's own subsistent being. When the effect does not express the fullness of the ontological content of the cause, but does have a share in this perfection, it is said to participate in that cause, and so Thomas speaks of created being as a participation in God's being.

The Problem of Pantheism

Does this bestowal of being imply that the creature has a part in God himself? This seems to have been implied by the pantheism of the Neoplatonic tradition. But while the Neoplatonic tradition takes being as the summit of the intelligible world, yet something still derived from the One, Thomas identifies *esse* with God himself. He drops the mediatory role that being has in Neoplatonism, and as a result, the being of creation is seen as directly created by God, as having a direct participation in the divine order.[25]

It is precisely by his distinctive meaning for participation that he guarantees the metaphysical distinction between Creator and creature. Created beings do not possess part of God—this is totally excluded by reason of God's transcendence and unicity, by the perfect identity of God's essence and existence, and by the fact that this perfect identity occurs only in God. His point is rather that a limited perfection can only exist because the original exists in all its purity. The transcendental unity of being (that God and creatures share in being analogously) requires us to locate the distinction between God and creatures in a "confinement" or "contraction" of the fullness of being in whatever is created.

Participation then takes place by means of creation, the work of God's efficient and exemplar causality. Creatures are formed according

---

24. Garden City: Image, 1956, *e.g.*, pp. 35-44.

25. See Aertsen pp. 123ff. In particular, cf. SCG I, 26 (contra Kremer): God is not the formal *esse* for other things or the *esse* by which each of them exists. God would then not be *above* all things, but *inter omnia*.

to the exemplars in the mind of God, with the result that each thing in its own way manifests some aspect of divine fullness in a graduated series of perfections.[26] Each limited perfection is only real by the uninterrupted partaking in its source, and this sort of reference to God as *fons et origo* is the metaphysical basis of the inclinations that are so important a part of natural law theory.

Final Causality and the Doctrine of Participation

How does this consideration of participation help us? Let one example suffice at present to suggest that this is an important road for the future of Thomism.

Although the terms *nature* and *creature* tend to be used interchangeably, with reliance on context to provide the necessary qualifications being assumed, explicit attention to participation in an analysis of these terms, such as Jan Aertsen has recently provided in his new book *Nature and Creature*, shows that they have different orientations and directions. Further emphasis on these different orientations and directions could get the natural law debate beyond the question of whether one must intuit *per se nota* goods.

The terminus of generation lies in the intrinsic nature or essence of the thing, while the terminus of creature is being (*esse*), that which the creature has from another, that is, from God, as a gift. Nature suggests what the being is in itself, its specific essence, which is preserved by the eternal recurrence of the same in the causality of generation. What "creature" suggests is the condition of being-related-to-God, (both the radical distinction between God and the creature and the direct relation of creation to God, not some more or less mediated one as in Neoplatonic or gnostic systems), and the religious directedness of all that is back to this Origin, each in the way suited to its nature according to the order or hierarchy of beings.

For natural law discussions, this immediately suggests an *order* of goods *perfective* in *different ways*, an ordering of the creature to the creator that is in one sense *simply given* by the fact of the participation of composite creatures in existence, but in another sense an ordering that *must be achieved and developed* (participation as imitation) according to a pattern of goals and perfections. Metaphysical consideration of human participation in the life of the divine gives a much different color to what otherwise tends to be a minimalist, least common denominator approach to natural law.

---

26. Cf. James Ross, "Aquinas's Exemplarism; Aquinas's Voluntarism" in *American Catholic Philosophical Quarterly* 64: 2 (Spring 1990): 171-98.

That Thomas manages to reformulate some of the doctrines he most valued from Aristotle in the ostensibly Platonic language of participation—but only a corrected version of participation—indicates the virtue he discerned in this approach. And the sense of "valuable inclusion" within God's providence which "participation" suggests today makes me think that any energy we commit to thinking things through in terms of participation will yield ample fruit.

Thomism and Romantic Confusions of the Good: Beauty Is Truth, Truth Beauty

Marion Montgomery

> For the realist, whose thought is concerned with being, the Good, the True and the Beautiful are in the fullest sense real, since they are simply being itself as desired, known and admired. But as soon as thought substitutes itself for knowledge, these transcendentals begin to float in the air without knowing where to perch themselves. This is why idealism spends its time "grounding" morality, knowledge and art, as though the way men should act were not written in the nature of man, the manner of knowing in the very structure of our intellect, and the arts in the practical activity of the artist himself.
>
> Étienne Gilson, *Methodical Realism*

You will have recognized that my subtitle alludes to those famous concluding lines of John Keats's "Ode on a Grecian Urn," the highly debatable lines that read:

> "Beauty is truth, truth beauty"—That is all
> Ye know on earth, and all ye need to know.

The lines are debatable as a proposition, of course, but there is a question preliminary to that debate, though a part of it. Keats punctuates the lines differently in two manuscripts, raising the question whether there is one speaker or two. Whether the urn is to be understood as "saying" the whole of the two lines, or whether the last line and a half are the poet's own response, his turning upon the urn as it were, saying that such a proposition is well and good if one happens to be an urn or a poem, but is cold comfort if one happens to be an urn-maker or a poet.

You will also have recognized in my epigraph from Gilson a clear, precise putting of a central Thomistic point about "being itself" as the pivotal recognition separating the Thomistic realist from the Cartesian idealist. What interests me in putting these texts together is the light Gilson sheds on that large and amorphous intellectual movement in Western thought we speak of as "Romanticism," and particularly that movement as reflected in literature in English. Gilson makes his observation in the early 1930s, just as a very significant modern "Romantic" poet, T. S. Eliot, is becoming a realist—or rather is recognizing that almost unknown to himself, so sophisticated a Romantic has he been, that he has metamorphosed from secular idealist into a Christian realist. And it is at this same time that Eliot as critic begins to praise John Keats, after long disdain of the English Romantics. His praise, at heart, is for Keats's having recognized so clearly the difficulties to the poet in the Cartesian ambiance of thought that dislocated the poet increasingly from his desired position in community after the sixteenth century. To have recognized the difficulties is not, of course, to have overcome them, being only the first step necessary to a recovery from intellectual confusions. Much stumbling may, and does, follow for Keats and to an extent for Eliot before he at last comes to rest in what is essentially a Thomistic realism.

When Gilson in our epigraph says that "as soon as thought substitutes itself for knowledge," those transcendentals—the Good, the True, and the Beautiful—"begin to float in the air without knowing where to perch themselves," he puts the Romantic's dilemma rather clearly. The proximate perch of those transcendent realities is in the intellect, as the poet knows intuitively. Intellect is but a visitation site for the transcendent, for finite intellect is at best an uncertain roosting place, save through grace. Losing sight of this truth about the limits of finite intellect, modern philosophy, aided and abetted by the emerging empirical sciences, has since the Renaissance increasingly insisted that the desired, the known, and the admired are causally occasioned by finite intellect: that the Good, the True, and the Beautiful exist by and through the operation of finite intellect. The poet, intuitively disturbed by such a position, should he extend metaphor out of Gilson's figure of the floating transcendentals might well liken his own circumstances in this confused age to those of the falconer whose birds remain leashed, though circling near his outstretched but carefully gloved hand—that controlling perch of his own intellect. Such a violation of the reality of intellect through metaphorical *attribution* (in this Thomistic sense) will call forth at last an eruption, perhaps such a one as William Butler Yeats cries in famous lines:

> Turning and turning in the widening gyre
> The falcon cannot hear the falconer;
> Things fall apart; the center cannot hold;
> Mere anarchy is loosed upon the world . . .

So apt are Yeats's words to the breaking asunder of intellect and reality in our century that they are his most quoted ones, characterizing as they do our centripetal intellectual chaos. Few philosophers dealing with that chaos can resist this very Romantic poet, whose work is a rich source of epigraphs to the explorations of our age's malaise in which intellect gasps as order dissipates—order being the intellect's necessary medium.

I think we may properly explore this confusion as signalled by our Romantic poets generally, and thereby rescue what has been too casually called the "Romantic" impulse. I rather take that impulse to be in its actuality a Thomistic intuition unrealized as such, and most often by the poet himself. It is a gift of intellect in its very nature, and so timeless, though in certain times and places more highly visible in the arts when an intellectual community begins to lose a common consent to the necessity of particular and communal order. In a recovery of the intuitive as legitimately real lies the significant future of Thomistic realism: in its clarification and then restoration to an ordinate service of intellect's complementary gift, the rational. Still, I am uncomfortable in speaking of a "future" of Thomism, even as I am restive when "Romanticism" is seen as a Western movement beginning in the eighteenth century. Sufficient unto the present moment of intellectual unrest are the evils of intellect misapplied. What is always at issue is the recovery of the particular soul's proper relation to complex reality, which is a relation possible only in this present moment. That recovery is by intellectual vision restored, a recovery of intellect to its proper engagement to reality.

And so I value Josef Pieper's cautionary words to my point: in respect to intuitive knowledge as it may be distinguished from rational knowledge, he reminds us, there is no "tension toward the future" in the intuitive, one of whose functions is to call unified intellect to the exigencies of this very moment. Now if the stirring in the poet's intellect caused by his intuitive gift fails in his rational exercise through a confused excess, neither his attempt nor the intuition are themselves wrong of necessity. Notably, when our Romantic poet fails in consequence of intuitive stirrings, it is likely to be because he has wrongly associated the intuitive with the temporal circumstances through which he struggles toward vision. That is, the failure is likely to be occasioned by a rational distortion of the nature of the soul's presence in time and place, the nature of this crucial present moment of its being. He inclines to make time the enemy, whereby he becomes time's pawn, increasingly enthralled either by nostalgia for an imagined moment in the past or an imagined moment in the future: enthralled by an Eden lost or by some

Eden yet to be established, the one occasioning passive lament, the other activist assaults upon time future.

The struggle to recover intuited reality through our intuitive nature to a respect by rational intellect, so conspicuous in nineteenth-century literature, is revealed most variously in theme and in genre. For instance, the attempt is very much present in those "Romantic" novels of Sir Walter Scott, which our gnostic humorist Mark Twain makes such fun of in his own attempt to recover Adam as his own possession, namely his *Adventures of Huckleberry Finn*. The failures of Twain's own Romanticism, we note in passing, are forced upon him even as he ridicules the nostalgic Romantic. *A Connecticut Yankee at King Arthur's Court*, pitting a modernist "Yankee" against Scott's medieval dream, ends most darkly, followed by Twain's many dark works reflecting despair in him. Intuitive stirrings such as those in Scott one finds also in Keats's nostalgic texture of "The Eve of St. Agnes," through whose sensual details a swooning of the senses is encouraged, and even sometimes effected, at least in sophomores who have not yet lost or had distorted entirely the virtues of their sensual nature, through which one is properly drawn toward the Good by fleeting glimpses of the Beautiful flickering in young love. For who in flowering youth can resist moonlight through those stained windows that are ripe with "quaint" devices of "carven imag'ries," falling with "warm gules on Madeline's fair breast." Not only Porphyro grows faint.

But these, alas—both Madeline and Porphyro, the old crone and the beadsman—are gone "ages long ago," leaving one to confront this present, fleeting moment. Both Scott and Keats share a turning back toward the medieval world in an attempt to regain faint stirrings of the Good, the True and the Beautiful. If they ignore or downplay unbeautiful particulars in that historical period, our century has been delighted to recover those particulars, in a derision of medievalism and in support of our favorite epithet for it, the "Dark Ages," only to be left with the recognition that derision does not effect vision, as Twain so sadly discovered.

Our century has exercised a proprietary authority over this dilemma to consciousness, its mislocation in contentions of time future with time past, which though mislocated speaks an intuitive hunger for a restitution of a fullness of intellect to reality. Such are intellect's stirrings after its long wanderings in Cartesian shadows of being, though we must be reminded often that such wanderings are not limited to either an age or a country or a literary movement. Which is to remind ourselves that, in posing Thomistic realism as it contends with Cartesian idealism, we are posing inherent intellectual difficulties not to be sufficiently accounted for by historical designations. One might, with world enough and time, discover such contentions operative in the intellect of Homer or Aeschylus or Dante.

* * *

However much the poet may become confused or willfully stubborn within the stifling idealist oppressiveness that is subversive of his hunger for order, that hunger continues in some degree present in his actions of making. So long as one is a maker, he has not yet completely lost a certain likeness to the cause of his given nature as maker. That is, he will not have lost that aspect of existing "in the image of God," existence itself of necessity an image of the Cause of existence in some degree. And so there remains in his concern and action as maker an awareness that it is the good of the thing made that is the guiding principle of making. The good of the poem as poem is at issue, but in which principle there is also implicit an intent to his own proper end through his participation in being by the action proper to his nature. We recall St. Thomas's insistence that "art does not belong to moral knowledge, which concerns things to be done (*agibilia*), since art is right reason about things to be made (*factibilia*)" (*ST* 2-2, Prologue). The maker as judged by his making is commendable by virtue of "the quality of his work." The work does not demonstrate a moral good as its primary principle of being but a good in itself in respect to order, proportion, and the like. As for the maker himself, however, there is an inescapable moral dimension to his actions whereby he is realized as participating in actions of making. The practical intellect, governed by the virtue of prudence, is necessary to the act of making, so that making, in its effect upon the maker, can never be absolutely removed from the necessity of moral order. Art, like fire, is indifferent in itself to the moral dimension of existence, but that is only to speak of art itself as removed from culpability in respect to the spiritual agent, the artist. The relation of beauty to truth for Keats's urn, the question of a moral dimension to the truth or beauty proper to art itself, is irrelevant to the urn or the poem as art. But the habit of making perfected by the maker is relevant to the good of his spiritual state as person, a state realized in part through that habit of making which is salient in that creature, the embodied soul.

While we may not justly indict either an art or a science which happens to be pervasive of a particular age is the case of a person's failure in his calling as a "maker" to the fulfillment of his person as a gifted, particular, specific being, the complex of intellectual circumstance, the intellectual climate coincident to his particular history as a person, must be recognized. But a person's failures as maker is ultimately a spiritual consideration, and rests in his own will. Thus one must engage, as a soul in progress, the conditions impinging upon that progress. For his "calling" as maker is circumscribed by the finitudes of existence, by his own limited gifts which are potential and less decisively the immediacy of history as a context of his nature. Thus his own deportment as person he bears residually as a personal history, in response to the history of his age and the history of his civilization to which he responds by actions of intellect. At issue is his prudent response to circumstances. Pervasive of our age's history is the idea that he is determined in his response by circumstance, an idea quite distinct from saying that he is circumscribed by circumstances natural and historical. The deterministic idea is reductionist in its logical extension, making man an effect of nature and history. One may argue the idea by logic, but the evidence of experience underlines persuasively the innate resistance to that determinate pressure of circumstances. One need only pursue the argument with its advocate in pressing upon the advocate himself to discover that, while he may hold all other men determined, he himself will not consent to determination as the first and final principle of his own existence. In this respect his silence in the face of argument might possibly be his strongest argument, since the purely determined creature has no necessity of describing his state, the very description already intellect's taking a stand beyond the principle he insists is inclusive. Nevertheless, untenable ideas have effects seductive of imprudent intellect, and the deterministic principle has been generally operative in sociology and psychology in particular. It has seemed to justify the proponents in exceeding the descriptive limits of science by presuming philosophical authority in the question. As intellectual creature, one is required to understand the position as a circumstance to the pursuit of the truth of things. One remarks here the stifling oppressiveness upon the "maker" in our world, affecting his breathing through the virus of Cartesean idealism advanced as if fully established by empirical science.

Since the Enlightenment especially, intellect in its necessarily empirical address to the circumstances of being has tended in its communal authority to declare the reductionist end of idealism. This is to say that idealism and empiricism have too-much cooperated in the divorce of intellect from reality, nowhere more conspicuously than in the academy for this past hundred years and more. Like Chaucer's Physician and Apothecary, each has made the other for to win in the struggle over being against the realist. That struggle requires from that position a domination over other intellects. To understand this circumstance of history is to safeguard oneself against one's own abuse of knowledge.

For empirical science yields truth not to be reasonably denied. And *cogito ergo sum*, as Gilson says, expresses a philosophical truth, though "it is not the starting point" to an acceptable epistemology. To understand the limit in particular knowledge as learned through science is at once to value that knowledge in its limits and to move toward an understanding of that knowledge, the responsibility peculiar to intellect. It is the tensional response to circumstance by intellect, in its freedom of response, and within the mystery of limit that is thematic in what we recognize as that historical movement, Romanticism.

If order and proportion signify a Beauty that is worth the intellect's admiration and courtship through language, that order and proportion must rest at last, and in an ultimate way, in an absolute, lest the concepts themselves be left merely floating in the air, tenuously attached to intellect itself, which finds for itself no firm ground in being. This is to say that if the Beautiful is merely sprung from intellect's primary assertion of the True, which is an assertion as well that the Good is also determined by finite intellect, then intellect alone seems necessarily the primary cause of the good, the true, the beautiful. It creates for itself the desired, the known, the admired. But despair must be the final end of such conclusion. Narcissus may be the first captivated by the illusion of his own beauty, but the spiritually debilitating effect of *ennui* waits upon him, the most ancient of dragons. Wallace Stevens came at last to concede the point at the end of his life by his conversion of Christianity, having spent a lifetime as poet denying all power over being except that of the poet's imagination, the "necessary angel" as he called it, an agent at finite intellect's command executing those "supreme fictions" as the only absolute. Eliot realizes the danger earlier than Stevens, and from "Ash-Wednesday" to the end treats as the central issue to intellect the contention of hope and despair for his soul, a contention in the soul of the maker who cannot escape the reality of his existence as in the image of the First Maker. If one were to put the recognition in Thomistic terms, one might say that Eliot recognizes as the poet's danger a temptation to rivalry with the Holy Ghost over the power of *to make*. (Consider on this point the *Summa*'s Question 14, of 2-2, concerned with blasphemy against the Holy Ghost.)

The necessity of some source of Beauty beyond the poet's own absolute power to make a beautiful thing is fleetingly recognized by Keats, as his great Odes discover to us. The urn seems to echo an abiding Beauty and Truth, though those transcendents as transcendents are prevented from Keats's visionary power. They are prevented largely by the reduction of his flickering vision to rather desperate aphoristic shibboleth—words clasped in a moment of intellectual despair which crowds out the virtue of hope. Despair consequently makes dead ashes of his personal history which by a forced imaginative act he prematurely scatters onto the static, teasing urn. He is trapped in a reduction of himself as person by the accidents of his immediate circumstances. Similarly, that moment of transport in another Ode in an English garden, that erratic flight by willed imagination as if on the nightingale's wings, stirs intellect to the border of a stranger vision-held country which is suddenly lost. And because lost, that country is declared illusional, is declared a shadowy "thing" sprung from helpless daydreaming.

As if rebuking Keats's weak faith in art as savior to the finite intellect, William Butler Yeats is adamant. Art is the one possible transport of finite intellect beyond the clutches of time. In "Sailing to Byzantium," Yeats insists that intellect by its own power of making, or by its power through a Keatsean negative capability to enter the made thing of art as the vehicle of transport, may transcend its temporal and corporal entrapments. Keats's aphorism is thus certified as holy vision to the maker of things, though abandoned by Keats. Art, the "golden bird," transforms the natural bird and thereby becomes a timeless medium to transcendent reality. "Set upon a golden bough" beyond nature's decay, it sings a truth beyond "what is past, or passing, or to come" in the decaying world. Through its beauty, time's and space's seeming authority are reduced by a transcendent truth: the beauty of Idea—that old Platonic shadow concept that has haunted Western thought since the Renaissance in one guise or another. For Yeats, truth is the transcendent beauty of form faintly perceived through art, revealed as separate, self-subsistent forms beyond the ravages of temporal finitude.

Art, those artifacts strewn through history which Yeats in a memorable phrase calls "monuments of unaging intellect," thus solves for him history's enigma. Or so Yeats insists. But for Eliot as for Keats, Beauty must have primal cause more real and immediate to the world than an imagined or faintly remembered self-subsistent form among forms, even as it must be more real than an effect certified by the poet's assumed autonomous power of imagination in the making of monuments to itself. The truth of the soul's existence seems not sufficiently spoken to by art so conceived. Yeats's monuments therefore still leave in doubt for Keats and Eliot the makers of those monuments. One might, as maker, as well be sod to art's high estimate of transcendent truth and beauty, if truth and beauty are gnostically separated from the here and now in which intellect acts. In time and place, art if understood as by Yeats becomes at best but requiem for that collapsing sod, the poet. In brief, what is sensed is lost, as not rescued, is the *person*, the peculiar discrete maker, this poet the world knows as John or Thomas Stearns or William Butler, though pinned and wriggling to the wall of our common memory in time as Keats, Eliot, Yeats by their piercing poems.

The prudent Romantic poet may in the end fear that metaphor is built only by attribution, thus leaving the poet isolated not only from the transcendent, but from the immediacy of creation itself whereby the potential of *person* moves toward perfections. Its monuments thus built to celebrate unaging intellect against the despair of isolation may prove but an effect of fancy, sand therefore far removed from the truth which intellect desires by its very nature. For mere metaphor of attribution dooms art to fancy's province and so proves insufficient to the intuitive desire to understand, a perfection of intellect beyond merely knowing. Intellect, by understanding, might thus be both at home in its own mode of existence as finitely particularized and additionally more comfortable with being, with creation, beyond a walled-in autonomy that so much depends upon metaphor of attribution as the defense of its autonomy. For by building "supreme fictions" through attributive analogy, intellect would deflect the intrusiveness of reality as understood Thomistically.

The prudent Romantic, then, may well detect a desperation in a Stevens or a Joyce or Pound. Or in a Shelley, in whose words histrionics overwhelms poetry. Which is to say, overwhelms signs ordinately related to the complexity of being itself as encountered in diverse creation when there is a proper intensity of intellectual attention toward the mystery of being as known through actual experience of creaturely existences. That "knowing" is prelude to both conceptual knowledge and to artful articulations of that knowledge. Of course being is not inaccessible to sign: it is only always larger than any concept's or sign's power to contain it through and aggressive presumption of power over being by concept or sign. Shelly exhibits such an excess, as in his "Hymn to Intellectual Beauty." But Keats to the contrary, in a rare moment of vision upon his intellectual limit, speaking of his desire for the faculty of negative capability, recognizes the necessity in that faculty: intellect must consent to exist "in uncertainties, Mysteries, doubts, without any irritable reaching after fact & reason" forced by its desire to control that gift of power called negative capability—the power of harmony in being.

A species of Shelley's desperation is in the early Eliot, though without Shelley's rhetorical excess against uncertainty. Eliot at first modifies and, to a degree, governs his desperation through ironic detachment, though that irony increasingly turns sardonic, that symptom of a festering intellect. The sardonic reflects an increasing uncertainty in him till he must abandon irony altogether. We witness this change when we read his early poetry against his late poetry, his "Preludes" or "Love Song of J. Alfred Prufrock" against "Ash-Wednesday." Relatively late in his career as poet and critic, we find him recovering himself to a reconciliation with existence larger than that self self-loved which is so fearfully present in the early work. And he recovers through a Thomistic deportment of intellect, the self opened to being.

It is, incidentally, consequent to this change that Eliot reports his youthful infatuation with Shelley, whom he now finds intolerable. And along with this late acknowledgement comes his recognition of kinship with Wordsworth and Keats, a kinship that all along has been insipiently present. Eliot's desire has stirred him increasingly toward the Good, the True, and the Beautiful through intuitive intellect. Thus what he comes to value in Wordsworth and Keats is the presence of their person in the poetry itself, a presence reaching beyond sheer rationally decreed intellectual autonomy as poet which so easily burdens art with the merely autobiographical. The principle of intellectual autonomy, which comes to flourish in Western thought with the rejection of metaphysics, Eliot sees as portending spiritual cataclysm such as we witness pervasive of the intellectual community in our century, the chaos which leaves our intellectual community in disarray.

It is worth noting as more than an aside to this point that, as we lose the understanding of the *personal* which lies at the heart of Scholastic metaphysics, we become more and more obsessed with the vague ghost of the personal, the "self." And we observe that the literary genre of the autobiographical becomes dominant, the poet or novelist such as Eliot or Joyce feeling the strain of exorcising the "personal" history in their art, with less success than they desire. Eliot's personal experience of intellectual disarray, consequent upon his embracing modernist ideology, leads him to speak more and more in anticipation of our own pending disarray, after he has overcome ideological possession through an exorcism of making art of his "personal grouses," such as his *Waste Land*. His forewarnings to intellectual community are in both his *Four Quartets* and in his prose. His changing perspective as critic is conspicuous in *The Use of Poetry and the Use of Criticism* (1933), in which lectures he emphatically rejects Shelley as Romantic and embraces Wordsworth and Keats.[1]

---

1. Note for instance, Eliot's remark that Wordsworth's "critical insight, in this one *Preface* and *Supplement*, is enough to give him the highest place." A decade earlier, Eliot had dismissed Wordsworth's argument in this "Preface," without ever naming the work or Wordsworth directly. By 1932, however, he finds in Wordsworth's

We may now recognize as Wordsworth's and Keats's problem the same one experienced by Eliot. Having accepted, if but passively, the reductionist view of intellect whereby intellect is separated from reality, intellect finds itself islanded. It becomes endangered by an overwhelming melancholy, the emotional effect of the soul's growing despair. For melancholy is symptom of soul's disorder. In that uneasy circumstance of the soul as experienced by Wordsworth and Keats, we observe, they do not turn back to the "Dark Ages" in their best art. Each is rather concerned to satisfy an immediate hunger of intellect for its present moment in existence—a hunger to be reconciled to that which is not intellect itself but a current to intellect flowing through present circumstances. St. Thomas might say of this disturbing intimation to these poets of some presence. The thing they encounter is a timeless abiding "thing," namely being itself, however much time-designated and determined it might appear to the encountering intellect. It is experienced in *this* time and in *this* place, and so appears to bear an aura of circumstantiality, as if it were ultimately designed by history. But what intellects in their varying particularities thus discover are rather hints of the ground of existential reality, treasured by memory, which intellect by its proper operations must reconcile itself to through concept and sign.

One understands how the poet, perhaps more than the philosopher might, becomes time-trapped in such a moment in which intellect finds itself at the border of vision. The absence from memory of the once known appears time-related, since what was present as a knowledge (so memory insists) is now seemingly absent or at best only partially present. And even this present moment of knowing seems fading, grasped at by intellect through images but held only fitfully in memory as now already "one moment past." Such seem the conditions to memory. St. Augustine speaks tellingly to the relation of intuitive desire as supported by memory in his *Confessions*. The argument in his "A Philosophy of Memory" and "Time and Eternity" (Books 10 and 11) proved a rescue to Eliot in his "Romantic" dilemma of intuition besieged by time, as they well might have to Wordsworth and Keats under their circumstantial labors.

The very finitudes of intellect thus seem to entrap intellect in history, seem to decree that memory in relation to desire dooms intellect to an entrapment by its own past as past event weighting memory residually and seemingly preventing a present encounter with truth by the dislo-

---

"poetry and in his Preface, a profound spiritual revival, an inspiration communicated rather to Pusey and Newman, to Ruskin, and to the great humanitarians, than to accredited poets of the next generation." One surely adds to the list Eliot gives Gerard Manley Hopkins.

cation of desire to its own history, to time past and passing. It is this confused reduction of memory's office that both Keats and Wordsworth struggle to surmount, for they would escape history's entrapment, that graveyard of nature vividly in decay. And so each is in this respect *modern*, if we may wrest that term from its abuse and transform it to a deeper Thomistic dimension. If Thomistic realism is valid, its salient nature is that it is always modern in that it is concerned most of all with this present moment of this particular, concerned soul. That soul by its concern is always presently vulnerable to the distortions of its realistic position if it fail to orient its inescapable attention to past or future by reference to an abiding present. That is the danger Eliot encounters when he comes to see at least, with the help of St. Augustine, I believe, a dimension to memory larger than the limit of history:

> This is the use of memory;
> For liberation—not less of live but expanding
> Of love beyond desire, and so liberation
> From the future as well as the past.

Such is the "key" that both Wordsworth and Keats almost recover to the rescue of each's person in a present moment bordering upon vision.

Eliot is surely right in praising Wordsworth as a great philosophical poet, since Wordsworth is intent upon the significant question of intellectual existence in its present circumstances. Wordsworth's concern is first for an epistemology that might rescue intellect from its isolation from reality and restore soul to a reality intuited in the present sensual moment. Surely Gilson is right, in *Methodical Realism*, to chide us for a modernist obsession with epistemology. But surely that is a concern to be anticipated once Cartesian ideology has so generally separated intellect from reality. Happily, the soul is always attempting to come to terms with reality in this moment of its existence—in a presence of itself to being—whatever tangential uses it may make of time past, or passing, or to come. It can do so, it supposes, only if it regains a confidence in its capacity to know reality here and now, beyond the shadowing of knowledge by time. That is, in Eliot's term, the soul first and last (such is the burden of discursive intellect) seeks a *still point* in the turning world. In Wordsworth's less well-known term, it seeks a *spot of time*.

What these prudent Romantics Wordsworth and Eliot reach toward intuitively through such metaphor, attempting to put time in its subordinate relation to being, is a recovery to intellect of what we term Thomistic realism. They do so at risk of melancholy if not deep despair if they fail. Moved intuitively, the poet struggles to recover a knowledge of being beyond mere thoughts about being, however ill-equipped he may be as philosopher to do so, or however much he may think himself by the pervasiveness of Cartesian idealism. We ought to note that actually this idealism in Western thought has been principal antagonist to the poet's recovery in community at least since the advent of Renaissance Humanism, a demarcation point recognized to a degree by the nineteenth-century Romantic, as evidenced by his attempt to return to the Middle Ages to discover where we began wandering in the darkening woods of this world, sometimes led, sometimes followed by the poet. One need only recall Pico della Mirandola's words in his *Oration on the Dignity of Man,* whereby Pico puts words in God's mouth addressed to Man: "You shall determine your own nature without constraint from any barriers, by the means of the freedom whose power I have intrusted [to] you.... I have made you neither heavenly nor earthly, neither mortal nor immortal so that, like a free and sovereign artificer, you might mold and fashion yourself into that form you yourself shall have chosen." A sufficient license to the poet as freed artificer is implicit, Pico prophetic of Joyce's Stephen Dedalus.

And so it may be an irony suited to the amusement of a Socrates that our age, which so highly values its sophistications of intellect, is so much obsessed with the problem of epistemology. For that is a problem early to philosophical approaches to a metaphysics, whose analogy might perhaps be the child's wonderful awakening amid multitudinous existences, his struggling to keep straight the names of things. Eliot of course shared with his nineteenth-century predecessors—as do we all—a capacity of recovery to reality limited by epistemological confusions. That is why he at last sees himself like them and not superior to them as he had at first supposed. For he comes to know all too well that the poet's and the philosopher's medium, the sign, much decayed in that authority anchored in reality, proves increasingly uncertain in its manifestations through idealist dislocations of thought. But uncertainty about knowing does not prove the uncertainty of that reality itself toward which poet and philosopher reach through signs:

> Words strain,
> Crack and sometimes break, under the burden,
> Under the tension, slip, slide, perish,
> Decay with imprecision, will not stay in place,
> Will not stay still.

It will never occur to the Thomistic realist, Gilson says, to make "thought the starting point of his reflections, because for him a thought is only possible where there is first of all knowledge." Such is the truth lost to Keats and to Wordsworth, leaving them threatened by thought as somehow alien to their true nature. For it seems to them that thought intrudes as if an invading malignancy, reducing intuitive knowledge to an illusion. The truth which is held as knowledge from an intellectual experience of being is thus obscured, leaving only an ephemeral beauty, faintly remembered from past experience, a forlorn means to rescue. As Keats puts the concern, here in this time and place we find that

> but to think is to be full of sorrow
> And leaden-eyed despairs.

The experience of a being *per se* which is anterior to thought appears to thought itself as always "past," just how long past not the issue. Only its pastness seems of concern. Thus Wordsworth returns to his childhood in an attempt to solve the mystery of memory. Keats in the instance of his "Ode to a Nightingale" remembers a transport through the nightingale's song freed of thought's curse. But it *was* a moment, a past, though "but one moment past."

It is only by a wavering faith in beauty that this illusive truth may be certified as having existed if one lose the experience of that truth which is the gift of being *per se* to intellect, a gift requiring no desperate certification by thought. What is required first of all is an open acceptance of that gift. But, alas for ephemeral Beauty! It is inadequate in that "Romantic" arrest to establish Truth. In that perspective as divorced from reality—the recognition to the soul of its exile—Beauty cannot be itself established intellectually as resting in Truth. And merely to interchange terms, to declare that "Beauty is Truth, Truth Beauty," is to bite the ashes of being, an empty sign. Intellect is thus reduced to that Keatsean condition wherein *person*, either as poet or as man, "grows pale and spectre-thin and dies" toward the oblivion of nonexistence, through having declared all existence illusional. That is Keats's personal prospect as a young man struggling to reconcile Beauty's fading attraction to intellect as he has experienced it in the world's conspicuous decay. It is also Gerontion's prospect as Eliot dramatizes this Keatsean dilemma in the "little old man" who speaks his poem, and in "Gerontion" Eliot is himself still endangered by despair.

A reconciliation of mind and heart, of rational and intuitive modes of intellect, is not satisfactorily made by assertion alone, but the will's forcing signs beyond their proper limit of measure of reality by finite intellect, however strong the desire for reconciliation or how moving the words that would justify desire in the user of words. Very soon after

"Tintern Abbey," Wordsworth experienced the shock of a death close to him, the death of a person who apparently only at the moment of her death was approaching the age Wordsworth remembers as his own when "like a roe" he

> bounded o'er the mountains, by the sides
> Of the deep rivers, and the lonely streams
> Wherever nature led.

Nature, through death, seems at last to have betrayed that child despite her opening love for creation. The experience left the high sentences of "Tintern Abbey" empty, those that declare that "Nature never did betray the heart that loved her." The famous "Lucy" poems are in this respect a recantation of the argument of "Tintern Abbey," and after those poignant poems Wordsworth turns somewhat desperately toward Platonism as reflected in his "Ode on Intimations of Immortality from Recollections of Early Childhood," in which he attempts to go back earlier than the roe-like stage that seemed visionary at the time of "Tintern Abbey." Such a visionary moment, he comes now to believe, was actually an illusion advanced through the trickery of thought. Lulled by thought's "remoter charm," thought's seeming separation of consciousness from reality it now appears, he must now conclude himself seduced thereby into a "slumber" of spirit in which his intellect sojourned still disjoined from waking reality.

That is the way Wordsworth puts it in those two moving quatrains beginning "A slumber did my spirit seal." In that slumber he "had no human fears," since he saw "Lucy" as a "thing that could not feel/ The touch of earthly years." Now she is a "thing" in quite another sense, being dead: a thing with no "motion . . . no force," who "neither hears nor sees" her loved things in nature. A pathos of loss in the words prevents self-excoriation, or a direct recantation of those high, now seemingly empty pronouncements recorded in "Tintern Abbey," though even in his lamentations Wordsworth cannot at last entirely reject the memory of visionary moments. For in that recovery of emotional balance called the "Intimations Ode," itself heavy with illusional high sentences, he cries that loss as once real. This present May day world, and a memory of other days in glad nature, now speak only to him "of something that is gone":

> Whither is fled the visionary gleam?
> Where is it now, the glory and the dream?

That gleam out of nature, a "glory" hallowing creation, will be spoken to more effectively by a later "Romantic" poet, Hopkins.

Meanwhile, it remained to Eliot to pick up Wordsworth's "Tintern Abbey" slumber in his opening gambit as anti-Romantic poet. Wordsworth had declared the "mind" a "mansion for all lovely form" and "memory . . . a dwelling place/ For all sweet sounds and harmonies." This metaphor Eliot gives a sardonic twist. Not a mansion, but a run-down tenement wherein are housed "a thousand sordid images" holding awareness itself hostage. It will not be till Eliot reaches the point of view upon reality reflected in "Ash-Wednesday" that he will be prepared to rescue from Wordsworth, and from Keats, their intuitive inclination of intellect which by their "thought" becomes reduced from truth to illusion. And in that rescue intellect becomes enabled to move the soul beyond nature and history, from which rescue follows a return to nature and history to see them "for the first time," the poet having learned at last both "to care and not to care."

In that movement which Eliot experiences, vision is a possibility to intellect in its pursuit of truth which is relatively independent of nature and history, a possibility through which the soul through grace may at any moment or in any place of its journey find light through the dark woods it journeys. Such is that "still point of the turning world" in which the world and history and time are "redeemed." Thus intuition restores a present vision, aided by memory but beyond a memory supposed limited by history, either personal or general. Memory is thus no longer circumscribed by and reduced to the world, including that little world of the finite particular intellect seemingly confined and "peculiar and private" to itself as F. H. Bradley asserted of it. What is restored is a possibility of a present experience of reality through which the soul may recover its prospect upon timeless being: this *very* present, in which alone intellect ever sees truly the truth of things, sees into "the life of things," to quote again from "Tintern Abbey." In that recovery, intellect beholds all things sustained in being by their cause and proper end, each thing according to its given nature. Intellect, thus having made a journey from a pre-conceptual harmony with being, discovers itself possessed of a knowledge antecedent to its conceptual awakening and journeying toward the soul's proper end. It is enabled thereby to return, as Eliot has it, to the "place" from which it set out and "know the place for the first time." Such is the possible reconciliation of the soul to time and place, once freed of the entrapments of time and place. Then the soul may conclude that, in the words of Dame Julian and Eliot, "all manner of thing shall be well." It will have learned how "to care and not to care."

It is in this circumstance of intellect alive to being that one may also conclude with Gilson that "the Good, the True and the Beautiful are in the fullest sense real, since they are simply being itself as desired, known and admired." As for the poet or philosopher, this new life of intellect depends for its proper feeding upon those correspondences discovered in existent things as proper to the thing in its own nature and limit, and not an attribution *upon* the thing by intellect itself as dictator of the order of conception. For conception is anchored in reality and not imposed by the willed desire for order by intellect. What is thus to be discovered is the limits of the truth of particular things within—a community of being. It is here that significant metaphor at last must rest—*significant* signing of the thing's truth rather than form imposed by intellect upon the thing and declared the thing's truth by virtue of intellectual imposition. Or so Thomistic realism holds. There must follow, from poet or philosopher, the obligation of his peculiar art whereby he recovers sign, he recovers metaphor and analogy beyond the impatient inclinations to mere attribution. In brief, the labor is to recover sign as oriented by being itself as seen in the light of the concept of that proper proportionality whereby things *are* as they *specifically* are.[2]

That growth to intellectual liveliness requires no formulaic concept, though intellect may profit from concept prudently formulated, a necessity to intellectual community as distinct from the reflective and meditative harmony possible to the separate, distinct soul. Nevertheless, the end suitably issuing from communal intellect, from minds engaged in a common recovery of the meaning of the mind's journey in reality, a recovery on the soul's behalf, is a rediscovery of the meditative state suited to the solitary, though not lonely, intellect in its reflective journeying. This is to say that the discrete participant in intellectual community tends, intentionally if not tacitly so, toward a post-conceptual harmony of soul such as contemplation sometimes allows the solitary soul. That is why St. Thomas sets contemplation as the intellect's highest office. Intellect moves toward contemplation through metaphysical reflection, aided by such rationalized pursuit of metaphysical vision as St. Thomas's "principle of proper proportionality."

In the end, each of us is "Romantic," whether poet or philosopher, and may be strengthened in our intuitive journey, through which in the end we return to the place from which we set out intellectually, return to a recognition that intellect possesses knowledge as a gift from an initial and initiating experience anterior to the movement of intellect through concepts. That recognition justifies, in a Thomistic sense, the

---

2. The phrase "things *are* as they *specifically* are" intends to catch the relation between *being* and *specific* being, between the thing as it shares being and the thing which is concomitantly—even as it is consequentially—the thing that it is by essence.

journey, accommodating the will to knowledge as always a gift to intellect. One of the immediate ways of strengthening intellect on its journey is to turn to St. Thomas's "On Being and Essence." The poet will find there a protection against the temptation to constitute his awareness as a little world revolving arrogantly or helplessly on the uncertain axis of his own self-awareness, as it seemed to do to Eliot at his setting out. Nor will he feel justified by the illusion of autonomy, as if freed by awareness of all worlds other than the signing self, supposing that self thereby empowered to reconstitute being by attribution. That proved an irresistible temptation to Joyce and Stevens and Pound as poets.

If we fail to determine this proper point for intellect's embarkation, we shall be endangered by an illusional state of mind whereby thought attributes being to the intellect as being's causal agent. To make that error is to find in our signs only a reflection of our lone self, an intolerable company to keep in the increasingly isolated state, more and more separated from the inexhaustible wonder of encompassing being through which one makes his way toward that end of perfection of gift which the Fathers and Doctors call Beatitude. Failing that drawing of our intuitive inclination to a proper end, one can hardly escape such despair as threatens Keats, "where but to think is to be filled with sorrow and leaden-eyed despair." Joyce at the end feared darkly such error: that as maker he had succumbed to fancy over the gift of liberating imagination. Pound, in the final fragments of his *Cantos*, feels forced to confess "I am not a demigod,/ I cannot make it cohere" and to call for "A little light, like a rushlight/ to lead back to splendour." *Splendour* here seems to touch, whether intended to do so or not, on Wordsworth's lament over having lost that "splendour in the grass," that halo of presence in being which is beyond the power of attribution.

Symbol, sign, has for a hundred years and more gradually turned mirror of the self, rather than a window opening the self to reality. For the most part, our poets, however much entrapped by confusions out of Cartesian idealism (a generic term we have said and not historical), continue disquieted by the entrapment in their own signs. That is why our age in its letters has been the Age of Melancholy, the Age of Alienation from being, the Age of Emotional Pathos. Such is a state of intellect little propitious to the highest prospects of art's celebrations of Beauty. Our "Romantic" poetry nevertheless, even in its failures, bears witness to a truth to be pondered beyond Beauty's allure. It bears witness to the timeless, continuing hunger in intellect stirred toward recovery of a key to open intellect to reality, both to its own reality and to the diversity of that modernist philosophical mystery, the Other, from which it senses its disturbing isolation. That opening may at last issue upon the transcendent as intellect's proper causal end no less than its giving beginning. Such is, I believe, always the proper "future" of Thomism, which is not a future of temporal implication but a present still point in which the soul is reconciled to time past, passing, and to come. In such still points come visionary glimpses of an abiding Presence, which Eliot came to speak of as the "Word in the desert." Those glimpses, which is knowledge understood, however limited that knowledge and that understanding by intellectual finitude, is a glimpse of the reality of that Cause of intellect and of its journeying. We may well say *glimpse*, rather than *vision*, for such is our impatience that vision seems to promise a continuing resting of the intellectual eye upon truth. St. Thomas might well remind us that it is given only to the Eye holding all creation to rest in vision in what is metaphorically an unwavering and everlasting "seventh day." Granted only glimpses of that Presence, from Whom all things have (as Eliot say of those roses in a garden at Burnt Norton) the look of things that are looked at beyond our limited sight—granted only such glimpse of being seen as we struggle to see as struggle we must, we may be content to rest while journeying. One may, as Eliot found necessary be at once "still and still moving." Or, in Keats's version, one may find himself "being capable of being in uncertainties, Mysteries, doubts," content in knowing if not fully understanding that all manner of thing shall be well at last.

Thomism and Practical/Public Philosophy

Vittorio Possenti

It is well known that studies on public philosophy and public ethics have greatly increased in number over the past twenty years, fostered as they have been by the *Rehabilitierung der praktischen Philosophie*, which has mainly interested the practical philosophy of Aristotle and Kant. For a while now, the question of practical reason has been placed at the center of the debate, with contributions from the main schools: phenomenology, hermeneutics, critical theory, neo-Aristotelianism, neo-Kantism, critical Rationalism, analytical philosophy, etc. Regardless of the final judgment made on that debate, whether or not the results are to be judged positively or not, or whether they have underlined the serious limits of contemporary research into moral philosophy, it must be stated that the Thomistic school has not significantly contributed to it except marginally. And yet it would seem that this school possesses solid arguments for a revival of practical philosophy linked with ontology and anthropology, which method has normally been set aside by many contemporary moral philosophies. What is more, the collapse of Marxism has accentuated the need for a long-term confrontation between Thomistic-Christian ethics and the rationalist, "liberal" and emotivistic ones. I would like to thematize the above arguments, beginning with a few reflections on the relationship between ethics and metaphysics and on the status of practical reason.

I. Metaphysics and Ethics

Over a pluri-millenary period, the task of ethics can fundamentally be reassumed in replying to the three questions around which moral discourse rotates: (a) what is good and what is evil, and why? (b) what is the *summum bonum* for man? (c) how must one live, given that he who acts well perfects himself, while acting badly he degrades himself? The very meaning of these interrogatives establishes the nature of ethics as a knowledge of a speculative-practical type: speculative in its structure and practical in its object (human action) and its aim (directing action).

Since the Enlightenment, the answer to these interrogatives has become a real riddle, despite the great vitality which qualifies contemporary ethics. This is mainly due to the crisis of the notion of the Good.

The passages thanks to which the question of Good, of vital importance in Greek and medieval thought, has ceased to occupy a satisfactory place in modern philosophy are sufficiently known. I am not simply referring to the substitution of the scheme of virtues with that of the passions inaugurated by Hobbes, nor to the much less developed treatment of the problem of the Good in the great modern philosophers. In these, there has been such a shift that the central problem of practical philosophy is no longer the teleological orientation of human action toward the Good, but rather the critical-justificatory discussion on moral obligation, values, norms or, more simply, the means of the *Pursuit of Happiness*. Equally linked to this shift is the abandoning of the problem of the *summum bonum* for man already remarked on by Kant: "The question of the *summum bonum* seems to have fallen into disuse, or at least it has become a merely secondary question."[1]

Noncognitivist currents have adopted procedural and "weak" versions of the theory of the Good. It is not clear what the area of the universal on which it bases itself might be, faced as it is with a conflicting plurality of ethical codes. The call to democratic pluralism and democratic tolerance is insufficient, as it does not constitute a rational criterion of choice, but merely a variable empirical parameter. Without a common rational base, it is difficult to avoid tolerance for all positions. Versions of "neo-Enlightenment" public ethics are alive today in the dichotomy between the area of the universal (progressively minimal) and tolerance for every code (progressively maximal).

In underlining the function of theoretical philosophy, do we assume overly onerous obligations for public philosophy? In order to answer this question, it might be helpful to distinguish between the philosophical level and the practical level. In the former it is necessary to assume "metaphysical obligations," because this is in keeping with the nature of philosophy as an attempt to see the very nature of reality: only what is valid in principle for everyone can pretend to be considered obligatory for everyone. In the field of concrete action the problem is a different one, because to live and cooperate within society it is not indispensable, although desirable, for everyone to share the same speculative principles. It might well be sufficient to agree to, albeit for very different reasons, a certain "practical frame" of norms and values.

After Kant, it has become a commonplace to separate metaphysics and morals. Positivism and neopositivism have accepted this assumption: for these currents, "nature" is only physical nature, a vast complex of phenomena subjected to determinism and therefore deprived of any relationship with morality. Without this notion of nature, in which the

---

1. *Critica della ragion pratica* (Bari: Laterza, 1963), p. 82.

Kantian heritage is very tenacious, and from which every ontological connotation and finality have disappeared, it would not be possible to maintain Hume's "great division" between "is" and "ought." We do not oppose the world of (human) nature, of being and *telos* to the world of morality and freedom, but we root the latter in the former: the world of freedom/morality necessarily presupposes that of being, at least that of human nature of which freedom is one of the attributes. It is therefore necessary that practical reason requires theoretical reason for several grounds: (1) moral good is a particularization of ontological good; (2) the notions of value, aim, norm, law, merit and freedom, that is all the fundamental systematic notions which along with the notion of the Good give structure to ethics, possess analogical meaning and are at least in part studied by metaphysics; and (3) what is more, existential moral truth is measured in reference to the rectitude of will, directed toward the real aims of human life. And these are not known to practical reason without the intervention of theoretical reason, which reveals some of the premises regarding the being and the absolute, which qualify as meaningful the search for an aim.

II. Speculative Knowledge and Practical Knowledge

Moral philosophy therefore presupposes speculative philosophy and ethics metaphysics. This does not imply that the former be reduced to only a partial aspect or a mere deduction of the latter, because the respective paradigms of rationality are different, given that practical knowledge is subdivided into numerous levels so as to match the extremely complex structure of moral experience. Once this has been admitted, there still remains the fact that metaphysics is, for practical knowledge, an illuminating support which discloses its sense. In his *Scienza nuova prima*, Vico observes that there cannot be a science of moral things without the fundamental help of the truths conquered by metaphysics. This is linked with the unity of the intellect: the speculative intellect, the aim of which is the consideration of truth, and the practical intellect, aiming at ruling human action, are not two separate faculties but a single one. *Intellectus speculativus per extensionem fit practicus*, said the Scholastics.

The difference between speculative knowledge and practical knowledge can briefly be summarized as follows (the scheme, in fact, should be divided up even further):

(1) (relative) autonomy of *praxis* from *theoria*;
(2) difference between *praxis* and *techne* (between ethical-po-

litical-practical knowledge and technical knowledge);
(3) value of practical knowledge, which lies between the necessary knowledge of speculative cognition and purely opinable knowledge (*doxa*);
(4) difference both in the aims (knowledge for the sake of knowledge in theory; knowledge for the sake of action in practical philosophy) and in the argumentative procedure (apodeictic=theory; topical-dialectical=practical knowledge).

The rift between metaphysics and morals, between ontological nature and freedom, renders the situation of ethics very precarious. The terminal point of the process is the thesis of "ethics without truth," which, incidentally, is the equivalent of a death sentence in reference to both morality and moral philosophy. On the other hand, the refusal of the Aristotelian tradition in moral philosophy, a central event in the moral science of the last few centuries, began at a theoretical level with the critique and the abandoning of the notions of *telos*, of human essence with its aim/*telos*, and of the possibility of knowing good. In Aristotle, the framing of practical knowledge requires the availability of theoretical knowledge, without however having to accept the thesis according to which the former is merely deduced from the latter. That it is not possible to recover practical Aristotelian knowledge without also taking up his metaphysics has been affirmed, for example, by Manfred Riedel. Phronesis/prudentia is not, by itself, able to build up practical knowledge. The rehabilitation of practical philosophy along Aristotelian lines has attempted to go beyond this aspect. But in the long run, it is fruitless to consider as valid Aristotelian practical philosophy when Aristotelian metaphysics has been dismissed as dead.

III. The Basic Scheme of Moral Science: Some Indications

There are four contributions that must come into play in the constitution of ethics as a science: an anthropological notion, articulated according to the two aspects of human nature—"as-it-is" and "as-it-ought-to-be-if-it-were-aware-of-its-essence-and-reached-its-*telos*"; a notion of the Good; a set of norms on good and evil. By operating on these levels, what is constituted is, for the essential or at its peak, moral science. We must be careful, however, that the various phases of practical rationality, which also incorporates the institution of the relationship between *phronesis*, virtue, eudaemonia, etc. are not exhausted. The moral science scheme, mentioned above and handed down up to the Enlightenment, is essentially given in the *Nicomachean Ethics* and is teleological.

It is well known that much of the Aristotelian argumentation is polarized by the determination of the best *telos* for man. An anthropological notion is also introduced, or rather the idea of human nature, along with the doctrine of the rational parts of the soul and of its more noble part which is open to the divine. The indication of "man-as-he-ought-to-be" is another strong aspect of the scheme, which also presupposes the doctrine of the act and of power: the movement from "man-as-he-is" to "as-he-ought-to-be" is a growing actualization. In its turn, good, which is what all things desire, is the aim. By attaining it, man accomplishes and actualizes his essential nature. Markedly teleological, Aristotelian ethics left somewhat in the background the concepts of value and absolute obligation, which had already been hinted at by Plato and which later received new light from Christian ethics.

It is intuitively acceptable that to leave out one or more of the four contributions cited above from the building of ethics would be equivalent to disorganizing it and throwing it into confusion. Yet this is how many Enlightenment and post-Enlightenment ethics operated, generally using their weapons against the concept of human *telos* and of "man-as-he-ought-to-be-if-he-were-to-realize-his-essence" (which is a notion that some thinkers have attempted to stifle in ethics), and against a certain metaphysics of good and of value. From this point on, the task of moral science became the burden of Sisyphus, as there is no rational mediation capable of linking the two residual levels, which therefore remain extraneous to one another and reciprocally unintelligible: what have man as he is and how he acts, in fact, to do with the universe of moral norms? What origin, foundation or sense does this possess? The task of ethics becomes a desperate one because moral laws cannot be deduced from empirical facts (and in this Hume was quite correct), if not in the statistical form of customs and average social behavior. But in this case, we are no longer at the normative level of moral philosophy, but rather in the field of the sociology of morality.

Kant, who inherited the outline of the moral problem from the Enlightenment, adding his objections regarding metaphysics and finality, tried to escape an almost impossible situation, without however being able to completely conceal the *impasse* in which moral philosophy found itself. Once speculative reason failed to give its support in knowing the *telos* and the Good, there was nothing for it but to base the imperatives of moral law on themselves, that is on the self-legislation of pure practical reason. This was a coherent solution, given the premises; that it is also a solid solution is another matter. In Kant, the project still maintains a certain stability, because it was secretly nourished by the influence of the Christian moral tradition, which was still rather diffuse in his era and which outlined a sufficient profile of the *bonus vir* and his virtues. But after him? Basing morality on itself means exposing oneself to the temptation of reworking it *ad libitum* and of denying it, in the end, any cognitive value. The two paths have not infrequently been followed by post-Enlightenment moral philosophy. Among the most noteworthy consequences of the process there is the risk of a dissolution of the practical character of moral philosophy, represented by the "knowledge to direct action" sequence. In the noncognitivist position, moral philosophy cannot know; therefore it cannot expect to direct action except on emotivist and irrational bases, which would no longer be a "directing" but rather a "letting" things occur as they occur. Loss of the practical character of ethics is a direct consequence of the loss of its cognitive character.

IV. The Impasse of Modern Ethics and Nietzsche

The project of modern moral science, regardless of its variegated and extensively diversified nature in many details, is unified at least negatively, as it has more or less moved away from the principles of moral science itself. Hume based morality on the passions; Kant on the self-legislation of pure practical reason; Kierkegaard on the general (ethics for him is the general, and in that he remained dependent on Hegel in his opposition); Scheler on emotional intuition; Sartre on freedom; Moore maintained that the idea of good was undefinable. Opposed to one another in several assumptions and notions, each criticizes the others and yet all of them refute the linking of metaphysics and ethics, nor do they succeed in giving back to reason its command over ethics. "From then on," writes Alasdair MacIntyre, "the ethics of culture which preceded us (and therefore also our own) lost all logical basis and publicly acceptable justification. In a world of secular rationality, religion could no longer give such a background and common foundation for moral discourse and action; and the fact that philosophy had failed in its attempt to furnish what religion was no longer able to give was one of the most important causes for its loss of a fundamental cultural role and its transformation into a marginal, strictly academic issue."[2]

---

2. Alasdair MacIntyre, *Dopo la virtù* (Milan: Feltrinelli, 1988), p. 68. For the current paper, I have drawn inspiration from MacIntyre's diagnosis, according to which the Enlightenment project of a justification of morality was destined to fail because of the intimate incoherence of the underlying conceptual scheme, but I have added to his diagnosis an essential point which *Dopo la virtù* overlooks or in any case leaves too implicit: that is, the beginning of the dissolutive process in the Aristotelian

The crisis of modern moral science, which had gained ground in the eighteenth century and reached its peak in the nineteenth, came about in two phases: in the first, there was a disintegration of classical moral science, and in the second philosophy was no longer able to substitute it with another, equally powerful one capable of legitimately replying to the vital questions posed by moral experience. Many versions of moral science were born, each of them in disagreement regarding the task of reason in moral experience, whether, that is, its role should have been executive or auxiliary, on the function of the passions, interests, and so on. Ethics was split into two directions: one logical-normative, the other empirical-positivist.

The heritage we are faced with in ethics is the crisis of rationalism, which in various versions leads to a complete dualism between "is" and "ought," which it declares itself incapable of mediating. At this point, rationalism is reversed into the irrationalism of ethics without truth and ethical emotivism, with which it eliminates itself: the use of reason is invoked in order to suppress reason. And the choice for reason is intended as an act of faith: in this case it will be necessary, as in Popper, to speak of the irrational basis of rationalism.[3]

But the person responsible for pushing the *destructio* of ethics to its extreme was Nietzsche with the conjoined use of the genealogical method and that of suspicion. In his writings, the modern *volo* reaches its terminal stage, marked as it is by the abandoning of the capital doctrine of *nous/intellectus*. Nietzsche has demonstrated in negative that moral reason crumbles if the light of the theoretical one is extinguished and if the intentional opening out of the *intellectus* to being does not take place.

V. Recent Attempts at Renewal: Hermeneutics and Ethics of Discourse

Hermeneutics and the ethics of discourse currently constitute two paths followed by moral research. The former has promoted, with

---

tradition and the incapability of the *novatores* to establish ethics were due to the crisis of theoretical reason, with the consequent decline of the intellectual perception of Good/Value.

3. Let us cite just one of Popper's many assertions: "It . . . is certainly impossible to demonstrate the correctness of any ethical principle or talk in its favour as if it were a scientific assertion. Ethics is not a science. But even when there is no scientific-rational basis for ethics, there is however an ethical basis for science and rationalism" (K. R. Popper, *Die öffene Gesellschaft* [Bern-München, 1970], 2: 283). According to Popper, all of the discussions on the definition of the Good or on the possibility of defining it are absolutely useless.

Gadamer's fortunate *Warheit und Methode*, the rehabilitation of practical philosophy, maintaining the actuality of Aristotelian ethics and its concept of *phronesis*: in this it has found allies in the work of Hannah Arendt, Wilhelm Hennis, and Joachim Ritter. The hermeneutic method tends to interpret documents and traditions belonging to the past, adroitly giving them life and grasping their potential meaning for the present. However, as the direct access to being is still precluded along this path, it is only with difficulty that the hermeneutic method in ethics can go beyond a wise comprehension of the situation, a discerning homage to rules arising from the past, or a recuperation of the link between reason and decision. It can conciliate reason and decision by virtue of phronetic or prudential knowledge capable of guiding action; but only within a cultural horizon assumed as given and almost untranscendable, in which the act of interpreting is for the most part never closed off and always in process. Gadamer claims: "A definitive interpretation would in itself be a contradiction."[4] One might well ask: Where would the contradiction be? His hermeneutic method adopts a "weak" neo-Aristotelian paradigm because in taking up elements from the Aristotelian practical philosophical, hermeneutics has detached them from the overall scheme of his speculative philosophy, which is no longer held to be acceptable. The division that separates what once formed a unity runs the risk of invalidating the very recuperation of practical discourse. It is not clear if Gadamer's hermeneutics, in its resolute opposition to the models of rationality proposed by positivistic scientism, is able to find an access to being which is different from the infinite process of interpreting, mediated by the various cultural languages (juridical, theological, artistic, classical texts).

Despite their merits, the communicative ethics themselves, based on a pragmatic-universal method (Habermas) or a pragmatic-transcendental one (Apel), assume as given a ground which is not subject to careful scrutiny: the complete disconnection of ethics from metaphysics. And in this, as in other factors, they are still part of the Kantian school. Both are aware of having tried to reformulate Kantian moral theory on the problem of the foundation of norms through the categories of the theory of communication. Despite these common intents, there are three points which divide Apel's and Habermas's ethics from Kant: it relinquishes the distinction between the intelligible and the phenomenic; it goes beyond the interiorizing and monological Kantian framework, aiming at a public intersubjective discourse; it thinks it has resolved the foundational problem of ethics eluded by Kant via a deferment to the "fact of reason" (the experience of being obliged by duty).

---

4. *La ragione nell'età della scienza*, p. 83.

The specific performance assigned by Apel to the ethics of discourse is that of a rational "final foundation" of the *moral point of view*, and along with this that of a "confutation of moral skepticism and relativism."[5] His position, and that of Habermas, is *cognitivist* (but in a restricted sense as it excludes the discourse on *telos*, virtues, and happiness from the arguments that can be treated in ethics), *formalistic* because it does not indicate material contents and norms, universalist, *anti-relativist*, and, within certain limits, *deontological*. These are also the characteristics of Kantian ethics, which also adds a particular emphasis to duty and intention: do what you have to do, whatever happens. As for the foundation of material norms, this is left to "practical discourses" (Apel), despite the reformulation of the categorical imperative according to an ethics of responsibility carried out by Apel. The traits we have just listed, which represent the advantages of the ethics of discourse, do not, I think, make up for its limits: procedural ethics, completely cut off from metaphysics, light years away from our substantial moral intuitions.

VI. Ethical Neo-Aristotelianism (MacIntyre) and Thomism

In his *After Virtue*, Alasdair MacIntyre has undertaken a brilliant study of moral philosophy through the history of philosophy. His text has been amply read and commented, and this precludes the necessity of a wide-ranging introduction. Going straight to the point, I would like to state what I consider to be the positive points and the less convincing aspects of his diagnosis.

The following should be ascribed to the positive aspects: (1) the close and documented critique of Enlightenment and post-Enlightenment moral philosophy; particularly noteworthy are the diagnoses of analytical philosophy and ethical emotivism; (2) the suggestion that the Aristotelian ethical tradition should be recovered once more in one of its various forms as the suitable path in order to elude the bankruptcy of contemporary moral science; (3) the idea that a moral scheme as tested and ancient as the one set out in the *Nicomachean Ethics* must have grasped some essential note in human moral experience if, despite its age, it comes up again and again and has been integrated, albeit with some corrections, into Christian thought; and (4) the underlining of the condition of undecidability in contemporary moral discourse.

As for the less convincing aspects in MacIntyre's discourse, they might be summarized as follows:

---

5. K. O. Apel, "Limiti dell'etica del discorso?" in *Etiche in dialogo*, ed. K. O. Apel et al. (Genoa: Marietti, 1990), p. 31.

(1) the connection between ethics and metaphysics is never explicitly thematized, even if there are interspersed hints which offer the possibility of further analysis. The failure of the Enlightenment moral project does not begin with the abandoning of the paradigm of Aristotelian ethics, but with the attack on metaphysics and concepts such as *telos*, nature, and good, necessary for the constitution of ethics. Let us spend some time on the concept of the Good, the analysis of which depends, precisely, on metaphysics. In reference to this, the horizon is the same as the one put forward twenty years ago by John Rawls in *A Theory of Justice*, that is, the irrelevance and perhaps the unsolvability of the problem of good in public philosophy, the need to assume a *thin* theory of it and, above all, the priority of the Just over the Good. In reference to this, Michael Sandel has spoken of Rawls's liberalism, calling it precisely "deontological liberalism." Rawls's entire work is based on this frequently reproposed assumption, which overturns the essential sequence of the systematic concepts of moral philosophy. This is: Good-Obligation-Right-Just. Therefore, the Just is never the fundamental notion of practical reason.

(2) the theory of *lex naturalis* as the fundamental law of human morality has been omitted. Here, neo-Aristotelianism is a little undefended because in the *Nicomachean Ethics* there is not a complete philosophy of what is in force according to nature and not according to convention. In order to develop this theme it would have been necessary to direct one's attention to Christian philosophy and especially to Aquinas's thought.

In the Thomistic doctrine, the concept of *lex naturalis* is elucidated according to the notions of *participatio, vis illuminativa et directiva, inclinatio* and *connaturalitas*, which are determined in metaphysics and anthropology. The philosophy of natural law, situated at the crossroads between ethics and metaphysics, requires a corresponding deepening of both fields.

According to Walter Lippmann, "public philosophy is known as natural law"; on the other hand, the aim of political society is the common good. We can therefore consider the two notions of common good and *lex naturalis* as the ultimate cardinal points of public philosophy, whose tradition found its apex in the Declaration of Independence and, in our era, with the writings of W. Lippmann, J. Courtney Murray, J. Maritain, etc.

MacIntyre's work is a good start for the renaissance of moral science and public philosophy. But in order to lead this renaissance to a good end, it is necessary that Aquinas's metaphysical wisdom and his school bear their fruits. The future of Thomism also depends on the Thomists: over the past decades they have perhaps not given sign of sufficient courage, farsightedness and presence within the debate. About 60-70 years ago, the difficulties of public philosophy arose from the harsh blow afforded by totalitarianism. Now, with the end of that phase, they derive from within nontotalitarian cultures and countries. Public neutrality and public agnosticism are not a good deal for democracy. The renaissance of political science and practical reason will be a "resurgence" (revival, renaissance), or rather a new dawn of values, a purification of tradition, a return to a violated ideal order. Even public philosophy, just like peoples and nations, can be restored and flourished again only thanks to a deepening of its own tradition.

Part III
Theological Contexts and Purposes

Thomism After Thomism:
Aquinas and the Future of Theology

J. A. DiNoia, O.P.

"Thomas *after* Thomism?" you ask. While you may question the wisdom, you surely will want to acknowledge the courage of a speaker who proposes to address such a topic in a symposium where the memory and achievement of that quintessential Thomist, Jacques Maritain, are revered. Still, you wonder: can any sort of rigorous inquiry proceed under so dubious a banner? Allow me to explain.

My objective in this paper is to commend to Christian theologians a new reading of Aquinas's *Summa Theologiae*. I understand this reading to be an alternative to one that appears to have been standard in the neo-Thomistic movement, particularly in Gerald McCool's account of it. Hence, the talk here of a "post-neo-Thomistic" theological appropriation of Aquinas. The suggested reading depends on an account of the properly theological uses to which Aquinas put philosophical analysis and construction as he sought to exhibit the intelligibility of the Christian faith. I shall illustrate the viability of this reading with reference to two topics, one drawn from the beginning of the *Summa Theologiae* (the doctrine of the triune God) another drawn from the end (the doctrine of the sacraments). This discussion will serve to indicate the potential range of Aquinas's contribution to present and future theology. Though I mean to appeal to theologians, I shall strive to do so in ways that will be of interest to philosophers as well.

I

Writing in *Church History* fifteen years ago, historian Marcia Colish remarked that "a consideration of the historiography of Thomas's place in modern thought reveals the fact that the Angelic Doctor's substantial postmedieval reputation has not generally been matched by an equally plentiful measure of historical understanding. For two generations, historians of the Middle Ages have made great strides toward the systematic recovery of the historical Thomas Aquinas. But the task of uncovering the historical significance of his thought within the changing contexts of postmedieval culture still awaits its Grabmanns and Chenus."[1] The kind of historical account that Professor Colish has in mind here—and of which her essay provides an enticing sketch—has yet to be written. Nonetheless, thanks to Gerald McCool's work, we now possess at least a comprehensive philosophical interpretation of the most recent phase of the postmedieval career of the thought of Aquinas.[2]

In Fr. McCool's interpretation, this properly "neo-Thomistic" phase of postmedieval Thomism runs roughly from a mid-nineteenth-century revival, through the official commendation of Aquinas in Pope Leo XIII's encyclical *Aeterni Patris* in 1879, to its demise as a movement sometime in the Vatican II era. What defines the neo-Thomistic movement in Fr. McCool's account of it was its endeavor to found Christian theology upon a reconstruction of a coherent philosophical system based upon Aquinas's philosophical and theological writings. But, according to Fr. McCool, this endeavor—despite its remarkable achievements—can no longer be sustained. The arguably irreversible pluralization of philosophical perspectives in the postconciliar Catholic world and within twentieth-century Thomism itself has effectively subverted the quest for a unitary philosophical basis for theology that was the hallmark of the neo-Thomistic project.

Ongoing historical study of nineteenth and twentieth century Catholic theology—of the sort advocated by Professor Colish—will undoubtedly entail some important revisions of Fr. McCool's complex thesis. I shall not be suggesting such revisions here. Rather, I want to let Fr. McCool's analysis of the rise and fall of neo-Thomism give me license to wonder about the shape of a possible "post-neo-Thomistic" theological career for Aquinas.

Elsewhere I have ventured an interpretation of the relative eclipse of Aquinas in much late-twentieth-century Catholic theology, with the telling exception of transcendental Thomism.[3] It was not simply that in postconciliar Catholic theological circles, neo-Thomism—and with it Aquinas himself—came to be associated with resistance to the prevailing agendas of *ressourcement* (reaffirmation of Christian identity by ap-

---

1. Marcia L. Colish, "St. Thomas Aquinas in Historical Perspective: The Modern Period," *Church History* 44 (1975): 433.

2. Gerald A. McCool, *Catholic Theology in the Nineteenth Century: The Quest for a Unitary Method* (New York: Seabury, 1977); *From Unity to Pluralism: The Internal Evolution of Thomism* (New York: Fordham University Press, 1989). See Robert E. Lauder's discussion of these books in "On Being or Not Being a Thomist," *The Thomist* 55 (1991): 301-319.

3. J. A. DiNoia, "American Theology at Century's End: Postconciliar, Postmodern, Post-Thomistic," *The Thomist* 54 (1990): 499-518.

peal to its ancient sources) and *aggiornamento* (renewal through the modernization of Christian thought and institutions). More to the point—and here my interpretation converges with Fr. McCool's—neo-Thomism cultivated a reading of Aquinas's theological works that seemed to construe their diffuse philosophical components as a philosophical system which had in turn provided the basis of Aquinas's theology. Rightly or wrongly, this perception of the neo-Thomistic project fueled the opposition to it on the part of a growing number of theologians throughout the twentieth century. Many Catholic theologians came finally to be convinced that systematic use of Aquinas in theology would require the prior commitment to adopt the philosophical system that neo-Thomists claimed to have distilled from his works. Increasing pluralization in philosophy made it hard to sustain this kind of commitment and, according to Fr. McCool, in the end it just collapsed.

I want to get clear on what I understand to be the validity of this complaint about neo-Thomistic readings of Aquinas. Two points are relevant here.

In the first place, I want to avoid charging neo-Thomists with a misreading of Aquinas—as if there were some standard reading that furnished a measure for assessing assorted construals of his thought. This leads to the largely fruitless debate among conflicting claimants to his legacy. Like the legacy of Augustine and other great thinkers, the legacy of Aquinas is rich enough for many heirs to lay claim to portions of it, neo-Thomists as well as transcendental Thomists, not to mention Thomists of the strict observance, Maritainians, or contemporary Christian philosophers. Thus, I see no reason to rule out a reading of Aquinas that strives to derive a set of coherent philosophical positions—in natural philosophy, metaphysics, philosophical psychology, and moral philosophy—from his theological and philosophical writings and to field a reconstruction called "Thomism."

Secondly, the use made of Aquinas by neo-Thomists can be defended on historical grounds. They saw the distillation of a *philosophia perennis* as crucial to mounting a response to the challenge of modernity. In the view of many neo-Thomists (and other theologians as well), this challenge was in large measure a properly philosophical one, resting as it did on a long tradition of philosophical reflection stretching back to Descartes. Furthermore, philosophical errors were regarded as the root of typically modernistic theological positions. In such circumstances, philosophically oriented neo-Thomistic readings of Aquinas could justly claim both plausibility and effectiveness.[4]

---

4. See Aidan Nichols's discussion of the neo-Thomistic revival in *The Shape of Catholic Theology* (Collegeville, Minnesota: The Liturgical Press, 1991), pp. 328-43.

But I want to suggest an alternative way of construing the philosophical component in Aquinas's theology, one that avoids the impression that his theological positions are largely parasitic upon a philosophical system derivable from his thought. The importance of such a reading is that it focuses on the properly theological role—the formal interest—that philosophical analysis and construction play in Aquinas's arguments in the *Summa Theologiae*.

According to this reading, philosophical analysis and construction are moments intrinsic to theological thinking in the *Summa*, that is, to the ordered and progressive explication of the doctrines of the faith in such a way as to exhibit their intelligibility. The interweaving of philosophical analysis and construction in the web of theological argument in the *Summa* is in the service of properly theological affirmation. The outcome is not a theological/philosophical system, but a highly ramified complex of interrelated dialectical arguments, always open to embracing or engaging alternative positions that can be rationally justified.[5] The principle of unity and coherence is supplied by the mysteries of the faith in their own interconnection and intelligibility, itself rooted in the *scientia divina*. The exigencies of doctrinal and theological affirmation are seen to demand an unflinching theological realism, and it is for this reason that wide-ranging appeals are made to philosophy and other non-theological disciplines. At each turn in the larger argument, such appeals function as needed to secure the intelligibility of the doctrine under consideration, whether it be the concept of relation in the Trinity, or the concept of making in creation, or the concept of end in moral life, or the concept of disposition in grace and the virtues, and so on.

Neo-Thomists saw this, but they tended to formulate their perception in terms of the reconstruction of an all-encompassing speculative system. Whether or not this historical judgment of neo-Thomism can be sustained in every case, such a position can be usefully contrasted with the reading that is being suggested here—a reading in which coherence and integration are seen to be functions chiefly of an overarching theological vision rather than a philosophical system.

The aptness of this construal of the role of philosophical arguments in the *Summa* can be confirmed by contrast with readings of this work that are misreadings in a true sense. I have in mind readings that approach the *Summa* as if it were a theological encyclopedia. In such misreadings the *Summa Theologiae* is consulted as a compendium of self-contained entries on an assortment of theological topics. Persistent

---

5. I have been influenced in my formulation of this point by Alasdair MacIntyre's discussion of Aquinas in *Three Rival Versions of Moral Enquiry* (Notre Dame, Indiana: University of Notre Dame Press, 1990).

objects of such misreadings are the arguments for the existence of God (read as if they had some entity other than the Father, Son, and Holy Spirit in view) or Aquinas's early discussion of the problem of evil (construed in isolation from his treatment of sin in the Secunda Pars and redemption in the Tertia). In fact, each topic is expounded in connection with the rest and can only be fully understood in the setting of the whole. In this connection, a helpful analogy for picturing the place of the reader of the *Summa* is to imagine him or her standing at the mid-point of a sphere upon whose inner surface the text has been inscribed. In this way—to return to our concerns in this paper—one recognizes that the more conspicuously philosophical components have their logical home in an overarching theological argument explicating the mystery of God's gracious dealings with humankind from creation, in the incarnation, passion, death, resurrection, and glory of his Son, and through the sending of the Spirit.

The *Summa*'s sparing methodological passages support this reading of the role of philosophy in the explication of the Christian faith. Though transposed to a new—a "supernatural"—level of activity, ordinary patterns of human perception, thought, and language are internal to knowledge and talk about God in faith and, ultimately, in vision. According to Aquinas, the life of grace involves not the infusion of a set of capacities geared exclusively to engagement with God, but the transformation and empowerment of natural capacities for exercise at a new level. Hence, wherever relevant and appropriate, the results of nontheological inquiries as well as the logic of assertion and argument can be brought to bear on the theological explication of the contents of Christian faith. With respect to its overarching formal interest, theology is thus a field-encompassing field, and nontheological disciplines contribute to its pursuit of understanding and explication of divine revelation. Because of the prominence of the role of philosophy here, these issues are usually considered under the rubric "theology and philosophy." But other nontheological disciplines contribute to theological understanding and explication, notably literary criticism, history, sociology, psychology, and the natural sciences.[6]

---

6. This paragraph gathers several strands of Aquinas's thought on the nature of theological thinking, drawn particularly from his commentary on Boethius's *De Trinitate* and from the more self-consciously methodological passages in *Summa Theologiae* Ia. 1; 12-13; 32-42. For more thorough discussion of these issues, see J. A. DiNoia, "Authority, Public Dissent and the Nature of Theological Thinking," *The Thomist* 52 (1988): 185-207, and "Knowing and Naming the Triune God: The Grammar of Trinitarian Confession," in *Speaking the Christian God*, ed. Alvin F. Kimel (Grand Rapids, Michigan: Eerdmans, forthcoming). For a congruent reading of

At this juncture, we need some illustrations to grasp the significance of the suggested reading of the role of the philosophical component in Aquinas's theological arguments.

II

Consider first Aquinas's discussion of the triune God in *Summa Theologiae* Ia. 2-43. Here is a glaring instance of the difficulties posed by treating the philosophical components as independent of the overarching theological argument. In part, these difficulties stem from the textbook division of Aquinas's unified treatise on the triune God that became standard in the historical transmission of Aquinas's thought. According to this division, Ia. 2-26 (concerning the existence and nature of the triune God) was taken to constitute the tract "De Deo Uno" and Ia. 27-43 (concerning the distinction of the persons in the triune God) the tract "De Deo Trino." When read back into Aquinas, the implication of this textbook distribution of materials is that the Christian doctrine of God—Father, Son, and Holy Spirit—functions as a kind of appendix to the purely philosophical account of the existence and nature of God. Whether justified as an account of subsequent theology, this constitutes a profoundly mistaken reading of Ia. 2-43.[7]

That the discussion of the existence and nature of God in Ia. 2-26 has a properly theological role to play is clear from Aquinas's prior description of the nature of theological inquiry (Ia. 1). To assert that theology gets its subject matter from revelation entails that faith in God constitutes one of the principles of the inquiry now getting underway. The triune God is already "in place," so to speak, in his full Christian characterization. The burden of the argument in Ia. 2 on the existence of God is to assert that the one confessed as Father, Son, and Holy Spirit is the cause of the world. Through an interweaving of philosophical and scriptural premises, the subsequent argument in Ia. 3-26 exhibits something of the kind of life the triune God enjoys as cause of the world.[8] The

---

Aquinas, see Michel Corbin, *Le chemin de la theologie chez Thomas d'Aquin* (Paris: Beauchesne, 1972).

7. In his otherwise brilliant book, *At the Origins of Modern Atheism* (New Haven, Connecticut: Yale University Press, 1987), pp. 341-43, Michael Buckley mistakenly reads the disjunction between "De Deo Uno" and "De Deo Trino" into Aquinas's *Summa Theologiae*. Nicholas Lash is critical of this misreading in his lucid discussion of the matter in "When Did the Theologians Lose Interest in Theology?" in *Theology and Dialogue*, ed. Bruce D. Marshall (Notre Dame, Indiana: University of Notre Dame Press, 1990), pp. 131-47.

8. See P. T. Geach's discussion of the connection between the Five Ways and the divine attributes in "Aquinas," in *Three Philosophers*, ed. G. E. M. Anscombe and P. T. Geach (Ithaca, New York: Cornell University Press, 1961), pp. 109-118.

force of these arguments is to secure the particularistic claim to universality which the Christian community makes for its doctrines.

Philosophically shaped arguments concerning God's existence function to secure this universal claim. Starting with observable features of the world, such arguments affirm the divine agency as the source of these features and of the world order as a whole. Whatever their logical merits or probative force, their position at the beginning of the theological inquiry signals the logical space that Christians' claims are understood to occupy. This discussion functions to locate Christian worship, nurture, practice, and belief with respect to the widest possible conceptual map.[9] The triune God who is adored, confessed, and proclaimed in the Christian community has not only a local, narrative, or contextual reference within the usage of a particular cultural and linguistic community. He is none other than the cause of the world.

While developed in connection with scientific and metaphysical claims, such arguments are subsumed in a properly theological and scripturally based inquiry. They do not displace, but rather presuppose the reading of Scripture as a "canonically and narrationally unified and internally glossed . . . whole centered on Jesus Christ, and telling the story of the dealings of the Triune God with his people and his world in ways that are typologically . . . applicable to the present."[10] In effect, philosophical analysis and construction enable Aquinas to address the question (here and in subsequent discussions of the divine nature and agency, of angelic and human natures, and, finally and decisively, of Jesus Christ as divine-human agent): what must be true of the main characters of the Christian narrative for it to have the features Christians claim for it, truth and "followability"? Philosophy and other nontheological disciplines contribute as needed to filling out these complex characterizations. A literary analogy may help at this juncture. In a critical study of Melville's *Moby Dick*, for example, the complex narrative need not be continually retold in the course of literary analysis of the motivations and structure of the main characters. In somewhat the same way in the *Summa Theologiae*, Aquinas presumes his readership's detailed familiarity with the Christian narrative in order to show—or, more accurately, to remove obstacles to seeing—that its central claims are true and its chief injunctions followable.

---

9. For a more thorough discussion of these issues, see J. A. DiNoia, "Philosophical Theology in the Perspective of Religious Diversity," *Theological Studies* 49 (1988): 401-416.

10. George A. Lindbeck, "Scripture, Consensus and Community," in *Biblical Interpretation in Crisis*, ed. Richard John Neuhaus (Grand Rapids, Michigan: Eerdmans, 1989), p. 75.

Aquinas thus provides a powerful model of theological affirmation and realism over against alternatives that locate the reference for Christian talk about God either in human experience of God or in the linguistic practices of the community.[11] The philosophical component in his discussion of the existence and nature of the triune God serves purposes internal to this properly theological project. In this discussion, the triune God is not left behind but presupposed. The burden of 1a. 2-26 is to affirm that the Father, Son, and Holy Spirit are together one God, sharing the single divine life of sheer existence (*ipsum esse per se subsistens*).[12]

III

For another illustration of the role of philosophical analysis and construction in theological argument in Aquinas's conception of it, let us turn to the final questions of the *Summa* concerning the sacraments (3a. 60-65). Extended consideration of this topic here will also serve to suggest ways in which Aquinas's discussion can contribute to current sacramental theology.

In its broadly neo-Scholastic textbook transmission, Aquinas's sacramental theology suffered a fate similar to that of his theology of the triune God. Again, a misconstrual of its philosophical component is at least in part to blame. For various reasons—not the least of which was the influence of the nominalist preference for contractual over ontological categories in theological explication—the textbook tradition came to view issues of sacramental efficacy largely in juridical terms. This juridical approach was wed to one or another theory of causality in establishing an excessively legalistic framework for treating questions of the effectiveness of sacramental actions and linking these with questions about validity, form, and so on. This conjunction of classical sacramental theology (often in some sense dependent on Aquinas) with juridicism made the metaphysical elements in that theology the object of

---

11. In his "Postmodern Dogmatics: Toward a Renewed Discussion of Foundations in North America," *Communio* 17 (1990): 180-191, Walter Kasper underscores the importance in theology of "passing beyond hermeneutics to ontological questions" (p. 189).

12. An otherwise philosophically rigorous work noteworthy for its lack of attention to the theological setting of Aquinas's discussion of divine simplicity is Christopher Hughes, *On a Complex Theory of a Simple God* (Ithaca, New York: Cornell University Press, 1989). For a philosophically oriented but more traditional treatment of these issues, see Leo J. Elders, *The Philosophical Theology of St. Thomas Aquinas* (Leiden: E. J. Brill, 1990). Ingolf U. Dalferth's *Theology and Philosophy* (New York: Basil Blackwell, 1988) casts light on all the issues discussed in this paper.

a sustained (though strategically indirect) attack in the preconciliar period in the approach to the sacraments characteristic of the *ressourcement*. The new style of sacramental theology appealed to biblical, patristic, historical, and liturgical studies to break the hold of neo-Scholasticism on the theology of the sacraments prior to Vatican II.

In order to appreciate the significance of the philosophical component in Aquinas's sacramental theology, it must be distinguished from the juridical terms in which sacramental efficacy came to be framed in textbook theology. Its potential contribution to the current discussion will be easier to identify.

The *ressourcement* theology generated a vast body of knowledge about the sacraments and provided the framework for the sorely needed renewal of sacramental liturgy and practice which was one of the first fruits of Vatican II. But practitioners of the *ressourcement* theology did not always possess the analytical tools, not to mention the philosophical interests, to press some of the conceptual issues posed and at least addressed by classical sacramental theology. Rahner and Schillebeeckx stand out in this period as systematic theologians who endeavored to appropriate the new knowledge about the sacraments in order to field well-developed sacramental theories dependent in part upon transcendental or phenomenological reconstruals (respectively) of Scholastic theology of the sacraments.[13] Two conceptual issues stand out: (1) integration (the need to bring together the variety of methodologies and subfields in a comprehensive theological approach to the sacraments) and (2) theological realism (the need to take account of the full breadth of Christian claims about what occurs in these activities). The philosophical component in Aquinas's sacramental theology can be understood to contribute to the elucidation of both issues.

The most obvious feature of the sacraments is that they are ritual activities in which the Catholic Christian community engages on special occasions and for designated purposes. Considered as activities, they can be "observed" to comprise a number of elements which can be listed more or less at random as follows: rites, forms of words, formal gesture and movement, use of sacred texts, symbolic actions, distinction of roles (ministers, recipients/candidates, assembly), worship and invocation of God, use of physical objects, ruled actions, sacred place and vesture, particular occasions in communal and personal life, memorializations or imitations of Christ's actions, enactment of intentions and purposes of the community with regard to itself as a whole or with regard to

---

13. See Karl Rahner, *The Church and the Sacraments* (New York: Herder and Herder, 1963), and Edward Schillebeeckx, *Christ the Sacrament of the Encounter with God* (New York: Sheed and Ward, 1963).

individual members, and the belief that this enactment realizes and mysteriously achieves divine purposes and intentions.

Given the complexity of the sacraments as activities, study of them can take a variety of different perspectives. To make this point more technically: a variety of different methodologies, involving distinctive scholarly specializations and interests, can fruitfully be applied to the study of the sacraments. Generally speaking, these specializations take one or more of the elements listed above as central to attaining an overall view of the sacraments en bloc. The following specializations come to mind: liturgiology, biblical studies, canon law, history, hermeneutics, scientific study of religions (anthropology, comparative religion, history and phenomenology of religions, and various subspecialities), canon law, sociology, and psychology. In addition to these disciplines, and often in combination with them, a variety of philosophical frameworks come into play: Scholasticism, phenomenology, personalism, existentialism, hermeneutical theory, analytical philosophy, etc. It has always been recognized that the sacraments are complex in this way and thus capable of study from different points of view (*e.g.*, Augustine applied a theory of symbols adapted from Neo-Platonic epistemology and aesthetics to the study of the sacraments). But the proliferation of specializations and methodologies, characteristic of contemporary scholarship in general, has come to be typical of current study of the sacraments.[14]

Since the sacraments are activities (admittedly complex ones) of the Christian community, it follows that an adequate description of them would have to take account of their place within the overall pattern of life which the Christian community commends and fosters. If the Christian pattern of life is seen as aimed toward loving union with God, then the sacraments should be viewed as central activities by which this personal union with God is deepened and enhanced in the participants in these sacramental actions. In the sacraments, we can see this overall aim embodied in a variety of activities: confession, renunciation, praise, petition, promise, pledge, commitment, commission, empowerment, consolation, forgiveness, initiation, intercession, etc. The sacraments, because of their richness as ritual, prayerful actions, affirm many of the central elements of the Christian faith. This factor becomes clear when we analyze, in a rough way, a sacrament like Baptism and discover there the intersection of many of the deepest Christian convictions repre-

---

14. For details of current sacramental theology, see Kevin W. Irwin's surveys of "Recent Sacramental Theology," *The Thomist* 47 (1983): 592-608; 52 (1988): 124-47; 53 (1989): 281-313; and "Sacramental Theology: A Methodological Proposal," 54 (1990): 311-42.

sented and enacted: God's gracious love in calling human beings to be in union with him, our need to be rescued from the consequences of our sinful condition, the prefiguration of our baptism in Christ's at the Jordan, our participation in the mystery of his death and resurrection, our renunciation of sin, our incorporation into the community of Christ's Church, our promise to foster this life of faith in ourselves and in others, our empowerment to participate in other sacramental activities of the community, and so on. Because of the richness of the sacraments in affirming and enacting the central convictions and intentions of the community, a variety of theological subfields contribute to a full account of the sacraments: Christology, soteriology, ecclesiology, theological anthropology, eschatology, etc. Contemporary theology of the sacraments reflects the interplay of all these theological subfields.

The foregoing sketch of the complexity of the subjects requiring attention in sacramental theology suggests, in the first place, the need for integration of the vastly enriched fund of knowledge about the sacraments generated by liturgical and historical studies. Although Aquinas encountered a simpler body of data and theological subfields, his sacramental theology supplies a model for the desired integration. Particularly germane is his conception of the way that theology relates to other disciplines. The theological appropriation of the results of nontheological inquiries (formally speaking) can only be successful if it strives to incorporate this knowledge into a synthesis shaped by a conception of theology as *sacra doctrina* with God as its primary object. According to this conception, theology is a field-encompassing discipline that re-shapes the knowledge provided by subfields according to its own interests and principles. Such appropriation occurs widely in all fields of scientific and humanistic studies when one discipline (*e.g.*, medicine) adopts the conclusions of other disciplines (*e.g.*, biology, chemistry, and so on) and adapts these to its own purposes. Theological appropriation of the findings of biblical, historical, patristic, liturgical, and other studies (which themselves have an integrity as disciplines in their own right) does not entail theological *imperialism*. Indeed, it is arguable that only appropriation at a higher level protects a broad field, requiring interdisciplinary studies—like sacramental theology—from being co-opted by one or another parallel discipline—like canon law or liturgics.

Furthermore, as Aquinas's example demonstrates, an adequate theology of the sacraments cannot avoid the difficult conceptual problem posed by the Christian belief in the conjunction of divine and human agency in the accomplishment of sacramental effects. The issue of sacramental realism cannot be addressed simply by rehearsal of the historical development of sacramental theology or by a description of the symbolic richness of the sacramental ritual. Some conceptually sophisticated account of what philosophers like to call the problem of double agency is fundamental to securing the sacramental realism of Christian affirmation.

At issue in the question of how a double agency comes into play in the sacraments is the conviction that the effects believed by the community to be achieved by the sacramental activities surpass what human beings are capable of achieving on their own: for example, in baptism the conferral of grace entails an alteration of the interior states of persons to an extent beyond anything a human agent can achieve; in the eucharist, the bread and wine are changed into the body and blood of Christ; and so on. So an adequate sacramental theology will need to address not only the question of the convergence of two agencies in the achievement of a particular effect, but also the question of how the effect of the human agent can be embraced by the purposes and intentions of the divine agent. It is not clear how such issues could be sorted out without some appeal to philosophical analysis and construction. Aquinas turned to available scientific and metaphysical accounts of causality in trying to deepen theological understanding of the mystery of this double agency in the sacraments. When firmly distinguished from the juridicized conceptuality in which his sacramental theology has been transmitted, this philosophically shaped account of sacramental efficacy can be acknowledged and deployed as a potent instrument for theological affirmation.[15]

IV

The topic of this conference has been the future of Thomisms. I take the reading of Aquinas's use of philosophy in theology proposed here to be vital to the future of theology.

Various observers have suggested that this future will be a postmodern one—in which case I find myself in the unenviable position (linguistically at any rate) of commending a post-neo-Thomistic Aquinas to postmodern theologians. But I will forebear to adopt this fractious babble. David Tracy recently remarked that we are in an age in doubt about how to name itself. Are we living through an extended modernity,

---

15. The potential of the kind of reading of Aquinas's sacramental theology suggested here is brilliantly realized in Colman E. O'Neill's *Sacramental Realism: A General Theory of the Sacraments* (Wilmington, Delaware: Michael Glazier, 1983) and *Meeting Christ in the Sacraments*, rev. ed. Romanus Cessario (New York: Alba House, 1991).

postmodernity or antimodernity? he asks, implying that these are labels not for the times but for the positions we adopt towards them.[16] To be sure, there is a shift away from the sorts of concerns that dominated modern consciousness—its turn toward inwardness as Charles Taylor has brilliantly described it in his *Sources of the Self*.[17] But, as Taylor makes clear, modernity continues to maintain a vigorous afterlife. If the term "postmodern" has any value as a description of theological trends—as Walter Kasper has recently suggested—it is a heuristic one that signals a shift towards objectivity, nonfoundationalism, and a realism of sorts.[18]

I have suggested elsewhere that there are reasons to believe that a reading of Aquinas like the one sketched in this paper can play an important role in theology's postmodern future.[19] In these final remarks, I want to consider briefly the pluralism of theology's postmodern present and future to which Fr. McCool has drawn our attention. The intellectual environment of Catholic theology has undergone pluralization in at least three areas: pluralism of specializations, philosophical pluralism, and religious pluralism. Aquinas has relevance for each.

First, a marked internal pluralization of theology arises from the diversification of theological specialities. This development is not something new, but continues trends already well established in Protestant theology in the nineteenth century. At the present time, a powerful countertrend seeks not so much to suppress the new specializations as to recover the conception of a unified inquiry that can integrate theology's assorted subfields.[20] My brief discussion of sacramental theology will have to suffice to suggest that Aquinas's notion of theology as a field-encompassing field (in technical Thomistic language, the "subalternation of sciences") has a significant contribution to make to the current quest for unity in theology.[21]

Secondly, the more or less common framework of discourse furnished for past Catholic theology by various cognate forms of Scholastic philosophy has yielded increasingly to philosophical pluralism. For one thing, this kind of pluralization makes conversation across theological

---

16. David Tracy, "On Naming the Present," *Concilium* (1990/91): 66-85.

17. (Cambridge: Harvard University Press, 1988). See James J. Buckley, "A Return to the Subject: The Theological Significance of Charles Taylor's Sources of the Self," *The Thomist* 55 (1991).

18. Kasper, "Postmodern Dogmatics," p. 190.

19. DiNoia, "American Theology at Century's End."

20. For a penetrating discussion of these issues, see Edward Farley's influential *Theologia: The Fragmentation and Unity of Theological Education* (Philadelphia: Fortress Press, 1983), and his subsequent essays collected in *The Fragility of Knowledge* (Philadelphia, Pennsylvania: Fortress, Press, 1988).

positions more difficult. The challenge is not simply one of communication, however, but also one of constructive assessment. Strategies for appraising and appropriating alternative philosophical conceptions are needed to maintain unity in faith in the midst of diversity in theology. According to Alasdair MacIntyre, Aquinas provides a striking model of such strategies in operation. Describing Aquinas's appraisal and use of Augustinian and Aristotelian traditions, MacIntyre notes that Aquinas strove "to enable Augustinians to understand how, by their own standards, they confronted problems for the adequate treatment of which, so long as they remained in the confines of their own system, they lacked the necessary resources; and in a parallel way to provide the same kind of understanding for Averroistic Aristotelians."[22] What this means in practice, MacIntyre indicates, is that for Aquinas "no claim to rational superiority . . . can be made good except on the basis of a rationally justifiable rejection of the strongest claim to be made out of the opposing point of view." MacIntyre continues: "For one view to have emerged from this encounter with its claim to superiority vindicated it must first have rendered itself maximally vulnerable to the strongest arguments which that other and rival view can bring to bear against it."[23] Aquinas's strategy for entertaining and assessing alternative positions furnishes a model for Catholic theology in its philosophically pluralistic environment.

Finally, Aquinas also has something to contribute to Catholic theology's encounter with the alternative systems of belief and practice embodied in the world's major religious traditions. Thus—to return to Aquinas's theology of the triune God and to introduce a concrete illustration—philosophical argument would be needed in conversations between Buddhists and Christians. Segments of the Buddhist community seem to be nontheistic in their doctrines, and their canonical and commentatorial literatures possess highly subtle explanations for the prevalence of theistic beliefs in other religious traditions. Presumably, in conversations with Buddhists, Christians would need to invoke patterns of argument analogous to those sketched by Aquinas in the Prima Pars of the *Summa* (and elsewhere). A readiness to advance such arguments would be a way of taking Buddhist objections to theistic

---

21. On Aquinas's account of the subalternation of sciences, see William A. Wallace, *The Role of Demonstration in Moral Theology* (Washington, D.C.: The Thomist Press, 1962), pp. 36-45. On the logic of the interrelation of fields of argument, see Stephen Toulmin, *The Uses of Argument* (Cambridge: Cambridge University Press, 1958).

22. MacIntyre, *Three Rival Versions of Moral Enquiry*, p. 173.

23. *Ibid.*, p. 181.

beliefs seriously. Given the empirical bent of Buddhist patterns of reflection and argument, there would be considerable scope here for empirically based discussions such as those elaborated in the Five Ways and similar arguments. Patterns of argument appealing to objective states of affairs would have an important role in the religiously pluralistic environment of current theology. Only these kinds of arguments presuppose a field broad enough to sustain interreligious conversations. The issues can be joined in a common logical field, so to speak, where rival particularistic claims to universality would be taken seriously and debated. The readiness to advance arguments would make it possible for a true meeting of minds—though not necessarily agreement—to occur. It seems clear that, in order to rise to the occasion (logically speaking), appeals to history, narratives, texts, personal experiences, and the like would need to be combined with philosophical arguments having features of objective states of affairs as their context. Aquinas's incorporation of such arguments in his theology provides a model for Christian engagement in interreligious conversation.[24]

* * *

For the question "Thomas after Thomism?" read "Is there a theological life for Aquinas after the gradual displacement of the neo-Thomistic synthesis in Catholic theology underway for several decades?" I have argued here that an affirmative response to this question depends at least in part on a more dialectical and less systematic construal of the philosophical component of Aquinas's theology. It remains to be seen whether theologians will find this kind of reading both viable and serviceable.

---

24. See DiNoia, "Philosophical Theology in the Perspective of Religious Diversity" and "Pluralist Theology of Religions: Pluralistic or Non-Pluralistic?" in *Christian Uniqueness Reconsidered*, ed. Gavin D'Costa (Maryknoll, New York: Orbis Books, 1990), pp. 119-34. For application of Aquinas to various issues posed by religious pluralism, see my *The Diversity of Religions: A Christian Perspective* (Washington, D.C.: The Catholic University of America Press, forthcoming).

Christology, Public Theology, and Thomism: de Lubac, Balthasar, and Murray

David L. Schindler

Martin Marty suggests that the term "public" in public theology identifies the place where "strangers [can] meet on common ground."[1] This suggestion will suffice to indicate the general concern of the present paper.

Among the issues that must be taken up by Christians who would address this concern for establishing common ground with non-Christians is that of the integrity of human nature. More exactly, the question is: how are we to understand the form of nature relative to the form of grace given in Jesus Christ? This question indicates the christological context of my concern.

Finally, with respect to the third term in my title, "Thomism": the past two days of discussion have made it abundantly clear how vexed is the question of who most adequately represents the mind of Aquinas or indeed authentic Thomism, and I will not enter directly into that debate here. Rather I am going to assume for present purposes that de Lubac, Balthasar, and Murray are all indebted to St. Thomas in some significant if not uncontroverted sense. This assumption permits a focus on what to me is a prior and indeed more important question: namely, which of their "Thomisms," if we allow them all to be called such, is most faithful to the Gospel as interpreted in the central Christian tradition?

It would be irresponsible to make any pretense of providing, within present limits, anything approaching a complete argument with respect

---

1. "From Personal to Private, From Political to Public Religion," Inaugural Lecture on Religion and Public Life, Cushwa Center for the Study of American Catholicism, University of Notre Dame (February 9, 1984), p. 11.

Robert McElroy in his recent book on John Courtney Murray defines public theology as "the effort of the mainstream Christian churches and theologians in the United States to articulate a substantive role for spiritual values in public life which does not violate the spirit of American pluralism"; in *The Search for an American Public Theology* (New York: Paulist Press, 1989), p. 5. Again, David Tracy suggests that the concern of a public theology is to establish a discourse that is "available to all persons *in principle*"; in David Tracy and John B. Cobb, Jr., *Talking About God: Theology in the Context of Modern Pluralism* (New York: Seabury Press, 1983), p. 3.

to our three theologians. The intention is merely to try to identify the terms which seem to be the necessary and most basic ones for addressing properly the concern noted above—though of course I recognize that establishing terms is already the important beginning of an argument.

I will consider in turn: first, some texts which I take to be indicative of the respective positions of our three theologians on the relation of nature and grace; secondly, the sense of the public character of (Christian) theology, that is, of the "common ground," which follows from these different positions; and, thirdly, the hermeneutical question. For reasons which will become evident, the issues raised here lead us directly into the interpretation of conciliar documents, not only of Vatican II but of earlier councils.

I. Christology: Nature and Grace

(1) I begin with a quotation from Balthasar's *Glaubhaft ist nur Liebe* (*Love Alone*):

> For the creation, the forms of nature, have developed and opened themselves in spirit and in love to the unending fruitfulness of grace, receiving their final form from above so that everything natural is reformed, recast and re-orientated. The archetype of this whole development is found in the way Christ's human nature stands out—ecstatically —in relation to his divine person, from which he draws his human existence; the mission he receives from the Father forms not only his office and destiny as Redeemer, but the essential traits of his individual nature.[2]

The points to which I wish to draw attention with respect to this quotation are two. First, that the forms of nature receive their "final form from above"; secondly, that the archetype for this is found in Jesus Christ, in Christology.

Regarding the first point, then: it is Balthasar's position, following the patristic and High Scholastic tradition, that grace orders nature from the beginning of nature's existence. Firmly maintaining the distinction between nature and grace, Balthasar's affirmation is nonetheless meant to exclude dualism of both a "hard" and a "soft" sort. It excludes the hard or cruder form of dualism found in the "pure nature" hypothesis characteristic of much of the modern period, according to which nature was conceived first in terms of its own finality, to which was then "superadded" a second, now "supernatural," finality. But Balthasar's theology excludes a softer or more subtle form of dualism as well:

---

2. New York: Herder, 1969, pp. 101-102.

namely, one that accepts that there is, *de facto*, only one ultimate end for nature, a supernatural one, but which nonetheless fails to take sufficient account of the fact that this end already gives direction and thus (in some significant sense) *form* to nature. Balthasar's theology, in other words, excludes as well any view that fails to recognize that the one (ultimate) finality of nature, which is for the God of Jesus Christ, in ordering nature from its beginning, thereby orders nature (and all of its penultimate ends) *from within*. In short, Balthasar rejects the notion of a mere harmony between the two orders, insofar as such harmony is conceived, however subtly or unconsciously, in terms of an extrinsic relation.

Evidently, several qualifications are important for proper understanding here: first, the gratuitousness of the supernatural ordering of nature and that of the creation of nature must be distinguished, even though both occur simultaneously. Secondly, the order of creation and the order of redemption, and their corresponding "graces," must be distinguished. Thirdly, the supernatural ordering of nature must be seen as established, not independently of the historical person Jesus Christ, but precisely in virtue of Jesus Christ, and indeed of the church which is Christ's body. These qualifiers cannot be developed here; but it is important to take note of them.[3]

---

3. Perhaps most especially the third one, since it is the sense of Jesus Christ and indeed the church as the a priori for every presence of grace in the cosmos that determines the crucial differences between the major streams of Catholic thought in recent decades represented by Balthasar on the one hand, and Karl Rahner on the other. It is beyond the scope of this paper to give detailed attention to such differences.

For Balthasar's sense of those differences, see, *inter alia*, his *Karl Barth: Darstellung und Deutung einer Theologie*, 4th ed. (Einsiedeln: Johannes Verlag, 1976), pp. 308-313; *Henri de Lubac: sein organisches Lebenswerk* (Einsiedeln: Johannes Verlag, 1976), p. 60; *The Moment of Christian Witness* (Glen Rock, New Jersey: Newman Press, 1969), pp. 60-76 and passim. Fundamentally, the issue is this: once one affirms a (*de facto*) unity (within distinctness) of the natural and the supernatural orders, there remains the crucial question of how one is to interpret the "a priori" character of this relation. How one understands this "a priori" determines the relative sense of "symmetry" (and indeed "mutuality" of relation) between the two orders. For Balthasar, the relation that is given "a priori" must be viewed first "from above." For Rahner, on the other hand, the tendency is toward an "a priori" viewed first transcendentally or "from below." These different tendencies are of momentous consequence: what is at stake is nothing less than whether (in what sense) nature (man; reason; world) will be the measure for grace (God; revelation; Church), or grace for nature. See also the discussion of Rahner in Joseph Ratzinger's *Principles of a Catholic Theology* (San Francisco: Ignatius, 1987), pp.161-71; and de Lubac, *The Mystery of the Supernatural* (New York: Herder and Herder, 1965), p. 132, fn 2.

In sum, then, my first concern with respect to the text cited above is merely to insist that, for Balthasar, nature, wherever it is found, always-already bears within its depths the vestige of—an internal *ordering* toward—the form of love revealed by the trinitarian God in Jesus Christ.

The second point of the text is that, for Balthasar, the relation of nature and grace indicated here has its archetype in Jesus Christ. That is, it takes its meaning—by way of analogy, if I may introduce a term that needs to be treated with care[4]—from the formula of the relation of the two natures in Christ. The crucial point to note is Balthasar's emphasis: the *unity* of Christ's divine person penetrates Christ's human nature, even as it leaves that nature its essential distinctness—indeed, creates that distinctness. Jesus draws his human existence from the Father and from his divine person; and the mission he thereby receives from the Father forms not only his office and destiny, but the essential traits of his individual nature. In an "analogous" manner, our human nature takes its deepest meaning from being brought into the service of God's revelation, that is, by virtue of the downward movement of God's grace and love which affects us (already and not yet) from the moment of our created existence.[5]

---

4. The required qualifications here are at least two: first, in accord with the formula of the Fourth Lateran Council (1215), the similarity between the divine-human relation in Jesus Christ and the divine-human relation in all other persons does not rule out but on the contrary presupposes an infinite difference between those two relations. Secondly, then, those relations are nonetheless "analogical" rather than merely equivocal in character: but only with the crucial qualification that the analogy is Christ's doing and not our doing. The analogy is "from above" first, and only consequently "from below." (There is a sense in which Balthasar's "ana-logy" is first a "kata-logy": cf. Wolfgang Treitler's discussion in his article in *The Life and Work of Hans Urs von Balthasar*, ed. David L. Schindler [San Francisco: Communio Books/Ignatius Press, 1991].) There is only one hypostatic union. The pertinent point is simply that Jesus Christ has nonetheless utterly freely offered to share with creation his relation to the Father and not some other relation, and this offer serves to order creation from the beginning (already and not yet).

It is beyond our purpose to develop Balthasar's understanding of analogy as indicated here. But see, for example, the brief but pertinent discussion, "The Cross and Philosophy," in *Mysterium Paschale* (Edinburgh: T & T Clark, 1990), pp. 56-66, where Balthasar charts a course between too much continuity between Jesus Christ (the Cross) and the structures of the world (philosophy) (*e.g.*, as in the case of Hegel) on the one hand, and sheer paradox (*e.g.*, as in the case of Luther) on the other. And cf. also fn. 5 below.

5. Cf. the following statement by Balthasar: "Christ is the one and only criterion, given in the concrete, by which we measure the relations between God and man, grace and nature, faith and reason; and Christ is, though he has a human nature, a divine Person. This is the determining factor in the relationships. His humanity is the

This, then, indicates Balthasar's interpretation of the formula given at Chalcedon and developed in subsequent councils: the two natures which are ever distinct ("in duabus naturis inconfuse") nevertheless actualize this distinctness only *from within the unity* of the one divine person ("indivise"; "unam personam atque subsistentiam"). Balthasar's sense of the way unity (of divine person in Jesus Christ) establishes the context within which alone distinctness (of divine and human natures in Jesus Christ) can be properly understood, provides the archetype (analogy) for his understanding of the unity and distinctness of grace and nature.

(2) We turn, then, to Henri de Lubac. The text I offer is from an article written in 1932, and was in fact cited by John Courtney Murray in the context of their—de Lubac's and Murray's—common rejection of Robert Bellarmine's theory of the Church's indirect power over the temporal order.

De Lubac says as follows:

> The law of the relations between nature and grace, in its generality, is everywhere the same. It is from within that grace seizes (*reprend*) nature, and, far from diminishing nature, raises it up, in order to make it serve its own ends. It is from within that faith transforms reason, that the Church influences the state. As the messenger of Christ, the church is not the guardian of the state; on the contrary she ennobles the state, inspiring it to be Christian and thereby more human.[6]

---

expression and instrument of the divinity, and by no means is the divinity the expression and instrument of the humanity. In every respect, the humanity is fulfilled in that it sees itself, with all its upward stirrings, brought into the service of God's revelation, into the downward movement of his grace and love" ("Characteristics of Christianity," in *Verbum Caro* [San Francisco: Ignatius Press, 1989], pp. 161-80, at 162-63.

6. Henri de Lubac, "Le pouvoir de l'église en matière temporelle," *Revue des Sciences Religieuses* 12 (1932): 329-54, at 343-44. It should be noted here that de Lubac is writing prior to and therefore independent of Murray's distinction between state and society. It would be anachronistic—not to mention false—to charge de Lubac with anything like a theocratic tendency in the text cited. It is the very point of this article, as well as of a lecture on the same topic given at about the same time (1931), to reject theocracy. Nonetheless, the theological presuppositions that inform de Lubac's rejection of theocracy are significantly different from those of Murray. Though the point cannot be argued here, the difference between them is indicated in the fact that, for de Lubac, the proper purpose of the church, that is, even in the temporal order, is sanctification (because *all* of human being has its end and salvation in Jesus Christ), whereas, for Murray, the proper purpose of the church in the temporal order is humanization and civilization (because and insofar as one must distinguish the spiritual and temporal ends of human being: see, to take but one example, Murray's "Governmental Repression of Heresy," in *Proceedings of the*

There are two points in this text to which I wish to draw attention. The first, consistent with what we already saw in Balthasar, is that grace (or faith) acts from within nature (or reason), and thus trans-forms nature. The second is that the influence of grace (faith) thereby makes nature (reason) more—and not less—human. Grace's transformation of nature neither leaves nature be nor modifies it merely "accidentally," nor does it turn nature into something essentially different.[7]

The pertinent point for present purposes, then, is that what nature is is most fully revealed (*de facto*) in its order to grace; what nature truly is (in the one concrete order of creation) is revealed progressively more, the more it is transformed in and by grace. It is crucial to take note of what is implied in de Lubac's way of formulating this truth: *because* and insofar as one is Christian, one is *thereby* more human. Given the primitive relation between grace and nature, it follows that in some significant sense grace and nature each tell us something about the other. But de Lubac's understanding of this sense is missed if one fails to notice the asymmetry implied in his formulation: to wit, that the human informs us properly about grace, about what is truly divine, not "in itself" or as *separate* from grace, but only as itself anteriorly ordered by grace. In a word, grace's interpretation of what is natural is the anterior condition for nature's interpretation of what is "graced" or indeed compatible with the order of grace.[8]

Catholic Theological Society of America 3 [1948]: 26-98, at 65-66, where he says that the Church must seek to animate from within the various rational structures and processes of society, but only to help these achieve their own finalities as determined by their nature.)

De Lubac's article cited above, as well as the 1931 lecture, are reprinted with several slight modifications in Henri de Lubac, *Theological Fragments* (San Francisco: Ignatius, 1989), pp. 199-233 (the lecture appears on pp. 222-33, as a supplement to the article).

7. On the term "transformation" (as preferable, for example, to the term "elevation"), see de Lubac, *A Brief Catechesis on Nature and Grace* (San Francisco: Ignatius, 1980), pp. 81-99; and p. 49. See also *The Mystery of the Supernatural*, pp. 291-311, esp. p. 294.

De Lubac points out that the term "accident" is in fact susceptible of a correct use with respect to the grace-nature relation (*A Brief Catechesis*, p. 46f.). What is necessary is that one recognize the extent to which a more conventional ("Aristotelian") sense of the terms "accident" and "substance" needs to be deepened and expanded to accommodate the uniqueness of this relation: on this, see Balthasar, "Der Begriff der Natur in der Theologie," in *Zeitschrift für katholische Theologie* 75 (1953): 455.

8. The asymmetry implied here indicates the point on which turn the crucial differences between de Lubac on the one hand, and Karl Rahner on the other, for example, with respect to the understanding of nature and "common human ex-

Of course, the sense of this priority must be properly understood. Certainly it is possible to have some knowledge of the integrity of nature directly through experience, and thus both "before" and as distinct from the order of grace. The point is simply that this knowledge will in any case be of a grace-related nature (of a nature always-already concretely ordered, positively or negatively, consciously or unconsciously, to the God of Jesus Christ) and thus not of a "pure nature," whether one is aware of this relation (or ordering) or not.[9] Such knowledge therefore

---

perience" in Christian ethics. For those who follow Rahner, "the resources of Scripture, dogma, and Christian life are the fullest available 'objectifications' of the common human experience" (Richard A. McCormick, S.J., "Does Religious Faith Add to Ethical Perception?" in *The Distinctiveness of Christian Ethics*, ed. Charles E. Curran and Richard A. McCormick, S.J. [New York: Paulist Press, 1980], pp. 156-73, at p. 162); or again, Christian faith provides motivating power for insights which are in principle available to all human beings (*ibid.*, p. 170). For those who follow de Lubac, Jesus Christ, in assuming human nature and thus natural law, thereby already establishes the basic horizon for the latter's proper meaning. Jesus Christ is thus, in a sense that is inclusive and not exclusive of "natural law," at once the formal-universal and the concrete-personal norm for moral life (see Balthasar, "Nine Theses in Christian Ethics," in *The Distinctiveness of Christian Ethics*, pp. 190-206, at p. 191, and passim).

For views consistent with that of McCormick as expressed here, see Josef Fuchs, S.J., "Is There a Specifically Christian Ethics?" in *The Distinctiveness of Christian Ethics*, pp. 3-19; idem., "Christliche Moral: Biblische Orientierung und menschliche Wertung," *Stimmen der Zeit* 205 (1987): 671-83; and John Langan, "The Christian Difference in Ethics," *Theological Studies* 49 (1988): 131-50. For views consistent with that of Balthasar, see Joseph Ratzinger, "Magisterium, Faith, Morality," in *The Distinctiveness of Christian Ethics*, pp. 174-89; and Angelo Scola, "Christologie et morale," *Nouvelle revue théologie* 109 (1987): 382-409.

Robert McElroy, in *The Search for an American Public Theology*, indicates the fundamental agreement of Murray with the view of Fuchs that "the material content of Christian ethics is identical with that of the human ethics produced by reason," and thus that "the superiority of Christian ethics over natural ethics is a superiority of horizon and motivation, not a superiority of action or behavior" (pp. 150ff). This claim of agreement between the two authors seems to me both interesting and accurate. It is nonetheless beyond the scope of this paper to develop the point: namely, to show the sense in which the autonomy of the natural order on the part of Murray and Fuchs is understood in similar ways, albeit from different directions ("neo-Scholastic": Murray, and "transcendental": Fuchs); and to show further how this similarity-in-difference leads the two thinkers to—respectively— "neoconservative" and "progressive" senses of the autonomy of the cultural-social order relative to Christianity.

9. The point of this paragraph is emphatically not to deny the possibility and legitimacy of a distinctly philosophical understanding of nature (regarding the distinction between the natural/philosophical and supernatural/theological or-

must be judged *by* the order given in Jesus Christ, as the necessary condition for determining finally the sense in which what it tells us is truly compatible *with* that order.

It does not seem to me necessary to belabor the evident agreement between de Lubac's understanding of the grace-nature relation here and that of Balthasar as noted earlier:[10] the context that is established in and by the order of grace provides the horizon within which the integrity of what is distinctly natural must—in the real order of things—ultimately and most properly be understood. A useful analogy here is that employed by de Lubac regarding the spirit-body distinction. As de Lubac points out, the true integrity of the body is secured best within an anterior unity of spirit-body (Thomism), and not in the body as pushed outside of or made extrinsic to spirit (Cartesianism).[11]

(3) We turn, then, to John Courtney Murray. The quotation I offer is from a long article originally presented to the Catholic Theological

---

ders, one must always keep in mind the following: "duplex ordo cognitionis, proprio objecto, propria methodo" [Denzinger 1795, 1799]). The issue is simply whether the integrity of nature (philosophy) which indeed is required in the Catholic tradition entails a "purity of nature," or entails the claim at least to be able to abstract such a "pure nature"—in suchwise that one could be certain that what one had thus abstracted had no traces whatever either of the supernatural or of sin. Regarding this point see the important discussions by Balthasar in *Theologik*, vol. 1, *Wahrheit der Welt* (Einsiedeln: Johannes Verlag), pp. xi-xvii, especially xi-xiii; and "Von den Aufgaben der Katholischen Philosophie in der Zeit," *Annalen der Philosophischen Gesellschaft Innerschweiz* 3 (December-January, 1946/47): 1-38, especially pp. 5-6. See also, generally, Part Three ("Denken und Denkform im Katholizismus") of Balthasar's *Karl Barth*, pp. 263-386. Balthasar's view on this matter turns on a central principle: the more complete and concrete one wishes one's philosophy to be, the more one must recognize the historical order of things—wherein there has always been some purification due to faith, or some obscuring due to sin.

10. On the differences between himself and de Lubac on the grace-nature distinction, see Balthasar, *Henri de Lubac*, p. 61, fn. 36. De Lubac logically distinguishes three moments in God's plan: (1) creation of spiritual being; (2) the supernatural finality imprinted in its nature: (3) the free offer of participation in God's life. Balthasar asks whether (1) and (2) do not coincide conceptually. That is, if one starts theologically from the point of the unity of God's salvific plan, is not the whole an indivisible act of God's freedom which can, in the order of execution, be conceptually analyzed only into two moments—(1-2) and (3)?

11. See *The Mystery of the Supernatural*, pp. 42-43.

In connection with my discussion of de Lubac in the present article, see *A Brief Catechesis*, pp. 43ff, where de Lubac suggests that the perfect model for understanding the union in difference between the creature and its Creator is to be found in the circumincession of the three Persons of the Trinity.

Society in 1948, entitled "Governmental Repression of Heresy." In the context of his discussion regarding the work of John of Paris (d. 1306), Murray states as follows:

> [The relations between the two powers—between the spiritual and temporal—] are to be determined on theological principles—basically, those that govern the relations between nature and grace—and not by considerations of political reality, or by feudal concepts of social unity. As grace does not destroy nature, so the institution of the Church has not destroyed the spontaneously natural aspirations of man to a good political society; and this society is as autonomous as the social instinct that produces it. Again, as the harmony of nature presupposes their enduring distinction, so the harmony of the two powers is conditioned by the fidelity of each to its own nature and end; each obeys the one God and ministers to the one man, but each does so in its own order. Finally, as grace completes nature, not by invading the order of nature but by elevating it, so the spiritual and temporal powers complete one another, not so that one assumes the other's functions, but so that each favors the performance by the other of the other's own functions, the favoring being done by each *suo modo*.[12]

First, two preliminary comments. Although clearly I cannot offer additional textual evidence in this forum, I take the distinction between nature and grace as formulated here to be representative of Murray's published work throughout his career. That distinction, albeit in terms which shift with context, is decisive in each of the key areas of his concern throughout his life.[13]

Secondly, then, it is important to note that Murray himself, as the text already makes clear, sees this distinction as establishing the basic horizon within which he takes up each of his concerns. But it is equally important to recognize that he nonetheless sees the distinction as one that can be taken for granted, at least by Catholics. Murray therefore sees no need for extensive argument on its behalf and on its own terms. Rather, he sees his task largely as that of developing the as-yet unseen consequences of the distinction for the social-political order, that is, in the light of the new circumstances of modern democracy. We will need

---

12. "Governmental Repression of Heresy," p. 57.

13. I attempt to document this claim in some detail in a forthcoming book. Perhaps I should note here that I take the claim to be accurate, even granting Leon Hooper's argument on behalf of a later (post-1959) influence of Lonergan on Murray: that is, precisely in terms of an evolution in Murray from a more "timeless" or "abstract" appeal to natural law to a more historically sensitive appeal (cf. J. Leon Hooper, *The Ethics of Discourse* [Washington, D. C.: Georgetown University Press, 1986]). But this is matter for discussion elsewhere.

later to comment on Murray's mode of procedure here. But first we need to ask the obvious question: isn't Murray's assumed distinction between grace and nature one that a Catholic can and indeed must adopt?

In addressing this question, it must suffice for present purposes to draw attention to the ambiguity resident in Murray's language, an ambiguity, that is, which I believe is brought into relief by the theology of Balthasar-de Lubac. "Harmony," "completing," "fidelity of each to its own nature and end," and the like: these terms are indeed all tradition-honored terms, and are susceptible of authentically Catholic interpretation.[14] At the same time, what the work of Balthasar-de Lubac I think makes clear is that the sense of that interpretation is hardly self-evident. The terms "harmony" and "completion" (and indeed all the key phrasings of the text cited) as indicative of the relation between the two orders can be understood in at least two ways, depending on the relative priority one accords unity and distinctness in one's conception of that relation. A priority—anteriority—of unity entails a relation between orders which is first from within; a priority of distinctness entails a relation between orders that is first from without. The difference, in other words, is between a relation that is intrinsic and a relation that is extrinsic, and consequently between contrasting senses of the integrity of what is distinct. What is at stake in these contrasting senses is nothing less than the difference between the primary meaning of integration on the one hand, and of fragmentation (or indeed secularization) on the other.

My proposal is that it is just this difference between an intrinsic (*de facto*, not *de jure*) and an extrinsic relation between the orders of grace and nature that is implicated in the different formulations of Balthasar-de Lubac and Murray regarding grace and nature. The issue which Balthasar-de Lubac bring into relief with respect to Murray is whether Murray, notwithstanding his affirmation of one end as common to the two orders, does not still conceive these orders, even if unconsciously or with great subtlety, as lying alongside each other, as if they were first outside of each other; or again as layered on top of each other, as if grace came *after* nature. From the perspective of Balthasar-de Lubac, it seems clear to me that Murray does in fact conceive the relation between the two orders in just this sort of extrinsic way.[15]

---

14. Cf., for example, Balthasar, "Analogie und Natur," *Divus Thomas* 1 (1945): 3-56.

15. Another way of indicating what I am attempting to get at here: de Lubac characteristically says that what is Christian is "thereby more human." Murray more characteristically makes statements such as that the order of human society determined by reason represents a common "Christian ground" indeed, but only because it is common human ground ("Intercredal Co-operation: Some Further

But with this let me reiterate again the limits of the present paper. My intention is to suggest, first, that there are important substantive differences between Balthasar-de Lubac and Murray regarding the grace-nature distinction which are carried in what may appear to be only subtle differences of language; and, secondly, that these substantive differences are decisive for how one conceives the task of Christianity in relation to the world.[16] That there are differences and that these are laden with consequences for Christian praxis (to which topic I will turn momentarily) seems to me not likely to be disputed by interpreters of Murray. What is more likely to be called into dispute is the legitimacy of suggesting that terms like "extrinsic" or "fragmented"—and hence "secularized"—aptly characterize Murray's position. Clearly the use of such terms presupposes an argument on behalf of the Balthasarian-Lubacian perspective which it nonetheless cannot be my concern to provide here. Once again, my intention in the present forum is merely to identify the argument that needs to be taken up—on both sides—and to set the terms of that argument. Of course central to that eventual argument will be the question of which perspective—Balthasar's or Murray's—best interprets the main Catholic tradition. I will return to this point in the third part of my paper.

II. The Public Character of Christian Theology

If Christian theology is to "go public" in a pluralistic society, it must of course be able to give an accounting for the common ground that is a necessary condition for communication between Christians and non-Christians. All three of our theologians see the need to speak publicly as part of the essential mission of Christian theology. The difference between them turns not on *whether* a Christian must seek "common ground," but *on what terms*. My purpose will be merely to indicate how

---

Views," *Theological Studies* 4 (1943): 103). The different senses of distinctness and consequent symmetry in the grace-nature relation that are suggested in these different formulations I believe are indicative of a fault-line that runs between the respective theologies of the two men. Regarding the nature of this fault-line, cf. the discussion of de Lubac above, as well as the comments in fn 9 and fn 22.

16. See, for example, Balthasar, "Der Begriff der Natur in der Theologie," pp. 452 and 461, where he points out how the interpretation of the grace-nature distinction affects one's understanding of the structures of metaphysics, ethics, apologetics, politics, and the entire praxis of Christian life. And see the general discussion regarding "christocentrism" in the third part of my paper. Joseph Komonchak's "Theology and Culture at Mid-Century: The Example of Henri de Lubac," *Theological Studies* 51 (1990): 579-602 provides an interesting look at de Lubac which is pertinent here.

their different understandings of the grace-nature relation set those terms.

All of our theologians, then, recognize that some appeal to a "common nature" is necessary in the doing of "public" theology. The difference is that Balthasar-de Lubac's sense of this "common nature" takes its primary meaning from within the order of person: from the ontological order of love and relation as revealed by the trinitarian God in Jesus Christ in and through the *fiat* of Mary and the church. Balthasar understands human nature first (ontologically) by way of analogy[17] to the "Abba" expressed by Jesus to the Father, and again to the Cross of Jesus—and thus to the agapic and kenotic love revealed in Jesus. Balthasar's approach here does not imply that one must invoke the name of Jesus Christ, and indeed of the trinitarian God, Mary, and the church, in every public conversation. It does imply that, though one can, for purposes of discussion and communication, distinguish nature in its integrity from within the fundamental horizon given in grace, one can nonetheless never (in one's own understanding) *separate* nature from that more fundamental horizon—and hence from the personal order of love whose ontological meaning is given in Christology, trinitarian theology, ecclesiology, and mariology.[18]

In a word, then, the key for Balthasar-de Lubac is that nature from the beginning is embedded (de facto) in only *one concrete historical order*: namely, that of person and love, as these are ultimately revealed in the life and death of Jesus Christ. There is no actual human nature—anywhere, even in America—that is not ordered from its depths to the transforming love of Christ's life-in-death; there is no human heart within which this call to love does not resonate.

Murray's difference from Balthasar-de Lubac on the meaning of "common ground," then, hinges on the different way in which he distinguishes the order of nature from the order of grace. Drawing on what we said earlier, we can summarize here by saying that Murray seeks to establish "common ground" on the basis of a nature which is (first) separated from the order—and hence *form*—given in grace. The meaning of the nature to which Murray appeals as common thus is not one that takes its beginning from the meaning of person and love as

---

17. That is, with the qualification recorded in footnote 4 above.

18. For the sense in which the concept of person takes its ultimate meaning from within theology, see Balthasar, "Zum Begriff der Person," in *Homo Creatus Est* (Einsiedeln: Johannes Verlag, 1986), pp. 93-102; and Joseph Ratzinger, "Zum Personenverst ndnis in der Theologie," *Dogma und Verkündigung* (Munich: Erich Wewel Verlag, 1973), pp. 205-23. These articles appear in the North American *Communio* in Spring, 1986 (Balthasar) and Fall, 1990 (Ratzinger).

revealed in Jesus Christ; and it is consequently not one that has intrinsic need of transforming love for it to be rationally accessible.

If I might put all of this in the most general terms, I would say it as follows: both Balthasar-de Lubac and Murray affirm an analogy of being—and thereby are able to identify structures of reality that are "common," indeed universal. The difference between them lies in the way they see it as possible or appropriate to detach the analogy of being from the analogy of faith.[19]

Of course this summary leaves the difference between the theologians expressed schematically and indeed in largely negative terms. For present purposes, it will suffice to illustrate the positive sense of that difference by the different models for public discourse to which our theologians characteristically appeal. Murray's model is the person of civility; the tradition to which he most readily appeals is what he calls the "tradition of reason." Balthasar's model, even—precisely—for public discourse, is on the contrary the saint;[20] the tradition to which he most

---

19. See in this connection the following statements by Balthasar: "In this sense Christ can be called the 'concrete analogy of being,' since he constitutes in himself, in the unity of his divine and human natures, the proportion of every interval between God and man. And this unity is his person in both natures. The philosophical formulation of the analogy of being is related to the measure of Christ precisely as is world history to his history—as promise to fulfillment, the preliminary to the definitive. He is so very much what is most concrete and most central that in the last analysis we can only think by starting with him; and every question as to what might be if he did not exist, or if he had not become man, or if the world had to be considered without him, is now superfluous and unnecessary" (*A Theology of History* [New York: Sheed and Ward, 1963], pp. 74-75).

"Herein lies the solution to the theological problem of universals. . . . (Christ) himself is the idea made concrete, personal, historical: *universale concretum et personale*" (*ibid.*, p. 89).

"In the last analysis there are not two lines of progress because there are not two universalisms existing side by side, for the human (abstract) universal of the natural order is always subordinate to the (concrete) universal of Christ, in whom all things are brought into unity" ("God Speaks as Man," in *Verbum Caro*, pp. 69-93, at 90).

On the theological problem of "universals," see also "Characteristics of Christianity," pp. 170-71; on the connection between the analogy of faith and the analogy of being, see also *Karl Barth*, p. 390 and passim.

20. Or indeed the witness unto death (in, with, and for Jesus) called a martyr: cf. *Who Is a Christian?* (Westminster, Maryland: Newman Press, 1968).

The more general point here involves the whole of Balthasar's undertaking in his trilogy: there can be no seeking and indeed speaking of the truth (no being truly reasonable) without the engagement of one's "subjectivity" and one's action: it is no accident that Balthasar's "logic" (*Theologik*) is preceded by his "aesthetics" (*Herrlichkeit*) and his "drama" (*Theodramatik*). Of course, the burden of this sug-

readily appeals, precisely for examples of reasonability, is that of the communion of saints. The differences of emphasis represented in these models are not merely happenstance; they are functions of different convictions about when and how one might legitimately abstract from the personal order of love revealed in Jesus Christ.[21]

We conclude our brief treatment here, then, with two important qualifiers. First, with respect to Murray, it is of course true that Murray is open to an eventual appeal to transforming love as necessary for a full and complete employment of reason by a Christian. The point is merely that this eventual appeal to love, from the perspective of Balthasar-de Lubac, will always come too late and too extrinsically (*i.e.*, positivistically), in terms of both the form (subject) and the content (object) of one's public discourse.[22]

With respect to Balthasar-de Lubac, then, what needs to be emphasized is that their insistence on a concrete context of loving witness does not remove them from a context of natural law. There is much discussion in ethics today about the difference between a so-called ethics of discipleship or narrative on the one hand, and a natural law ethics on the other. Balthasar's position includes even as it transcends both these approaches to ethics. It does so for a christological reason: Jesus Christ has assumed, not destroyed, nature (natural law), even as his divine person now reveals the deepest—ontological—meaning of that nature.[23]

III. The Hermeneutical Question

In conclusion, then, I would like to speak briefly to the hermeneutical question which is raised by the foregoing discussion, at least for anyone who takes seriously the conciliar tradition of Christianity.

---

gestion is entirely missed if one fails to see that Jesus Christ is that in terms of which subjectivity and action are ultimately and most properly to take their meaning.

21. Cf. Balthasar: "Christ did not leave the Father when he became man to bring all creation to fulfillment; and neither does the Christian need to leave his center in Christ in order to mediate him to the world, to understand his relation to the world, to build a bridge between revelation and nature, philosophy and theology" ("Theology and Sanctity," in *Verbum Caro*, pp. 181-209, at 195).

22. Cf. here the statement of de Lubac: "To humanize before Christianizing? If the enterprise succeeds, Christianity will come too late, its place will be filled. And do they think that Christianity has no humanizing value?" (*Paradoxes* [Paris: Seuil, 1959], p. 46).

23. For a discussion of Balthasar pertinent to the sketch I have offered here, see the outstanding overview by Marc Ouellet, P.S.S., "Balthasar and the Christian Foundations of Ethics," *Communio* 17 (Fall 1990): 375-401.

In a monograph on Vatican II's "Declaration on Religious Freedom" prepared two years ago for the Heidelberg Academy of Sciences, Walter Kasper states that the true significance of this declaration lies without doubt in its "solemn confirmation that man has a right to religious freedom."[24] Warmly endorsing this achievement, Kasper nonetheless goes on to point out what were the limits of the declaration. These limits are to be found in the declaration's lack of a comprehensive theology of religious freedom (p. 39; cf. pp. 31-41). Kasper's point is not that it was the task of a conciliar declaration to provide this comprehensive theology, but that in any case this theology is still needed, to fill out, deepen, and interpret properly the meaning of the declaration.

Essentially, what such a theology must do, according to Kasper, is develop the christological roots of religious freedom. As St. Paul says (Gal. 5:1), it is Jesus Christ who has made us free. As *Gaudium et spes* states, Jesus Christ is "the key, the center, and the purpose of the whole of man's history" (*GS* 10; cf. also *GS* 45). What remains still to be developed, then, is how human dignity and freedom are anchored in Jesus Christ: how Christ's hypostatic union is both the foundation for and gives the primary meaning of man in his or her relation to God and indeed to all else in God. This task involves showing the sense in which truth, love, and freedom mutually imply one another, how each is a necessary condition for the other.[25]

Elsewhere, in a chapter of a recent book, Kasper takes up the question of the hermeneutics of conciliar statements generally.[26] Acknowledging that, as has been frequently noted by others, the texts of Vatican II often leave so-called conservative and progressive statements side by side, with no attempt at reconciliation (p. 170), he goes on to insist that it is in fact completely within the conciliar tradition for such juxtapositions to remain: that the "theoretical mediation of these positions is a task for the theology that comes afterwards" (p. 171).

In the light of these suggestions by Kasper, then, my comment for present purposes is a simple one: namely, that an important example of juxtaposed statements in the documents of Vatican II that require further theoretical mediation are those that accord priority to what has been called christocentrism on the one hand, and to the autonomy of the created order on the other.[27] My proposal is that the theologies of

24. *Wahrheit und Freiheit* (Heidelberg: Carl Winter Universitätsverlag, 1988), p. 36.
25. It is perhaps worth noting here that, as Kasper remarks, the necessary connection between truth and freedom was insisted upon by Karol Wojtyla in an intervention during the third session of the council in 1964 (p. 26f).
26. *Theology and Church* (New York: Crossroad, 1989), pp. 166-76.
27. For texts of the council that affirm a legitimate autonomy of the created order,

Balthasar-de Lubac and Murray are illustrative of these contrasting statements of the council—or better, that their respective theologies serve in important ways to *undergird* the different interpretations of the council that stem from these contrasting statements.[28] The question of

---

see for example: *GS* 36; 41; 56; 76. Cf. McCormick's gloss on *GS* 41 ("Does Religious Faith Add to Ethical Perception?" p. 168f.) for an illuminating sense, especially in light of what was said in fn 8 above, of the alternative interpretations that are apparently available. See also here de Lubac's discussion of Schillebeeckx's "L'Eglise sacrement du monde" in *A Brief Catechesis*, Appendix B, pp. 191-234; and Angelo Scola's "Cristo 'Lumen Gentium'," in the Italian *Communio* (September-October 1987), pp. 5-17, where, among other things, he discusses the striking expression used by John Paul II in his first trip to Argentina, when he defined the Church as *"forma mundi."*

28. See in this connection the following discussions regarding the council: Balthasar, "Das Konzil des Heiligen Geistes," in *Spiritus Creator* (Einsiedeln: Johannes Verlag, 1967), pp. 218-36; de Lubac, *Athéisme et sens de l'homme: Une double requete de Gaudium et spes* (Paris: Les Éditions du Cerf, 1968); Joseph Ratzinger, "The Church and Man's Calling," in *Commentary on the Documents of Vatican II*, vol. 5, ed. Herbert Vorgrimler (New York: Herder and Herder, 1969), pp. 115-63. Cf. in particular the trenchant comment by Ratzinger: "[I]t seemed to many people... that there was not a radical enough rejection of a doctrine of man divided into philosophy and theology. They were convinced that fundamentally the text was still based on a schematic representation of nature and the supernatural viewed far too much as merely juxtaposed. To their mind it took as its starting-point the fiction that it is possible to construct a rational philosophical picture of man intelligible to all and on which all men of goodwill can agree, the actual Christian doctrines being added to this as a sort of crowning conclusion. The latter then tends to appear as a sort of special possession of Christians, which others ought not to make a bone of contention but which at bottom can be ignored. This was the real reason for the protest against the 'optimism' of the schema [all these objections refer to Text 4]. It was not a question of imposing a pessimistic view of man or of constructing an exaggerated theology of sin because of a certain correspondence with some forms of Lutheran thought. The text as it stood itself prompted the question why exactly the reasonable and perfectly free human being described in the first articles was suddenly burdened with the story of Christ. The latter might well appear to be a rather unintelligible addition to a picture that was already quite complete in itself. Consequently the text was blamed for only apparently choosing a theological starting-point in the idea of man as the image of God, whereas in reality it still had a theistically-coloured and to a large extent non-historical view. As opposed to this, it was urged that the starting-point should be Christ, the second Adam, from whom alone the Christian picture of man can be correctly developed. Advocates of this position could point to the fictitious character of a supposedly rational picture of man and therefore say that the only realistic picture must start from the actual Christian creed which, precisely as a confession of faith, can and must manifest its own intelligibility and rationality..." (pp. 119-20 [regarding *GS* 12]).

the nature-grace distinction, or again of "public" theology, whatever else it is, is also, and fundamentally, the question of the christological meaning of the created order.

Let me put the matter more sharply: it has become commonplace to assert that Vatican II has vindicated the theology of Murray.[29] There is of course an obvious and important sense in which this is true: religious freedom has been vindicated. But the question that is nonetheless still begged in such an assertion—or so it seems to me, in the light of both the theological claims of Balthasar-de Lubac and the hermeneutical comments of Kasper—is that of the christological context and ordering of human freedom implied in and by Murray's work. Specifically: Murray's work relative to the "Declaration on Religious Freedom" is guided by a definite sense of human (social-political) autonomy which in turn represents but the concrete carrying through of a definite sense of the grace-nature distinction. It is clear that the council has affirmed religious liberty. What is not clear, when one takes note of the many christocentric texts of the council, particularly in the light of theologies such as those of Balthasar and de Lubac, is that the council has thereby embraced the sense of autonomy, and thus of the grace-nature distinction, which mediates Murray's interpretation of religious liberty.

But let me repeat what I said earlier. Murray himself was explicit about how decisive the grace-nature distinction was for his work. The problem, as we indicated, is that he nonetheless took his sense of that distinction as something which was evident, at least for Catholics, and which therefore had merely to be applied to the social-political order—that is, in the light now of the new circumstances of modernity. The burden of the work of Balthasar-de Lubac, it seems to me, is that Murray's sense of grace and nature in fact cannot be taken as self-

---

29. See for example: Dennis P. McCann, *New Experiment in Democracy* (Kansas City: Sheed and Ward, 1987), p. 26; David Hollenbach, "Foreword," in Leon Hooper, *The Ethics of Discourse*, p. ix; Avery Dulles, S.J., *The Reshaping of Catholicism* (San Francisco: Harper & Row, 1988), p. 8. It seems to me worth pointing out here that John Courtney Murray's understanding of religious liberty is no more (and no less) normative for interpreting Vatican II's "Dignitatis humanae" than is Joseph Kleutgen's understanding of the faith-reason relation normative for interpreting Vatican I's "Dei filius." I do not make this statement for polemical purposes; nor do I intend the comparison to bear first on the detail of the respective textual histories. Rather, I mean merely to recall what seems to me a central principle of Catholic hermeneutics: namely, that the meaning of a conciliar text, however much it is (of necessity) anchored in the concrete thought of a given person or group of persons, nonetheless becomes complete only when and insofar as it is integrated with texts from earlier councils and indeed the whole of the main Christian tradition. I have indicated in the body of my paper what this implies in the present case.

evidently true in or for the Catholic tradition; that it must on the contrary now be argued and defended on its own terms.

In sum, then, my point is this: that the distinction for which Murray—and those who would follow him—must yet give an accounting is not, first or most fundamentally, that between the social-political order of the Middle Ages and of modernity, or again between the liberalism of Jacobin France and of revolutionary America; it is rather the distinction between divine person and human nature in Jesus Christ and, in this context, between divinity and all of humanity.

For those who still might be inclined to think that we are quibbling here over fine theoretical issues that have little practical import, it seems to me worth recalling in conclusion that the early church was occupied for centuries in her councils in an effort to get clear about some very fine christological distinctions. She knew that what was at stake in understanding properly the sense of the unity and distinctness of natures in Jesus Christ was nothing less than whether there had been an Incarnation. What I am suggesting is that it is this same issue, in a truly analogous form, that is before us in the present case: namely, whether or in what sense there is or can be a continuing extension of God's incarnation into the time and space of the cosmos. Only in addressing this question of God's presence in Jesus Christ and his church, and in turn in the world created in Jesus Christ, can we situate ourselves properly to judge whether we are in fact, to use Murray's words, truly "revers[ing] the secularist drift," or on the contrary merely contributing to it.

The Example of John Courtney Murray

Jude P. Dougherty *

In its cover story of 12 December 1960 *Time* magazine used John Courtney Murray to symbolize the coming of age of American Catholicism.[1] John F. Kennedy had just been elected president of the United States and would become the first Catholic to hold that office. Significantly, Murray was pictured against the backdrop of a sixteenth-century manuscript of Robert Bellarmine's "Disputationes de Controversiis Christianae Fidei." A diagonal yellow banner bore the title of the cover essay, "U.S. Catholics and the State." Murray, a theology professor at the Jesuit seminary, Woodstock College, was then a major academic participant in a debate concerning the nature of American democracy and its presuppositions. It was the time of a vigorous and self-confident Catholicism. Issues were sharply defined as Murray challenged both secular liberal and Protestant social and political thought.

Many things have changed since Murray wrote. In the political order Vietnam was yet to come; in the religious, the culmination of the Second Vatican Council was six years off. Murray never lived to witness the fall of Saigon or to experience a Church recreated in the "spirit" of Vatican II. He was sixty-three years of age in 1967 when he was stricken with a heart attack while riding in a taxi in his native New York City. The subsequent collapse of the American will to prosecute to a successful conclusion a war in Southeast Asia would not have surprised him; the dissolution of his beloved Catholic church into a friendly, mindless, liturgically impoverished religious body would have come as a shock. Murray had more confidence in the Catholic church than he did in the United States, principally, because, in his view, the Church possessed a tradition much wider and deeper than any that America had elaborated, and, with a history many times as long, it commanded the intellectual resources indispensable to the formulation of a public philosophy. He was under no illusion that the United States could, in fact, develop a public philosophy, but he was convinced that the country needed one. He was confident that the materials required were available in the natural law tradition carried within the Catholic intellectual community. He was pleased to observe that the Catholic church in America was

---

*Jude P. Dougherty's article originally appeared in *World & I* and is reprinted here with the kind permission of its and editors and the author.

1. *Time*, 12 December 1960, p. 65.

not divided into Left and Right as was the case in France. With confidence he could represent an essentially unified Church, articulating what he took to be a common outlook with respect to the fundament of law. That fundament in its ideal formulation is what he called the "public philosophy," and insofar as it was broadly accepted, he was willing to call it the "public consensus."

No doubt the experience of war years had led many public figures to reflect on the difference between the American republic and the totalitarian regimes which it had just defeated and others which were seen as emerging. The debate was many-sided and its participants represented a wide range of disciplines from philosophy and theology to sociology and economics. Prominent among those engaged in this debate were Mortimer Adler, Will Herberg, Sidney Hook, Walter Lippmann, Jacques Maritain, and Gustav Weigel.[2] There was a sense that things were changing and that it was necessary to elucidate, to use Lincoln's term, "the American proposition." In retrospect, it is clear that the nation was moving from a Christian past to a secular future, a drift that was even then dimly perceived. Many thought that America was entering a state of ideological disarray, having lost the certitudes that formerly were provided by metaphysics and religious faith. Throughout the 1950s, the sociologist Will Herberg could say, "To be American is to be religious, and to be religious is to be religious in one of three ways, as a Protestant, as a Catholic or as a Jew." Sidney Hook would dissent. America is not simply a pluralist society in the sense of religiously plural. For Hook, to be an American is to be religious or irreligious.

Murray was an attractive and articulate speaker and was a frequent lecturer throughout the country. In 1960 he collected a number of his speeches and published them as *We Hold These Truths*.[3] In his book, Murray described for a Catholic audience the truths they held as Americans, as Catholics, and as Catholic-Americans. But in a sense Murray was after bigger fish. He wished to find those truths which all Americans pre-

---

2. Mortimer Adler, *Philosophy Law and Jurisprudence* (Chicago: Encyclopaedia Britannica, 1961), *Scholasticism and Politics* (New York: Macmillan, 1940); Will Herberg, *Judaism and Modern Man* (New York: Atheneum, 1970) and *Protestant-Catholic-Jew* (Garden City, New York: Doubleday, 1955); Sidney Hook, *Political Power and Personal Freedom* (New York: Criterion Books 1959), *Reason, Social Myths and Democracy* (New York: John Day, 1940), *Education for Modern Man* (New York: Dial Press, 1946); Walter Lippmann, *Essays in the Public Philosophy* (Boston, Massachusetts: Little Brown and Company, 1955); Jacques Maritain, *Christianity and Democracy* (London: Geoffrey Bles, 1946), *Man and the State* (Chicago: University of Chicago Press, 1951); Gustav Weigel, *Faith and Understanding in America* (New York: Macmillan, 1959).

3. (New York: Sheed and Ward, 1960).

sumably shared by virtue of citizenship. The basic problem, he was convinced, was not one of the relation of church to state, but of the intellectual unity required for a nation to act. The nature of the "public philosophy" is the issue which would bring Hook, Lippmann, and Murray into the same forum. All three were to ask, is there a constitutional consensus whereby the people acquire an identity, a sense of purpose as a collective, sufficient to serve as the basis for action? "Can we or can we not," Murray wrote, "achieve a successful conduct of our national affairs, foreign and domestic, in the absence of a consensus that will set our purposes, furnish a standard of judgment on policies; and establish the proper conditions for political dialogue?"[4] To Murray the civic consensus is constructed neither of psychological rationalizations nor of economic interest nor of purely pragmatic working hypotheses. "It is an ensemble of substantive truths, a structure of basic knowledge, an order of elementary affirmations that reflect realities inherent in the order of existence."[5] But he recognized that any systematic formulation of these truths is apt to meet resistance.

If there was once an American consensus, if the Founding Fathers knew what they meant by liberty, law, and by God, that consensus does not exist today. "The ethic which launched Western constitutionalism and endured long enough as a popular heritage to give essential form to the American system of government has now ceased to sustain the structure and direct the action of this constitutional commonwealth."[6] Murray was convinced that the grounds for such a consensus still exist, at least ideally, in the natural law philosophy of Aristotle, the stoics, and Aquinas. It is that tradition, reflected in the writings of Richard Hooker, John Locke, and others, which provided the principles on which the nation was founded. It is a philosophical tradition which surmounts religious difference, an intellectual tradition that is confident that the order of nature can be discerned and that what is good for man can be established.

For Murray, political life aims at a common good which is superior to a mere collection of individual goods. The fruit of common effort must, of course, flow back to the individual. But he was disturbed by the question, in the absence of a common way of looking at things, can there be an ascertainable common good? Murray's answer contrasts sharply with that entertained by John Dewey and Sidney Hook, who subscribed to an essentially Hobbesian account of the social order. From the point of view of Hobbes, society is not one entity but a collection of action

---

4. *Time*, 12 December 1960.
5. *We Hold These Truths*, p. 9.
6. *Ibid.*

groups each pressing for advantage. According to Hobbes the source of government is the consent of those governed, taken one by one. The individual is the sole source of the right or the good and as an autonomous agent is subject neither to given norms nor to a naturally determined end. Hobbes makes no attempt to subordinate the individual act of self-aggrandizement to the public good. Self-interest, he holds, is not only the dominant motive in politics, but enlightened self-interest is the paper remedy for social ills. Men, he believes, are constituted differently in temperament, biography, and intelligence, and consequently identify the good for themselves in radically different ways. Self-interest is not to be taken as evidence of moral defect but as evidence of disparate personality. In the absence of a common good, separate from and superior to the private goods of individual men, the function of government becomes that of conflict management. Given the fact that litigious subjects are likely to press for special privileges and exemptions for themselves, bargaining and negotiating are natural features of public life. The sovereign is not the representative of the common will; he is the common object of separate wills. In the exercise of his authority, the sovereign is restrained by the diverse purposes of his subjects. The sovereign assists his subjects in the pursuit of happiness not by defining the goals which the members of society ought collectively to pursue, but by removing obstacles to happiness, privately defined. Public order thus has its sources in negotiations between individually situated political actors.

In North America this Hobbesian analysis of society is nowhere more evident than in the area of sexual morality. Sexual union has been made a purely personal affair with society's interest downplayed. Abortion, divorce, homosexuality, and pornography are sanctioned as if their presence had no social repercussions. It is also evident in various rights movements where an invocation of the common good is thought to be a betrayal of a social agenda. In both theory and practice, those who defend special interests do not acknowledge any need to attend to the perceptions or reactions of others who do not share their view. Rights are to be pushed no matter what the consequences. This, in spite of the fact that many communities are presently suffering from the effects of a one-sided pressing of rights, a pressing that in the making identified success with the achievement of a particular gain, even if that gain meant the loss of the setting where that gain might have became meaningful. To offer one notorious example, in Washington, D.C., in the 1950s a Federal judge struck down a "track system" in the public schools of the District of Columbia because its purpose to discriminate between the gifted and not-so-gifted also seemed to discriminate against the blacks. The result was the flight of white families to other school districts and a

D.C. public school system in which 97 percent of the students enrolled were from black families. The gifted black students who remained in the system were themselves disadvantaged by the ruling which prevented instruction on the basis of talent. A judicial emphasis on equality of treatment failed to recognize that the common good demands appropriate education for the gifted. After decades of inferior education, the District of Columbia school system is only now beginning to reverse its losses. It is doubtful that Hobbes himself would have looked with favor on the extremes to which his doctrine has been carried.

To return to my theme, in the absence of a common way of looking at things can the notion of the common good play a role in thinking about the ends of government? Lord Patrick Devlin, the English jurist reflecting on the social order in his own country, not unlike Murray, saw the need for a public philosophy which would provide a secular as opposed to the fading Christian underpinnings of his nation's laws and culture.[7] Devlin, also like Murray, realized that any single candidate for the title "public philosophy" is unlikely to gain universal acceptance. But one may ask, is it necessary that a philosophy prevail in order to exercise a beneficial influence in the social setting? Is it not sufficient that it keeps alive and defends a vantage point? May not calls to attend to the common good have their effect on policy even if the philosophy underlying the concept is imperfectly understood or flatly rejected? Murray's answer is that a working consensus need not embrace all sectors of the society and that it need not embrace equally those which do share it. The existence of intellectual conflict, suggests Murray, is not evidence that there cannot be agreement on very important matters. The acceptance of principles such as the rule of law, the separation of powers, the freedom of belief, the freedom of association, and the representation of beliefs and interests do not depend on metaphysical agreement, though these principles obviously need a defense. Sidney Hook, normally an opponent, would concur. The danger of course is that in the absence of a set of commonly acknowledged principles special interest groups may prevail. Irving Babbit saw this when he wrote in *Democracy and Leadership*. "No movement illustrates more clearly than the supposedly Democratic movement the way in which the will of highly organized and resolute minorities may prevail over the will of the inert and unorganized mass."[8]

Interestingly, when Murray attempts to articulate the truths we hold as a people, the list is surprisingly long. On his account, we can readily

---

7. Patrick Devlin, *The Enforcement of Morals* (London: Oxford University Press, 1965).

8. (New York: Houghton Mifflin, 1924), pp. 290-91.

identify the broad purposes of the nation, or, if you will, the aims of government. With respect to means, standards of judgment may vary and there will be policy differences but we can speak about these things because there is a basis of communication, a universe of discourse. "We hold in common a concept of the nature of law and its relationship to reason and to will, to social fact and to political purpose. We understand the complex relationship between law and freedom."[9] As a people we have in common an idea of justice, we believe in the principle of consent, we distinguish between law and morality, and we understand the relationship between law and freedom. We also recognize criteria of good law, that is, norms of jurisprudence. As a people we "grasp the notion of law as a force for orderly change as well as social stability."[10] Most law is rooted in the shared idea of the personal dignity or sacredness of man, *res sacra homo*. This sacredness guarantees him certain immunities and endows him with certain empowerments, and this is universally recognized.

Neither ideally nor in the United States, need consensus prevent dissent. In the United States the dissenter is not placed beyond the pale of social or civil rights. Those who refuse to subscribe often came from the ranks of the literati and have the media at their disposal. They are not only the academicians, the professional students of philosophy, politics, economics, and history but also the politicians, writers, journalists, and clergy. Murray calls them "clerks." Oxford professor, John Gray, in a recent essay, calls them "intellectuals" and is wary of them because of their nonconformist tendencies.[11] They lack the same stake in society which those responsible either for economic production or for governance possess. They are apt to be disruptive in any scenario.

To readdress Murray's big question. "Can we or can we not achieve a successful conduct of our affairs, foreign and domestic, in the absence of a consensus that will set our purpose, furnish a standard of judgment on policies, and establish the proper condition for political dialogue?"[12] Murray's answer is "no." In Murray's judgment the United States of his time was doing badly. He uses the words "insecure" and "political bankruptcy." Writing thirty years later, John Silber begins the Introduction to his volume, *Straight Shooting*, with the observation "Our society is in trouble and we all know it. We know that something is terribly

---

9. *We Hold These Truths*, p. 81.
10. *Ibid.*
11. John Gray, "Society and Intellectuals: The Persistence of Estrangement and Wishful Thinking," *The Many Faces of Socialism* (New Brunswick, New Jersey: Transaction Books, 1987).
12. *We Hold These Truths*, p. 86.

wrong—the way we might know in our own bodies that we are seriously ill."[13] Silber is forced to address many of the issues previously explored by Murray and comes to many of the same conclusions. Only now the nation is further down stream and the problems more serious, showing how prescient was Murray's analysis. The cause of our weakness, Murray thought, is not simply the Soviet threat. If the Communist empire and communist ideology were to disintegrate overnight our problem would not be solved. We would be worse off in many ways. Anticommunism is not a public philosophy. This is never more evident, he thought, than in discussions concerning the structure, content and orientation of military policies. We have not articulated, for example, the political and moral ends for which we are prepared to use force. Murray could in 1960 cite Kissinger's book *Nuclear Weapons and Foreign Policy* (1957) and its chapter, "The Need of Doctrine," in support of his own outlook. "It is not true that America can intelligently construct and morally put to use, a defense establishment in the absence of a public philosophy concerning the use of force as a moral and political act."[14] Until we can articulate an American consensus with regard to our truths, our purposes, and our values, unless we can agree on fundamentals, "public policy will continue to be projected out of a vacuum in the governmental mind into a vacuum in the popular mind."[15] The only bright spot is that in the absence of intellectual agreement, our instinctive wisdom permits us to cope and survive.

Murray is careful to note that consensus does not mean majority opinion. "Public opinion is a shorthand phrase expressing the fact that a large body of the community has reached or may reach specific conclusions in same particular situation. Those conclusions are spontaneously, perhaps emotionally reached usually from some unstated but, very real premises. The 'public consensus' is the body of these general unstated premises which came to be accepted. It furnishes the basis for public opinion."[16] The consensus is a doctrine or a judgment that commands public agreement on the merits of the arguments for it. "The consensus is not in any sense an ideology; its close relation to concrete experience rescues it from that fate."[17] The public consensus is a moral conception. "Only the theory of natural law is able to give an account of the public moral experience that is the public consensus. The consensus itself is simply the tradition of reason as emergent in developing form in

---

13. John Silber, *Straight Shooting* (New York: Harper and Row, 1989), p. xi.
14. *We Hold These Truths*, p. 91.
15. *Ibid.*, p. 95.
16. *Ibid.*, pp. 102-103.
17. *Ibid.*, p. 106.

the special circumstances of American political-economic life."[18] Murray is aware that the doctrine of natural law is associated with Catholicism. He is quick to point out that the doctrine has no Catholic presuppositions. Its presuppositions are threefold: "that man is intelligent; that reality is intelligible; and that reality as grasped by intelligence imposes on the will an obligation that it be obeyed in its demands for action or abstention."[19] The assumption is that rational human nature works competently in most men, although intellectual judgment alone is not enough. Not only knowledge but rectitude of judgment is required.

"Natural law theory does not pretend to do more than it can, which is to give a philosophical account of the moral experience of humanity and to lay down a charter of essential humanism."[20] It does not show the individual the way to sainthood, but only to temporal fulfillment. "It does not promise to transform society into the city of God on earth, but only to prescribe, for the purposes of law and social custom, the minimum of morality which must be observed by the member of society, if the social environment is to be human and habitable."[21] To inquire what natural law is, means to inquire, on the one hand, what the human mind is and what it can know, and on the other hand, what human society is and to what ends it should work. Its hallmark is its empirical character, its fidelity to evidence derived from common experience and from the sciences. Natural law is best considered as a meta-ethic. As a meta-ethic it amounts to this advice, proceed with confidence that intelligence can determine in a general way what is good for the human race. Put another way, natural law encourages the observer to look for regularities in nature, human and nonhuman. Regularity indicates structure and a knowledge of structure will in turn yield functional explanation, which has a major role in the determination of moral norms. Systematic reflection on human nature will reveal certain constants which are the same everywhere and remain the same from generation to generation. But there are variables too which differ with culture, economic situation and even topography. But Murray was engaged in formulating a public philosophy not on a global scale but for the nation.

An interesting study of contrasting views on the nature of the public philosophy and its justification is provided by an examination of the views of Murray and Sidney Hook. For Murray, democracy is an effective mode of government. The democratic charter is not to be made

---

18. *Ibid.*, p. 109.
19. *Ibid.*
20. *Ibid.*, p. 297.
21. *Ibid.*

an object of faith. The Constitution and the articles of its First Amendment, "Congress shall make no law respecting an establishment of religion nor prohibiting the free exercise thereof," are articles of peace, not part of a secular credo which renounces a role for religion in civic affairs. "If history makes one thing clear it is that these clauses were the twin children of social necessity, the necessity of creating a social environment, protected by law, in which men of differing faiths might live together in peace."[22] The American solution to the relationship between church and state was purely political. Among the various churches vying for allegiance none was to be preferred for the nation as a whole; although in the beginning of the American Republic nine states had established churches, eventually this principle was to be applied to the states as well. The result was political unity and stability without uniformity of religious belief and practice. The Gallic, "One law, one faith, one king," had been replaced by "political unity in the midst of religious plurality." But it does not follow from this that political unity can long endure in the absence of a moral consensus. "Nor has experience yet sawn how, if at all, this moral consensus can survive amid all the ruptures of religious division, whose tendency is inherently disintegrative of all consensus and community."

In 1960 Murray could write "In America we have been rescued from the disaster of ideological parties."[24] Where such parties exist, the struggle for office becomes a struggle for power, for the means by which the apposing ideology may be destroyed. In contrast to certain Latin countries, the American experience of political unity has been striking and to this the First Amendment has made a unique contribution. Murray is convinced that the Church has profited from the American arrangement. In Latin countries, the Church has alternately experienced privilege and persecution. Where it is thought that the business of government is the fostering of the commonwealth as ascertained by the Church, the fortunes of the Church wax and wane with transfer of political power. "In contrast, American government has not undertaken to represent transcendental truth in any of the versions of it current in American society."[25] It has not allied itself with one faith over another, but it has represented a core of commonly shared moral values. In a religiously plural society, government must be neutral; it cannot set itself up as a judge of religious truth. But pluralism is the root of certain problems. How much pluralism and what kinds of pluralism can a

---

22. *Ibid.*, p. 57.
23. *Ibid.*, p. 73.
24. *Ibid.*
25. *Ibid.*, p. 74.

pluralist society stand? Thus the debate concerning the need for a public philosophy.

As we have noted, Murray's public philosophy is one grounded in the natural law which he believes is accessible to all, believer and nonbeliever, Protestant and Catholic, though he recognizes that the Catholic church in a unique way is the bearer of the natural law outlook. The principal function of the public philosophy is the articulation of a set of standards external to the civic order against which the actions of the state can be measured. The standard is right reason shaped by a time-transcending metaphysics and anthropology.

Orestes Brownson, writing in 1856, was similarly confronted with the problem of holding the state accountable, but came to a conclusion which Murray rejected. In an essay, "The Church and the Republic," Brownson argued that the Church is necessary to the state.[26] Surveying American political and social life, Brownson found two powerful and dangerous tendencies: on the one hand, an excessive power of the state leading to social despotism, and on the other, an excessive individualism leading to anarchy. Brownson thought that the Catholic church provided a necessary corrective to both tendencies. As an institution, carrying a moral tradition, it could call the state to account; it could also mitigate, in a way in which Protestantism could not, a destructive individualism by fostering a respect for authority and tradition. But the Church had to exist as an institution with the power not only to teach but to provide moral sanctions. In the interest of the common good, it could not avoid political engagement. Brownson's was the classic notion of political engagement, with antecedents in Greece and Rome, which Murray happily found absent on the American scene. Brownson, himself, was reacting to the Jacobian separation of the Church from the civic order and the denial to it of any influence. Murray stands somewhere between Brownson and Sidney Hook who can be taken as a representative of the Enlightenment Program.

For Hook there can be only one society, one law, one power, and one faith, namely, a civic faith that is the unifying bond of the community. Hook would banish from the political sphere the divisive force of religion. He has no quarrel with religion taken as a "purely private matter." What alarms him is religion in an institutional form, visible, corporate and organized, a community of thought that presumes to sit superior to and in judgment on the community of democratic thought. Religion possessed of social structures by means of which it can voice its judgments and perhaps cause them to prevail is foreign to Hook's concept of civic life. Civil society is the highest societal form of human

---

26. *Quarterly Review*, reprinted in *Works*, vol. 12, p. 409.

life. Civil law is the highest form of law and is not subject to judgment by pure ethical canons. Thus Hook would decry the existence of the parochial school system, while recognizing its legality, as "educationally and democratically unsound," because it separates out a large segment of our youth and imbues them with quite a different outlook.[27] For Hook there is no eternal order of truth and justice; there are no universal verities which command assent, no universal moral law which requires obedience. The ultimate values espoused by society do not flow from the recognition of same antecedently derived notion of the common good. Rather, ultimate value is to be identified with the democratic process itself. The democratic faith is belief in the efficacy of the process.

Both Hook and Murray would agree that democracy is a form of political judgment and as such is to be measured by the extent that it achieves more security, freedom, and cooperative diversity than any of its alternatives. But Hook also speaks of democracy as a way of life; a set of procedures for critical discussion and discovery, which are preeminently exhibited in the work of the scientific community. Even so, democracy as a social philosophy is to be considered an hypothesis. Considered as an hypothesis, Hook believes, it is justified by experience. For Hook the essence of democracy consists in the equal treatment of persons of unequal talent and endowment. "This method of treating human beings is more successful than any other in evoking a maximum of creative, voluntary effort from all members of the community."[28] It enlarges the scope of our experience by forcing us to understand the needs, drive, and aspirations of others, without abandoning our own viewpoint. In nurturing the capacities of each, it adds to the existing stores of truth and beauty. "Regard for the potentialities of all individuals makes for less cruelty of man toward man, especially where cruelty is the result of blindness to, or ignorance of, others' needs."[29] Essential to the democratic process are the methods of public discussion, criticism, and argument. Though these are postulates themselves, they are the postulates of democracy. To undertake their justification is to begin "a new inquiry into a new problem."[30]

Murray's natural law philosophy and Hook's pragmatic naturalism lead to many of the same conclusions, and both recognized this. Their

---

27. As quoted by the *New York Times*, 10 October 1963.

28. "The Justification of Democracy," *Political Power and Personal Freedom* (New York: Criterion Books, Inc., 1959), reprinted in *The American Pragmatists* (New York, Meridian Books, Inc., 1960), p. 396.

29. *Ibid.*, p. 397.

30. *Ibid.*, p. 398.

differences illustrate the metaphysical and epistemological difference between a Dewey-type instrumentalism and an Aristotelian-Thomistic natural law outlook. For Murray there exists a body of truths about human nature and about that which is required for human fulfillment which can be passed from generation to generation. Thus the ancients, no less intelligent or observant than we, can speak to us across the ages, about an essentially unchanging human nature, and it behooves us to return to those authors whose works have been appreciated and commented upon for centuries. That body of truths rests on a set of metaphysical assumptions, viz., that there is such a thing as human nature and that certain ends can be identified as proper to it and others as not. Thus one can say that a life of the mind is preferable to a "simple sense life," that the laws of the state should promote those structures and activities that contribute to self-fulfillment, that self-fulfillment cannot take place apart from community, that the state, for example, is obligated to defend the family, the rights of private property and ensure access to a basic education for all of its citizens. Those commonly accepted truths serve as principles in the prudential order. The prudential judgment itself does not share in the certitude characteristic of the universal or time-transcending principle. The prudential judgment is made in context; its value is determined not solely by principle but by the empirical data available. Concrete options may even foster a reexamination of abstract principles. The further removed from the basic truths regarding human nature and society, the more precarious the judgment. Thus Murray, recognizing the importance of the family for personal growth and for the stability of the social order could never sanction contraception, divorce, abortion, or voluntary euthanasia for the hopelessly afflicted, as Hook would. Of a different order is the judgment, for example, to place an aging parent in a nursing facility when care could be rendered by the family. "Respect for one's parents" taken as a principle does not dictate a specific conclusion. Circumstances direct prudential decision.

The pragmatist's preference of solving each problem in the context in which it arises does not abrogate for him an appeal to principle. He too will invoke principle, but he is not willing to weave those principles into a consistent whole or anchor them in a particular conception of human nature or conception of human fulfillment. Thus contradictory principles may be appealed to in different contexts without inconsistency. If a principle itself is challenged, it too is defended in the context at hand without recourse to a set of constants. For this reason the pragmatist is often considered to be slippery in argument. The metaphysics to which he is committed often goes unstated and placed beyond direct confrontation.

The history of philosophy in the United States can provide many examples of pragmatism. Lovejoy in his famous work identified thirteen. That form which has dominated the American scene, however, has been the instrumentalist or pragmatic naturalism of the Dewey-Hook variety. Murray finds this outlook nothing less than "barbarous." He was, of course, not the first to find it wanting. Writing a generation before, Irving Babbit in his *Democracy and Leadership* (1924) came to the conclusion that the influence of Dewey and his kind on education "amounts in the aggregate to a national calamity."[31] The ill effects of "progressive education" were apparent to Murray in the fifties and are even more so now.

The pragmatic naturalism of the Dewey-Hook variety reduces science to technology, to problem-solving of the sort where answers are not so much to be expected as are reliable predictions. Though it eschews metaphysics, it is nevertheless a materialism which rules out the existence of God and therefore the need for religion in the lives of the people. The beauty attendant the temple, ritual, and feast is held to be built on chimerical foundations. Man is regarded as through and through physico-chemical, having his origin, growth, and decay in nature. This has implications for ethics, since there is no transcendent end for human life. The most one can aspire to is to make this a better place for future generations. Hence the emphasis on training for service and power. Dewey's educational philosophy, with its assumption of "progress," its insistence on personal experience and its orientation to an idealized future, tends to denigrate the inherited and even the study of history. Classical languages are not required to gain access to an irrelevant antiquity. For Dewey, one of the primary aims of education is that of challenging the inherited. Education does not consist in an appropriation of the literature that has nourished the West since classical Greece, but is rather a training for change.

Thus Murray could speak of the new barbarism which threatened the life of reason embodied in law and custom. The perennial work of the barbarian is "to undermine rational standards of judgment, to corrupt inherited wisdom by which the people have always lived, and to do this not by spreading new beliefs but by creating a climate of doubt and bewilderment in which clarity about the larger aims of life is dimmed and the self confidence of the people destroyed."[32] Murray in his day was not optimistic that the West could in the near future recover its patrimony. He would have even less grounds for optimism today. Many

---

31. First published (Boston, Massachusetts: Houghton Mifflin, 1924); reprinted (Indianapolis, Indiana: Liberty Classics, 1979), p. 339.

32. *Ibid.*, p. 13.

outside his Church look to it to supply the intellectual and moral void which is increasingly apparent. Yet that Church as a visible organization in North America appears as muddled and as confused as the larger society which it seems more to reflect than to challenge. But the legacy is there and can be tapped for the direction it provides. The key, of course, is the learning which gives one access to Athens and Rome and medieval Paris and Padova. A respect for the time-transcending wisdom of the ancients follows acquaintance. The Greeks can teach us much about human nature, about the nature of science and about the requirements for virtue. The Romans can instruct us on the subject of law and on the nature of religion and its importance to civic life. Their medieval commentators can weave both into a synthesis that contains a third element, namely, revealed religion.

Revolution and reformation notwithstanding, there is a great literature which remains to be explored by the open mind. But Murray would not be content simply with its recovery. A heritage is to be appropriated, built upon and utilized. That is exactly what Murray did in his own life.

The Relation of Law and Practical Reason in Aquinas

Daniel Westberg

The revision of moral theology in the past generation can be seen as a rejection of the legalism of the manual tradition, and the search for a more biblical foundation of Christian ethics on the life in Christ, the gifts of the Spirit, and the development of the virtues. There is a parallel development in moral philosophy in which the teaching of Aristotle on practical reason has seemed to offer welcome relief from the impasse of the arguments between utilitarians and deontologists.

For many Catholics, the association of Thomas Aquinas with legalism has been so strong that in many quarters his thought is little regarded; and even where his teaching is still used as a source, as in the moral theology of Finnis and Grisez, the interpretation is presented more as a reconstruction than a faithful presentation of Thomistic ethics.

A major part of the problem is the contradiction we think we see between an ethics based on law and one described in practical reasoning in which the agent acts to achieve what he desires. The contrast between the two was a problem not only for Kant (who absolutized the divide between duty and inclination), but goes back to the Stoics, reflected in their attempts to combine Aristotelian psychology of action with natural law.

One way of eliminating the tension is just to say that practical reason simply *is* reasoning from rules. This certainly applies to many interpretations of Thomas (and not just the handbooks); and it can be seen as well in some modern interpretations of Aristotle's theory. The author of a standard account of Aristotelian ethics writes that his theory of human action amounts to "practical rule-keeping" in which what the agent needs to perceive is that he is in the kind of situation to which the rule applies.[1] A number of writers have strongly argued that the association of rules and practical reason in Aristotle is a faulty interpretation.[2]

---

1. W. F. Hardie, *Aristotle's Ethical Theory* (Oxford: Clarendon Press, 1980), p. 240.
2. See A. Kenny, *Will Freedom and Power* (Oxford: Oxford University Press, 1975), p. 71; and Martha Nussbaum, *Aristotle's De Motu Animalium* (Princeton, New Jersey: Princeton University Press, 1978), Essay No. 4, pp. 165 ff.

Since the tension between rules and practical reason precedes Christian thought, and therefore seems to indicate two inherently different ethics, how are we to understand the moral theology of Thomas Aquinas, who not only incorporates the two approaches, but gives both law and practical reason masterful systematic treatment? Many have objected to the practice of excerpting the "treatise on law" (*ST* I-II qq. 90-105) as though its context in a profound moral theology did not matter; but the fact remains that it is located well away both from the treatment of the process of practical reason and from the discussion of specific virtues and vices, giving the impression that it is there for some other purpose, or at least that there is less than a full integration in Thomas's ethical system. We are well aware of (and properly suspicious of) the possibility of constructing the discussions of the virtues into a legalistic system; and it is also possible (which some have found a refreshing change) to marginalize the account of law in the *Summa* and argue for the dominance of practical reason and its perfection in the virtues. Thus Vernon Bourke, to whom we owe many valuable insights, wanted to argue for seeing Thomas primarily as a theorist of right reason.[3] This might imply however that Thomas somehow was not fully aware of the contradictions in his account, or that he made a shift from an emphasis on law in his earlier teaching to a later concentration on the virtues.[4]

There are interpretations of Thomas which try to recognize both the philosophy of Aristotle and the theology of Augustine, but produce false explanations of the combination of an ethics of law and of practical reason in Thomistic terms. These treat the theory of Aquinas as a kind of hybrid between law and practical reason: that he used Aristotle's terms and concepts but that the constraints of the moral tradition of law, sin and conscience force practical reason into a quite different Christian framework.

Thus it is possible to appreciate the Aristotelian structure of the account of morality in the opening of the *prima secundae*, and then to see the account of sin (which follows the general description of the virtues) and of law as the Christian modification. Pere R.-A. Gauthier is a good example here. He is thoroughly at home with both Aristotle and Aquinas, having written a lengthy commentary on the *Nicomachean Ethics* as well

---

3. "The theory of right reason seems to me to take precedence over the theory of natural law"; Vernon Bourke, "Was Aquinas a Natural-law Ethicist?", *The Monist* 58 (1974): 66.

4. This is argued by G. Abba, *Lex et Virtus: Studi sull'evoluzione della dottrina morale di san Tommaso d'Aquino* (Rome: LAS 1983).

as having a significant share in the editing of key texts for the Leonine edition of St. Thomas. For Gauthier, the notion of practical wisdom is restricted in Aquinas (from its function in Aristotle) by the notion of *synderesis*, the knowledge of the first principles of natural law. Thus the freedom of the agent is circumscribed, and the role of prudence contracted. Further, the Christian concepts of sin and the role of the will (derived through St. Augustine, of course) introduce into practical reasoning alien notions with the result that it is only the terminology of Aristotle which survives in Thomism, not the spirit.[5]

A different estimate of the achievement of Thomas is provided by Alan Donagan, who argues for a kind of teleological deontology. He states quite categorically that "early and late, St. Thomas thought of morality as a matter of law ... and of law as resting on a teleology of pre-existent ends."[6] In other words, obedience to law is the foundation of morality; but instead of a deracinated Enlightenment notion of intellect and will, the agent is linked to certain ends which are established, and expressed in the form of law (for the Christian, the two summary commands of our Lord). The will is somewhat less awesome than the Kantian one, not so starkly autonomous, but the spring of action clearly remains a conception of recognizing the motive force imposed by understanding obligation.

Such approaches, whether they envision Thomas starting with Aristotelian practical reason and modifying it by fixed rules and conscience, or starting with the concept of duty or obedience to law but anchored and enriched with relations to certain specified ends, do not provide us with satisfactory accounts of what Aquinas's project really was.

That is why it is important to note Alasdair MacIntyre's recent appreciation of the accomplishment of St. Thomas's project of harmonizing the theology of law from St. Augustine with Aristotelian practical reason. He writes that Aquinas was able to combine an Aristotelian account of nature, theoretical and practical, in such a way that "Aristotle's account of the rational world became recognizably the prologue required for an Augustinian theology."[7] MacIntyre rightly perceives the possibilities of mutual enrichment at a profound level: ". . . both the achievements of Augustinianism and Aristotelianism had been inte-

---

5. Gauthier-Jolif, *L'Ethique a Nicomaque* (Paris: Beatrice-Nauwelaerts, 1970), I. 1, p. 276.

6. A. Donagan, *Human Ends and Human Actions*, Aquinas Lecture, 1985. (Milwaukee, Wisconsin: Marquette University Press, 1985), p. 17.

7. Alasdair MacIntyre, *Three Rival Versions of Moral Enquiry* (Notre Dame, Indiana: University of Notre Dame Press, 1990), p. 123.

grated in such a way that what were, or should have been, recognized as the defects and limitations of Augustinianism as judged from an Augustinian standpoint and the defects and limitations of Aristotelianism as judged from an Aristotelian standpoint had both been first more adequately characterized and then corrected or transcended."[8] We might also note that this represents a growth in insight on MacIntyre's part from his earlier expression of a problem in "overcoming the conflict of traditions,"[9] which shows that the synthesis is by no means obvious or easy to appreciate.

What makes the synthesis of Aristotelian practical reason and Augustinian law so difficult to understand, simply on the level of reading it, is their complete and utter separation in the account of the *Summa Theologiae*. Not only are the treatments widely separated; the vocabulary of law and rules does not enter into the description of the psychological process of action. Reference to law is not made in the description of intention, deliberation, choice, and execution which form the detailed process of human action presented in I-II qq. 12-17. *Synderesis* and conscience are discussed in the anthropological section in the *prima pars*; reference to *synderesis* is made in discussing prudence; but in the section on human action referred to, where the actual operation of intellect and will is presented in relation to action, Thomas does not make use of these terms. Even more to the point is the fact that the "first principle of practical reason" (the correct description of which has recently been so problematic) is not described in the section on action, but in the section on law (in I-II 94.2). If human action is to be explained as following this basic principle and the specifications to be made from it, the basic principle at least would be introduced in the earlier section, with the more detailed explanation deferred to the alter law discussion. This is not the case however. The description of human action given is strictly Aristotelian in flavor, faithful to the principles of the *Nicomachean Ethics*, improved and systematized, and enriched with some material (especially in describing execution where Aristotle was vague) from the Stoic tradition mediated through Nemesius and Chrysostom.[10] We must note that it is not here that law, or rules, even in the basic form of the first principle, make an appearance.

It is of the utmost importance to see correctly the implications of this separation. Motivation for action is not obedience to law or duty,

---

8. *Ibid.*, p. 120.

9. See Alasdair MacIntyre, *Whose Justice? Which Rationality?* (Notre Dame, Indiana: University of Notre Dame Press, 1988), chap. 10.

10. I present a detailed description of this in *Right Practical Reason: Aquinas on Prudence and Human action* (Oxford University Press, forthcoming).

whether this is understood as exterior authority or the inner voice of conscience. The agent does not use his intellect to discover what he should do and generate a "command" for himself to follow. The notion of duty as motivation is wholly absent from the description of the process of action.

Why the stage of *imperium* in the process of action (*ST* I-II 17) has been so confusing is explained by a fundamental misunderstanding of what Aquinas is describing. Since the notion of an inner command—*imperium*—seems to correspond so well to the judgment of conscience (and the Kantian notion of a self-legislating agent), this seems the basis on which to understand duty and obligation in moral reasoning. But Thomas places *imperium* after choice (*electio*) where the decision is already made, and seems from this viewpoint to be badly confused. It is not surprising, given his desire to read St. Thomas in Kantian terms, that Donagan speaks of the "blunders" of Aquinas and tries to correct the account of Thomas by moving *imperium* to coincide with choice.[11] But Thomas's account is not confused; it is a description of action not in terms of rules and inner commands, but in psychological terms, and what *imperium* represents is the mind of the agent controlling the execution of action.

Just as it is clear that no notion of obeying law is to be used in explaining the agent's motivation, so we need not puzzle over what Thomas does say is the motivation—it is understood good (*bonum intellectum*); good, presented as an end (*finis*) is what activates the will.[12] This means that at a very deep level both intellect and will are involved (as specification and exercise) in the process of action. This applies to intention, to deliberation when this is required, to choice and execution. At each stage it is the natural dynamism of the will toward good, which for any given action requires cognition to specify the object and identify the characteristics which make it attractive. Thomas develops a much more systematic description than Aristotle, and integrates it with his metaphysics of act and potency and being, good and truth; but the fundamental dynamics and explanation of the process of action are not a distortion of Aristotle but a clarification and development.

---

11. A. Donagan, "Thomas Aquinas on Human Action," in *The Cambridge History of Later Medieval Philosophy*, ed. N. Kretzmann, A. Kenny, J. Pinborg, (Cambridge: Cambridge University Press, 1982), pp. 642-54.

12. *ST* I 82. 4: "Et hoc modo intellectus movet voluntatem, quia bonum intellectum est obiectum voluntatis, et movet ipsam ut finis." See the detailed development of this in I-II qq. 9 and 10.

Law and Providence

How then, if human action is described without reference to rules or law, is the treatment of law to be integrated in the account of human action? The clue to the principle of integration is not the first principle of practical reason, or conscience and the practical syllogism; it is given to us in the structure of the *prima pars* itself. When Thomas introduces the topic of habits in I-II q. 49 he states (in the prologue) the overall sequence of treatment: after treating the acts and passions, he says, the principles of human actions must be considered. There are "intrinsic" principles as well as "extrinsic." The intrinsic principles are potency and *habitus*, and this introduces the discussion of dispositions and virtues. This occupies Aquinas for the next forty questions, which include an account of the effects of sin on human character. Then when he begins the section on law at q. 90 he says in the prologue, "Now we must consider the exterior principles of actions." Thus the discussion of law is not the provision of more details for understanding practical reason; it is the consideration of human action from an entirely different point of view.

It is useful to pause here and spell out how the organization of the *Summa* relates to the treatment of human action. Thomas alludes in the prologue to I-II q. 49 that the powers of the soul, namely intellect, will, sensation, appetite, and so on, had already been treated in the *prima pars*. Then in the *secunda pars* he treats of the activation of these powers in the process of action (in intention, deliberation, choice, and so on), with a lengthy account of the role of emotion. These powers can be seen also as aspects of character, that is, operating in a pattern of action over time and not just in particular actions, so that habits and virtues come into the picture. All of this teaching, the intrinsic principles of action, makes up the treatment of action from the point of view of the agent.

Action can also be described however from the exterior viewpoint, as a consideration of law, which Thomas first defines as "the rule and measure of actions, according to which someone is led to, or drawn away from, the doing of something."[13] Properly speaking, law is related to reason, a point which is the foundation of the whole treatment of law. But there is a secondary sense, recognized by Aquinas, in which law applies to anything which is regulated and measured—and in this sense "law is in all things which are inclined to something from some law,"[14] although this is not law in its essence but by a kind of participation.

---

13. *ST* I-II 90. 1: "lex quaedam regula est et mensura actuum, secundum quam inducitur aliquis ad agendum vel ab agendo retrahitur."

14. *ST* I-II 90. 1 ad 1: "Et sic lex est in omnibus quae inclinantur in aliquid ex aliqua lege."

To clarify this point we refer to *ST* I-II 1.2. It is a property of all agents (rational and otherwise) to act for an end (*omnia agenta necesse est agere propter finem*). An agent does not move except from an intention for an end. If an agent were not determined toward some effect, he would no more do this rather than that. Now in a rational creature this direction of appetite towards an end (which is what intention means) is through the will, the rational appetite; in other beings the direction is through natural appetite inclined to a form. In other words, in nonrational creatures intention in action (direction towards an end) is still present, but it has been placed there from without.

Agency in creatures without will is a matter of being moved toward an end by some other agent, just as an arrow tends to a determined end by being directed by the archer who directs its action to the end. Thus creatures lacking reason tend toward an end through natural inclination, moved as it were by another, since they are not able to have cognition of the end. Thus all of nature which is irrational relates to God as an instrument relates to the principle agent.[15] It is important to note that the principle of intending an end applies to all agents in creation, and that irrational beings carry out the intention of someone else (in strengthening Aristotelian teleology St. Thomas depends on a Christian doctrine of creation).

This direction toward an end, placed there by God, is the way in which St. Thomas defined providence, and it encompasses all being: "Since providence is nothing other than the rational ordering of things to an end, it is necessary that all things, to the extent that they share in being, be subject to the divine providence."[16]

The description of all law as the direction of all being toward an end by God's wisdom is made explicit in the section on the divine law in *ST* I-II 93.1: Just as the character of the divine wisdom, inasmuch as all things have been created through it, has the character of art, or exemplar, or idea, so the character of divine wisdom moving all things to the proper end attains the character of law.[17] In this way, Aquinas says, the

---

15. *ST* I-II 1. 2: "Illa vero quae ratione carent, tendunt in finem propter naturalem inclinationem, quasi ab alio mota, non autem a seipsis; cum non cognoscant rationem finis, et ideo nihil in finem ordinare possunt, sed solum in finem ab alio ordinantur. Nam tota irrationalis natura comparatur ad Deum sicut instrumentum ad agens principale."

16. *ST* I 22. 2: "Cum ergo nihil aliud sit Dei providentia quam ratio ordinis rerum in finem, necesse est omnia, inquantum participant esse, intantum subdi divinae providentiae."

17. *ST* I-II 93. 1: "Unde sicut ratio divinae sapientiae inquantum per eam cuncta sunt creata, rationem habet artis vel exemplaris vel ideae; ita ratio divinae sapientiae moventis omnia ad debitum finem, obtinet rationem legis."

eternal law is nothing else but the nature of divine wisdom, according to which it is directive of all acts and motions.

Unlike creatures lacking reason human beings are moved through an intrinsic principle, which requires cognition, so that they not only act, but that they act on account of (*propter*) an end. This is what voluntary action means: that creatures with rational appetite act knowingly and willingly for an end.

Animals with some sensation have a degree of cognition of the end, and can react; and Thomas calls this "imperfect cognition" in *ST* I-II 6.2. What distinguishes human cognition in relation to action is that the thing which is the end is not only recognized, but that the rationale of the end is perceived, and the proportional relation of the action to the end is known.[18]

An animal such as a dog runs, or lies down, or digs up a bone as his appetite responds to objects represented by sensation. The reason why these are not fully voluntary actions is not because the dog lacks a sense of obligation, but because he has no means-end structure to give reasons for his actions. From an exterior point of view there is a means-end structure to the movements (which can be described in terms of nourishment, exercise, play, and so on), but the animal is not aware of his actions as fulfilling these purposes.

This is precisely the difference in human acts. A person might be running, and could give a number of explanations—he is running away from something, or hurrying to catch a train, or he is jogging for exercise. It is true that a dog might be running to catch something, or away from a threat, or just for play, but it could give no account (assuming the possibility of communication) of how this particular action fits in to his life as a dog; whereas a human being could talk about the desire to lose weight, the urgency of the meeting he is hoping to attend, and so on.

Human beings have the freedom to choose actions, particular actions for a certain purpose. Each action is the result of a choice made by the operation of intellect and will, which is how *electio* (the *prohairesis* of Aristotle) is defined in *ST* I-II 13.1. Wrong choices and bad decisions are made, and this is the result of human beings having free choice. Since the goodness or badness of actions depends not only on having good purposes but also on other factors such as the object of the action, and the circumstances (where, when, why, how, and so on), both the exterior action (the actual act) and the interior action (disposition of the will) need to be correct. Thus awareness not only of the goal but of the

---

18. *ST* I-II 6. 2: "Perfecta quidem finis cognitio est quando non solum apprehenditur res quae est finis, sed etiam cognoscitur ratio finis, et proportio eius quod ordinatur ad finem ipsum."

appropriateness of the means and the suitability of the occasion must inform the judgment of the human agent in deciding to act.

We need to make clear at this point that the knowledge which attends action, and makes it a human and voluntary action, is not described as the knowledge of rules but knowledge of the purposes of action, and awareness of how the actions in the present circumstances are properly directed to those ends. In other words the agent needs to know the end as an end, needs to know the character of his action, both in relation to his purposes and to the situation; and he needs the wisdom to be able to judge these elements correctly.

The capacity for free choice, which gives human beings a power over their actions (*ST* I-II, prol.), would seem to lift human agency from the realm of providence, the ordering of actions to a certain end. Since the will is not determined to any particular goods (the way an animal's is), how then are voluntary human acts to come under the category of law and providence? In the question dealing with God's providence Thomas specifically states that man is not excluded from this providence. He writes that "because the act of free choice is reduced to God as cause, it is necessary that those things which arise from free choice be subject to divine providence; for the providence of man is contained under the providence of God, as a particular cause is contained under the universal."[19]

Participation

It is in the concept of participation that Thomas brings together practical reason and virtue, the interior principles of action, with law, the exterior principle of action. The intellect itself is described as a sharing in the divine light, by which we know and judge things.[20] Thus the intellect is not directly infused with knowledge, but is able, by the certainty of the first principles, to make correct judgments about objects of cognition and so acquire truth.

It is this capacity to form judgments which applies also to practical reason, and which is central to prudence. All actions proceed from judgments made about them (see *ST* I-II 13.1 ad 2); and again, it is the certainty of the first principles of practical reason (which Thomas described as *synderesis* and which he separated from conscience) which enables the agent to make correct choices for action, just as the certainty

---

19. *ST* I 22. 2 ad 4: "Sed quia ipse actus liberi arbitrii reducitur in Deum sicut in causam, necesse est ut ea quae ex libero arbitrio fiunt, divinae providentiae subdantur; providentia enim hominis continetur sub providentia Dei, sicut causa particularis sub causa universali."

20. *ST* I 12. 11 ad 3.

of the first principles of speculative reason enable true judgments to be made.

The function of law then is to inform the mind with principles by which to judge particular actions, so that they are correctly directed to the ends. This right ordering of action to an end implies correctness in counsel, judgment, and execution; and since they are all required for the right ordering of action, they come within the purview of providence.[21]

Thus the principle of union between law and practical reason is not at the level of conscience—that *synderesis* informs the conscience of what the agent should do, and then practical reason deliberates about how to achieve that. That is a complete distortion of Thomas's account of action. The link is at a much higher or profound level, the link between prudence and providence. Prudence is the developed ability of the practical reason to deliberate, decide and execute, expressed in terms of the correct ordering of means to an end. Providence, as we have seen is also the correct ordering of actions to an end, on the universal level of the governor of the universe.

Law is an expression of the wisdom of God as governor, and the same human mind which can learn to recognize and choose actions correctly is the same mind which can participate in the wisdom of God. And that is why an identity can be expressed between knowledge of truth and participation in the eternal law.[22]

Thomas does provide a direct link between participation in the divine law and the description of human action. This is found in *ST* I-II 19.4 where he asks whether the goodness of the will depends on the eternal law. In the reply Aquinas states that the fact that the human reason regulates the will, by which the will's goodness is measured, derives from the eternal law which is the divine reason.[23] It is instructive that in explaining this and referring to Psalm 54.6 Thomas does not say that we have this light when we know the rules for human action, but that the light of this reason is in us to the extent that it shows to us good things, and regulates our will.[24] When we know and desire the proper *fines* of human life, then we share in the light of the eternal law.

The description of participation by a human agent which we are attempting here would be incomplete if we did not include a wider

---

21. *ST* II-II 49. 6 ad 3: "in recta ordinatione ad finem, qui includitur in ratione providentiae, importatur rectitudo consilii et iudicii et precepti, sine quibus recta ordinatio ad finem esse non potest."

22. *ST* I-II 93. 2.

23. *ST* I-II 19. 4: "Quod autem ratio humana sit regula voluntatis humanae, ex qua eius bonitas mensuretur, habet ex lege aeterna, quae est ratio divina."

24. *Ibid.*: "Lumen rationis quod in nobis est, intantum potest nobis ostendere bona, et nostram voluntatem regulare."

conception of sharing in the life of God through charity. Although the impression is given above that sharing in the eternal law is primarily a matter of informing the intellect, the way in which St. Thomas develops the doctrine of the new law, the *lex evangelica*, shows that it also involves the will, the seat of charity. The new law is principally the very grace of the Holy Spirit, says Aquinas, which is given to believers in Christ.[25] Although in content there is a continuity between natural law and the old law, because there is the same end involved, what makes the Gospel law new is that it is the law of perfection, because it is the law of charity.[26]

With this connection made between charity and law, we may turn to the treatment of the virtue of charity to find a most profound summary of the union of providence, goodness, wisdom, and love in the notion of human participation. In responding to the argument that charity belongs to God and is therefore not something belonging to the human soul, Thomas puts forth the following reply:

> The divine essence is charity, just as it is wisdom, and as it is goodness. Thus just as we are said to be good by the goodness which is God, and wise by the wisdom which is God—because the goodness by which we are formally good, and the wisdom by which we are formally wise is a kind of participation in divine wisdom—so also the charity by which we formally love our neighbour is a kind of participation in divine charity.[27]

It is interesting to read in the same reply that Thomas assigns this terminology to Platonic language used by Augustine, but incorporates it in the Aristotelian categories of voluntary action, act, potency, and habit used in the main response. This is a striking example of how Thomas has been seen in the study of Fabro to incorporate the Platonic conception of participation with a richly expanded version of Aristotle's act-potency scheme.[28] The union of law and practical reason is only an instance of a much grander synthesis underlying the *exitus-reditus* structure of the entire *Summa Theologiae* and seen as early as I q. 5 where

---

25. *ST* I-II 106. 1: "Et ideo principaliter lex nova est ipsa gratia Spiritus Sancti, quae datur Christi fidelibus."

26. *ST* I-II 107. 1: "lex autem nova est lex perfectionis, quia est lex caritatis."

27. *ST* II-II 23. 2 ad 1: "ipsa essentia divina caritas est, sicut et sapientia est, et sicut bonitas est. Unde sicut dicimur boni bonitate quae Deus est, et sapientes sapientia quae Deus est, quia bonitas qua formaliter boni sumus, et sapientia qua formaliter sapientes sumus, est participatio quaedam divinae sapientiae. Ita etiam caritas qua formaliter diligimus proximum est quaedam participatio divinae caritatis."

28. I am following the interpretation of C. Fabro's *La nozione metafisica di partecipazione secondo S. Tommaso d'Aquino* provided by Helen James John, *The Thomist Spectrum* (New York: Fordham University Press, 1966), ch. 6.

St. Thomas combines in the definition of good both the Aristotelian definition *bonum est quod omnia appetunt* and the Dionysian notion that *bonum est diffusivum sui esse*.

Conclusion

The concept of law can be combined with practical reason because they describe two different points of view—the agent's and God's. On the level of the psychological explanation of action, therefore, Aquinas can follow Aristotle faithfully, and his teaching on law does not affect the psychological description of potencies and their activation in intention, deliberation, and choice. The notion of law does not introduce the concept of obligation into the motivation for action.

The doctrine of law is a description of the exterior principle of action, the expression of God's providence directing actions to an end. Without a doctrine of creation and a wise and loving God who desires to share his being this perspective is hardly possible, which is why we do not find this in Aristotle (who had to use the commonly recognized wise person as the standard for practical wisdom).

Prudence was described by St. Thomas as the perfection of practical reason, requiring the development of other moral virtues, but not a notion of law as obligation. Nevertheless Augustine's doctrine of law fit well with a Christian view of prudence, because the agent who understands the correct means and ends for his life and is able to order them properly is the one who by the Holy Spirit participates in both God's wisdom and charity.

Virtue Theory and the Present Evolution of Thomism

Romanus Cessario, O.P.

Over the past decade, a quiet revolution has been gathering momentum in the fields of moral philosophy and Christian ethics. These disciplines are undergoing a decisive shift as duty, obligation, and decision yield their central role in the understanding of the moral life lo the long-neglected concepts of virtue, character, and action.[1] In the English-speaking world, Alasdair MacIntyre remains the chief spokesman for the effort. It may interest some to learn that several years before he published *After Virtue* in 1981, the Faculty of the Dominican House of Studies in Washington, D. C., had decided to reinstate instruction in speculative moral theology, especially treating the matter of virtue theory. In the late 1960s, that is, shortly after the conciliar directive *Optatam totius*, No. 16, urged that the development of moral theology "should be nourished more thoroughly by scriptural teaching," such instruction had been dropped from the curriculum and replaced by courses such as the "Biblical Foundations of Morality."

In some respects, we can credit British scholarship within the analytical tradition as providing the impetus toward a contemporary study of the virtues.[2] Peter Geach, for instance, renders a complete account of classical virtue theory in his small book, *The Virtues* (Cambridge: Cambridge University Press, 1977).[3] In this work, the author

---

1. In *The Moral Virtues and Theological Ethics* (Notre Dame, Indiana: University of Notre Dame Press, 1991), I provide an overview of the nature of the moral virtues, their relation to the intellectual virtues, the centrality of prudence in the moral life, and the structures of the acquisition and development of virtues.

2. Amelie Rorty, ed., *Essays on Aristotle's Ethics* (Berkeley, California: University of California Press, 1980), collects a number of essays which discuss specific aspects of Aristotle's ethical arguments. Arthur Flemming, "Reviewing the Virtues," *Ethics* 90 (1980): 587-95, provides a survey of the literature up to that date. For a recent example of moral philosophy's interest in Aristotle, see D. S. Hutchinson, *The Virtues of Aristotle* (London: Routledge and Kegan Paul, 1987). Finally, J. O. Urmson delivered the 1989 Aquinas Lecture at Blackfriars, Oxford entitled "Aristotle on Excellence of Character," *New Blackfriars* 71 (1990): 33-37.

3. The chapters were originally delivered as the Stanton Lectures (1973-74).

treats the four cardinal virtues, prudence, justice, fortitude, and temperance, as well as the three theological virtues, faith, hope, and charity. Notwithstanding the inclusion of the theological virtues, Geach's work remains a philosophical text. "Faith is God's gift," he writes, "I try here only to remove obstacles to faith." While Geach obviously relies on the texts of Aquinas for his apologetical argument, the majority of ethicians in the back-to-virtue movement contented themselves with Aristotle and other non-Christian sources of moral truth. This may help explain why contemporary debates in Christian ethics actually center on issues other than the development of virtue and moral character. Of course, developments in philosophy usually do require some time to influence theological discussion. Nonetheless, it remains safe generalization to say that virtue theory occupies a small place in the current renewal of moral theology, at least in Roman Catholic circles. Still, it is useful to inquire why the virtue tradition that at one time dominated so much of Christian thinking on moral matters scarcely receives attention today, even from those whose stated purpose includes the revision of Roman Catholic moral theory and practice. This includes the majority of Roman Catholic thinkers who accept St. Thomas Aquinas as a source for theological reflection.

Before the II Vatican Council, two prominent Christian writers did produce properly theological studies on the virtues: Josef Pieper, *The Four Cardinal Virtues* (originally published as three separate treatises between 1954 and 1959 by Pantheon Books, Inc.), and Romano Guardini, *The Virtues* (Wurzburg, 1963). Even though the prevailing casuistry within official Roman Catholic moral theology relegated these essays to the field of Christian spirituality, these books still merit attention. Guardini in fact titled his work *Meditationen Über Gestalten Sittlichen Lebens*. This reflects the general view held earlier in this century and officially endorsed (by Pius XI) which held that discussion about virtue belongs to the realm of ascetical or mystical theology, but does not pertain to the warp and woof of hard moral theology.

In the United States, the Protestant ethicist Stanley Hauerwas again opened the eyes of the theological ethics community to the importance of virtue for moral theology. *Character and the Christian Life: A Study in Theological Ethics* (San Antonio: Trinity University Press, 1975) certainly merits an honored place in the history of virtue renewal. But according to Eilert Herms, "Virtue: A Neglected Concept in Protestant Ethics," Hauerwas's inspiration attained neither wide nor immediate recognition.[5] The history of Protestant thought also witnessed a similar eclipse of interest in virtue theory. But now the tide is turning.

---

4. *Ibid.*, p. viii.
5. *Scottish Journal of Theology* 35 (1982): 481-85.

In recent years, a number of substantial works have appeared in the fields of moral theology and philosophy which take serious account of the place which virtue holds in the moral life. And in these publications, the texts of Aquinas invariably surface. I have chosen to chronicle an evolution of Thomism which is going on mainly in continental thought: in Germany (Tübingen), the theologian Eberhard Schockenhoff; in German-speaking Switzerland (Zurich), the philosopher Martin Rhonheimer; in *la Suisse Romande* (Fribourg), the Belgian Servais Pinckaers, O.P.; and in Italy, the Spanish Ramon Garcia de Haro. However, since Alasdair MacIntyre's recent Gifford Lectures published as *Three Rival Versions of Moral Enquiry* (Notre Dame, Indiana: University of Notre Dame Press, 1990) clearly merits him a place in some future history of Thomism, I would also like to include the American theologian Jean Porter in my survey. In a forthcoming book from Knox/Westminster Press, Miss Porter clearly acknowledges her reliance on Professor MacIntyre for her reading of Aquinas's virtue theory.[6]

The extensive use of Aquinas's *corpus* forms the only criterion for calling the authors of these works Thomists. And pluralism, I submit, accurately describes the present state of Thomist morals. Because few of these "evolving" Thomist moralists are well known in the United States, this summary account of their positions on virtue will introduce them to the American audience. Beyond meeting that objective, I also wish to indicate briefly certain "orientations" of Thomist moral philosophy and theology.

First, the Tübingen theologian Eberhard Schockenhoff and his scholarly study *Bonum Hominis: Die anthropologischen und theologischen Grundlagen der Tugendethik des Thomas von Aquin* (Mainz: Matthias-Grünewald-Verlag, 1987). Although the author considers the roots of Aquinas's thought in both the biblical commentaries and early systematic works, this 613-page model of German erudition principally inquires into the moral theology of the *Summa Theologiae*. The investigation unfolds in six major moments: First, concerning the doctrines of the *imago Dei* and *beatitudo* as, respectively, the origin and destiny of the human person; second, on Aquinas's conception of human freedom as the basis for his doctrine on virtue; third, on the role and function of

---

6. This list excludes an author who deserves mention in any account of contemporary Thomist moral theology. I refer to the work of Michel Labourdette, O.P. As the veritable "doyen" of Thomist moralists, Fr. Labourdette belongs to the generation of du Lubac and company. But he still teaches at the Dominican studium in Toulouse. Until recently, his complete commentary on the *secunda pars* has existed only in mimeographed copies. Recently however, I learned with great pleasure that his editor plans a printed edition for next year.

human emotions in virtue; fourth, on *habitus* as the psychological foundation for virtue; fifth, concerning the specific notion of what constitutes a virtue; sixth and finally, on the notion of infused virtue and the working of divine agency on the human creature. A final section of the book considers each one of the theological virtues.

On Schockenhoff's account, "Bonum hominis" ("Das Gut des Menschen") forms the "Leitidee" of both human and Christian morality. In brief, the author adopts a concordist view concerning the relationship of imperfect and perfect beatitude, that is, human flourishing possesses at least some concrete relevance for beatifying *beatitudo*. In a similar way, since faith remains a virtue of the intellect, it can serve as a point of convergence for philosophy and theology. As much as the whole person engages in the moral life, virtue-shaped emotions facilitate our spiritual desire to achieve its final goal, the bonum hominis. Finally, freedom and (infused) virtue converge in the pursuit of a good which itself terminates the (ultimate) spiritual desire of each person.

Interestingly, Schockenhoff argues that one can measure the stability of a *habitus* not only by reference to the quality of the acts which it produces, but also by reference to the quality of the object which specifies it. Because of this view, the author can ascribe to the infused virtues a greater firmness than that which the acquired moral virtues enjoy. For this author, the infused virtues even provide the prime analogue, that is, the best concrete example and gauge, of all operative *habitus*. Whether or not this view represents the position of Aquinas, the author does draw our attention to the "receptive" side of a *habitus*. The stance, moreover, prepares us for the author's strong insistence on the place of the theological virtues in the Christian moral life.

Eight final theses indicate the various relevances which Aquinas's virtue theory holds for contemporary discussion in moral theology. For example, Schockenhoff contends that Aquinas's notion of virtue allows us to recognize moral science even in concrete and specific actions. He points out that moral science, practical judgment, and actual experience constitute a sort of dynamic circle which links elaborated moral knowledge with individual moral behavior. All in all, *Bonum Hominis* embodies a reliable contemporary version of Aquinas's moral theology.

Martin Rhonheimer's *Natur als Grundlage der Moral* (Wien: Tyrolia-Verlag, 1987) pursues a slightly different objective, one which challenges the use to which some German moral theologians put the distinction between the "categorical" and the "transcendental" in moral decision-making. Since he defines virtue as the "place" where reason and natural inclination integrate, the author stresses the importance of virtue for a correct understanding of natural law theory. However, because it enlarges on the account of virtue in his book, I am citing from a more recent article by Rhonheimer, "Naturgesetz, Prinzipien der Praktischen Vernunft und Menschliches Handeln," an abridged translation of which will appear shortly in *The Thomist* under the title "Human Action, Natural Law, and the Moral Virtues." In both works, Rhonheimer grounds his "metaphysics of action" in Aquinas's discussions about the eternal and natural law. He insists that we envision natural law, not as an "order of nature," but as an "ordinatio rationis," that is, as an achievement of human reason.

Because he submits Aquinas's moral theory to a powerful Augustinian exegesis, Rhonheimer can easily take issue with those who cite Aquinas to support the existence of an autonomous ethic. For example, Rhonheimer notes the *Tenth Quodlibetal Question* q. 2, a. 2 where Aquinas interprets verse 6 of Psalm 4, "Signatum est super nos lumen vultus tui, Domine" as meaning that divine truth establishes the ground and cause for all human cognition. The same biblical text is to be found at *Summa Theologiae* Ia-IIae, q . 91, a. 2 when Aquinas affirms that "the light of natural reason by which we discern what is good and what evil, is nothing but the impression of divine light on us." Given this confidence in human reason's direct enlightenment concerning moral truth, Rhonheimer, perhaps understandably, defines moral virtue as those dispositions which guarantee that the appetitive powers will not frustrate practical judgments. In other terms, moral virtue constitutes Augustine's "ordo amoris" (*De civitate Dei* 15. 22). Or again, moral virtue remains the condition for natural law to govern effectively in concrete and particular choices of action. As I said, Rhonheimer refuses to distinguish a (transcendental) theonomous from a (categorical) autonomous domain in human actions. Why? In his judgment, such a view effectively disengages both human freedom and moral activity from their privileged participation in the divine perfection of light.

Servais Pinckaers presents his study of moral theology under the title *Les Sources de la morale chrétienne* (Paris: Editions du Cerf, 1987). The Belgian Dominican represents an older generation of scholars who continue to develop the moral teaching of Aquinas. What makes Fr. Pinckaers especially noteworthy in this survey is his long-standing insistence on the importance of a moral theology based on the virtues, gifts of the Holy Spirit, and evangelical beatitudes instead of a moral doctrine based on commandments and rules. Although somewhat eclipsed by the developments in moral theology immediately after the Council, Fr. Pinckaers conserved Aquinas's fundamental intuitions on the moral and theological virtues. Curiously, however, I can find no reference to Fr. Pinckaers in Alasdair MacIntyre's recent writings.

Two elements of Pinckaers's virtue theory deserve special attention. First, Pinckaers stresses the unique character of Aquinas's notion of *habitus*. In an early article, Pinckaers played with the notion that virtue is not a habit. Why? Because virtue insures that our human capacities accomplish their optimum, and this does not imply routine. Of course, a correct understanding of *habitus* leaves room for virtuous originality, and indeed makes it possible. Yet some critics have misunderstood Pinckaers's reasons for talking about virtuous *habitus* as "inner principles" of action. Morals, these critics insist, mean decisions, not inner dispositions. But Pinckaers responds that only virtue insures the full and complete performance of a correct choice.

Secondly, Pinckaers stresses the teleological framework of Aquinas's moral teaching: Augustine, not Aristotle, however provides the key to understanding this moral finality. Inspired by the five major themes which Augustine discloses in the Sermon on the Mount (*De Sermone Domini in Monte*, Bk. 2), Pinckaers signals the search for *le bonheur*, the active pursuit of happiness as the architectonic for Christian living. As a theologian, Pinckaers prefers talking about the role of the Holy Spirit in the moral life instead of elaborating on the function of practical reasoning in discerning moral absolutes. But, as the title of one of his books indicates, there still exists "Ce qu'on ne peut jamais faire," that is, actions intrinsically evil by reason of their constitution. By definition, such deeds do not make us happy.

In his recent book *Cristo, Fundamento de la Moral* (Barcelona: Ediciones Internacionales Universitarias, 1990), the Spanish priest Ramon Garcia de Haro devotes a concluding chapter to virtue. For Garcia de Haro, virtue serves as a cipher for divinization. In itself, this does not distinguish him from the position of Schockenhoff or Pinckaers on the infused virtues. But the program for reaching a virtuous state varies considerably from how the classical moral tradition interpreted the *secunda pars*. Garcia de Haro begins with Christ's teaching as the sole means to establish the grounds for true human dignity, and continues with "metaphysical harmonies" which he discovers between the notions of person, law, liberty. The author continues by emphasizing the role of a conscience which remains sympathetic to both moral law and magisterium, and in two chapters, by enlarging on sin and sinning. The casuists, as you will recall, relied on many of these same categories to develop their school positions.

As the title indicates, Garcia de Haro represents what I will provisionally call "Christocentric Thomism." The members of this school share an active interest in the writings of the Angelic Doctor, but they also choose to place Aquinas within a larger context of specifically evangelical objectives. These objectives, whether they derive from a reading of the conciliar documents, such as *Lumen gentium*, the encyclicals of John Paul II, such as *Redemptor hominis*, or the distinctive purposes of a founder, such as Josemaria Escrivá de Balaguer, require that the person of Christ always functions as the starting point of all legitimate theological enquiry. Of course, we recognize how this method runs counter to that which many interpreters agree Aquinas himself follows in the *Summa Theologiae*. Nevertheless, the custom of reading Aquinas as if he were St. Bonaventure is gaining increasing respectability, and therefore must be considered one of the evolutions to which Thomism submits.

Finally, Jean Porter's *Recovery of Virtue: The Relevance of Aquinas for Christian Ethics* (Louisville, Kentucky: Westminster/John Knox Press, 1990). This book aims at drawing the thought of Aquinas into a clearer dialogue with those who write about theological ethics in the United States. Accordingly, Porter prefaces her study with a brief survey of Catholic moral theology since Vatican II (where Germain Grisez and Richard McCormick, S.J.—it will come as no surprise—represent the major positions) and summary accounts of the dominant themes in the works of Protestant theologians Gene Outka, James Gustafson, and, indeed, Stanley Hauerwas. She then turns to a "reconstruction of the more strictly philosophical components" of Aquinas's moral theory as contained in the *Summa Theologiae*. In chapter two, Porter explains some basic notions which undergird Aquinas's general theory of morals, for example, his notion of goodness as something real; the premise that what is good or best for anyone is so in virtue of its being of a certain kind; the assertion that the self remains a legitimate "object" of theological charity; the view that one discovers intelligibility and organization within the created order; and finally, the conviction that the final perfection of the rational creature transcends the limits which creatureliness itself imposes. In chapter three, Porter gives an account of Aquinas's action theory, illustrated by some good examples. Chapters 4-6 provide her account of the *secunda pars*: the affective virtues, justice, and, in one chapter, "Prudence; Cardinal and Theological Virtues." But ultimately the author proposes that Aquinas can serve only as a starting point for morals, for "we can no longer accept [his] account as it stands" (*Recovery of Virtue*, p. 180).

Fr. McCool's thesis (in *From Unity to Pluralism: The Internal Evolution of Thomism*) concerning the pluralistic evolution of Thomism in the twentieth century surely holds true for the present state of Thomist moral philosophy and theology. Although I run the risk of sanctioning premature and, consequently, artificial divisions for a process which only now has begun to emerge, I would like to suggest some characteristics which allow us to identify certain recognizable strains in the pluralism. In sum, I think we can verify two leanings among Thomist moralists nowadays.

First, the "Teleological Thomists." These emphasize Aquinas's insistence on final causality as both specifying and energizing the course of a good moral life. The theologians Schockenhoff and Pinckaers especially dwell on the significance of *beatitudo* in Thomist moral theology. The vision of God ultimately specifies the kind of life which the Christian must lead and at the same time draws the individual believer to follow that path of blessedness. But, alas, teleology can easily become a dangerous notion. Interpreters, for instance, sometimes confuse teleology with questions about intention and purpose in moral conduct. For example, Jean Porter asks whether Aquinas's teleological frame of reference allows for performing actions "without reference to any wider aim" (*Recovery of Virtue*, p. 76). And in a noteworthy article, Lisa Sowle Cahill points out that some who read Aquinas even interpret his teleology as a species of consequentialism.[7] Thomas Gilby once remarked that end so dominates the *secunda pars* that it should be read to say what it means. I suggest that today this remains an apt remark.

Secondly, the "Christocentric Thomists." As I have said, Garcia de Haro transparently represents this perspective. The Roman theologian Carlo Caffarra reads Aquinas along similar lines (*e.g.*, in his *Living in Christ* [San Francisco, California: Ignatius Press, 1987]). This perspective of course reintroduces some issues which preconciliar Thomism never quite got around to solving. I refer to the discussions between those who inaugurated the return to les sources of Christian thought, judging them indispensable for the continued viability of the theological enterprise, and those who took issue with this judgment, maintaining that only a realist metaphysics could preserve stability in theology. We usually think about the "New Theology" crisis as related to dogmatic concerns, but it has significance, I submit, for moral theology as well. It was none other than the late Fr. Chenu who felt obliged to explain why Christ appears so infrequently in the *secunda pars*.[8]

Does this mean that some evolving Thomist soon will produce a contemporary version of R. Garrigou-Lagrange's 1937 article, "L'instabilité dans l'état de péché mortel des vertus acquises"?[9] I think

---

7. "Teleology, Utilitarianism, and Christian Ethics," *Theological Studies* 42 (1981): 601-29.

8. See his *Toward Understanding St. Thomas*, trans., A.-M. Landry, O.P. (Chicago: Henry Regnery Company, 1964), pp. 313-17.

9. *Revue Thomiste* 42-43 (1937): 255-62.

not. But the distinction between grace and nature still haunts ethics, theological or otherwise.

Some authors, such as Pinckaers and Garcia de Haro, clearly address themselves to Christian believers. They respectively represent a theological teleology and a confessional Christocentrism. But Rhonheimer and Porter, for different reasons, do not intend their studies to serve as examples of confessional literature. Rhonheimer calls his work philosophy, but he likes to emphasize the "identity" of the eternal law and natural law. "Reason," he argues, "does not know eternal law in an 'objective natural order'; rather, reason unfolds and explicitates the eternal law through a 'ratio naturalis' so that one can speak about a natural law. The eternal law is to be found, then, in the 'spirit of God' and participatively in the rational creature's inclinations and proper activities." His emphasis on participation leaves open the question as to how this differs from that participation which we call the grace of the moral virtues. On the other hand, Porter expressly undertakes a "reconstruction of the more strictly philosophical components" of Aquinas's moral theory as contained in the *Summa Theologiae*, but also considers both the theological and infused moral virtues. Although she enjoys the company of a growing number of scholars who analyze the arguments used in theological discourse, her approach raises the question as to how a philosopher can enquire about matters which surpass the competence of reason, such as divine charity, Christ, and the Holy Spirit.

By way of conclusion, I submit that, in order to recognize how imperfect beatitude, what we sometimes hear referred to as "human flourishing," and Christ respectively shape a distinctively Thomist moral theology, we will need to take up again the distinction between the infused and acquired virtues. Only Schockenhoff appears willing to review those discussions frequent in the neo-Thomist period, but clearly based upon divergent school positions held by thirteenth- and fourteenth-centuries theologians, which sought to untangle the relationship of the infused moral virtues to their acquired counterparts. This discussion will certainly involve renewed reflection on Maritain's thesis, as expressed in Appendix VII of *The Degrees of Knowledge* (trans. Gerald B. Phelan [New York: Charles Scribner's Sons, 1959]): "We do not think that, in the state of fallen and redeemed nature, a complete moral wisdom of the purely philosophical order is possible, be it speculative or practical in mode" (p. 463).

Ultimate End and Common Good
In *Summa Theologiae*, Secunda Pars

Gregory Froelich

In human action what is last in execution is first in intention. For just this reason Thomas Aquinas begins the *secunda pars* of the *Summa Theologiae* with a consideration of man's ultimate end. It is the end and the end alone that renders intelligible all those choices and activities that human life comprises. "Finis enim dat speciem in moralibus" (*ST* 2-2 43.3; cf. 1-2 1.3, 18.6). Both the intellect in its practical activity and the will in its inclination share the same starting point. "The point of departure," Thomas says, "in the activity of rational appetite is the ultimate end" (*ST* 1-2 1.5). And: "The first principle in human deeds—the subject matter of practical reason—is the ultimate end" (*ST* 1-2 90.2); accordingly, "what first falls into the apprehension of practical reason is the good" (*ST* 1-2 94.2). Clarity on this point therefore must be had at the outset of moral discourse (whether philosophical or theological) to ensure success; confusion spells disaster. Hence Thomas devotes the first questions of the *secunda pars* to a consideration of the ultimate end. He had, as it were, no choice. Only then does he proceed to consider human actions in themselves and their intrinsic and extrinsic principles. In my brief comments I wish to call your attention to a feature of Thomas's discussion concerning that extrinsic principle he calls law. For there beginning with question 90 of the *prima secundae* an explicit consideration of the ultimate end arises once again but with a precision which is, I think, sometimes misunderstood within the Thomistic tradition.

It is obvious that Thomas's discussion in *ST* 1-2, leading up to the definition of law (q. 90), takes its cue from the familiar sense of the term, that is, human positive law. This is perhaps no more obvious than in the second article where Thomas argues that all law (eternal, divine, natural, and human) is ordered to the common good. As the rational rule and measure of all human action, so the argument goes, law must first take into consideration the ultimate end; but since human perfection at every level is achieved only in society (human and divine), the ultimate end is in fact nothing other than the common good. In a way to confirm this Thomas refers to the fifth book of the *Nicomachean Ethics* where Aristotle speaks of legal justice as procuring and preserving the happiness of political community. He then reminds us that in the *Politics* Aristotle calls the perfect community "the city" (*civitas*). Strange references for a theologian, unless we realize that Thomas is not restricting his discussion here to divine law only and in fact is focusing on its better known yet secular counterpart in order to shed light on it and the other forms of law. When Thomas identifies the ultimate end with the common good, therefore, he has chiefly in mind the human ultimate end attainable in this life and the political common good, that is, political community.

This identification is precisely what a Thomist such as Henry Veatch denies.[1] As he sees it, the common good or political community is considered good just so far as it is an expedient means to the welfare and happiness of each and every individual citizen. It is not a good worth choosing for its own sake, let alone an ultimate end. Veatch's own description of the common good resembles the *bona communia* that Thomas refers to in his discussion of distributive justice (*ST* 2-2 61.1), namely such goods as money, honors, water, land (natural resources in general), and "anything else in the class of exterior goods" (*ibid.*). The sum of these, together with the roles, offices, responsibilities, and "institutional arrangements" that ensure their maintenance and usefulness, is Veatch's common good.[2]

For Thomas this is indeed a common and indispensable good, but nevertheless a common good on the level of utility and not choiceworthy in itself. For it falls within an order toward an even more indispensable common good—a good that is, as Jacques Maritain argued repeatedly,[3] in the class of *bonum honestum*, noble, choiceworthy for its own sake, and perfective of the human agent. Thomas identifies this common good as the life of political community itself, for as a part of this communion of persons, just as within a friendship, the individual finds an essential element of his or her flourishing. In other words, for Thomas (and Aristotle), political community is a basic human good (cf. *ST* 1-2 94.2); in fact, so far as it is perfect the life of the community contains even all other natural human goods and for this reason can be considered an ultimate end (though of course not the absolute ultimate end).

Interestingly enough, while Veatch denies that the political common good could possibly have the character of an ultimate end, he nonetheless argues that "the love and association of others" is an

---

1. *Human Rights: Fact or Fancy?* (Baton Rouge, Louisiana: LSU Press, 1985], pp. 124-34.

2. *Ibid.*, p. 122.

3. *The Person and the Common Good* (Notre Dame, Indiana: University of Notre Dame Press, 1966), p. 53; *The Range of Reason* (New York: Charles Scribner's Sons, 1952), p. 142; *Man and the State* (Chicago: University of Chicago Press, 1963), p. 149.

integral part of an individual's flourishing.⁴ But is not political community a form of love and association, of *philia, amicitia,* friendship? Doubtless Aristotle, Thomas, and Maritain thought so and for that reason considered the city to be an intrinsically choiceworthy good, in fact, an ultimate end. Not only does Veatch neglect this constant and evident teaching of the tradition he claims his own, he even (perhaps unwittingly) contradicts it. His confusion on this point, I suggest, stems both from his oversight of the distinction between objective beatitude (*finis cuius*) and formal beatitude (*finis quo;* cf. *ST* 1-2 1.8) and from his attempt to reconcile two fundamentally disparate political schools (those of Aristotle and of Locke).

John Finnis's discussion of the common good in *Natural Law and Natural Rights* surpasses Veatch's in clarity and fidelity to the tradition but is not completely immune from criticism. For his working definition of the common good seems strikingly similar to Veatch's: "A set of conditions which enables the members of a community to attain for themselves reasonable objectives, or to realize reasonably for themselves the value(s), for the sake of which they have reason to collaborate with each other (positively and/or negatively) in a community."⁶ I say "seems similar" because of other remarks Finnis makes in *Natural Law and Natural Rights* that in fact run counter to such an interpretation. For example, he also calls the common good a "value" and "objective," the "flourishing of all members of the community," and the "object of all justice." In this last sense, the common good "is not to be confused with the common stock, or the common enterprises, that are among the means of realizing the common good."⁸ Finnis in fact offers a threefold division of the common good: (1) the seven basic values (life, knowledge, play, aesthetic experience, friendship, religion, and freedom in practical reasonableness) taken together; (2) each basic value taken separately; and 3) a set of conditions . . ., which is the one "commonly [but by no means exclusively] intended throughout this book."⁹ He sees this third type as ordered to bringing about the first and second types of common good (cf. p. 156).

Thomas himself admits that "common good" is used in a variety of ways, but not exactly in the ways Finnis mentions.¹⁰ For among those

---

4. Henry Veatch, *Human Rights,* p. 129.
5. (Oxford: Oxford University Press, 1984), pp. 134-60.
6. *Ibid.,* p. 155.
7. *Ibid.,* pp. 154; 174, and cf. 303, 372; 168, 194.
8. *Ibid.,* p. 168.
9. *Ibid.,* p. 155.
10. See Gregory Froelich, "The Equivocal Status of *bonum commune,*" *The New Scholasticism* (Winter 1989), pp. 38-57.

seven basic values or goods Thomas would point out only one that is truly common in the way a good is properly common, that is, as a common end or goal ("communitate causae finalis," *ST* 1-2 90. 2ad2). That good is friendship. Life, knowledge, and the others, since realized (or instantiated) in the individual as such, are common only in definition ("communitate generis vel speciei," *ibid*.). Although we both may be knowing the same truth, my act of knowing is not yours. Knowledge, properly speaking, is a purely personal good. Friendship, on the other hand, in its very particularity is as common to the friends as is the room they may be sharing. Indeed, as Thomas argues, the common life of friends is the most choiceworthy thing in friendship (*In IX Ethic*, lect. 14). Hence for Thomas it is precisely this kind of common good above all that law must respect. This finds vivid expression in Aristotle's insistence that the principal intent of human law is to produce friendship among the people (*Nic. Ethics* 1155a25). Thomas adds that even divine law has friendship chiefly in view—the friendship of course between man and God (*ST* 1-2 99.2).

Yves R. Simon once warned that "an inquiry into the common good must involve constant awareness that its object may, at any time, be displaced by deadly counterfeit."[11] For it is a highly equivocal term. But equivocity does not always preclude one of the many senses from ranking first. I have tried to indicate what kind of common good an authentic Thomistic moral theory would place foremost: the common good as ultimate end. In this view, an individual citizen chooses to participate in the common good of his community as an integral component of his flourishing, and not as a mere means. Fortunately, this is not a uniquely Thomistic view. The authors of *Habits of the Heart* (New York, 1985), for example, seem to accept it, and in fact have argued that everybody seems in one way or another to assent to it, even though the prevailing language at the moment is that of individualism. For even natural law, the set of first and immediate principles of practical reason present to everyone, has as its principal object the common good.

---

11. *A General Theory of Authority* (Notre Dame, Indiana: University of Notre Dame Press, 1962, 1980, 1991), p. 27.

Contributors

Benedict M. Ashley, O.P. is Professor of Theology at the John Paul Institute for Studies on Marriage and the Family. He is author of *Healthcare Ethics: A Theological Analysis.*

David C. Burrell, C.S.C. is the Theodore M. Hesburgh Professor of Philosophy and Theology in the University of Notre Dame. He recently co-edited *God and Creation: An Ecumenical Symposium.*

John C. Cahalan, author of *Causal Realism*, is an independent scholar living in Methuen, Massachusetts.

Romanus Cessario, O.P. is Associate Professor of Systematic Theology at the Dominican House of Studies in Washington, D. C. and the author of *The Moral Virtues and Theological Ethics.*

W. Norris Clarke, S.J. is Professor Emeritus of Philosophy at Fordham University. He is author of *The Philosophical Approach to God: A Neo-Thomist Perspective.*

Vincent M. Colapietro, author of *Pierce's Approach to the Self*, is Associate Professor of Philosophy at Fordham University.

Raymond Dennehy, Professor of Philosophy at the University of San Francisco, is author of *Reason and Dignity* and President of the American Maritain Association.

J. A. DiNoia, O.P. who teaches in the Department of Religious Studies at the Dominican House of Studies in Washington, D. C., is the Editor of *The Thomist.*

Jude P. Dougherty is Dean of the School of Philosophy at The Catholic University of America and Editor of *The Review of Metaphysics.*

Desmond J. FitzGerald is Professor and Chair of the Department of Philosophy in the University of San Francisco.

Gregory Froelich is Adjunct Assistant Professor of Philosophy at The Catholic University of America.

Robert F. Harvanek, S.J. is Professor Emeritus of Philosophy at Loyola University of Chicago.

Deal W. Hudson is Professor of Philosophy at Fordham University. He is co-editor of *Understanding Maritain: Philosopher and Friend* and current Vice President of the American Maritain Association.

John F. X. Knasas is Professor of Philosophy at the University of St. Thomas Center for Thomistic Studies. He is author of *The Preface to Thomistic Metaphysics*.

Joseph W. Koterski, S.J. is a member of the faculty of the Weston School of Theology, Cambridge, Massachusetts.

Gerald M. McCool, S.J. is Professor Emeritus of Philosophy at Fordham University. He is author of *From Unity to Pluralism: The Internal Evolution of Thomism*.

Marion Montgomery is Professor Emeritus of English Literature at the University of Georgia. Among his many books on modern culture is his three-volume *Prophetic Poet and the Spirit of the Age*.

Josef Pieper, author of *Leisure: The Basis of Culture*, is well known for his numerous publications on Thomism and modern philosophy.

Vittorio Possenti is a member of the philosophy faculty of Università degli Studi de Venezia. He is author of *Maritain e Marx: La critica del marxismo in Maritain*.

Juha-Pekka Rentto teaches Philosophy in the University of Turku, Finland; he is author of *Prudentia Juris: The Art of the Good and the Just*.

David L. Schindler is on the faculty of the John Paul Institute for Studies on Marriage and the Family and is Editor of *Communio*.

Edward A. Synan is Director Emeritus of the Pontifical Institute of Mediaeval Studies and author of several books on medieval subjects.

Daniel Westberg teaches in the Department of Religion at the University of Virginia. He is the author of *Right Practical Reason: Aquinas on Prudence and Human Action*.

Index of Names

Adler, Mortimer J., 7, 92, 266
Aertsen, Jan, 195
Aeschylus, 201
Albert the Great, 60, 183
Al-Farabi, 165
Apel, Karl Otto, 224, 225
Aquinas, Thomas, 1, 2, 3, 4, 7, 8, 9,
  13, 14, 15, 16, 17, 19, 28, 43, 45,
  52, 53, 54, 55, 56, 57, 58, 59, 60,
  61, 62, 63, 77, 79, 80, 81, 83, 85,
  86, 87, 88, 89, 90, 92, 93, 96, 97,
  98, 100, 105, 106, 109, 112, 113,
  114, 115, 117, 118, 119, 120, 121,
  123, 124, 127, 128, 130, 131, 133,
  134, 136, 137, 138, 140, 141, 142,
  143, 144, 145, 146, 147, 149, 150,
  152, 153, 156, 162, 163, 164, 165,
  167, 169, 171, 172, 181, 182, 183,
  187, 188, 189, 190, 191, 192, 193,
  194, 196, 201, 207, 213, 215, 226,
  227, 231-45, 247, 267, 279-290,
  291-99, 301-304
Arendt, Hannah, 224
Aristotle, 14, 30, 31, 37, 43, 55, 56,
  74, 75, 80, 81, 86, 87, 97, 101,
  104, 165, 167, 172, 188, 189, 190,
  191, 217, 220, 267, 279, 280, 281,
  282, 283, 286, 292, 296, 301, 302,
  303
Ashley, Benedict M., 14-15
Augustine, Aurelius, 56, 60, 86, 87,
  207, 208, 233, 240, 280, 281, 289,
  290, 295, 296
Avicenna, 165, 182, 183
Ayer, A. J., 79

Babbit, Irving, 269
Bacon, Francis, 129
Balthasar, Hans Urs von, 247-64
Balthasar, Nicolas, 52

Bañez, Domingo 163, 167, 182
Bellarmine, Robert, 265
Bergson, Henri, 52
Billot, Louis, 78
Boethins, 80, 182
Bohr, Niels, 129
Bonaventure, Saint, 17, 86, 297
Bouillard, Henri, 56, 57, 77
Bourke, Vernon, 54, 83, 280
Bradley, F. H., 212
Braine, David, 167
Brownson, Orestes, 274
Buber, Martin, 80
Buchler, Justus, 97
Buckley, Michael, 79
Burrell, David B., 18-19

Caffarra, Carlo, 298
Cahalan, John C., 17
Cahill, Lisa Sowle, 298
Cajetan, Thomas de Vio, 89, 90
Cessario, Romanus, 17
Chaucer, Geoffrey, 202
Chenu, Marie-Dominique, 2, 3, 56,
  58, 232, 298
Chesterton, G. K., 41, 45
Chrysostom, Saint, 282
Clarke, William Norris, 2, 5, 11, 18,
  56, 62, 63
Colapietro, Vincent, 18
Colish, Marcia L., 231-32
Collins, James, 9, 54
Coreth, Emerich, 54

Dante Aligheri, 201
Deely, John N., 137
Dennehy, Raymond, 13, 14, 86
Descartes, René, 4, 27, 44, 45, 46, 87,
  88, 89, 92, 129
Deulin, Lord Patrick, 269

Dewan, Lawrence, 119
Dewey, John, 267, 277
DiNoia, Joseph A., 16
Donagan, Alan, 281, 283
Dondeyene, Albert, 52
Dougherty, Jude P., 16
Duhem, Pierre, 129
Duns Scotus, John, 89, 138

Edwards, Sandra, 137-138
Eliot, T. S., 14, 198, 203-215
Escrivá de Balaguer, Josemaria, 297

Fabro, Cornelio, 2, 53, 120, 136
Finance, Joseph de, 91, 92
Finnis, John, 279, 303
FitzGerald, Desmond J., 13
Freddoso, Alfred J., 4
Froelich, Gregory, 15

Gadamer, Hans-Georg, 106, 224
Garcia, Jorge, 4
Garcia de Haro, Ramon, 293, 296, 97, 298, 299
Gardeil, Ambroise, 3, 52, 57, 60
Garrigou-Lagrange, Réginald, 3, 52, 57, 141, 162, 298
Gauthier, R. A., 280, 281
Geach, Peter, 291, 292
Geertz, Clifford, 94
Geiger, L. B., 53, 120
Gilby, Thomas, 9, 298
Gilson, Étienne, 2, 7, 9, 13, 15, 40, 45, 46, 51, 53, 54, 56, 57, 58, 78, 83, 86, 87, 88, 89, 90, 91, 109, 111, 113, 120, 136, 139, 169-83, 197, 198, 203, 208, 209, 212
Gleason, Philip, 93, 94, 96
Goethe, Johann Wolfgang von, 29
Gray, John, 270
Grisez, Germaine, 279
Guardini, Romano, 292
Gustafson, James, 297

Habermas, Jürgen, 224, 225
Hals, Franz, 45
Harris, Errol, 97
Hart, Charles, 94
Harvanek, Robert F., 18
Hauerwas, Stanley, 292, 297
Hegel, G.W.F., 24, 79, 80, 81, 92, 97, 126, 222
Heidegger, Martin, 35, 36, 54, 79, 100, 102, 103, 113, 137
Henle, Robert J., 83
Hennis, Wilhelm, 224
Herberg, Will, 266
Herms, Eilert, 292
Hobbes, Thomas, 218, 267, 268
Homer, 201
Hook, Sidney, 139, 266, 267, 269, 272, 274, 275, 277
Hooker, Richard, 267
Hudson, Deal W., 39
Hume, David, 79, 92, 100, 103, 104, 113, 145, 154, 167, 221, 222
Husserl, Edmund, 100

Ibn Sinâ, *see* Avicenna

Jaeger, Werner, 37
Jaspers, Karl, 30, 35, 36
John of Paris, 255
John of St. Thomas, 90, 138, 163
John Paul II, Pope, 86, 297
Journet, Charles, 164
Joyce, James, 205, 209, 214

Kant, Immanuel, 4, 36, 37, 56, 57, 70, 71, 79, 87, 88, 92, 103, 104, 105, 106, 145, 217, 218, 221, 222, 224, 279
Kasper, Walter, 243, 261, 263
Keats, John, 13, 21, 197, 200, 201, 203, 204, 205, 206, 207, 208, 210, 215
Kennedy, John F., 265

Kierkegaard, Søren, 79, 222
Kissinger, Henry, 271
Kleutgen, Joseph, 60, 84
Klubertanz, George P., 54, 83
Knasas, John F.X., 14, 15
Koterski, Joseph, 15

Labourdette, Marie-Michel, 57
Lawrence, Nathaniel, 31
Le Blond, Jean-Marie, 57, 65, 85
Leclerc, Ivor, 97
Leclerque, Jacques, 52
Leibniz, Gottfried Wilhelm, 97, 110, 120
Leo XIII, Pope, 1, 8, 9, 51, 55, 56, 65, 83, 84, 86, 90, 96, 111, 232
Lescoe, Francis, 84
Liberatore, 84
Lincoln, Abraham, 266
Lippmann, Walter, 226, 266, 267
Little, Arthur, 56
Locke, John, 61, 267, 303
Lonergan, Bernard, 2, 9, 14, 18, 19, 58, 60, 63, 79, 85, 86, 90, 109, 123, 127, 128, 139, 161-68
Lovejoy, Arthur O., 277
Lubac, Henri de, 20, 56, 58, 85, 162, 247-64

McCarthy, Michael, 129
McCool, Gerald A., 10, 13, 15, 17, 18, 65, 77, 79, 80, 84, 85, 86, 88, 90, 142, 161, 231, 232, 243, 297
McCormick, John, 94
McCormick, Richard, 297
Macelwane, James, 95
McInerny, Ralph, 11, 123, 125, 126, 127, 128, 129, 135
MacIntyre, Alasdair, 2, 3, 12, 14, 20, 21, 81, 155, 222, 225, 227, 244, 281, 282, 291, 293, 295
Macmurray, John 80
Manser, Gallus, 56

Marcel, Gabriel, 53, 79, 80
Maréchal, Joseph, 2, 3, 15, 52, 57, 65, 86, 111, 143
Maritain, Jacques, 2, 3, 5, 7, 9, 10, 13, 14, 15, 18, 19, 20, 39-47, 52, 61, 67, 76, 78, 83, 86, 90, 108, 109, 111, 112, 113, 123, 124, 127, 128, 135, 136, 139, 140, 144, 145, 161-68
Marty, Martin, 247
Maurer, Armandy, 54, 83
Mercier, Désiré, 52, 77, 111, 141
Molina, Louis de, 163, 167
Montgomery, Marion, 13-14
Moore, George, 222
Murray, John Courtney, 16, 226, 247-64, 265-78

Nemesius, Bishop of Emesa, 282
Neville, Robert, 97
Newman, John Henry, 29
Nicolas, Marie-Joseph, 57
Nicolas, Jean-Hervé, 164
Nietzsche, Friedrich, 20, 223
Nys, Désiré, 52

O'Connor, Flannery, 7
O'Donnell, James, 46
Outka, Gene, 297
Owens, Joseph, 11, 54, 80, 183

Panikkar, Raimundo, 81
Paul of Tarsus, 261
Paul VI, Pope, 86
Pegis, Anton C., 54, 56, 83, 89, 91
Peirce, Charles S., 80
Phelan, Gerald B., 54, 299
Pico della Mirandola, Count Giovanni, 209
Pieper, Josef, 7, 9, 16, 19, 123, 125, 126, 128, 199, 292
Pinckaers, Servais, 293, 295-96, 298, 299

Pius XII, Pope, 85
Plato, 30, 34, 36, 55, 56, 80, 86, 97, 101, 188, 189, 191, 192
Plotinus, 86
Poinsot, John, see John of St. Thomas
Polanyi, Michael 106, 107
Pompanazzi, Pietro, 90
Popper, Karl R., 223
Porter, Jean, 293, 297, 298, 299
Possenti, Vittorio, 14
Pound, Ezra, 205, 214

Quesnell, Quentin, 134, 138, 139, 140, 143
Quine, W. V., 137, 144, 145

Raeymaeker, Louis de, 52, 53
Rahner, Karl, 2, 78, 81, 85, 86, 90, 239
Rawls, John, 226
Reutto, Juha-Pekka, 17
Rhouheimer, Martin, 293, 294-95, 299
Riedel, Manfred, 220
Ritter, Joachim, 224
Roland-Gosselin, M. D., 52
Ross, James, 4
Rousselot, Pierce, 2, 10, 52, 56, 60, 61, 62, 65
Royce, Josiah, 9

Sandel, Michael, 226
Sartre, Jean-Paul, 35, 43, 222
Scheler, Max, 80, 222
Schelling, F.W.J., 24
Schillebeeckx, Edward, 239
Schockenhoff, Eberhard, 293, 294, 298, 299
Scott, Sir Walter, 200
Shelley, Percy Bysshe, 205, 206
Shook, Laurence K., 54
Silber, John, 270-71

Simon, Yves R., 7, 9, 137, 144, 304
Socrates, 37, 74, 129, 209
Spinoza, Baruch, 97
Stevens, Wallace, 203, 205, 214
Synan, Edward A., 13, 54

Taylor, Charles, 243
Tracy, David, 242
Trimalchio, 46
Twain, Mark, 200

Van Riet, Georges, 52
Van Steenberghen, Fernand, 2, 52, 91
Veatch, Henry B., 15, 302, 303
Vico, Giambattista, 219

Wade, William, 91
Wagner, John V., 119
Weigel, Gustav, 266
Weisheipl, James A., 2, 54
Weismann, David, 97
Weiss, Paul, 97
Whitehead, Alfred North, 16, 24, 31, 34, 97
Wilhelmsen, Frederick, 11
Wippel, John F., 190
Wittgenstein, Ludwig, 32, 79
Wojtyla, Karol, 2, 5, 80, see also under Pope John Paul II
Wolff, Christian, 110, 111, 112, 113
Wordsworth, William, 14, 206, 207, 208, 210, 211, 212, 214
Woznicki, Andrew, 84
Wulf, Maurice de, 52

Yeats, William Butler, 198-99, 204, 205

The text of this book was set in Palatino, and the titles in Helvetica. Pages were prepared with Aldus Pagemaker and typeset with a laser printer. Layout by Martin A. Foos, 77 Lincoln Road, Tiffin, Ohio 44883.